Visionary Milton

Medieval & Renaissance Literary Studies

VISIONARY
MILTON

*Essays on
Prophecy and Violence*

Edited by Peter E. Medine,
John T. Shawcross & David V. Urban

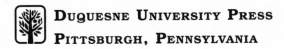

DUQUESNE UNIVERSITY PRESS
PITTSBURGH, PENNSYLVANIA

Published in the United States of America by
DUQUESNE UNIVERSITY PRESS
600 Forbes Avenue
Pittsburgh, Pennsylvania 15282

Library of Congress Cataloging-in-Publication Data

Visionary Milton : essays on prophecy and violence / edited by Peter E. Medine,
John T. Shawcross, and David V. Urban.
    p. cm. — (Medieval & Renaissance literary studies)
    Includes bibliographical references and index.
    Summary: "Scholars discuss Milton's focus on prophecy and violence and
how these themes—which function as a context in Milton's life and as a mode
for an extended analysis of Restoration politics in Milton's poetry—add to an
understanding of Milton as a visionary, extending the literary discussion of
Milton's work into a larger geopolitical area"—Provided by publisher.
    ISBN 978-0-8207-0429-6 (cloth : alk. paper)
    1. Milton, John, 1608–1674—Criticism and interpretation. 2. Milton, John,
1608–1674—Political and social views. 3. Milton, John, 1608–1674—Religion.
4. Prophecy in literature. 5. Violence in literature. 6. Politics and literature—
England—History—17th century. 7. Religion and literature—England—
History—17th century. I. Medine, Peter E. II. Shawcross, John T. III. Urban,
David V.
    PR3592.P64V57 2010
    821'.4—dc22

                                                                    2009053468

∞ Printed on acid-free paper.

For Michael Lieb

— *colleagae optimo doctissimoque*

Contents

Acknowledgments

The editors wish to thank Calvin College for its support and the University of Arizona for its generous subvention of publication costs.

The editors wish to pay tribute to the late Professor Albert C. Labriola, without whose early support and guidance this volume would not have been possible.

Introduction

> The invincible Warriour Zeale shaking loosely the slack reins drives over the heads of scarlet Prelats, and such as are insolent to maintain traditions, bruising their stiffe necks under his flaming wheels. Thus did the true Prophets of old combat with the false.
>
> — *Apology for Smectymnuus*

1. *The Visionary Mode*

The visionary mode is by nature prophetic. It envisions not only the future but also the past and the present. The scope is therefore capacious and can accommodate itself to virtually all subjects and all literary genres. The mode is interpretive as well; it revises and re-envisions what is established, received, and expected. The process is twofold. Typically iconoclastic, the visionary author reforms and reinvents the texts that lie behind him or her. The result is a restatement, a new form, and from this perspective the process is aesthetic. In the second place, the visionary author reinterprets reality and critiques the historical moment. The subject of the critique stems ultimately from violations of the first and second commandments — against idolatry and graven images — which have become institutionalized in social norms and structures. These in turn do violence against God and humans and require aggressively stringent correction. Hence the distinctive iconoclasm and politics of the visionary mode. But the visionary is not simply destructive. As a teacher, a bearer of a message, he or she undertakes to rebuild, if only to anticipate a renewal in a distant space and time. In this way the mode is transformative: the originating vision transforms the one receiving it, and the aim then becomes to transform the reader—to make all God's people prophets and visionaries. Finally, the authority of the visionary mode is theological; it is God in the case of sacred prophecy and the muse in the case of visionary poetry.

2. *The Scholarship of Michael Lieb on the Visionary Mode*

Michael Lieb has long studied the visionary mode and the culture of violence, paying special attention to matters of vision and violence in Milton, subjects that form the theme of this collection and to which Lieb has made such a significant contribution. In his *Dialectics of Creation: Patterns of Birth and Regeneration in* Paradise Lost (1970), Lieb approached Milton's epic as a polemic work, the "great Argument" of which emerges not from "a straightforward presentation of answerable propositions and verifiable conclusions" (6) but rather through the violent oppositions of dialectic that inform the epic. In asserting that *Paradise Lost* is fundamentally dialectic, Lieb draws upon *Areopagitica*'s vision of Truth and Falsehood engaging in a kind of "rhetorical warfare" so that the genuine seeker of truth may gain a higher level of knowledge. A similar dialectic takes place in the "great Argument" of Milton's epic, one that surfaces amid the various aspects of creation throughout the poem.

Interest in the polemic nature of Milton's writings continues in *Achievements of the Left Hand: Essays on the Prose of John Milton* (1974), which Lieb coedited with John T. Shawcross, and *Poetics of the Holy: A Reading of* Paradise Lost (1981). Like *Dialectics*, several of the essays in *Achievements* do much to break down the boundaries between Milton's poetry and prose, demonstrating the artistry of the prose and recognizing in Milton's prose fresh and instructive approaches to the poetry. Lieb's essay in the volume, "Milton's *Of Reformation* and the Dynamics of Controversy," analyzes Milton's use, within his own combative polemical rhetoric, of "prevailing modes of discourse in order to transcend them" (56). *Poetics* challenges the secularized notion of the "demythologized" Milton presented in Mary Ann Radzinowicz's *Toward Samson Agonistes* (1978) and argues that "Milton's religiosity not only aligns [him] with an outlook that is fundamentally sacral but causes him to become...the poet of 'the other' par excellence."[1] This investigation of the holy in Milton's epic marks Lieb's first book-length inquiry into matters of prophetic vision and contains his first sustained discussion of Milton's depiction of the Chariot of Paternal Deitie in book 6 of *Paradise Lost*, which becomes the ultimate embodiment of the oft-violent nature of Milton's visionary mode.

In *The Sinews of Ulysses: Form and Convention in Milton's Works* (1989), Lieb presents in the final chapter a detailed analysis of *Samson Agonistes*. His argument holds that Samson's renovation takes place in conjunction with the progressive return of his God-given strength, a renovation that is perfected in his violent, divinely ordained destruction of the Philistine temple. This "regenerative" reading of Samson was squarely at odds with the challenging analysis put forth by Joseph Wittreich, whose influential *Interpreting* Samson Agonistes (1986) was the first book-length assertion of the increasingly popular scholarly interpretation of Milton's Samson as a misguided and unregenerate figure.[2] In the final chapter of *The Sinews of Ulysses* and other studies soon to follow, Lieb argued that, modern distaste aside, Milton is an author whose works—*Samson Agonistes* in particular—are strikingly and often disturbingly comfortable with the notion that violence may be a divinely sanctioned method for punishing the wicked and rewarding the righteous.

Lieb broadened his study of visionary art and surveyed the contexts of prophetic vision in *The Visionary Mode: Biblical Prophecy, Hermeneutics, and Cultural Change* (1991). The analysis rests on Ezekiel's *visio Dei* (the *merkabah* [chariot] of Ezekiel 1:4–28), and affirms that the "thunderous otherness" of this *visio Dei* reflects the essence of the visionary mode (1). Drawing on the theories of Carl Gustav Jung—who coined the phrase "visionary mode"—Lieb describes the visionary as that which is mysterious, unfamiliar, unknowable, and beyond human comprehension, which can only be transmitted by seers and prophets—"poets of the highest order" through whom the visionary is articulated in poetic form (4).

In *Milton and the Culture of Violence* (1994) Lieb investigates matters of violence and gender through a biographically informed analysis of many of Milton's poetic and prose works. Explicitly "concerned with a darker, more unsettling side of Milton's personality" (12), the book argues that Milton's personality and art emerge from pervasive fears of bodily dismemberment (akin to the *sparagmos* of Orpheus) and underlying anxieties concerning his own sexuality. These fears and anxieties reflect the culture of violence in which Milton lived and figure prominently in works as diverse as *Areopagitica*, Sonnet 18 ("Avenge O Lord thy slaughter'd Saints"), *Ad Patrem*, *Lycidas*, Milton's sixth Prolusion, *A Mask*, *Paradise Lost*, the divorce tracts, *Defensio secunda*, *Pro se defensio*, and, perhaps most significantly, *Samson Agonistes*. The study concludes that for Milton violence is, paradoxically, an agent of both renewal and destruction.

Lieb's interest in the *merkabah* led to *Children of Ezekiel: Aliens, UFOs, the Crisis of Race, and the Advent of End Time* (1998). This study again takes Ezekiel's *visio Dei* as its point of departure, and, after defining as the children of Ezekiel the many "Inventors, scientists, technologists, evangelicals, and poets...visionaries all" who attempt "to harness the power that gives rise to technology," Lieb discusses the way these "children" "reinvent...re-create...[and] 'technologize' [Ezekiel's vision] in their own terms" (3). Not surprisingly, the first child of Ezekiel that Lieb examines is Milton and his depiction of the Chariot of Paternal Deitie. The discussion of Milton's poetic vision reveals how Milton's Chariot "embodies the technological impulse on a grand scale" (4) and proceeds to manifestations of Ezekiel's chariot in the eighteenth century and the Industrial Revolution of the nineteenth century.

Later chapters address the relationship between Ezekiel's *visio Dei* and the UFO furor of the middle and late twentieth century, the Jehovah's Witnesses and their expectation of Armageddon, the apocalyptic fervor that characterizes much of twentieth-first century evangelical Christianity, and the nuclear tensions between the Soviet Union and the United States (with special attention paid to Ronald Reagan and how his belief in biblical prophecy affected his policies). The second half of the book contains a detailed analysis of the way Ezekiel's vision has figured into the teachings of the Nation of Islam under the leadership of Elijah Muhammad and Louis Farrakhan.

Of several densely theological essays of the 1980s and 1990s, the 1996 *Milton Studies* article, "'Our Living Dread': The God of *Samson Agonistes*," illustrates particularly well Lieb's developing interests as they found full expression in the new millennium. The article builds on his previous work in *The Sinews of Ulysses* and *Milton and the Culture of Violence* and analyzes Samson as a regenerate character whose violence is orchestrated by God himself. In contrast to Radzinowicz's argument for the rational and ultimately understandable God of *Samson Agonistes*,[3] Lieb contends that the deity of Milton's drama is terrifying, inscrutable, even primitive, localized, and nonrational. Moreover, God's servant Samson, in his destruction of the Philistine temple, essentially "subsumes within himself the divine role…and becomes that force, that *tremendum* through which 'our living Dread' [Israel's God] is made manifest…. [Samson] is 'our living Dread' incarnate" (16). The argument recurs in expanded form in part 2 of *Theological Milton: Deity, Discourse, and Heresy in the Miltonic Canon* (2006), where Lieb examines Milton's God as portrayed in *Paradise Lost* and *Samson Agonistes*, focusing on the more disturbing aspects of Milton's God—including his hatred—and paying significant attention to God's violence in these works. This section of *Theological Milton* also addresses the changing emotions of the passible God of *Paradise Lost* and *De doctrina Christiana*, observing that Milton's portrayal of a passible deity stands at odds with the teaching of the most prominent church fathers and Reformed theologians, including Calvin. Throughout the study, Lieb cautions against associating Milton too closely with any particular system of belief. He affirms that Milton's theology (and, for that matter, Milton's God) is *sui generis*—unique, a type of its very own.

In short, from his first to his most recent work on Milton, Lieb has shown that for no other author has iconoclasm and violence been more of a hallmark and that for perhaps no other author in what has been described as the "line of vision" has the model of visionary and prophet been more definitive than for Milton. Addressing themselves to the works of Milton, the essays of the present collection take up topics and perspectives that Lieb's scholarship on the visionary mode and violence has suggested over the last four decades.

3. *Prophesy and Violence*

The three essays of part 1 introduce the collection by focusing on the visionary mode in Milton's early poetry, on the visionary mode throughout the poetic oeuvre, and on the appropriation of Milton's post-Restoration biography and works to critique a form of political violence during the 1950s in the United States. The four essays of part 2 deal with various contexts of the visionary mode in Milton's works and include a discussion of Milton's contemporary, the political philosopher Thomas Hobbes; an analysis of the subject of pain in the war in heaven in *Paradise Lost;* and studies of the prophetic hermeneutics of *Paradise Regain'd* and of the shifting contexts of artistic representations of *Samson Agonistes.* The essays of part 3 explore various perspectives on *Paradise Regain'd* as a visionary poem; part 4 concludes the collection with an essay on the three great poems that cap Milton's career as visionary and prophetic poet, demonstrating the complexity of their final vision or visions.

In the opening essay of part 1, "Milton and the Visionary Mode: The Early Poems," John T. Shawcross describes the "visionary mode" as one that dominates the "fundamental hope in and assertion of Eternal Providence that is the epic *Paradise Lost.*" He then demonstrates the importance of visionary prophecy in 14 poems that antedate *Lycidas* (1637), a work that Milton himself as well as many later critics have regarded as prophetic. Prior to 1637 the visionary mode looms largest in the ode on the Nativity. In the crucially significant fourteenth stanza of the hymn of the Nativity ode, for example, Milton presents a version of the eschatological vision that recalls the book of Revelation. Finally Shawcross extends his discussion to a reconsideration of "The Passion" as a "sequel" or "companion Poem" to the Nativity ode—it seems to have been written four months later, March 1630—a claim that he elaborates upon by indicating the substance of prophecy and the visionary mode of the poem. Shawcross concludes that in revealing Milton's "vatic experience" and delineating a "theosis that allows an experience of deification," these early poems point to *Lycidas* and the first intimations of *Paradise Lost,* which later criticism has demonstrated to represent Milton's full realization of the visionary mode.

In "Milton and the Culture Wars," Barbara K. Lewalski broadens the scope of Shawcross's discussion of the prophetic Milton to the whole of his poetic oeuvre. She focuses on the role Milton self-consciously assumes as a prophetic teacher who undertakes a cultural transformation through a radical revision of the canonical literary genres. As Lewalski sees it, the project is militant and offensive, an "aesthetic contestation through the transformations his own poems manifest." The poems would invite readers to "contrast his poems with others in the respective genre he deems corrupting or debased." For example, she finds in *Lycidas* that the "apocalyptic and prophetic overtones" threaten violent retribution and "transform the genre of pastoral elegy." In *Paradise Lost,* she sees Milton aspiring to the position of "prophet-poet" above his classical and modern predecessors. And she suggests that the note on the verse "aggressively" challenges current poetic norms and associates the verse form with a restoration of English freedom from Stuart tyranny. Lewalski concludes that "Early to late, Milton hoped that his revisionist poetry" would transform his readers and effect their "liberation."

Like Shawcross and Lewalski, Sharon Achinstein sees Milton as a visionary prophet in quest of transformation. Her essay, "Red Milton: Abraham Polonsky and *You Are There* (January 30, 1955)," centers attention on a mid-twentieth century appropriation of Milton to critique a form of political violence that undermined civil liberties in the mid-twentieth century United States. She reflects on a historical moment in U.S. history which she suggests witnessed a confusion of the two sorts of violence described by Walter Benjamin as law-preserving violence and divine violence. This was the early 1950s, in which—in anticipation of the post-9/11 era—"domestic and international security were made to trump civil liberties, and...a law-preserving violence justified the abandonment of humanitarian principles." She focuses on a television script, "The Tragedy of John Milton," written by the blacklisted Abraham Polonsky for the prime-time network program *You Are There*. Set in August 1660, the drama opens in a London bookshop where Milton's works are being pulled from the shelves for burning and ends with the blind Milton fleeing in disguise from government officials and a likely death sentence. As Achinstein points out, the "equation between destroying books and destroying men" runs throughout *Areopagitica,* and she observes further that in his script Polonsky explored the "psychological no less than the political dimensions of such acts of violence." Polonsky thus appears a visionary figure himself as he adapts the historical Milton in a transformative critique of the politics of his own day.

4. *Contemporary and Later Contexts*

In the first of the four essays of part 2, "Milton's Visionary Mode: Contemporary and Later Contexts," Stanley Fish addresses himself to seventeenth century political theory and the dangers of political violence. In "How Hobbes Works," Fish contextualizes Milton's fear of the "barbarous dissonance" that threatens the individual in society, its institutions, and the idea of liberty by exploring the thought of Thomas Hobbes. Like Milton, Hobbes fears chaos—what Hobbes refers to as the state of nature. For

Milton, preservation—not to say salvation—comes from faith in an ultimately unknowable God. That faith, the strength to believe in such a God, can come only from within. For Hobbes, the only thing that can come from within is destructive, particular passions and appetites the gratification of which would reduce society and civilization to primordial chaos. Against this Hobbes asserts the "Leviathan," the supreme authority—the elaborate structure of government. To this authority every member of the body politic will "submit their Wills...and their Judgements.... This is the Generation of that great LEVIATHAN...of that *Mortall God*, to which we owe under the *Immortal God*...peace and defense." Fish shows that Hobbes would buttress the whole arrangement with a network of "Artificiall Chains, called Civill Lawes" that are sustained only by mutual agreement and can be easily broken. In this respect, Hobbes resembles his great antinomian contemporary John Milton. At a crucial point of *Paradise Lost*, Raphael points out that the only guarantee of happiness of truly free individuals is an "act of obedience rooted in nothing firmer than itself: 'On other surety none' (*PL* 5.538)." For both poet and philosopher, order and security in the world are fragile and at every moment in peril. Though one looked within and the other looked without, the two authors coincide in their positions against what Fish calls "facile rationalists—the believers in perspicuous and easy solutions in their day and ours."

In "God's 'Red Right Hand': Violence and Pain in *Paradise Lost*," Diana Treviño Benet examines the seventeenth century context of the violence and pain portrayed in Milton's epic in a discussion of contemporary medical and spiritual attitudes toward pain and of religious teachings about violence in Christian warfare. The materials bear on a notoriously problematical feature of *Paradise Lost*, the war in heaven narrated in books 6 and 7. Benet interests herself in the poetic obstacles the war raised for Milton, particularly the difficulty of presenting a conflict between two sides, one of which cannot suffer physical pain and another of which can. The discussion enables her to focus on one of the enduring critical questions of Milton scholarship and criticism: pain and the violence that causes it may be rationalized variously by contemporaries and may be represented variously in *Paradise Lost,* but all pain in the poem stems from the Father. Poetically speaking, Milton is obliged "to mitigate the violence, the 'red right hand' of God." It is, Benet comments, the "intractable problem," and points to the complex of issues associated with the *odium Dei* that informs Milton's theodicy and the epic task of justifying the ways of God to men.

The next two essays of part two enlarge the discussion of Milton's visionary mode and preoccupation with violence from the contemporary to the broader contexts of the early modern and modern periods. Joseph A. Wittreich addresses himself to Milton's reshaping of the scriptural sources of the temptation narrative into the visionary mode of *Paradise Regain'd.* "A World with a Tomorrow: *Paradise Regain'd* and Its Hermeneutic of Discovery" begins with a reprisal of the current criticism of Milton in which "*Fissures, rifts, crevices, conflicts, inconsistencies, contradictions*" have come to be regarded as "acts of poetic engineering." Placing the poem within the sweep of exegetical and poetic readings of the Gospels' temptation narrative from the seventeenth to the twentieth centuries, Wittreich sees Milton not eliding or erasing contradictions and conflicts in the materials but embracing them. The differences include the questions of whether the sequence of the temptations should be read literally or figuratively and of whether Jesus' experience on the mountain and the pinnacle are actual or visionary. Milton departed from his contemporaries who would harmonize the narratives into totalized statements and gravitated to those who would recognize the differences. The effect of this version of the temptation story is to shift "attention to the interiority of the Son's journey, to its concerns with self-definition and discovery within a theater of the mind." Wittreich sees Jesus as completing a period of contemplation and pointing directly to a life of action as he comes to understand his roles as prophet, king, and priest; as both man and God. Having so defined his mission, and now complete within himself, Jesus is "ready to do his work of deliverance."

Like Wittreich, Wendy Furman-Adams and Virginia James Tufte discuss Milton's scriptural sources and the ways in which they were variously read. In "'Shifting Contexts': Artists' *Agon* with the Biblical and Miltonic Samson," Furman-Adams and Tufte approach *Samson Agonistes* as a work very much in the visionary mode of revision of the prophetic text and explore the ways in which painters and illustrators have literally envisioned the Samson narrative and Milton's *Samson Agonistes*. Their aim is not to provide yet another interpretation of what has become Milton's most contested work. It is to deepen the understanding of what Wittreich calls the "fissures, rifts, crevices, conflicts" that seem to lie deep within the narrative materials and emerge, subside, and re-emerge in "readings" over the centuries. Surveying visual renditions from the early Christian period to the late twentieth century, they point out that nearly all recent critical readings of *Samson Agonistes* are anticipated by the hundreds of illustrators and painters who have represented the biblical account in Judges and by 15 illustrators of *Samson Agonistes*. The Samsons rendered by the artists extend from "types of Christ to types of Satan" and from "terrorists to romantic victims." In the case of illustrations of *Samson Agonistes*, the renditions are characterized less by "extroverted violence" than by "profound interiority." The most recent illustrator discussed is Robert Medley, who in a 1979 edition of *Samson Agonistes* published a series of illustrations that are not representational but abstract. The illustrations not only suggest aspects of Samson's "interiority" but also, as Furman-Adams and Tufte discuss, extend to a suggestion of the Holocaust and, when viewed and read from a post-9/11 vantage, to more recent occurrences of political violence. No less than readings presented in other essays, Furman-Adams and Tufte's discussion reveals the profoundly prophetic nature of Milton's visionary mode.

5. *Paradise Regain'd*

Part 3, "Milton's Visionary Mode and *Paradise Regain'd*," begins with "Why Is the Virgin Mary in *Paradise Regain'd*?" by Mary Beth Rose. Rose examines the importation of five references to the Annunciation by the angel Gabriel to the Virgin that she will be the mother of the Son of God and the detail concluding the poem that Jesus returns to his "Mother's house" (*PR* 4.639). Such revision of source material is very much part of the visionary mode and leads Rose to her characterization of the poet's prophetic intention as the exaltation of the Son. The discussion historicizes the resulting narrative by taking into account some broad cultural shifts that gender studies have identified during the early modern period. One is the transformation of the literary representation of heroism, which came increasingly to idealize and celebrate "passive fortitude" and to move away from "deeds of killing and conquest." The shift entails the "elevation in the status of private endurance over public adventure," and this, Rose suggests, further "involves a transformation in the gendering of heroism," from masculine to feminine. The other development noted is the emerging critique of maternal authority, which Thomas Hobbes articulates. Though he concludes that the traditional patriarchal arrangement should continue, he argues with clarity and force that there is no "natural" difference between the mother's and the father's claim to authority. Milton appears to be even more radical than his contemporary. Besides "erasing" any reference to Joseph from Jesus' life narrative altogether, Milton elaborates Mary into a major character whose insistent presence "confirms the Son's origins and provides knowledge of his birth," and solidifies the "Son's identity, making it perfect: both human and divine."

Like Rose, Stella P. Revard in "Charles, Christ, and Icon of Kingship in *Paradise Regain'd*" historicizes the visionary mode of Milton's brief epic but focuses on the poem's covert criticism and ultimate rejection of Charles's and his supporters' assertion of legitimate kingship. She cites contemporary court poets—Abraham Cowley and John Dryden among others—who throughout the 1660s wrote encomia of the restored Charles as inheritor of the "mantle of the Old Testament prophets and kings" and even as a figure of the Messiah. In *Paradise Regain'd* Milton's strategy is to compare Jesus' role as the "new Moses, Joshua, and David" with Charles's claims to these types and to contrast Jesus as the true Christ with Charles's alleged role as "anointed king or Messiah." Revard demonstrates how Milton proceeds through the three temptations to evoke these contrasts. But from the beginning to the end of the poem, the defining issue is of Jesus as the Davidic king, an issue, Revard suggests, that is as important as that of his person as the Son of God. The question of the nature of the earthly kingdom Jesus is to rule receives elaborate expression in the temptation of the kingdoms in book 4. Here Jesus rejects various kingdoms offered by Satan, but "he does not deny kingship itself." Instead, as the legitimate heir of David, he "lays claim to a kingdom that will transcend both and displace all the corrupt tyrannies of the world"—of that kingdom "there shall be no end" (*PR* 4.151). So for Revard, the prophetic vision of *Paradise Regain'd* lies not only in its critique of the contemporary Restoration monarchy and culture but also in its anticipation of the Second Coming—a type of restoration—of the true Messiah and true kingship. While the government may have curtailed the freedom Milton had earlier exercised as a pamphleteer, he still spoke out in *Paradise Regain'd*, a statement combining politics and prophesy to reject the "false icon of kingship and to set up the true image of the king that the returned Son will eventually erect."

In the next essay, "From Last Things to First: The Apophatic Vision of *Paradise Regain'd*," Michael Bryson does not historicize the poem as Rose and Revard do, but very much in their vein of inquiry he concerns himself with one of the chief critical questions: the nature of its final vision. Bryson examines the problem by approaching both *Paradise Lost* and *Paradise Regain'd* as examples of the "visionary mode," which is a "way of representing, if not bridging, the gap between God-with-qualities and God-without-qualities." The mode is dynamic and moves from that which is external ("last things") to that which is internal ("first things"). The movement is "apophatic"; its opposite is "cataphatic" and moves from first to last things. The latter dynamic informs *Paradise Lost*, as Adam and Eve proceed from paradise in their unfallen state to the world and history in their fallen state. *Paradise Regain'd* embodies the first dynamic, as the narrative unfolds in an ascent, a kind of "reclamation" of the "paradise within" through a complete recognition of the sense of "divine similitude." Jesus moves in this way through the three temptations and his rejection of what Bryson regards as the same temptation: essentially an effort by Satan to trick the Son into identifying himself "with, and through, externals and a focus on last things." The climax of the movement comes with the rejection and defeat of Satan by Jesus' riposte: "Tempt not the Lord thy God." Bryson takes these words to mean, "Not only do not tempt me (that is, Jesus) and anyone else," but also, "Do not tempt yourself," that is, Satan. The reading depends on the apophatic movement toward first things, which above all include an "inner awareness of divine similitude" and a movement away from last things, which above all include idolatry. Bryson concludes that while the Jesus of *Paradise Regain'd* does not "regain Eden or shed a drop of blood," he acquires and reveals his knowledge of the "paradise within."

6. Last Poems

In the single essay of part 4, "Milton's Visionary Mode and the Last Poems," David Loewenstein's "From Politics to Faith in the Great Poems?" focuses on *Paradise Lost, Paradise Regain'd,* and *Samson Agonistes* and addresses itself to the question of whether in the post-Restoration years Milton retreated from the life of engagement and controversy to a kind of quietism. Loewenstein takes as a basic assumption about the last poems the poet/narrator's assertion in the invocation to book 7 of *Paradise Lost* that though "fall'n on evil days" and amid "evil tongues," Milton continues "with mortal voice, unchang'd / To hoarse or mute" (*PL* 24–26). It is a poetic stance that predicates the visionary mode of serious critique and commitment to courses of political action. The main point of discussion is that when regarded more comprehensively, the vatic Milton of the great poems does not speak univocally. Milton responds with "multiple, diverse, even conflicting voices" to the "hostile, dissipated, and idolatrous world of Restoration England." In readings of the prophetic vision of books 11 and 12, Loewenstein demonstrates "impulses" to reject history and withdraw from it as well as to persist in expressions of radically charged religious and political involvement. Both voices are evident in what are often "unstable, haunting passage[s] narrating the uneven course of postlapsarian history." Loewenstein proceeds to detect a comparable variety of poetic statement in the 1671 volume of *Paradise Regain'd* and *Samson Agonistes*. Not only are there allowances in the first work for extreme political, even militaristic, responses but also there is evidence that Milton took pains in the second work to provide that Samson is not a suicide or a terrorist. "We need," Loewenstein concludes, "a historicized criticism...that acknowledges that even within dense passages of Milton's great poems we may find conflicting impulses and weltering reactions to the pressures of contemporary postlapsarian history and the political sphere of post-Restoration England."

As the above summary suggests, the 11 essays of this collection take up the subjects of the visionary mode and violence with different emphases and different points of view. But all the discussions bear on Milton's appropriation of the visionary mode and engagement with the iconoclasm and violence that his vocation as a visionary poet and his historical circumstances called him to. It is testament to the scholarship of Michael Lieb that his work on these subjects should make possible such a rich and instructive variety of essays on the poetry and prose of John Milton.

Part I

Milton's Visionary Mode:
Prophecy and Violence

1 ⟜ Milton and the Visionary Mode
The Early Poems

John T. Shawcross

Writing "Of the Original and right use of Poetry: with the manner of its Corruption by later Poets," Thomas Jackson remarked upon authors who

> were any way disposed by nature to the Faculty, were inspired with lively and sublimate affections, apt to vent themselves in such Poetical Phrases and resemblances, as we cannot reach unto, unless we raise our invention by Art and imitation, and stir up Admiration by meditation and study. And because neither our senses are moved with any extraordinary effects of Gods *Power*, nor our minds bent to observe the ways of his *Wisdom*, so as we might be stricken with true Admiration of them, we have fewer good sacred Poems, then of any other kind.[1]

He thus epitomizes the false and the true *vates*, the literary "prophet" or "visionary" who, observing God's wisdom, can predict what the future will bring. As is clear in Jackson's thought, the term carries a religious connotation, the true vates being one who is moved with the power of God and who is struck by the ways

3

of God's wisdom no matter what humankind experiences. John Milton's much quoted line from *Paradise Lost:* "And justifie the wayes of God to men" echoes here for us as evidence that Milton believed in his truly being inspired by God.[2] The Holy Spirit of God and his wisdom dominate the proems to books 1, 3, 7, and 9 as Milton pursues his "great Argument." He has assumed and has put on the mantle of vates, one who through (poetic visionaries), by the grace of God offers the means of regaining "the blissful Seat." First he delineates the cause (or causes) of its being lost, which cause (or causes) must be repudiated, thwarted, reversed to enable human redemption. And the path to "justifie the wayes of God to men" is opened by asserting "Eternal Providence" (25) to humankind who would seem to have forgotten God's power and wisdom. God's Providence is the Son, whose Incarnation will lead to the means to salvation—the Christ, the "one greater Man," who will "Restore us, and regain" that paradise for those faithful mortals who "Acknowledge [their] Redeemer ever blest" (*PL* 12.573).

The prophecy that Milton elaborates within *his* "sacred Poem" is built on many "visions," of the past, of the future, and of the sinister present that suffers from political blight and human degeneracy and especially religious apostasy. This underlying sense of foreseeing what lies ahead, particularly if the future stays its course, and its reflection in poetics have been analyzed as "the visionary mode," which Michael Lieb has discussed as the "thunderous otherness" of Ezekiel's *visio Dei,* a manifestation of the religious experience with its transformative power.[3] The term, as Lieb points out, is one mode of artistic creation which Carl Jung analyzed as derived from the "hinterland of man's mind," the primordial dynamism, the propensity to change, the transformative experience that defines and redefines itself.[4] Vatic texts are underlain by texts of an "originary event whose mysteries they seek to illuminate"; "The new text, the new reading, is in effect the source not only of a new awareness but of a reenvisioning of the originary event."[5]

Lieb's important and explicitly detailed study answers a call for the attention to visionary literature that Leland Ryken made some years before: "Its two main subtypes in the Bible are prophecy and apocalypse. Visionary poetry is a notoriously elusive form, and a great deal more descriptive work remains to be done in the biblical texts (especially their characteristic imagery and rhetoric).... The more we learn about the poetic strategies of visionary poetry in the Bible, the better we will understand some of the most striking effects in Milton's major poems."[6] Ryken's earlier investigation of *The Apocalyptic Vision in Paradise Lost* set forth the various motifs of apocalypse and apocalyptic imagery, and demonstrated how these various elements of the visionary unify in the poem to achieve what Joseph Anthony Wittreich Jr. will later distinguish as "a line of vision." Of the subtype prophecy Wittreich, remarking that "Prophecy is a way of seeing and a way of writing; that is, it is system of aesthetics," maintains that "Isolated from the visionary line, the prophet is speechless; touching it, he becomes articulate, even to the point of engaging...in corrective criticism.... They all derive their vision from Christ; they are all ministers of the Word."[7] Ryken also speaks of the "*prophetic* element in literature": "it turns out that we are really talking about a quality of discourse, a stance of the writer as a person and narrator, and a set of poets and rhetorical techniques, not about a genre of literature."[8] Ranging over a number of works, William Kerrigan established "the poetic and prophetic inspiration of John Milton," a vates who through "visionary song and zealous prose" moved "to participate in the prophetic history of the private motions of God." Two sentences in Kerrigan's interrogation of "The Prophetic Milton" provide a kind of summary of what I have cited before, and imply the distinction that is the foundation of Jackson's comment: "In *Paradise Lost*, then, God invents prophecy to complete the process begun with the first fallen prayers, revealing to Adam that the apparent discontinuity of his time is in fact the initial act of a providential drama. Milton knew that the divine poet, like all the champions of God, would have to recreate this original paradigm—one [such paradigm] began a sacred song with 'devout prayer.'"[9] Kerrigan views Milton's epic as proffering a new Scripture, and Barbara Lewalski, discusses the proem to book 3 and stresses the illumination of celestial light, which Milton petitions: "he does not claim the extraordinary visions of a John of Patmos. Rather, he hopes for the mediated poetic vision of Dante, who, in his dream, imagined himself blinded at first by the dazzling light of God but then accorded stronger vision."[10]

The forms of vision Lieb discusses at length—gnosis, theosis, poetics—can lead to knowledge that transforms the reader to become a partaker of divine existence; can allow an experience of deification where God condescends, causing "the contemplative to undergo a transformation through which the human participates in the divine"; and can move through the art that displays God's power and God's wisdom from one vision to another to still a higher vision. The capstone is "To see," which is "to behold the self: to know God is to look inward as God Himself looks inward." The result should be the "return of the individual soul to its beginnings" (the *Urerlebnis*) *and* the anticipation of the "final conflagration when all those who are saved will undergo an ultimate theosis."[11] "It is this sense of return that is all important." This process of visionary poetics is, in Wittreich's conspectus, like "the breaking of each seal" in the book of the Apocalypse (Revelation), which "denotes a new discovery, an unfolding of visionary meaning, the breaking of yet another manacle as the mind moves progressively toward total consciousness.... Within each prophecy, vision combines with commentary, the obscurity of the one being mitigated by the clarity of the other.... Each vision is, then, an exit into another higher vision."[12]

Echoing for us in the foregoing are three important concepts Milton envisions in book 3 of *Paradise Lost*. First, God the Father makes clear that each "step" humankind takes can lead to an advancement and ultimate regaining of the blissful seat, and that it is through "inwardness" that such positive steps occur:

> And I will place within them as a guide
> My Umpire *Conscience*, whom if they will hear,
> Light after light well us'd they shall attain,
> And to the end persisting, safe arrive.   (*PL* 3.194–97)

Second, the Son, who is the vertex of God's Providence, will make possible the redemption of humankind through his "love divine," through his sacrifice, through his binding of the powers of darkness, to allow those who "persist" to "safe arrive." And third, the chorus of faithful angels hymn God's mercy and the Son's "Heav'nly Love," and the shutting of "Hell her numbers full" (3.332) forever, but

> Mean while
> The World shall burn, and from her ashes spring
> New Heav'n and Earth, wherein the just shall dwell
> And after all thir tribulations long
> See golden days, fruitful of golden deeds,
> With Joy and Love triumphant, and fair Truth.
>
> . . . .
>
> God shall be All in All.[13]   (*PL* 3.333–41)

The visionary mode dominates this fundamental hope in and assertion of eternal Providence that is the epic *Paradise Lost*. This visionary mode will persist, and it has not sprung into existence in just one moment of meditation; it has existed for Milton throughout his life although not always so explicitly stated or demonstrated. He has not necessarily expressed these beliefs as vatic prophecy through which other mortals will learn, yet they exist as basic themes and often take the form of imagery or allusion.

This visionary mode has been examined in works from *Lycidas* on, but in the poetry written prior to 1637, when Milton altered his "studious retirement" to a more active poetic life, it has not specifically been looked at as prelude to an anticipated vatic life.[14] Instanced by his writing of the pastoral elegy and, some few months later, by his trip to Italy, that vatic life is most specifically planned upon his return to England. Drafts for *Paradise Lost* in 1640–42 and the biographical "Preface" to book 2 of *The Reason of Church-Government* (1641–42) proclaim such hope for his "new" career. Here I examine some of the evidence that the earlier poetry implies for his envisioned vatic role, especially in the variously read and usually unappreciated aborted poem, "The Passion."

In these earlier poems we recognize the seeds that will grow into full flower: the belief has always been there and its properties and manifestations perceived. We are not apprehending a "changed" mind, nor an "unchanging" mind as that designation seems usually to be meant. As with all people who mature, we are witnessing a Milton who, at least in certain religious positions and faith, has honed his world into an exacting, demonstrable, and expressible literary exemplum.

The first two completed poems that we have from Milton's hand, dated 1624, are translations of psalms. The Passover psalm number 114 is paraphrased to emphasize God's omnipresence and omnipotence as he wrought the miracle of separating the waters of the Red Sea for the Israelites' exodus from Egypt, and the recoiling of the waters of the river Jordan to deliver them to "*Canaan Land.*" The nullifying of the impossibility of having "glassy flouds" emerge from "rugged rocks" and "soft rills from fiery flint-stones gush" attests to God's omnipotence, and Milton exhorts the people of this "earth" "at the presence [to] be agast / Of him that ever was, and ay shall last." God, as the Chorus proclaims in the last completed poem of Milton's oeuvre, *Samson Agonistes*, "Oft . . . seems to hide his face, / But unexpectedly returns" (echoing and answering Psalm 27:9, "Hide not thy face far from me," and Psalm 88:14, "Lord, why castest thou off my soul? why hidest thou thy face from me?"). The headnote in the Geneva Bible expresses the message of the psalm: "the wonderful miracles, that God wrought at that time Which put vs in remembrance of Gods great mercie toward his Church, who, when the course of nature faileth, preserueth his miraculously." The vision which the psalm produces in the 15-year-old Milton is concerned with the prophecy that God will look out for his faithful servants and looks forward to a new life in Canaan—the Promised Land, the similitude of heaven—for them, for all faithful servants of God.

Ten years later Milton translated the psalm (rather than paraphrased it) into Greek and sent it to his teacher and friend Alexander Gill (junior), referring to it in a letter of December 4, 1634: "I send . . . what is not exactly mine, but also that truly divine

poet's, this ode of whom, only last week, with no deliberate inten-
tion certainly, but from I know not what sudden impulse before
daybreak, I was rendering, almost in bed, to the rule of Greek
heroic verse."[15] Perhaps we may infer a psychological source here:
an iteration of hope for his life in God's providence when, in 1634,
in the midst of his "studious retirement," he did not have direction
for hiș life, now and in the future not a clerical one, and thus with
anxiety over what the future would bring. In the letter he refers to
having written "some things of my own of this kind," that is, the
hendecasyllabics that Gill had sent, "but which I should in no way
rate worthy of sending in a contest of equality of gift with yours."
These verses do not survive, perhaps because they were indeed
inferior and did not foretoken success as a poet, a vates. A final
sentence in the letter indicates the lack of direction for his life and
displays the need for only the assurance "All is...As ever in my
great task-maisters eye" (Sonnet 7, dated around 1631 or 1632).
Indeed, the sonnet likewise dwells on the lack of "bud or blossom"
defining his "lot."[16] These last lines—and his continuance in this
somewhat floundering circumstance—are reassured by Saint Paul:
"For I say, through the grace given unto me, to every man that is
among you, not to think of himself more highly than he ought to
think; but to think soberly, according as God hath dealt to every
man the measure of faith.... Having then gifts differing according
to the grace that is given to us, whether prophecy, *let us proph-
esy* according to the proportion of faith" (Rom. 12:3, 6). Milton's
prophecy for himself is the lot "Toward which Time leads [him],
and the will of Heav'n." The psalm that he translates thus provides
the rationalization and consolation that God does not hide his face,
that he will act to aid the true believer. Milton in 1634 would seem
to need that reassurance, for the future is a blank.

The same themes of God's omnipotence, the deliverance of the
Israelites from pharaoh land, God's subduing of their enemies, his
mercy, and his faithful presence pervade the other psalm para-
phrased in 1624, Psalm 136. This "moste earnest exhortation
to giue thankes vnto God for the creation and gouernance of all
things," as the Geneva headnote reads, celebrates "Gods merciful

prouidence toward man" (to cite one of its glosses). The psalm is not prophetic or particularly visionary, but Milton significantly adds two verses not in the original, at the end of his paraphrase:

> Let us therfore warble forth
> His mighty Majesty and worth.
> For, &c.
> That his mansion hath on high
> Above the reach of mortall eye.
>   For his mercies ay endure,
>   Ever faithfull, ever sure.   (89–96)

These stanzas laud the vatic voice that Milton has been exercising in Psalm 114 and would envision God's heaven, except that that is beyond the ken (the sight, the knowledge) of *mortal* humans, but, it subtly intimates, not him who has been saved. Implication of the visionary mode lies beneath these singular additions to a well-known psalm, and one might suppose that as Milton wrote he thought of John 14:1–2: "Let not your heart be troubled: ye believe in God, believe also in me. In my Father's house are many mansions."

These early poems provide evidence for what has become a standard conception of the "prophetic" or "visionary" Milton. Occasionally, however, Milton's poems display qualities of both what is called the "line of prophecy" and the "line of wit."[17] Comparing "Elegia tertia" with "In obitum Præsulis Eliensis" and "In obitum Procancellarii medici" tempers a blanket classification of Milton as a poet of prophecy, while suggesting that elements of the visionary mode do appear in less than dourly serious circumstances. Such employment should not jaundice serious uses of those elements, but it does raise questions about commonplace and traditional views of John Milton. He can and does sincerely impart the visionary mode and its prophecy depending upon subject and personal "involvement" *and* profane such sacred content and imagery depending upon specific subject and personal attitude. The intention of the author—Milton—separates the author as teacher, philosopher, preacher from the reader as perceptive and sensitive interpreter.

Such is the case of these three early poems (all 1626). His elegy on the death of Lancelot Andrewes, Bishop of Winchester, begins, "I was full of sadness…and many sorrows were clinging to my spirit." "Suddenly," he writes, "there arose a vision of the mournful destruction / which Libitina [the Italian goddess of the dead] wrought on English soil," referring to the visitation of the plague in 1625–26. He laments the demise of the "most worthy Bishop," "the great glory of Winchester"; he is "dissolved in weeping" and reproaches "Savage death" for envy of such "a noble breast," such "a half-divine spirit." "While, weeping, [he] meditated such griefs deep in [his] heart" that he envisions a shining world, the "father's kingdom," and sees Andrewes applauded by "the celestial multitudes," "the new companion" saluted "with an embrace and song," and hears one welcoming the bishop to "rest forever, my son, from harsh labor" as "the winged troops touched their harps." These greetings for the faithful servant of God presage the prophecy of Revelation, and not incidentally they echo that biblical book: "And I heard a voice from heaven saying unto me: 'blessed are the dead which die in the Lord from henceforth; Yea, saith the Spirit, that they may rest from their labours; and their works do follow them'" (Rev. 14:13); "And I heard a voice from heaven, as the voice of many waters, and as the voice of a great thunder: and I heard the voice of harpers harping with their harps" (Rev. 14:2).[18] The poem is built on the visionary mode, offering an encomium to the much-admired Andrewes and implying a belief in this prophecy for all good men.

Both poems on the deaths of Nicholas Felton, Bishop of Ely, and John Gostlin, vice chancellor of Cambridge and master of Caius College, are presented in different meters from the elegiac couplet, and thereby suggest derisive comment on the requirement of composing such poems for such notables, probably to be pinned to the bier as it proceeded to burial. In the first poem the injustice of life and death is alluded to, and then countered by the bishop's words rebutting the "deluded wretch" Death, "sent from the starry heaven," for she leads the faithful to God "into the presence of the eternal Father." Here, in this "crystalline realm and court paved with beryl" (see Rev. 21:19–21) he will enjoy its pleasures through eternity. The visionary mode underlies the poem, but the use of the Horatian iambic strophe points to satire and indecent invective: the line of wit has almost sabotaged the line of vision. The poem on Gostlin is even less positive, employing imperatives to the author to "learn to submit to the laws of destiny"; even physicians must succumb in retaliation for their "snatch[ing] so many / from the black jaws of death." In the author's leave-taking he wishes that the judge of the dead (Aeacus) will "be gentle upon [him]" and that he "forever among the fortunate / may...walk in the Elysian field"—hardly a commendable way of expressing it. The emphasis in the poem is not on "Death [is] the Gate of Life" "to the faithful" (*PL* 12.571), but that death is inexorable. The nature of the meter, the Horatian Alcaic, is a direct opposite to what the nature of the poem is. It is not personal, it is occasional; it is certainly not contemplative. This ironic use of meter, which Horace used to celebrate enjoyment and to exaggerate the unexpectedness and circumstance of death, circumvents what could have been a forthright vision of persistence, light after light well used.

"Elegia quarta" of March 1627, to his former tutor Thomas Young, refers to Young's exile to Hamburg, which was surrounded by actions of the Thirty Years' War. Young had refused to subscribe not only to articles concerning faith and the sacraments in the Thirty-Nine Articles of the state church, but also to those concerning rites and ceremonies. Milton berates their "Fatherland, hard parent," for exposing its "innocent children" to action wherein Justice and Truth have vanished. "Provident God" had sent such ministers to England to "bring joyous messages from heaven, and...teach the way which leads beyond the grave to the stars." Yet England lives in such "Stygian darkness" as that which beset Elijah and Paul and even Jesus when he cast out devils from the Gergesene demoniacs. Milton cannot foresee at this time in 1627 a nation and church that will not "perish by the eternal hunger of the soul," by denying those who "honor…primitive faith." Nor can he foresee anything more than "anxious hope" that Truth will ultimately triumph—not only in England, but also on the Continent where the victory of the Catholic Holy League over the Protestant forces of Christian IV of Denmark the year before might be interpreted as disclaiming "the copious volumes of the old fathers, / or the Holy Bible of the true God." The gloom continues into the following year in "On the Death of a Fair Infant Dying of a Cough," where his niece is analogized as Astræa, the goddess of Justice, or as Mercy or Truth. All are missing still in this "sordid world," this place of "slaughtering pestilence," this life of "Swift-rushing black perdition."[19] The visionary mode does not appear, but it underpins the hopes of "what creatures Heav'n doth breed, / Thereby to set the hearts of men on fire / To scorn the sordid world, and unto Heav'n aspire" (61–63).

The Milton engaging a wider visionary mode starts to appear with "Ode on the Morning of *Christs* Nativity" (1629), continuing with "The Passion" (1630) and underlying the three English odes, "On Time," "Upon the Circumcision," and "At a Solemn Music," all three precedent to its pervasive use in *Lycidas*.[20] These three odes *directly* employ the visionary mode, the imagery of which is imbued with assumption of change in humankind and its relationship with God in the afterlife of the "regained blissful Seat."

"On Time" looks forward to the prophecy of the "long Eternity,"

> When every thing that is sincerely good
> And perfectly divine,
> With Truth, and Peace, and Love shall ever shine
> About the supreme Throne
> Of him t'whose happy-making sight alone,
> When once our heav'nly-guided soul shall clime,
>
> . . . .
>
> Attir'd with Stars, we shall for ever sit.   (14–21)

"Upon the Circumcision," engaging the double vision of two related events that was almost a subgenre of poetic expression, envisions the circumcision of Jesus (eight days after birth according to Hebraic law, and thus celebrated on January 1) and his Crucifixion, which has "Intirely satisfi'd" "that great Cov'nant" made with Abraham, by which obedience to God's Will will bring salvation. The Son of God, through his "exceeding love" for humankind and his "obedience" to the Father, has suffered the "wounding smart / This day" but will suffer "Huge pangs and strong" "ere long." Not only is the visionary mode employed here, but it declares the "one greater Man" that God provides, it emerges from "the hinterland of man's mind" concerning afterlife and its attainment, and most importantly it is presented as the "transformative power" by which "we [who] by rightfull doom remediles / Were lost in death" will (as "On Time" expresses it) "Triumph over Death, and Chance, and thee O Time."

The third ode, "At a Solemn Music," calls upon Polyhymnia, muse of sacred song, and Erato, muse of lyric poetry, to "present / That undisturbed Song of pure concent / Ay sung before the saphire-colour'd throne / To him that sits theron" (5–8). It foresees that "we on Earth" can join "those just Spirits that wear victorious Palms... Singing everlastingly" (see Rev. 7:9), once they return to obedience to God and a "state of good." The transformation of those who experienced "disproportion'd sin" to "renew that Song" will "us unite" "To his celestial consort" "To live with him, and sing in endles morn of light." The word "consort" functions two ways: it is the song of the palmers before the throne of God and it is the "consortium," or marriage with Christ the bridegroom. The image will reappear in *Lycidas* when Edward King (and all the faithful who perish) through Christ ("him that walkt the waves") "hears the unexpressive nuptiall song / In the blest kingdoms meek of joy and love."[21]

These three odes relate to one another—contrast, expand, explicate the elements of prophecy and the visionary mode, and form a trilogy of poems unto themselves, becoming a prelude to the pastoral elegy. Unfortunately "Upon the Circumcision" has often been removed from this relationship and cast into one in which it joins "Ode on the Morning of Christs Nativity" and "The Passion," since each directly invokes an event in the life of Jesus: birth, circumcision, and Crucifixion, and the Passion. Not only is each of the 1629–30 poems an entirely different kind of poem from the three odic and prosodically experimental forms, but they also treat the *effect* (or hoped-for effect) of the Nativity and the Passion on humankind. The odes do not *advise*, they *foresee*. They assume the visionary mode; the earlier poems employ its elements to ponder the effect that the birth and sacrifice of Jesus can have, is hoped to have, is possible if humankind hears the "Crystal sphears," if "speckl'd vanity" indeed does "sicken soon and die, / And leprous sin" melts "from earthly mould," if his "sorrows loud" beget "a race of mourners on some pregnant cloud." The Nativity ode presents "the celebration of Christ's harmonizing of all life by becoming mortal man" (*Complete Poetry*, 63n1). Its compositional organization of four stanzas of rhyme royal (appropriate for a celebration of Christ the King and foreviewing his Second Coming) and 27 eight-line "original" stanzas has been examined by various critics,[22] as well as its numerological significances, particularly the importance of the number four as a symbol of Man, of 27 as a multiple of the number three (Trinity) and nine (defect amid perfection as well as God's will, being just short of ten), and of the importance of the center of the "Hymn" occurring in stanza 14 (my emphasis):

> For *if* such holy Song
> Enwrap our fancy long,
>   Time will run back, and fetch the age of gold,
> And speckl'd vanity
> Will sicken soon and die,
>   And leprous sin will melt from earthly mould,
> And Hell it self will pass away,
> And leave her dolorous mansions to the peering day.

The prophecy, the eschatological vision that Revelation presents, and the contrast with the mansion of Psalm 136 are central to the poem and focalize the difference between humankind's expectant view of what the Nativity can mean and its immediate influence and reality, for "wisest Fate sayes...This must not yet be so": "Our Babe...in his swadling bands" cannot yet "shew his God-head true."[23]

The conceived "sequel" or "companion poem" to "Ode on the Morning of *Christs* Nativity" that "The Passion" seems to be (written around four months later) should receive comparison, not contrast. The comparison does not make it a better poem than contrast would evaluate it, but it does refocus the subject and intentionality of the latter poem from what criticism has usually accorded it. The title of the Nativity ode does *not* take us to view the birth of Jesus (although references to the event are included): this is some morning many years later with the implication that all such commemorative mornings may partake of the visions (or some of the visions) and thereby the significance of the birth for humankind as here presented. "The Passion," in comparison—likeness being stressed—also views a long past event and not the Crucifixion of Jesus per se, but his suffering and what the significance of his suffering is (*should be*) for us living in later times, each time Passion Week is solemnized.[24]

The problem with "The Passion" for critics has been that it is aborted after an eight-stanza proem, and Milton's lack of direct confrontation of the Crucifixion as subject of a poem.[25] The often iterated endnote that appears with the poem's publication in 1645—"This Subject the Author finding to be above the yeers he had, when he wrote it, and nothing satisfi'd with what was begun, left it unfinisht"—has led to various interpretations concerning Milton's attitude toward the Crucifixion and soteriology, and the reason for including an "unfinisht" poem in his collection. That word does not necessarily indicate that nothing more was written: it was not finished and perhaps whatever else was produced simply did not establish a real unit unto itself, whereas the eight stanzas of *a proem* to the narrative hymn that might have followed (in parallel with the Nativity ode) do constitute a unit. In contrast to the four stanzas of the ode, emphasizing the Incarnation that is being celebrated, the eight stanzas of "The Passion" represents the day of justice, a concept attributable to Albert Magnus, and thus as the cube of two a seeming triumph of the infernal trio; *but* at the same time it is the prevailing of eternal providence and eternal regeneration in medieval number symbolism. The "passion" (its root means "suffering") emphasizes the first aspect, but it becomes the symbol of regeneration and the declaration of providence. The "suffering" pervades these stanzas—in their drama, in their imagery of danger, darkness, death, in their weeping and grief (with allusion to Jer. 9:10). Corrective symbolism is suggested in the reference to the "joyous news of heav'nly Infants birth," in the *Mask* and "disguise" of Jesus' "stooping regal head" and drops of "odorous oil down his fair eyes," in the vision of the Chariot and the Prophet [Ezekiel] whereby a cherub might transport the author's spirit to the Towers of *Salem*, in the author's "soul in holy vision [that sits] / In pensive trance, and anguish, and ecstatick fit" which may infect "a race of mourners." The substance of prophecy and the visionary mode is obvious. In parallel with the Nativity ode, we might expect the hymn that follows these introductory stanzas to have dealt with a more narrative picture of the Passion, moving to a statement of the race of mourners' need to "freely undergo" "Dangers, and snares, and wrongs, and worse then so" and still remain obedient to God. Herein will lie salvation, through the example of the Son, Jesus, the Christ.

For Wittreich, "Milton avoids the subject of the Passion for aesthetic *and theological* reasons.... Milton avoids the Passion because it is too fully elaborated in Scriptures; thus, to choose the subject is to choose the most intractable material imaginable. Besides, the emphasis on the Passion is wrong. It illustrates Christ's triumph at the divine rather than the human level."[26] I strongly disagree, for viewing the triumph of Jesus is at the human level; it is only *with* the act of obedience to the Father—and "Eli, Eli, lama sabacthani" (Ps. 22:1) is significant here to emphasize the human Jesus—that the example for humans can be grasped.[27] For Charles Huttar, stanzas 5 through 8 are no longer dealing with Christ's Passion because, he argues, the dominant tradition of seventeenth century Catholic and Protestant circles relating to the Passion was uncongenial: it urged an affective, devotional approach to the cross ("the Cross-as-Exaltation"). There should be "penitence and humility more than triumph."[28] But, we should note, the "personal response" that enters Milton's poem (the looking inward that Lieb remarked upon) is not really different from the author of the Nativity ode's "affording a present to the Infant God" (becoming one later who witnesses, as it were, "the Virgin blest" and the "sleeping Lord"), having been "toucht with hallow'd fire" and rather egotistically hoping for "the honour first, thy Lord to greet." Concerned that Milton did not directly employ the Crucifixion as subject, Huttar remarks, "The Cross is itself the Exaltation, from which the Resurrection and Ascension follow as (so to speak) appendages."[29]

Leading to an important analysis of "The Passion" for Marshall Grossman is the question of the "two natures" that the Son takes on in his kenosis. "Milton's view of the Passion would require the depiction of both natures in a distinct, and, if my argument is correct, an impossible way." His comment is based on Milton's statement in *De doctrina Christiana:* "the fact that Christ became a sacrifice both in his divine and in his human nature, is questioned by no one," and "the indistinguishability of the two natures." Unfortunately the translation is not what the Latin says: "divina et humana natura" implies not separate natures in this God-Man, but a being who is both divine and human at the same time, in some kind of coalesced being. Milton places himself as a witness to the Crucifixion (the allusion to Ezekiel is called "only a prefiguration") and thus the poem "is betrayed by his emphasis on the moment of death as the central and determining event of the Passion and of human history." This argument causes Grossman to assert that the "vision of the Passion must be understood in the silence of the Word" with its significance, therefore, "written inwardly on the softened stone of the heart."[30]

The difficulty with this interesting analysis is that it may not be dealing fully with what we have of the poem and what that proem may be setting up for the finished poem. We cannot be sure how the poem would have been completed or how the "two natures" of Jesus/Son of God in the Crucifixion would have been presented. (The kenosis of Phil. 2:6–8 has raised similar uncertainties and schismatic thought about the "two" natures or the "dual" nature or the total "emptying" of godhead.) Milton ponders this aspect of the redemption in *De doctrina Christiana,* citing 1 Peter 3:18 ("put to death in the flesh, but given life in the spirit"): "no part could be given life unless it were first dead. On the other hand, if *the spirit* is here intended to represent the cause of life, there are far less obscure passages which show us that this must be understood to mean a spirit of God the Father" (YP 6:440). He concludes this section: "It is moreover, necessary for the whole of a sacrifice to be killed. So it follows that Christ, the sacrificial lamb, was totally killed."

The Crucifixion in which the Passion culminates does cause difficulties of narrative description, but whether such description would have necessarily been part of the poem can be questioned (just as the birth of the infant is not detailed in the Nativity ode). As the birth was probed for its effect, its meaningfulness for humankind, the harmonizing it achieved, at least for a while, so "The Passion" may have probed what should have been its effect and meaningfulness for humankind. Whether the confined vision concentrates only on the Crucifixion is, I think, not certain; after all, the poem is on "The Passion," which consists of more than the death of Christ, but it does not include "His Godlike acts, and his temptations fierce, / And former sufferings." If the emphasis in the poem proper were on the meaningfulness for humankind, it would probably stress the sacrifice of the Son and the exemplum it indicates for humans who too will suffer. A comparison with "Upon the Circumcision" may instruct us about the details of the vision of the suffering that would have been reported and suggests contrast between underlying counsel in "The Passion" and encomiastic depiction of the two events of "Upon the Circumcision."

Grossman is quite right, I believe, in arguing that the "vision...must be understood in the silence of the Word" and is an inward theophany, but what is beyond Milton's years in content is the question that still besets human beings concerning the Incarnation, the Crucifixion, and the exaltation of the person who was called Jesus, as well as the sheer difficulty of putting any of this into meaningful words and analogies. Nonetheless we have in "The Passion" a line of vision, a recourse to the hope for eternal life (that "hinterland of man's mind") through the redemption of the Christ, a "transformation through which the human participates in the divine." This "participation" comes to those whose "echoes" and mourning proclaim comprehension of the sacrifice made on "that sad Sepulchral rock / That was the Casket of Heav'ns richest store," not simply through sorrow for such an event.

The problems that critics have advanced that impinge on the theological content of "The Passion" arise from later work such as *Paradise Regain'd* and *De doctrina Christiana* (the latter itself causing many extreme disagreements as to what is being said). They seem not to pay close attention to the poem as a product of March 1630 and a sequel/parallel to the Nativity ode; indeed the observation that from stanza 5 onward the poem is not about "The Passion" is not reading the poem that is being written. The poem that the critic thinks should be the content and continuous content of verse bearing that title is apparently the Crucifixion exclusively. Worrying about Peor and Baalim, Isis and Orus, or the "yellow-skirted *Fayes*" is not really about "the Morning of *Christs* Nativity" either. And to report the vision of the Passion and Crucifixion as a "witness" is akin to any creative writer's imagined worlds and its inhabitants. A poem is not a theological document. While Milton may have experienced various philosophical stumbling blocks in pursuing the completion of his poem, the main emphasis in his note appended to it is his inability to achieve in writing what he wanted: a worthy poem on the prophecy of salvation and one fully imbued with the vision that Ezekiel saw in emulation of David (as the allusion to the Towers of [Jeru]Salem adduces). The subject demanded exalted and inspiring expression: it is not a subject that he was ignorant of or incapable of seeing as a transformative act. And that subject is *not* the Crucifixion itself, although "The Passion" does include Jesus' death. What critics seem to expect—want—is a poem describing the scene and drama of the Crucifixion: "The Passion" completed would undoubtedly have detailed the *suffering* endured on the cross to achieve atonement for humankind, not just a graphic narrative of the Crucifixion,[31] but with the intention of instructing readers that even humans can sustain such suffering when it results from obedience to God. It would remind its readers of the great sacrifice that the Son of God had made in becoming man. It *should* beget mourners who will reform their lives and emulate the obedience of Jesus: "recreation is at the heart of Milton's thought."[32] But Milton finds himself incapable of achieving this goal. Kerrigan has said of the writing of "The Passion," Milton "does not, like the singing prophet of the Nativity Ode, move gracefully from time to time; the art of the poem never intertwines with the art of a Heavenly Muse," and Huttar talks of its "tactlessness" and "witty devices."[33]

The poem—*in the visionary mode*—is also partaking of the "line of wit." That should not condemn it as a poem, but the execution of that "wit" may be less than successful: it strikes one as puerile. One may question the decorum of referring to the printing practice of using a black title page with white letters for a funereal volume ("The leaves should all be black wheron I write, / And letters where my tears have wisht a wannish white"); or the appropriateness of balancing "the Casket of Heav'ns richest store" with "the soft'n'd Quarry" on which he would "score / [His] plaining vers as lively as before"; or the last lines ("I...Might think th' infection of my sorrows loud / Had got a race of mourners on som pregnant cloud") that Louis Martz labeled "The worst line he ever wrote."[34] But this "inept and overreaching" poem is nonetheless a work in the line of vision, advising the reader of the fruits of "Obedience to the Law of God," of "high Justice...appaid," of him who "shall endure by coming in the Flesh / To a reproachful life and cursed death / Proclaiming Life to all who shall believe / In his redemption" (*PL* 12.397–408).

Milton's belief in the eternal providence of God for all humankind is the foundation of the visionary mode for him: it underlies the foresight of what lies ahead and the heavenly goal sought. It defines Ezekiel's *visio Dei* and, with belief, transforms him who experiences such vision, who transforms that vision to prophecy. Its existence and the need to assert it for his readers begins Milton's

Paradise Lost and it becomes Adam and Eve's guide when they enter mortal life as the poem ends. While God provides numerous things for humankind, much (all?) of it is ephemeral; only the Son is eternal and God's eternally provident gift to humankind. "The hinterland of man's mind," the monomyth of the Son, of Jesus, of the Christ, of the true hero, is its subtext, and thus accordingly there is "a reenvisioning of the originary event." (The last two poems we have examined and "Upon the Circumcision" verify this aspect of the visionary mode.) These earlier poems exhibit the vatic experience for Milton: they may indulge a surface statement of the visionary mode as in the elegy on Andrewes, they may offer a didacticism for those reading them—and Milton's full oeuvre (poetry, prose, and life activity) iterates his "one Talent which is death to hide," teaching. But they also delineate a theosis that allows an experience of deification where God condescends to cause "the contemplative to undergo a transformation," such as *Lycidas* and the first treatments of *Paradise Lost* manifest. These early poems that we have looked at are indeed a "prelude" to these later ones in which criticism has shown us Milton's employment of the visionary mode.

2 ⇌ Milton and the Culture Wars

Barbara K. Lewalski

My title may seem anachronistic, yet I suggest that the intellectual conflicts of Milton's era merit the designation "culture wars" as much as or more than the controversies to which we now attach that label. A civil war, an established church dismantled, a king executed, and a monarchy replaced by a republic could only happen as a result of profound ideological and cultural conflicts. Moreover, several of the causes Milton fought for and the arguments he developed remain, in somewhat altered form, at the center of our own culture wars: his stirring defenses, despite some qualifications, of religious toleration, separation of church and state, a liberalized definition of marriage, an unfettered press, and the free exchange of ideas and opinions. Especially pertinent to our conflicts is his challenge to fundamentalists of all stripes who interpret holy texts with an "*alphabetical* servility" and an "obstinate literality."[1] His insistent argument that such texts must be interpreted by the principles of charity, reason, and the good of humankind was developed to answer his own compatriots who cited Matthew 19 to forbid divorce, but it extends to terrorists who suppose God commands the murder of infidels, defenders of creationism and intelligent design, and judges who hold to the constitution's "original intent."

That Milton saw his participation in such cultural controversies as a kind of warfare is evident from the martial imagery he employs in text after text—in keeping with that strain of Miltonic violence Michael Lieb has explored to other purposes.[2] In his *Apology against a Pamphlet* (1642) Milton defends his sharp satire in the antiprelatical tracts as a militant godly zeal allegorized as driving over enemies in a war chariot: "the invincible Warriour Zeale shaking loosely the slack reins drives over the heads of scarlet Prelats, and such as are insolent to maintain traditions, bruising their stiffe necks under his flaming wheels. Thus did the true Prophets of old combat with the false" (YP 1:900). In *Areopagitica* (1645), famously, he characterizes the "true warfaring Christian" as one who eschews a "fugitive and cloister'd virtue" and instead "sallies out and sees her adversary" (YP 2:515). And he constructs citizen-readers and writers who are engaged in "wars of Truth" analogous to heroic combat:

> When a man hath bin labouring the hardest labour in the deep mines of knowledge, hath furnisht out his findings in all their equipage, drawn forth his reasons as it were a battell raung'd, scatter'd and defeated all objections in his way, calls out his adversary into the plain, offers him the advantage of wind and sun, if he pleases; only that he may try the matter by dint of argument, for his opponent then to sculk, to lay ambushments, to keep a narrow bridge of licencing where the challenger should passe, though it be valour enough in shouldiership, is but weaknes and cowardise in the wars of Truth. (YP 2:562)

In the *Second Defence* (1654) he explains that instead of military service he chose a polemic role better suited to his talents but "no less perilous" (YP 4:1.552). He also refers to his answer to Salmasius in the *Defence* (1651) as an epic single combat with pens as weapons: he "was attacking us and our battle array...I met him in single combat and plunged into his reviling throat this pen, the weapon of his own choice" (553–56).

But I want to consider here Milton's construction of a less militant but no less zealous role for himself: the promotion and creation of poetry that helps produce a national culture able to nurture free citizens as opposed to slavish subjects of a king or bishop. He does so by setting up an aesthetic contestation through the literary transformations his own poems manifest, inviting readers to contrast his poems with others he thought corrupting or debased in the respective genres.

In the preface to book 2 of the *Reason of Church Government* (1642), the longest and most considered statement of Milton's poetics, he openly states his desire to reform English culture. He is concerned in this preface to explain and defend his right to engage in the controversy about prelates, but he is even more concerned to introduce himself—the first time by name—as a poet, albeit one who has temporarily laid aside that central work to answer an immediate call from God and the church. Logically, his long disquisition on his development as a poet, the genres and models he values, and the effects produced by several kinds of poetry has no real place in the argument of this tract: Milton could have explained his right hand/left hand distinction and his reason for turning to polemics in much briefer compass. But it is clear that he wants to explain what he thinks poetry is and can do in shaping the national culture. Auden might lament that "poetry makes nothing happen," but Milton seems to have believed it could have potent civic consequences.[3]

In "At a Vacation Exercise in the Colledge" he voiced his desire to write high poetry in English, in "Mansus" he imagined writing an English national epic, and in this preface he formally commits all his industry and art to becoming "an interpreter & relater of the best and sagest things among mine own Citizens throughout this Iland" (YP 1:811–12). He hopes to advance "Gods glory by the honour and instruction of my country" (YP 1:810), and he expects to have an advantage over those other choice wits of Athens, Rome, or modern Italy who created literature in their vernaculars, since he can draw upon the true subject matter available to a Protestant Christian. It is in no way surprising that Milton, like most Renaissance poets, signs on to the Horatian formula that poetry should teach and delight, or should teach by delighting, but Milton is especially emphatic about its educative and social role. In weighing whether he should write epic or drama he considers which genre would be "more doctrinal and exemplary to a Nation" (YP 1:815). He does not ask that question directly of lyric, but he does believe that lyric at its best will serve art and truth together. Those "magnifick Odes and Hymns" of Pindar and Callimachus are worthy for art but faulty in matter, whereas the biblical psalms and hymns rank far above all other lyric poetry "not in their divine argument alone, but in the very critical art of composition" (YP 1:815–16). That linkage is central to Milton's poetics: he does not suppose poetry devoted to truth will be in any way limited or deficient in art, but rather expects that, like the psalms, it can achieve the highest standards of art. The Platonic concept behind this assumption and behind Milton's poetics generally is that truth and beauty are finally one. He undertook to create poetry that served truth as he saw it, that sought to be "doctrinal and exemplary" to his own nation, and that became at the same time high art. He also hoped that his poetry would have a more universal reach: that he "might perhaps leave something so written to aftertimes, as they should not willingly let it die" (YP 1:810). He has of course done that; but in contrast to what we often suppose, he did not believe that these two aims—to reform his contemporary English culture and to write for the ages—are in any contradiction.

Like Sidney, Milton expounds the Horatian formula to mean dressing the truth elegantly and making the rugged paths of virtue seem easy. He supposes that poetry so conceived could supplant "the writings and interludes of libidinous and ignorant Poetasters" that now corrupt English youth and gentry (YP 1:818). Milton does not propose to censor or limit the circulation of poems by Lovelace, Suckling, Carew, and others, but he does suppose that better poetry might replace them and thereby "imbreed and cherish in a great people the seeds of vertu, and publick civility" (YP 1:816). He all-too-optimistically expected (unlike Thomas Gresham, who observed that bad money drives out good) that good poetry would drive out bad and so reform English culture. Beyond this, he proposed a national cultural program to reform "our publick sports, and festival pastimes" (YP 1:819)—the Sunday games, dancing, maypoles, and other festivities promoted by the king's *Book of Sports* and vehemently denounced by many Puritans. Milton wanted to reform, not like William Prynne abolish, public recreation.[4] His proposed cultural program called for "wise and artfull recitations" of poetry in various public assemblies to entice the citizenry to the "love and practice of justice, temperance, and fortitude, instructing and bettering the Nation at all opportunities, that the call of wisdom and vertu may be heard every where" (YP 1:819). He also proposed academies like those he so enjoyed in Florence as a means to "civilize, adorn, and make discreet our minds" (YP 1:819).

Milton probably did not have this full poetic program in mind when he composed his early lyrics, but some of its reformist goals are evident in many poems written at Cambridge, reflecting his commitment to a politics opposed to the Stuart court's policies and culture—anti-Catholic, anti-Laudian, critical of Stuart religious repression, supportive of Protestant militancy in Europe, prophetic. His Latin mini-epic, "In quintum Novembris," on the thwarting of the Guy Fawkes plot, exudes vehement anti-Catholicism, Protestant zeal, and Virgilian aspiration. Elegy 4, to his former tutor Thomas Young (composed at the same time his college peers were writing verses welcoming the royal favorite, Buckingham, to Cambridge) sympathizes with Young as victim of a harsh regime, exposed by Stuart policies to the dangers of the Continental religious wars: "O native country, hard-hearted parent,...is it fitting that you should expose your innocent children in this way."[5] Even Elegy 3, for Lancelot Andrewes, Bishop of Winchester, introduces what seems to be an extraneous lament for the lost Protestant heroes of the Thirty Years' War, "whom all Belgia had seen snatched up to the skies—Belgia, who wept for her lost leaders."[6] It is an implicit rebuke to those unheroic English leaders, James I and Charles I, who kept England from joining the continental Protestants in arms against Rome. Milton's first major English poem, the Nativity ode, written in 1629 at age

21, contains his self-definition as poet-prophet, like Isaiah "touch't with hallow'd fire" at his secret altar.[7] It also contains a very long passage about the expulsion of pagan idols at Christ's birth, a reflection of Puritan anxieties in 1629 about what they saw as the "papist idolatry" fostered by William Laud, whose influence was steadily increasing. Notably, Milton's muse entirely ignored the various royal and courtly occasions celebrated by his fellow university poets: he has no poems on royal weddings, births, coronations, funerals, visits, or the like.

If *Arcades* was written and performed in 1632, as I believe, it was Milton's first opportunity to present a reformed genre to a public audience—the "entertainment," a genre often employed to welcome visiting royalty or their surrogates to a noble house, praising them for bringing the benefits and virtues of the court ethos to their hosts. The term was also applied more generally to the pastoral entertainments sponsored by Queen Henrietta Maria at court. In Milton's reformed entertainment the visitors—the Countess of Derby's grandchildren and others—come in pastoral guise from the "Arcadian" court to pay homage to a far superior rural queen of a better Arcadia. The work undertakes to reclaim pastoral from the court, insisting on the superiority of these Harefield festivities to the queen's suspect pastorals. The countess replaces the king in the chair of state and displays royal qualities—a "sudden blaze of majesty" bursts from her "shining throne," which is also a "princely shrine" for an unparalleled deity: "Such a rural Queen / All *Arcadia* hath not seen" (*Arcades*, 2, 15, 25, 36, 108–09). The critique of the court is sharpened in a pair of lines added in the Trinity manuscript to the last two songs by Genius: "Though *Syrinx* your *Pans* Mistres were, / Yet *Syrinx* well might wait on her."[8] Those who knew the court, including some of the countess's grandchildren who had recently danced in Caroline court masques (*Cloridia* in 1631 and *Tempe Restored* in 1632), would know that Charles was Pan and Henrietta Syrinx. These lines explicitly exalt that noble Protestant lady, the countess, above Catholic Henrietta Maria and the Caroline court. Genius, the gardener/guardian of the place, embodies the curative and harmony-producing powers of music and poetry, indicating that the virtues of Harefield are nurtured by good art as well as by the ruling lady. Genius's last song calls on the visitors to leave off their Arcadian dances to serve this more excellent queen, associating the better aesthetics Milton is promoting with the virtues of a soundly Protestant aristocracy. Milton's reformed entertainment offers both to confirm and to educate these aristocrats in these virtues.

A Mask, commonly called *Comus*, carries on this program. It was presented at Ludlow in 1634, but the shorter acting version (probably close to that in the Bridgewater manuscript) was replaced in the first publication (1637) by the version in the Trinity manuscript with two quite substantial additions—an expanded epilogue and a long speech by the Lady extolling chastity and virginity, followed by Comus's awestruck testimony to that power in her. In form, theme, and spirit this is a reformed masque, projecting reformist religious and political values, as a comparison with contemporary court masques such as *Coelum Britannicum* or *Tempe Restored* clearly indicates.[9] The ideal masque world is Ludlow Castle, not the Stuart court, and it is attained through pilgrimage; it does not, as is usual in masques, simply appear and dispel all dangers. Nor are the monarchs—or even Bridgewater—the agents of cure and renewal. And the Platonism in this masque is a far cry from that of the Stuart court: external form here does not reflect internal worth and evil is conceived in Protestant, not Platonic terms. At the end of the masque evil remains, the dark wood is still dangerous to pass through, and Comus is neither conquered, nor transformed, nor reconciled. Moreover, as some critics have observed, Comus himself is a kind of court masquer, enacting "dazling Spells" and marvelous spectacles, but they only "cheat the eye with blear illusion" (*A Mask*, 154–55).[10] He deceptively claims the world of pastoral by his shepherd's garb, but instead of the promised "low / But loyal cottage" (319–20), he takes the Lady to a decadent court with an elaborate banquet and a beast-headed entourage—a none-too-subtle allusion to licentious Cavaliers. In masque terms, an audience would expect the court scene to be the main masque after the anti-masque of the dark wood, but instead it is another antimasque: the court is Comus's own residence.

As Cedric Brown notes, Comus is the right tempter for the occasion, presenting these young aristocrats with the refined, dissolute, licentious Cavalier lifestyle they must learn to resist.[11] Moreover, the rescue scene demystifies the direct divine interventions and male heroics common in masques: the brothers' brave but impetuous swordplay chases Comus away but cannot free the Lady. It is, appropriately, the female spirit Sabrina, herself transformed from victim to deity, who serves as an agent of divine grace from the Welsh countryside. As daughter of Locrine she calls up heroic myths of Aeneas, Anchises, Brut, and Trojan Britain as an impetus for national reformation, connecting the Egertons with that heroic past more than with the present Stuarts.[12] As a personage in Milton's poem and as a singer herself, she also figures the power of true poetry to counter unruly sensuality and Comus's debased "gay rhetorick" (790). She is the good poet whose elegant songs and rituals free the Lady from the spells of the bad poet and deceptive rhetorician, Comus. The shepherd's rustic dances at Ludlow Castle recuperate pastoral from Comus's and the court's deformation of it. Then the masque dances present the Lady and her brothers to their parents, imaging the virtuous pleasure, beauty, and art that accord with the life of chastity, best nurtured in the households of the country aristocracy. Milton's *Mask* again underscores the power of good poetry and art to help produce the good social order.

In 1638 the Cambridge memorial volume for Edward King, *Justa Edouardo King Naufrago* appeared, with *Lycidas* as its last and longest contribution. In virtually every respect, as well as, of course, aesthetic quality, Milton's poem differs from the other funeral elegies in the volume. Milton adopts the persona of lamenting swain but his focus is on himself, not on Lycidas/King. King had been both poet and minister, and Milton, by completely eliding King's royalist politics and poems, could take him as a kind of alter ego through whom to explore his own most profound anxieties about vocation, early death, belatedness, and unfulfillment, the worth of a poetic vocation, and the worth of service to the church. The other contributors to the volume—chiefly clerics and other college fellows like King—associate King closely with the church and the university he served while Milton sharply dissociates him from the corrupt church. In a furious diatribe, Saint Peter praises him as the single good minister (now lost) among unnumbered "blind mouthes" (119) who feed only their own bellies, and whose wretched sermons leave their flocks famished and prey to the Roman Catholic wolf. The vehemence of this diatribe, with its apocalyptic and prophetic overtones promising that some ambiguous though formidable "two-handed engine" (130–31) will soon smite the guilty and cleanse the church, goes well beyond previous examples of ecclesiastical satire in pastoral. Milton's poem further transforms the genre of pastoral elegy as it enacts the collapse of pastoral, displaying again and again the inability of its fundamental assumptions to deal with the wanton destruction of youth and beauty and noble ambitions. But at length the swain imagines Lycidas/King enjoying the perfection of pastoral in heaven, and so is able to devote himself again to poetry—the "Dorick lay" of pastoral and also the "pastures new" of other poetic kinds (189–93). Also, Joseph Wittreich argues, as the swain twitches his "Mantle blue" he assumes poetry's prophetic/teaching role, like Elisha receiving the mantle of prophecy from Elijah taken up to heaven.[13]

In the final months of 1645, after the fortunes of war had shifted to Parliament's side and peace was imminent, Milton evidently decided to collect and publish most of the poems he had thus far written; if he could not yet produce the great national epic, he could at least offer something on account. The publisher Humphrey Moseley's presentation of Milton is fraught with ambiguities: the title page resembles the one he produced for Edmund Waller six months earlier and would use later for Shirley, Suckling, Crashaw, and Cowley, associating Milton and several of these Cavaliers with the court musician Henry Lawes.[14] In his preface Moseley invites comparison of Milton's *Poems* with Waller's, but he allows that readers might prefer "more trivial Airs" than Milton's and properly

places him in the tradition of "our famous Spencer." He also com-
missioned, to Milton's dismay, the distorted engraved portrait of
Milton that claims to represent him at age 21 but makes him look
more like 51. The most obvious example of Milton's resistance to
this packaging of him is his witty satirical epigram beneath the
portrait, ridiculing it in Greek—a language the engraver Marshall
and probably Moseley did not know. Also, in his title page epigraph
from Virgil's Eclogue 7, Milton presents himself as predestined
English bard (*vati…futuri*), whose present collection is an earnest
of greater things to come, unlike Waller who in his preface casts off
poetry as a youthful toy, offering his *Poems* as "not onely all I have
done, but all I ever mean to doe in this kind."[15]

By his organization and self-presentation within the volume,
Milton separates himself sharply from Cavalier lyricists, Anglican
devotional poets, and court masque writers, offering poems
designed to reclaim and reform genres dominated by them: pastoral,
hymn, masque. He also claims a role shunned by them, prophecy.
Waller's volume, and most of the Cavalier lyric volumes published
or about to be published, are organized haphazardly, though they
usually begin with dedications to patrons and several poems to
King Charles and other royal personages and patrons. Otherwise
they contain mostly witty or elegant love songs. Milton's volume
is carefully organized, includes multiple languages (English, Latin,
Italian, Greek), and a striking variety of poetic kinds. His classi-
cal poems in Latin and Greek, most of them juvenilia, are placed
last—a book of elegies and epigrams followed by a book of *Sylvae* in
several meters ending with a Latin dirge for his good friend Charles
Diodati that reports a first attempt at epic. This classical part is
preceded by *A Mask*, again revised and expanded to underscore its
critique of the court masque and court ethos. The vernacular lyric
"book" is placed first. It contains no poems to the king or royal per-
sons but instead begins with the Nativity ode celebrating the birth
and desired return of the Divine King and proclaiming Milton's
dedication of himself as prophet-poet. It ends with *Lycidas*, given
a new headnote pointing to the poem's prophecy, now fulfilled, of
"the ruine of our corrupted Clergy then in their height"—a gesture

that deliberately links this volume with Milton's antiprelatical polemic. I think Milton saw his 1645 *Poems* as a worthy alternative to Cavalier lyric—a volume of learned, delightful, reformist poems that would advance the project he had proclaimed in 1642: to help transform English culture through good art.

During the 20 years Milton was engaged with polemics and the other duties incumbent upon him in service to the republic and to Cromwell, Milton wrote little poetry, but he often presents his polemic battles as contests of culture. In *Eikonoklastes* (1649) he casts King Charles as the embodiment of the bad author and artist; he is a masquer in his book as he was at court, devising fictions and using disguises, cosmetics, and costumes. The frontispiece of *Eikon Basilike* is "drawn out to the full measure of a Masking Scene...at Whitehall" (YP 3:342–43). Moreover he is a plagiarist, presenting as his own Pamela's prayer from Sidney's *New Arcadia*. His book, with its theatrical garb, false metaphors, and many fictions, might perhaps "be intended a peece of Poetrie" (YP 3:406), not political argument. That seems a strange sentiment from Milton the poet, but it is glossed by his earlier reference to "the easy literature of custom" (YP 3:339)—facile court genres that are the product of feigning and mere elegance. Milton would have readers see the king's book and his own strenuous treatise as examples of two kinds of poetry and two kinds of authors. The king's, patched up of facile and unacknowledged borrowings, pretense, and foolish metaphors, promotes indolent, credulous reading; it is an idol (as the king himself is) and it promotes idolatry. Milton's, like worthy poetry, is the product of "industrie and judicious paines" and inspiration (YP 3:339); it promotes diligent effort, careful judgment, and rigorous interpretation. In the *Second Defense* (1654) Milton presents himself as an epic bard (blind like the great classical poets and seers), celebrating "at least one heroic achievement of my countrymen" (YP 4:1.685). In form and tone, as David Loewenstein has argued, that work joins "epic vision to revolutionary polemics," to create a mythopoeic vision of an imagined good social order.[16]

During this long period Milton wrote a few sonnets, revising a genre usually engaged with matters of love or religious devotion to make that small kind take up immediate political and cultural topics. Three satiric sonnets defend his divorce tracts and three others address Fairfax, Cromwell, and Vane: the first urges that victorious general to turn his attention to the harder peacetime task of settling the government, the latter two seek to engage those statesmen to defend against threats to religious toleration. He also wrote a magnificent heroic sonnet on the Waldensian massacre, which is a unique amalgam of jeremiad and prophecy.

When Milton brought *Paradise Lost* to completion in the early 1660s he was all too aware that both he and his poem might suffer the fate of the archetypal poet Orpheus from Restoration maenads. In the proem to book 7 he implores his muse Urania for protection of poet and poem: "But drive farr off the barbarous dissonance / Of *Bacchus* and his revellers," whose "savage clamor" drowned out Orpheus's song, enabling them to tear him to pieces.[17] Milton had heard about and probably himself heard the mobs in the streets celebrating the grisly executions by hanging, drawing, quartering, and disemboweling of several of his erstwhile associates and friends who had supported the regicide. He also begged the muse to find for his poem "fit audience...though few" in a Restoration culture distinctly hostile to its moral seriousness, its politics, its idea of the heroic, and its blank verse form. Dryden and many others had appropriated the Virgilian heroic mode to celebrate the Restoration in what Laura Knoppers has termed a "politics of joy," a new golden age with Charles II as a new Augustus. Dryden rang explicit changes on those motifs in his *Astraea Redux* (1660): "Oh Happy Age! O times like those alone / By Fate reserv'd for Great *Augustus* Throne."[18] Dryden's heroic plays were also being produced and published, defining as norms for the heroic genres royalist politics, the pentameter couplet, and exotic subjects dealing with the conflict of love and honor.

In this milieu, Milton published his epic in 1667, and it is a daring effort to effect cultural and thereby political change even as it is also set forth as a poem for the ages by a prophet-poet who placed himself with, or above, Homer, Virgil, Ariosto, Tasso, and the rest. The epic undertakes a strenuous project of educating readers in the virtues, values, and attitudes that make a people worthy of liberty, encouraging them to think again, and think rightly, about monarchy and tyranny, religious and civil liberty, revolution, and what true heroism is. The poem's first gesture of resistance to Restoration culture is its ten-book format, as opposed to the expected Virgilian model in 12 books—a gesture that repudiates Virgil's celebration of an Augustan empire predestined by the gods. Instead, as David Norbrook persuasively argues, the ten-book format associates Milton's poem with the countertradition established by Lucan's unfinished *Pharsalia; or, The Civil War*, treating the resistance of the Roman Republican leaders to the victorious tyrant Caesar.[19] Milton also found in Lucan a model for the tragic epic: Lucan treats the loss of the Roman republic, Milton the loss of the earthly paradise.

Another formal gesture of resistance came in the second printing of the poem. In January 1667, several months before Milton's epic came forth in the fall, Dryden's *Annus Mirabilis* was published, offering a new model of the modern heroic poem, one based on contemporary events and serving royalist interests. He presented it as a historical poem that is nevertheless a branch of epic, and insisted that its rhyming stanzas are "more noble, and of greater dignity both for the sound and number, then any other verse in use amongst us." In his essay *Of Dramatick Poesie* published in or soon after August 1667, Dryden as Neander reiterated the claims for rhyme as the norm for modern poetry of all sorts, debunking blank verse as "too low" for tragedy or serious poetry.[20] Milton's publisher Simmons evidently recognized that readers in this milieu expected rhyme and asked Milton to supply an explanation for its absence. His note on the verse, added to the next printing in 1668, describes his poem as an example, "the first in *English*, of ancient liberty recover'd to Heroic Poem from the troublesom and modern bondage of Rimeing" (sig. A4). That statement, also contained in subsequent reprintings and in the 1674 edition, associates Milton's blank verse poem with ancient poetic liberty, and the resonances of these terms—ancient liberty, modern bondage—not only aggressively challenge these new poetic norms and the debased court culture and royalist politics that foster them, but also, as Steven Zwicker may have noticed first, identify Milton's freer verse form with the restoration of English liberty from the bondage of Stuart tyranny.[21] Milton thereby presents his poetic choice as a liberating act and an aesthetic complement to republican politics and culture.

The internal gestures of resistance to the dominant culture are also evident, among them Milton's incorporation into Michael's prophecy of several issues close to his heart for many years, now with special reference to Restoration circumstances: Christian liberty, the separation of spiritual and civil powers, the inviolability of conscience and individual faith. But the most interesting and enduring gestures require readers to work through complex issues and situations to right understandings, and thereby learn to be virtuous and liberty-loving citizens. Milton hoped to educate his fellow citizens, but his poem also challenges later readers to make rigorous moral and political distinctions, thereby cultivating habits of mind vitally necessary to citizens in a free society. Among the topics inviting such distinctions are monarchy and republicanism, political rhetoric, heroism, and the paradise within.

Monarchy and republicanism: The poem sets up an ongoing comparison of the monarchy of Satan and the monarchy of God, and also a comparison of monarchy and republicanism. Satan voices noble-sounding republican rhetoric in the service of liberty to justify rebellion against the monarchy of God and the Son, Adam shows himself a natural republican when told about Nimrod, the first king and tyrant who wrongfully assumes dominion over his equals, and the Israelites wandering in the wilderness establish a "great Senate" as their government. Abdiel models the kinds of distinctions required in book 5 as he answers Satan's republican rhetoric by granting him that it *is* unjust "that equals over equals monarch reign"—a principle that might apply to Satan's monarchy and certainly does apply to Nimrod's, though it cannot apply to God's rule as creator over his creatures.

Political rhetoric: Milton challenges readers to evaluate the complexities and deceptions of Satan's republican rhetoric and the historical revisionism of his version of the war in heaven and the creation of the angels. Also, Milton's unique version of Eve's temptation requires readers to deal with a fine-sounding but deceptive personal story as the serpent, inhabited by Satan, claims to have gained human powers of thought and speech by eating the forbidden fruit, arguing by analogy that Adam and Eve will rise to divine status by doing likewise. The parliament in hell presents a political institution in action, inviting analysis of several recurring political positions, rhetorical strategies, and political types: Moloch, the archetypal hawk who can only think of war regardless of the cost; Belial the smooth-talking Sophist who is without principles and can always "make the worse appear the better reason"; Mammon the archcapitalist who seeks wealth and a magnificent empire; and Beelzebub, the loyal chief minister who skillfully promotes his leader's plans.

Heroism: By presenting Satan as an attractive, eloquent, epic-like hero/leader and associating but also contrasting him with various epic and tragic heroes—Aeneas, Achilles, Prometheus, and others—Milton engages the reader in a poem-long exploration and redefinition of heroism.[22] Also, by exalting "patience and heroic martyrdom" as the highest heroism and truest epic subject, Milton challenges readers to consider whether this redefinition condemns all warfare (including the recent English civil war) or only that associated with wrongful imperial conquests such as those of Caesar and Alexander. God's command to the loyal angels in the war in heaven to defend their realm and conquer Satan's forces seems to legitimate some wars as necessary. Yet the good angels' inability to defeat the rebels, and the progressive escalation and degradation of their warfare, which almost destroys heaven itself, redefines war as tragic rather than gloriously heroic.

The paradise within: One issue is whether Michael's promise that Adam and Eve will gain a "paradise within thee, happier farr" (12.587) than the Eden they are leaving, if they attain true faith and perform answerable deeds of love, discounts their earlier happy life in Eden. Another is whether it promotes pacifism—cultivating one's own garden and retreating from the wicked public sphere. Yet the examples of Enoch, Noah, Moses, and others indicate that the just in every age have the responsibility to oppose Nimrods or Pharoahs or tyrannous kings or corrupt clerics.

Paradise Lost is at once a magnificent imaginative vision and also a poem-long exercise in making distinctions, moral and political, in complex and often deceptive circumstances, requiring the closest analysis of language, arguments, and engaging appearances. Though at the furthest remove from propaganda, this poem is nonetheless an ambitious effort to begin to transform English culture one reader at a time, through the challenging educative experience of reading a new kind of epic.

Published together in 1671, *Paradise Regain'd* and *Samson Agonistes* directly engage the contemporary situation as they carry forward Milton's effort to redefine the heroic for his age.[23] Even more directly than *Paradise Lost,* these poems challenge the aesthetics and cultural politics of the heroic drama of Dryden and others: its pentameter couplets and what Steven Zwicker terms "its bombast and cant...its spectacle and rhetoric...its exaltation of passion and elevation of empire."[24] Milton's largely dialogic brief epic celebrates in blank verse the heroism of intellectual and moral struggle as a higher epic heroism and entirely redefines the nature of empire and glory. And his severely classical tragedy, written in a species of free verse with varying line lengths and some irregular rhyme, eschews every vestige of exotic spectacle, links erotic passion with idolatry, and constructs a tragic hero whose intense physical suffering leads to spiritual growth. Milton's preface to *Samson Agonistes* explicitly sets his practice against that of his contemporaries, describing his tragedy as "coming forth after the antient manner, much different from what among us passes for best" (4).

Milton's paired poems have sometimes invited the conclusion that Milton now rejects and repudiates the Puritan revolution and all warfare, given the wholesale violence of Samson's final act and Jesus' repudiation of civil power and armed might as a means to advance his kingdom. But Jesus' repudiation pertains specifically to his own kingdom, the Christian church, and to his millennial kingdom, which has no need of it. I suggest instead that

Milton's paired poems are again fundamentally concerned with education, moral, political, and spiritual, dramatizing in different ways Milton's often reiterated principle in the prose tracts: that the attainment of liberty, the exercise of governance, and indeed any worthy action in the service of God and country are predicated on virtue, sound moral and political understanding, and openness to illumination that leads on from the status quo. These two poems offer Milton's defeated fellow citizens two models of political response to conditions of severe trial and oppression, and they challenge his readers then and now to consider what qualities and attitudes in the citizenry are required to preserve the values and liberties of a free nation.

Paradise Regain'd, composed according to Edward Phillips and Thomas Ellwood just after completion of the 1667 *Paradise Lost*,[25] presents in Jesus a model of unflinching resistance to and forthright denunciation of all versions of the sinful or disordered life, and all faulty and false conceptions of church and state—a model rather like that manifested by contemporary Quakers, as David Loewenstein proposes.[26] Jesus takes as his immediate kingly role "to guide Nations in the way of truth" (2.473), and the poem is primarily concerned with the realm of attitudes, values, and moral choices—with gaining the kingship within the self over "Passions, Desires, and Fears, . . . / Which every wise and vertuous man attains" (2.467–68).

The Jesus-Satan debates press readers to think rigorously and rightly about kingship, prophecy, idolatry, millenarian zeal, the proper uses of civil power, the uses of learning, and the abuses of pleasure, glory, and power, as they try to determine what is wrong with the intellectually complex and worthy-sounding arguments posed by Satan and just why Jesus refuses them. Why not turn stones to bread by miracle (if one can) to feed the hungry? What is wrong with partaking of a lavish banquet (whatever the source) if one is hungry oneself? Why not gain a destined kingdom as soon as possible and by force if necessary? Why not use all the resources of classical culture to "be famous" by wisdom and to spread the "empire" of the gospel throughout the world? Especially, why not use force to free those enslaved by the wicked Roman Emperor Tiberius or the ten lost tribes enslaved in pagan lands? Jesus' answer to this last proposition insists (overharshly, it has seemed to many) that as long as their idolatry makes them servile neither the Romans nor the ten tribes can be freed, because they would immediately enslave themselves again. Stated more generally and less pejoratively, this exchange opens the question whether it is right, or even possible, to "liberate" those who do not want or understand liberation in the would-be liberator's terms.

Alternatively, *Samson Agonistes* presents a warrior hero through whose catastrophic act the Danites might win their freedom, but only if, this time, they can seize the Machiavellian *occasione*. And that, in turn, depends on their virtue and political values. The political and religious issues faced by Samson, a defeated warrior enslaved by his enemies and commanded to participate in idolatrous ceremonies, resonate strongly, as Sharon Achinstein has shown, with the situation of the defeated Puritans after the Restoration.[27] Those issues are debated especially in Samson's exchanges with Harapha and the Philistine messenger: the relative claims of religious law and civil authority, the legitimacy of outward conformity, and the overriding imperative of divine inspiration.

With its dramatic form and absence of any authoritative voice, *Samson Agonistes* exercises readers with even more complex puzzles of interpretation, as its reception history clearly indicates. That challenge is sharpened by the drama's extended attention to the Chorus of Danites and Manoa as they try to understand the events of Samson's life and then the meaning of his death in the wake of his violent destruction of the Philistine theater. The poem achieves a brilliant mimesis of the confusions attending moments of political crisis and choice, requiring readers—especially the Puritans and dissenters of his immediate audience—to think through the hard questions raised by the failure of the revolution, so as, perhaps, to be better prepared should they be offered a new chance at liberty. In the poem's terms, the questions are posed in terms of divine providence. How is a nation to know the liberators raised up by God to promote change? What signs are reliable indexes of God's favor to, or God's rejection of, leaders or nations? How can would-be liberators know themselves to be chosen or repudiated? Can sinful humans be worthy leaders? Or, in broader terms, how far can we take the past as guide to the present? How can leaders know, or their followers know, when they are led by objective evaluations of circumstances, and when simply by their own desires or delusions? When if ever is it appropriate for them to act outside the law? And if they appeal to insights that lead beyond present codifications of law, what standards can be invoked to judge their actions?[28]

The scene with Dalila also forces readers to consider issues of cultural relativism. Samson intended his marriages to afford him the opportunity to act for Israel against the Philistines, and Dalila claimed to have betrayed Samson for her country's sake, in obedience to religious and civil authorities and the "grounded maxim" of *salus populi* (850–70). That defense recalls later analogues: parents in whatever country who sacrifice sons and daughters in suicide bombings or unnecessary wars on the authority of religious and civil leaders. Or leaders who invoke *salus populi* to justify torture or unlawful surveillance. Samson by contrast bases his actions upon what he takes to be divine inspiration and what he understands as higher, universal natural law. He counters Dalila's appeal to human authorities by the natural laws of love and spousal fidelity, and he counters Harapha's denunciations of him as a covenant breaker and murderous rebel against his rulers (echoing royalists' denunciations of the Puritans) by appealing to the natural law (a staple of Puritan and Miltonic justifications for the revolution) that allows armed resistance to those oppressed "when the Conquer'd can" (1206–07).

But Samson's claims are fraught with difficulties, to which John Carey responded strongly after 9/11, characterizing Samson as a terrorist.[29] Samson's antinomian appeal to "rousing motions"—presumably an augur of divine illumination—as he goes forth to perform in and finally to destroy the theater and the Philistine aristocracy within it seems to open the door to any action, however horrendous, if the person claims divine direction. Samson modifies that antinomian stance as he promises the Danites three times that his actions will fulfill the spirit of the law and the moral norms of the community: "of me expect to hear / Nothing dishonourable, impure, unworthy / Our God, our Law, my Nation, or my self" (1423–25)—but this is simply an appeal to the standards of a particular nation and culture. And as we know, one culture's terrorist is another's freedom fighter, with the label usually assigned by the victors who write the history. By such complexities, Milton's readers are led to consider whether there are "universal" moral norms and how we can know them.

The episode of Samson destroying the theater has apocalyptic overtones, evoking the final destruction of the Antichrist's forces as well as stories from the book of Judges of a wrathful God taking revenge on his enemies. As Michael Lieb insists, wrath and dread are aspects of Milton's God, as also of the biblical deity, and Samson can be seen as an agent of his fury.[30] Yet the violence wrought by God and Samson in Milton's drama is neither arbitrary nor inexplicable, being based rather on the natural law precept that Samson, Milton, and Milton's God share—that the conquered have the right to use force to gain their liberty from evil tyrants. Yet Samson cannot stand in for Christ at the Apocalypse; there was a lot of collateral damage, although the lower classes outside the theater were spared; and Samson's victory in death is very partial.

Milton underscores the problematics of interpretation and application for his readers by refusing to the Chorus and Manoa (our proxies for interpretation) any direct access to Samson's final act while at the same time devoting about one-fifth of the poem to their efforts at interpretation. Like them, readers must make what they can of signs and of the Messenger's report as to what he saw and heard of what Samson did and said. Significantly, he did not hear Milton's Samson pray for private vengeance as he did in Judges 16:28: "I pray thee, only this once, O God, that I may be at once avenged of the Philistines, for my two eyes." But neither Messenger nor reader can read the soul from external signs: Samson's head inclined and eyes fast fixed may indicate "one who pray'd, / Or some great matter in his mind revolv'd" (1636–38)—or both. Milton portrays the complexity and opacity of human motives as Manoa and the Chorus try to understand Samson's cataclysmic act by appealing to all the usual interpretations: revenge, suicide, action as God's faithful champion. Milton's much-mediated presentation forces characters and readers to distinguish between what is necessarily opaque—Samson's motives, his spiritual condition, his regeneration—and what they can know clearly: that God has restored Samson's prodigious strength, which has allowed him to strike a blow for Israel's liberation. That is consonant with the way Milton judges leaders in his political tracts: not whether they are or are not regenerate but whether they advance liberty.

At the end of the drama the responses of the Chorus and Manoa to the changed political situation remain confused. Manoa imagines a new future in which Samson figures as exemplum and challenge: his story might inspire other valiant youth to "matchless valour, and adventures high" (1740) even as his deed has already provided an opportunity for liberation: "To *Israel* / Honour hath left, and freedom, let but them / Find courage to lay hold on this occasion" (1714–16). The Danite chorus gives some indication of a new openness to illumination in their final ode, with its richly evocative imagery of eagle and phoenix representing Samson's restored vision and powerful action in blindness. But they fall back on sententious maxims again in the rhymed sonnet that ends the work, observing that "All is best" and that "in the close" we can best know the champions to whom God and history bear witness. But the drama has demonstrated that choices must be made and actions taken *in medias res,* in circumstances always characterized by imperfect knowledge and conflicting testimony. The Chorus has learned something but probably not enough: at the end we are led to contemplate the further tragedy that (like Milton's Englishmen) Samson's fellow citizens may be too servile to grasp the new chance for liberty he has won for them. Nor did they, as the biblical record shows.[31] Yet in the drama's historical moment, that future is not yet fixed and choices are still possible. As a final political insight, this drama invites readers to recognize the frailty and fallenness of all leaders and peoples, and in doing so to understand that any successful attempt at liberation requires a virtuous citizenry that understands the political stakes and values liberty. Early to late, Milton hoped that his revisionist poetry could help create such citizens.

3 ᕁ Red Milton
Abraham Polonsky and *You Are There* (January 30, 1955)

Sharon Achinstein

1. *Critiques of Violence*

In "Critique of Violence" (1921), Walter Benjamin makes a careful distinction between "law-preserving" violence and divine violence. The first, law-preserving violence, works to establish the sovereignty of the state, but the second threatens to overturn the very foundations on which the state is built.[1] Divine violence, outside the normative and legal, is capable of destroying in the name of justice, and resembles that Miltonic "living dread" that transcends ordinary ethics.[2] The terrifying enactment of God's violence in Milton's work, that "unsearchable dispose" that Michael Lieb has so eloquently undertaken to explain, gives Milton's *Samson Agonistes* perhaps the most troubling of all theological contours. It is only one place to look for the theologico-political occasions, even necessities, of God's violence.[3] Rather than explicate the nexus of theology and violence through recourse to the psychological or ideological—or set them aside as "archaic"—this essay shall engage a set of questions that burn today as the liberal political legacy is rethought, as the relations between ethical norms and transcendent possibilities are being reshaped by our own geopolitical climate.

The *9/11 Commission Report,* the document drawn up by an independent investigative team to analyze that cataclysmic event, states, "The terrorism fostered by Bin Laden and al Qaeda was different from anything the [U.S.] government had faced before. The existing mechanisms for handling terrorist acts had been trial and punishment for acts committed by individuals; sanction, reprisal, deterrence, or war for acts by hostile governments. The actions of al Qaeda fit neither category."[4] Philosophers are confronting the implications of this category lack: the editors of *The Philosophical Challenge of September 11* have found "all of our ready conceptual assurances confounded," and they write, "We are no longer certain about our analytic instruments.... We cannot diagnose the events of 9/11 by any simple application of the usual tools. They defy our sense of legible order, and we cannot say when our categories will adjust again."[5] Our political leaders, believing they face a new threat of global terrorism, are finding that cold war tactics, including conventions of international warfare, international diplomacy, and human rights (the Geneva Convention, for example), are now outdated, ineffective against the "new threats"; and that commitments to civil liberties, including freedom of speech and academic freedom, need to be rethought. New state-sanctioned violence is demanded to respond to these dangers. The legal theorist Alan M. Dershowitz has written publicly about the legalization of torture. As Dershowitz sees it, "new ways of thinking" are needed to "strike the appropriate balance between liberty and security in the context of entirely new threats."[6] As Slavoj Žižek puts it, "liberal warriors are so eager to fight antidemocratic fundamentalism that they will end up flinging away freedom and democracy themselves, if only they can fight terror." He is not the only one to lament that the "war on terror" has been the occasion for the diminishment of freedom in the homeland. Žižek finds this typically ironic: "If the 'terrorists' are ready to wreck this world for love of the other," he

writes, "our warriors on terror are ready to wreck their own demo-
cratic world out of hatred for the Muslim other."[7]

I want to turn to history to analyze, through comparison, another
moment when domestic and international security were made to
trump civil liberties, and where a law-preserving violence justi-
fied the abandonment of humanitarian principles, and that is the
period under the cold war repression, particularly during and after
the investigations of Senator Joseph McCarthy. During the cold
war era, John Milton seemed to be starting a new life, a liberal
voice to protest the illiberalism of the new regime of violence. The
author of *Areopagitica* would become a banner for civil liberties
under the new cold war state and social restriction of political dis-
sent with the cultural paranoia aroused by anticommunists.[8] The
1949 *Primer of Intellectual Freedom,* compiled by Harvard English
professor Howard Mumford Jones, reprinted most of Milton's
Areopagitica. Mumford Jones, who had refused to take the required
oath of loyalty that would give him employment at the University
of California, printed statements by current university presidents
who had recently defended academic freedoms, followed by a series
of documents from history including Milton's *Areopagitica.* Yale
President A. Whitney Griswold, in his 1954 address to celebrate the
bicentennial of Columbia University, cited Milton, among others
(including the Putney debaters, Locke, and the framers of the Bill
of Rights) for risking much to "bring freedom down to earth."[9]

While Milton, of course, is a figure who crops up in radical writ-
ing during numerous politically inflammatory moments—the
American Revolution; the French Revolution; the Russian
Revolution, for example—during the cold war, protests against the
red-baiters, Senator McCarthy included, brought about a new surge
of allusions to Milton.[10] This was Milton the prose writer, Milton
the defender of civil liberty. Name-dropped in many editorials
attacking persecutors such as McCarthy and the Senate investigat-
ing committees, and in a challenge to Red-scare book-bannings,
Milton was an emblematic figure in the history of the defense of
freedom of the individual against the state. This was the Milton

of the prose works, newly minted by Don M. Wolfe's magnificent edition of the *Complete Prose*, whose first volume was published by Yale University Press in autumn 1953. Milton's words seemed relevant to a time when there was much discussion of the limits of freedom of thought and of speech, and his resistance ("unchang'd though hoarse or mute") challenged the lived reality of repression.[11] Indeed, his writing allowed victims of cold war repression a chance to explore the conditions in which they found themselves, their position, within state-sponsored violence, as excluded, silenced. The battle over freedom of expression was not just a battle between Left and Right, victims and persecutors; indeed, fractures within the Left were precisely why Milton—a shared object of admiration—was a matter of interest.

This essay explores one moment in the adaptation of John Milton in this culture of repression, when the CBS prime-time television series *You Are There* aired "The Tragedy of John Milton" on January 30, 1955. The piece, set in August 1660, opens in a bookshop where Milton's works were being pulled off shelves for the bonfire, and it ended with Milton fleeing, in disguise, from his persecutors. Newsman Walter Cronkite introduced the "documentary," which also presented Andrew Marvell and Thomas Ellwood, Charles Davenant and Thomas Sedley, and the witch-hunting chief persecutor William Prynne, with his list of "names and crimes" of the "vermin" Roundhead regicides. This episode was written by Hollywood blacklisted writer Abraham Polonsky (1910–99), whose teleplay evoked not simply 1660, but the McCarthyite present. Polonsky, as we shall see, was himself a hunted man, ousted from Hollywood for his leftist activity. His creative output, which included novels, teleplays, and screenplays, returned again and again to themes of censorship, political repression, conscientious action, and betrayal. In *You Are There*, the character Milton quotes *Areopagitica*, speaking lines that resonated with the 1950s censorship and state-sponsored restriction of thought: "The great issue of our time is liberty, of conscience, of thought, of worship, of action. Tell me, any of you, do you know of one honest government that has fallen because its people were free to write, to speak, to think, to worship as their consciences bade them?"[12]

2. *Abraham Polonsky*: You Are There

While there has been some attention to Polonsky for his role in left-wing literary history, the story of his engagement with the poet John Milton has not been told.[13] Polonsky, the son of educated, left-wing New York Jewish immigrants, was educated at City College of New York and Columbia Law School. A screenwriter and occasional director, his most famous films, *Body and Soul* and *Force of Evil*, which he also directed, are classic film noir masterpieces created in 1947 and 1948.[14] With the first words uttered by the rags-to-riches but morally compromised Joe Morse in *Force of Evil*, "any day you don't get killed is a lucky day," Polonsky thrust his heroes on the knife-edge of morality, evoking the violence of the Hobbesian state of nature, life in the absence of civil society's protections. When called before the House Un-American Activities Committee on April 25, 1951, Polonsky was called "the most dangerous man in America" by Congressman Harold H. Velde, who labeled him as such because of Polonsky's immense talent with words, his Hollywood achievements, his Los Angeles labor organizing, and for his "black radio" work for the Office of Strategic Services during the Second World War.[15] Reporting the testimony, the *Hollywood Reporter* that week ran the headline, "Very Dangerous Citizen" in the article covering Polonsky's hearing.[16] Blacklisting silenced Polonsky as a filmmaker for almost 20 years. He was a novelist, with his *Season of Fear* (1956) exploring the psychological and dramatic ambiguities of the "friendly Witness," that is, a one-time friend and collaborator who produces testimony for the government against his own past; Myers, the hero of *The World Above* (1951) becomes a courageous opponent of McCarthyism. Themes running through his novels and films include loyalty and betrayal—to class, family, friends—and he introduced topics of economic, sexual, and racial radicalism through a realist prose style that did not flinch from the compromises of modern life. As an artist, Polonsky was obsessed with the risks of speech — in the words of Joe Morse, the central character in Polonsky's masterpiece, *Force of Evil* (1948), "A man could spend the rest of his life trying to remember what he shouldn't have said." The protagonist of *A Season of Fear* lives with the nausea of ill conscience for his failure to stand up to authority: "The truth was that he did not feel he was doing anything right at all. Nevertheless he had to do it, and this was more like life is than what life should be." This hero, Charley Hare, hunted like his rabbit namesake, spends the better part of four chapters destroying radical books that have been hidden in his cellar, poking at them in his incinerator with a "charred pointed stick that looked like a stake from an auto da fé."[17] When he is done destroying them, Polonsky writes, "He had slashed a way through the books and himself" (147). The equation between destroying books and destroying men echoes in Milton's *Areopagitica,* and in reviving Milton, Polonsky was exploring the psychological no less than the political dimensions of such acts of violence. The state-required, law-preserving violence is suicidal.

Polonsky had been a political activist, joining the Communist party in 1936. He had been a trade union organizer and had also taught English literature at the City College of New York, editing a newspaper for a radical faction in 1939–41, and he wrote scripts for radio and television in the late 1930s, including contributing to Orson Welles's famous radio series, *The Mercury Theater of the Air.* In 1943, he joined the Office of Strategic Services. He did a tour of duty in Occupied France (1943–45), producing "black radio" programs for the OSS and Free French Forces, broadcast from England. Purporting to originate in undercover stations in German-occupied countries and in the Reich itself, these masqueraded as patriotic Germans, loyal to the fatherland, but disturbed by, and critical of, Nazi leadership. Polonsky signed a postwar contract with Paramount Pictures, arriving in Hollywood in 1945.

Because of his long associations with the Communist party, Polonsky was a target for the attack on Hollywood workers; in his HUAC appearance (April 25, 1951), he refused to cooperate and, politely declining to answer questions, pleaded the Fifth Amendment protection against self-incrimination. This was the end of his Hollywood career until his rehabilitation in the 1970s. The Writers Guild of America restored his name in 1997. When, however, Polonsky scripted the 1991 screenplay *Guilty by Suspicion* (directed by Irwin Winkler), a story of a man persecuted by a McCarthyite political trial, he had his name removed from the credits when the ending was changed. In the original story, the hunted character played by Al Pacino was a communist; the revised version changed him to a liberal.[18] His experiences were explored in his novel *Season of Fear* when the idealist character is fired for refusing to sign the loyalty oath and his former colleagues call him "dead." This situation reveals the inadequacies of a law-preserving violence, and which Polonsky conveys with bitterness:

> He was dead because he could no longer be employed. He was through the way a man who dies is through. He was unemployed and unemployable and no one cared what happened to him. When they convicted a man of a crime they put him in prison and they took care of him. They fed him. When he got out they gave him another chance and got him a job. But a man like Al would be a "dead" one. (155)

In 1951, now out of work, Polonsky returned to New York from Hollywood, joining two other blacklistees, Walter Bernstein (*The Front*) and writer Arnold Manoff, creating scripts pseudonymously for the pioneering television series entitled, *You Are There* (1953–55).

You Are There was produced by Charles W. Russell, with famous newsmen Mike Wallace, Don Hollenbeck, Edward P. Morgan, and Walter Cronkite interviewing historical figures such as Galileo, Joan of Arc, Savonarola, Beethoven, Michelangelo, Socrates, and Freud, and also witnessing the Salem witch trials and the Dreyfus case. Sidney Lumet (*Twelve Angry Men, The Pawnbroker*) directed the episodes, and John Frankenheimer (*The Manchurian Candidate*) acted as assistant director for many shows.[19] The actors were well known, serious artists: Paul Newman, Rod Steiger, John

Cassavetes, Lorne Greene, Leslie Nielsen, Barry Jones, Mildred Dunnock, and even Louis Armstrong all took part in these 25-minute dramatic recreations. These were civics lessons offered by a dominant electronic medium for major corporate sponsors—the CBS television network, the Prudential Insurance Company of America, and America's Electric Light and Power Companies.

Premiering on CBS-TV in 1953, the scripts were written by the blacklisted writers operating under the cover of fronts. The show's subject matter and approach echoed the concerns of many on the Left: political repression, freedom of speech, vulnerability to power, cultural fracture, and betrayal. Years later, director Sidney Lumet recalled that his episode on "The Witch Trial at Salem" aired the same week as Edward Murrow's "A Report on Senator Joseph R. McCarthy" (March 9, 1954). "We like to think we were slight contributors to the general attack on him," he later recalled. Lumet's memory was a bit faulty; the witch episode had been broadcast in 1953. However, the episode of *You Are There* for the week of Murrow's broadcast—"The Trial of John Peter Zenger" (March 7, 1954)—was indeed a trial-based show that centered on freedom of the press. The point Lumet sought to make therefore stands.[20] Producer Walter Bernstein characterized *You Are There* as "guerrilla warfare" that won awards.[21]

This was a time when artists were using their creative powers to awaken citizen response and to comment on the climate of repression, with subject matter highlighting forensics, betrayal, social and political exclusion and persecution. Arthur Miller's *The Crucible* opened in January 1953; another notably political dramatic work included a revival of Ibsen's *Enemy of the People* (1882, 1950); the revival of Shaw's *Saint Joan* (1923, 1951); Charles Laughton's 1947 adaptation of Brecht's *Galileo*; Lillian Hellman's version of victimization in her translation of Jean Anouilh's *The Lark* (1953, trans. 1955). Novelists, too, shared these concerns—Herman Wouk's *The Caine Mutiny* (1951) and Arthur Koestler's *Darkness at Noon* (1951) are notable. As Brenda Murphy, who places *You Are There* in this activist artistic movement, argues, there was a widespread aesthetic practice under McCarthyism "that was firmly grounded on the representation of recognizable political events—events that drew an immediate emotional response from the spectator."[22]

The series *You Are There* did not simply invite its viewers to be spectators; it exhorted them to be participants, demanding an engaged audience response. Against the creeping passivity of American popular opinion, the show presumed that there was no such thing as an innocent spectator. Each episode opened with the narrator—most often Walter Cronkite—setting the scene, creating an illusion of documentary reportage, but breaking the frame of mimetic representation by placing historical events in the present tense and uttering the show's title refrain, *"You Are There."* Explicitly, then, the distance between viewer and object was being questioned, and the reality presented was to be one and the same with the viewer's experience. This immediacy spoke a moral request as well: no audience member could be a bystander; all were implicated in the action. The extensive use of close-ups, conspiratorial whispers to the viewers, and the application of the Aristotelian unity of time contributed to the viewer's participation.

3. *"The Tragedy of John Milton"*

The episode called "The Tragedy of John Milton" aired on January 30, 1955, the date a reminder of the execution of Charles I. Walter Cronkite gave the opening exposition:

> Walter Cronkite reporting. August 13, 1660. The restoration of Charles II to the throne of England continues smoothly as royalist politicians replace republican ones in all public offices, and former high church officials once again dominate the spiritual councils of the nation. In general the people seem happy and attend in great numbers.... Nevertheless, there have been a number of anxious inquiries from abroad about the fate of some distinguished republican Roundheads, notably the blind poet, John Milton.
>
> Each day as Parliament adds and subtracts names from the official list of those to be punished by death, imprisonment or other civil disabilities, new Puritan leaders have been arrested. The most notable of these are being held in the Tower of London. Others are being sought for throughout the land. Among the latter is John Milton

who disappeared from his home three months ago and has not been
seen or heard of since. The fact that Milton is blind makes it difficult
for him to travel and it is believed he is in hiding in London. We take
you to London where Parliament is in session.... All things are as
they were then except.... YOU ARE THERE.[23]

This was not history; it was writing for the present. But Polonsky
understood the present needs of history. As Polonsky claimed in an
interview, "History was dangerous in those days. History is always
dangerous."[24] Polonsky insisted, however, that the past was not
inert; it was, rather, the sum of the active choices people made,
choices that would bear consequences visible only in retrospect.
For those on the losing side of contemporary politics, such a his-
torical perspective was necessary. When asked why he maintained
his ideals despite the persecution, the lone principled character in
A Season of Fear replies, "Well, somebody has to be in the losing
fight or else nothing would ever happen" (168). Or, as the wise
psychologist in *A World Above* avows, "We do not try to please
any man. We seek the truth. If we do not forget this, we shall never
have any cause for regret, because even our failures will in the end
create the opportunity for those who follow in our path."[25] From
the existential present would emerge myriad possibilities, and the
show *You Are There* each time located its compact 25 minutes at a
crucial scene of choice, of moral decision and action; history would
depend upon these moments of choice.

As was the case in the other *You Are There* shows, the title
character of "The Tragedy of John Milton" was introduced late in
the teleplay; Polonsky took his time introducing other characters,
setting up the cultural conflicts and political positions offered by
friends, associates, and enemies. The casting of the show played
upon the reputations of the actors and developed the ethical
dimension offered by the text in rounding out the characters in
such a short space of time. The McCarthyite Prynne, who prom-
ises to "draw attention to these vermin [the Roundheads] and keep
their names and crimes before the members [of Parliament] and the
people" (331), was acted by the American character actor Philip
Bourneuf, who had been the wicked prosecutor in the 1948 film

Joan of Arc. In the film noir *Beyond a Reasonable Doubt* (1956) Bourneuf took on the role of the aggressive D.A. who maneuvers the apparently innocent Dana Andrews into the electric chair. The actor portraying the heroic and idealistic Andrew Marvell was Richard Kiley, whose rich, baritone voice was renowned; he won a Tony Award for Best Actor for his role of Don Quixote in *Man of La Mancha* (1966); later, he did the biblical narration for the gospel of Luke in the New Media Bible (1979). Marvell, in the Polonsky teleplay, represents the righteous opposition, the brave politician daring to challenge the repression, who boldly confronts Prynne to his face: "You are a fanatic, sir, hot for blood, your soul twisted, playing on the whims and fears of lords and commons.... No man is safe from you if he defies you. Your politics are born of your lust for power, your religion of your hate for mankind, not love. But I defy you, Prynne. Do what you can" (332). Prynne replies by stating that the writer John Milton is to be killed. The interviewer warns Marvell that such open speech subjects him to grave risk, but Marvell sticks to his principles, aware of the importance of each moment for the history that is to come: "I am not eager, sir," he says to the present-day interviewer, Harry Marble, "that my tombstone should read: 'Here lies a man who survived despite all.' He who dies after his principles have died, sir, has died too late" (332–33).

The past did not merely parallel the events in the present; the past, Polonsky insisted, contributed to each individual historical actor's deeds that shaped the present. In his Milton teleplay, the figure of Thomas Ellwood becomes typical of a persecuted religious group. Bodily harassed while examining Milton's now-censored works in a bookshop, Ellwood suffers the physical and verbal taunting of the royalists. He nevertheless offers a moving testimony of truth: "If I say the truth is no truth, it is still the truth. And if every man say [*sic*] it is no truth, it remains a truth. And if every man is killed who declares the truth, then the man born will see it, so why should I recant?" (338)—to which the mocking Sedley replies, "To save your life!" as he threatens him with his sword. To me, the scene recalls not simply the McCarthyite present, but the recent past of German anti-Semitism and genocide; the public humiliation and taunting of Ellwood replays the treatment of Jews on the street under the Nuremberg laws. Polonsky's figures of Ellwood and Marvell provoke the questions about what could be worth preserving when one preserved a "life."

In the "Tragedy of John Milton," the title character was played by Barry Jones, a British character actor who usually played intellectual aristocrats and whose roles included Aristotle in *Alexander the Great* (1955); Bluntschli in Shaw's *Arms and the Man*; Count Rostov in *War and Peace* (1956); and Professor Logan in *The 39 Steps* (1959). In *You Are There*, he is found reciting *Paradise Lost* to his amanuensis, "thus with the year / Seasons return" (341), a selection from one of the epic's most autobiographical moments, which the character Milton goes on to produce for his scribe (3.40–41). There, in what will become the invocation to book 3 of *Paradise Lost*, the character Milton's words reflect on the conditions of writing—physical, political—that gave force and pathos to his art: "but not to me returns / Day, or the sweet approach of even or morn.... But cloud instead, and ever-during dark / Surrounds me, from the cheerful ways of men / Cut off" ("Tragedy," 341–42; *PL* 3.41–46). Suffering on account of the material, social, and spiritual aspects of his isolation, the poet achieves resolve: "that I may see and tell / Of things invisible to moral sight" (3.54–55). Polonsky's art, too, won out of isolation, saw freedom and even inspiration in the darknesses of the human heart—subjects of the *film noir* work, subjects of modern life.

4. *Milton the Refugee*

The teleplay for "The Tragedy of John Milton" refracted several different aspects of the political repression of the McCarthyite present through the Miltonic past. We are delivered verbatim portions of Milton's *Areopagitica*, as Milton replies to his critics, "I cannot praise a fugitive and cloistered virtue, unexercised and unbreathed, that never sallies out to see her adversary" (346); and "assuredly, we bring not innocence into the world, we bring impurity much rather. That which purifies us is trial, and trial is by what is contrary" (346), adding that "only after a lifetime of struggle, of making a choice, doth a man live to die in innocence and virtue" (346), an addition that introduces not simply awkwardness of diction ("doth") but anachronism of belief (would Milton believe in "innocence" of this sort?). Polonsky's Milton goes on to proclaim the stirring lines from *Areopagitica*, "Who kills a man kills a reasonable creature, God's image.... [A] good book is the precious lifeblood of a master spirit embalmed and treasured upon a purpose to a life beyond life" (347). His Milton promotes the diversity of opinion barred in days past and in days yet to come, "Where there is much desire to learn, there of necessity will be much arguing, much writing, many opinions" (347). His handlers are in a hurry to spirit Milton off to his next hiding place, but the poet does not leave his viewers with his political polemic; rather, he leaves them reciting his poetry. With the flower passage from *L'Allegro,* Milton recalls the delight of poetry, adding to it a moral message about the necessity of vigilance in the pursuit of liberty: "I wrote those verses so many years ago...but now I think I see more richly the true flowers that adorn our mortal lives, the flowers of the human spirit, the flowers of life, the flower of reason, of thought, of love, and that greatest blossom and crowning wreathe upon the head of man, the love of liberty" (348).

While the situations of Ellwood, Marvell, Prynne, and John Milton reflect with great drama the cold war climate of political and cultural repression of civil liberty, there is another thread in the teleplay, indeed in Polonsky's whole oeuvre, and that is the question of survival as an exile within one's own country. When asked his opinion of the restored royal regime, Milton dryly comments, "Being exiled in my own country and a fugitive from his officers, I cannot have a very high opinion" (342) of it. (This, of course, runs counter to the actual Milton's own sense of *one's country being where it is well with one*). Polonsky saw the experience of the persecuted as one of betrayal and internal exile, as his protagonists repeatedly feel homeless on account of their consciences. The psychologist Curtin experiences internal exile in *The World Above:*

"The idea that shocked Curtin, the feeling he could not accommodate or even understand, was the notion of being banished, of having been pushed all at once beyond the security of his whole life, beyond the protection of society which he took for granted. He was outside, he felt himself outside" (*World Above*, 415). The character Beethoven in "Torment of Beethoven" for the *You Are There* series announces, "I am an exile...and yet, my conception of life is heroic...to seize fate by the throat and strangle it. I cry out that I will not be defeated" ("Torment," 322; ellipses in original). As various characters discover in the callings of conscience against which necessity and survival have dictated, they often feel in exile: indeed, this is the source of their art. Even as the morally compromised Charley Hare in *A Season of Fear* embraces this homelessness, his singing its song at a cocktail party becomes his pleasure, a "song coming from the inmost breath of him, coming from his lungs, his throat, the secret places of his soul." This song gives the refrain, "It looks like I'm never gonna cease / My wandering" (*Season*, 47).

Polonsky reflects on the status of hunted persons as a common theme throughout his writing. In his "Tragedy of John Milton," the title character is a refugee, a hunted man, and one without the security of a home. In *A Season of Fear*, he writes, "In today's world every man has the expectation of becoming a refugee. You can even be a refugee in your own country, or should I say especially in your own country?...Well, a refugee can retain his dignity only by becoming an exile, a man who passionately struggles to return home, to overturn the government which has banished him or pursued him. A man must love his native land and refuse to give it up" (54–55). When the hero, Charley Hare, refuses to help his co-worker, the blacklisted idealist, "he felt that he had become an exile and like every exile he yearned for respectability" (170). Guilty and innocent alike in that world have become exiles—the guilty because of the knowledge of their complicity, and the innocent without choice.

The outcast as refugee is more than a potent symbol: Polonsky touched upon significant philosophical and humanitarian issues

raised not simply by the cold war but also by the twentieth cen-
tury experience of atrocity and state-sponsored internal violence.
Polonsky's characters in the first pages of *The World Above,* are
described as "all waiting their turn in a hostile world" (*World
Above,* 8). The central figure of that work shares the Miltonic
ambition to accomplish great deeds, as Polonsky writes of the bril-
liant scientist Carl Myers, who will suffer betrayal by his closest
friend and colleague and who, at the end of the novel, goes on trial
for his political views. As in *Body and Soul,* the theme is betrayal;
but it is also ambition to do "things unattempted." Early in *The
World Above,* Polonsky writes that Myers "wanted something still
unnamed, still unsaid, still mysterious in the universe" (44). To
his mother, Myers announces, "I will never…do anything I do not
want to do just to make a living, you understand. And I will not
sacrifice myself to get the respect of the respectable, or the fools
who run this stupid world" (44). Victims of political repression and
social betrayal, these heroes typify Polonsky's idealism, but also
reveal the psychic costs of their heroism as well as the constitutive
role of the state in defining persons; Myers becomes a man who felt
himself to be "an enemy guest" (67).

The Italian philosopher Giorgio Agamben has written that "the
refugee is perhaps the only thinkable figure for the people of our
time and the only category in which one may see today—at least
until the process of dissolution of the nation-state and of its sover-
eignty has achieved full completion—the forms and limits of the
coming political community."[26] This philosopher has provided a
powerful lexicon, derived from analysis of Holocaust political the-
ology, for describing new contexts and modes of being in the world
for those deprived of human rights and who lack state protection.
Agamben draws a distinction between the citizen and what he
calls the "bare life" of outcast man, or *homo sacer,* who, although
alive, is excluded from the laws of the social and political com-
munity. Developing ideas from Benjamin's "Critique of Violence,"
Agamben sees this *homo sacer* as neither the prepolitical nor the
political subject, but revealing both the suspension of conditions
of the subject and the originary gesture of sovereignty. Agamben's

figure of *homo sacer* is both outside and inside the law; the excluded figure (such as the Jew or the Gypsy) is what guarantees the legitimacy of the human, the one to be protected and accorded citizenship under political power. In *The World Above,* the hero Myers, out of work and hitting rock bottom, declares, "My economic situation is such that I'm absolutely incapable of making moral decisions. I get a shock. I react. I live. Shock. React. Bing bang" (72). In "The Tragedy of John Milton," on the other hand, Polonsky explored the condition of humanity that meant more than mere survival, more than mere reactivity. Significantly, Polonsky's screenplay reveals that it is the social network that promotes the conditions necessary for the maintenance of ideals. Thomas Ellwood and Andrew Marvell are all necessary to sustain the ideals of Milton and his work.

Agamben's notion of the refugee is drawn from the thought of Hannah Arendt, and his analysis of the end of politics builds upon the figures of the excluded—the refugee, the Holocaust camp survivor, the object of torture. His politics of the "living dead" is indebted to the political theology of Carl Schmitt and Walter Benjamin, the one a member of the Nazi party and the other its philosopher victim. The Holocaust camp survivor in Agamben's account is one who has been made to pass beyond the bounds of the human and the moral because the concentration camp is a legal and political, *though not a moral* space. Agamben delineates with sensitivity and rigor how the absence of moral gradations inside the camp depend upon the very constitution of sovereignty in the political and juridical realm outside it. His work demands that current global-political regimes be understood as having created like conditions for those it cannot categorize, for those who are placed, through a permanent state of emergency, outside the political system; and where even sovereignty is taking "an existence outside of the law."[27] Living in the cold war era of fanatical fears, Polonsky, too, was concerned with the ways ordinary citizens could be reduced to faceless, impotent witnesses: outside rights, outside the political order, mere bodies to be pressed into the service of power.

Polonsky suggests that history may yet redeem meaning for such living dead.

Polonsky's Milton raises questions about the ethical meanings of state-sponsored repression, though without abandoning politics as the instrument of change. For Polonsky, able to work within the mediations of corporate America during the cold war, the words of the vulnerable, the stateless, the betrayed, still have a potency that history has yet to deliver. If Agamben is working to define a new "post-political" object of power, then Polonsky's Milton can help us think about the ways that emancipatory ideals can become mediations for the reassertions of justice. By engaging distinct historical experiences, ethnicities, and identities dialectically, one dares to confirm an essential uniformity or presentness of psychic and political life. That would be an idealism or enlightenment legacy that evades the peculiarity of history, as charges Dominic LaCapra, who offers a deep critique of Agamben's analysis. LaCapra wonders "how general this exceptional writing should be and whether it should function to provide the perspective from which all else is approached 'after Auschwitz.'"[28] The figure of the refugee, of bare life, risks assuming a postapocalyptic character, out of real time and real activity. Yet, to make this figure the truth of modernity is, as Polonsky insists, also to embrace history, to find media that permit the victims and perpetrators to come out of lawlessness into political and international community. Viewed from the current moment of post-9/11 thinking, the cold war—with its betrayal of civil liberties and refusing its citizens the very rights that defined them as Americans—shows the emergence of "post-political" thinking that is only beginning to be theorized by such thinkers as Agamben and Žižek. But this post-9/11 moment is also one in which we can observe how the great writer John Milton, a promoter of new concepts of freedom in his own day, can ever be a source of inspiration and reflection anew.

Part II

Milton's Visionary Mode:
Contemporary and Later Contexts

4   How Hobbes Works

Stanley Fish

In *Milton and the Culture of Violence* (1994) and in many other important writings, Michael Lieb has been concerned to show us what he sometimes calls the "darker, more unsettling side of Milton's personality" and Milton's God.[1] While poems like *Lycidas* and "At a Solemn Music" end in visions of a universal harmony of undifferentiated voices free of discord and jarring notes, Milton, Lieb tells us, was throughout his life haunted by the fear of the "barbarous dissonance" that attended the dismemberment of Orpheus.[2] The poet, in Lieb's account of him, was "desperate to avoid" the "return to the world of Chaos"—that "universal hubbub wild / Of stunning sounds and voices all confus'd" (*PL* 2.951–52)—that Orpheus's death at the hands of a "wild Rout" (*PL* 7.34) symbolized for him. Milton's response to the specter of violent chaos is to assert against it a faith in a power even more dreadful. Lieb quotes the place in *De doctrina Christiana* where Milton urges the practice of *timor dei*, "reverencing God as the supreme Father and Judge of all men, and fearing above all to offend him."[3] Assaulted by forces that threaten to overwhelm him, the Miltonic "I," says Lieb, always "seeks refuge in a power beyond itself."[4] That power, however, resides elsewhere—Lieb cites *Samson Agonistes*:

"our living Dread who dwells / In *Silo* his great sanctuary" (1673–74)—and one must affirm it in the face of *visibilia* that do not unambiguously declare it.

The strength to do so, if one has it, comes not from the world—which, considered in itself rather than as the creation of a power it cannot contain, points in too many moral directions—but from an internal resource that must be actively and willfully summoned. The danger is that the outward surface of things—mere forms—will overwhelm or obscure an inner truth that surfaces do not display; this inner truth, if recalled and clung to, not only dispels surfaces but also reconfigures them. The clearest example is the Lady in *A Mask,* who, surrounded by darkness and beset by a "thousand fantasies" of "beck'ning shadows dire" (205, 207), nevertheless relies on the anchor of her "virtuous mind" (211) and is rewarded both by a vision—"thou unblemish't form of Chastity / I see ye visibly" (215–16)—and by an alteration in the physical landscape—"there does a sable cloud / Turn forth her silver lining on the night" (223–24).

Milton is always imagining his heroines and heroes this way (including himself, as in the concluding sentences of *The Ready and Easy Way*), as solitary figures "In darkness, and with dangers compassed round" (*PL* 7.27) who reject the evidence of things seen and stake everything on a loyalty (to the God of dread) for which there is often no empirical support. The model is Abdiel, who alone dissents from the infernal council—Satan calls him a "seditious angel" (*PL* 6.152)—and receives this praise from his Lord: "for this was all thy care / To stand approved in sight of God, though worlds / Judged thee perverse" (*PL* 6.35–37). Abdiel, the Lady, the young Jesus in *Paradise Regain'd,* the poet in *Lycidas,* the Samson who finally frees himself from positive law, Milton in the *Apology*—they all exemplify Milton's conviction that "obedience to the Spirit of God, rather then to the faire seeming pretences of men, is the best and most dutifull order that a Christian can observe."[5] The word "order" is tendentious, for behind it is the recognition that in the eyes of those who abide by the order of worldly appearances ("the faire seeming pretences of men"), the lone dissenter will be seen as a figure of *dis*order.[6] The hero of faith in Milton's prose and poetry is always the one who marches not only to a different but also to an inaudible drummer and refuses to measure himself or herself "by other mens measures" (YP 1:904–05).

Other men's measures, by contrast, are the cornerstones of the philosophy of Thomas Hobbes (1588–1679), which receives its fullest expression in *Leviathan* (1651). For Hobbes, the private man who follows the inner promptings of his faith and prefers them always to public procedures and decorum is a figure not of heroism but of danger. It is he and others like him who precipitate and justify rebellion against established authority and thus bring about a condition of "continuall feare" and a way of life that is "solitary," but not nobly so as Milton would have it, for it is "poor, nasty, brutish, and short."[7] Where Milton distrusts surfaces because they distract the virtuous man and lead him away from the proper devotion to an internalized spirit, Hobbes valorizes and honors surfaces because they alone can protect us from the political fantasies of those who consult their own hearts and conclude from what they find there that it is necessary and good to kill a king.

Like Milton, Hobbes fears a return to chaos, but he identifies the coming of chaos with just what Milton celebrates—an antinomian virtue that knows no law except for the law written on the fleshly tables of the individual heart. Milton believes that discipline and order must come from within and cannot be imposed by external forms; a nation of transformed and regenerate people will naturally produce good and pious actions just as from a "sincere heart" the appropriate praise of God will "unbidden come into the outward gesture" (YP 1:941). Hobbes believes that external forms are all that stand between us and the war of all against all and that the claim of sincerity, because it is available to everyone and defies public verification, licenses everyone's crimes against life and property. Milton yearns for a transformation of vision in which everyone will be, like the Lady of whom *A Mask* says, "Sure something holy lodges in that breast" (246). Hobbes devises a technology of administration, not in order to encourage vision, but to hold it at bay. Milton worships a God who is removed from human

ways and must be arduously sought and found only by a few cho-
sen persons. Hobbes presents for our worship and fear a "Mortall
God" (227) who is the artificial construction of those who choose,
for entirely prudential reasons, to obey him. In short, if Milton, as
I have argued elsewhere, works from the inside out, Hobbes works
exclusively on the outside and regards the inside as a realm to be
avoided at (literally) all costs.[8]

The judgment of history has been kinder to the regicide than to
the arch-formalist, but in what follows I shall suggest that there
may be more to say for Hobbes than is sometimes assumed.

1.

Hobbes works by dismissing as absurd what many of his read-
ers will think of as obvious. This strategy is typically deployed
with a flourish and always points in the same direction. Here is
an example from chapter 7 of part 1 of *Leviathan*. It centers on the
idea of conscience, although that word does not appear until the
middle of the passage where it is redefined in a way that makes
Hobbes's usual point. The sequence begins with an account of how
public knowledge of a fact—knowledge based on what Hobbes
has earlier called "settl[ed] significations" (105), definitions gener-
ally agreed upon and placed at the beginning of any train of rea-
soning—binds men to certain verbal, and finally moral, actions:
"When two, or more, men, know of one and the same fact, they
are said to be Conscious of it one to another; which is as much to
know it together" (132). That is to say, their knowledge of the fact
is not an internal private matter—neither man looks inward for a
verification of it—but a matter of public record, and as a matter
of public record available to anyone, independently of his personal
inclinations, biases or desires. It follows then, says Hobbes, that
one who would deny this fact or replace it with some fanciful sub-
stitute has willfully departed from what he consciously knows to
be true and deserves to be condemned. It is at this point that the
word "conscience" is first used: "It was, and ever will be reputed
a very Evill act, for any man to speak against his *Conscience*, or to

corrupt or force another to do so" (132). What is surprising is that
the phrase "speak against his conscience" would usually be taken
to refer to someone who surrenders his or her private judgment of
what morality requires to some merely public formula. It is in this
spirit, for example, that Milton's Samson responds to the demand
that he come and entertain the Philistine nobility with feats of
strength. He refuses, and when the Messenger warns that the Lords
will be offended, and that he should take care to "Regard thyself,"
he retorts, "My self? My conscience and internal peace" (133–34).
Or, in other words, my first obligation is to the law written on the
fleshly table of my heart and not to the law of any state, be it either
Hebrew or Philistine. I will not act against my conscience in defer-
ence to the accident of political authority.

For Hobbes, however, conscience is violated precisely when
one does what Samson does—prefer the guidance within to the
guidance provided by publicly formulated definitions and obliga-
tions. Hobbes knows that the Miltonic sense of conscience is now
the standard one, but he regards it as a corruption. Once, he tells
us, conscience was understood as he understands it—a consci-
entious observance of the laws as they have been set down and
published—but at some point "men made use of the same word
metaphorically for the knowledge of their own secret facts and
secret thoughts" (132). That is, men departed from what they were
conscious of *together*—departed from meanings that in no way
depend on private perceptions—and opted instead for the mean-
ings concocted in the laboratory of their own individual ideas and
imaginings. Earlier, Hobbes has defined "metaphorically" as using
words "in other sense than they were ordained for" (102). The
ordination in question is not by God, but by agreed upon conven-
tions. "Conscience" is made metaphorical when it is taken to refer
to something unavailable to public inspection, and, once made
metaphorical, the word then gives rise to and legitimates a meta-
phorical world where nothing is fixed, and everyone is free—by
this perverted law of conscience—to assign meaning and value in
any way that pleases: "Men, vehemently in love with their own
new opinions, (although never so absurd), and obstinately bent

to maintain them, gave those their opinions also that reverenced name of Conscience" (132).[9] Misuse a word, and the next thing you know, private desires have invaded the sphere of public stability. Depart from a settled signification, and you are on the way to legitimizing the worst actions. As Hobbes observes in a later chapter (he has his eye on 1649), any man who wants to kill his king need only first "call him [a] Tyrant"; for then he does not have to admit to *"Regicide,* that is killing of a King," but only to *"Tyrannicide* that is, killing of a Tyrant"* (369). A little change in vocabulary, and what is unlawful is made lawful and an entire government is brought down.

Hobbes's entire philosophy and method can be extrapolated from these small examples. The method is simultaneously to introduce and scoff at standard meanings and concepts to which his readers are likely to be attached. You think that the word "conscience" refers to an inner voice that must be obeyed if you are to be moral? No, that is the very definition of *"im*morality," as anyone with a grain of sense should know. You think that "tyrannicide" is the name of a rational and defensible action? No, "tyrannicide" is a rhetorical device employed by men who would hide from you, and perhaps from themselves, the perversity and absurdity of what they propose. The philosophy is a philosophy of surfaces—of the superiority of procedural and conventional notions to substantive and internal ones. If any quarter whatsoever is given to private desires, idiosyncratic (nonpublic) definitions, religious revelations, or grand moral imperatives, the structure that holds things together and keeps men's instincts for plunder and self-aggrandizement in check will crack and tumble. The reason is simple: private desires, subject-centered definitions, religiously inspired agendas, comprehensive moral schemes are by definition plural—manifestations of the "difference in mens passions" that lead "some mens thoughts [to] run one way, some another" (135)—and in the absence of any natural or hard-wired measure of precedence and superiority, such a measure must be artificially devised ("artificial" is Hobbes's favorite honorific), and if it is to do its job, that measure must be as empty of substantive aspiration as possible. The trouble, however, is that in its present state our moral vocabulary is too full of substance, and therefore it must be purged of the pretensions that make it not only useless (because it has no single referent) but subversive (because it licenses precisely what must be curbed, the sway of private judgments). Hence the strategy, enacted over and over, of first invoking a word or phrase in its now impure form and then rescuing it from the corruption of positive morality.

Sometimes the strategy is performed almost as an aside, as when Hobbes begins a list of "absurd significations" with familiar examples like a "round Quadrangle" or "accidents of Bread in cheese" but ends it with "A *free Subject*; a *free-Will*; or any *Free*, but free from being hindered by opposition" (113). I know, he is saying, that many of you will believe that being free is the most desirable of states, the hallmark of your dignity; but think about the phrase "free subject": how can you be a subject, that is, a person living under magistrates and laws, and be free? It makes no sense; it is, as Hobbes says, (it is his favorite word of opprobrium) "absurd." And on the other hand, if you take "free" literally—that is, in the only way it should be taken, in the corporeal (not spiritual) sense of "free from being hindered," free to do anything you like without any restraint whatsoever—then you are by this definition free to be a menace to your neighbors as they, in turn, are free to be menaces to you. Far from being desirable, the life of freedom is the worst imaginable, as hordes of what Hobbes terms "masterlesse men" (266) go their marauding way without hindrance; the life of freedom is the life of total vulnerability and nonstop anxiety.

Later this small moment—it is, after all, a point made in the service of another—is expanded into a full chapter entitled "Of the Liberty of Subjects" (the title itself is a Hobbesian joke) (261–74). Here the argument is spelled out. Just as people corrupt the notion of conscience when they make it a private virtue rather than a resolution conscientiously to adhere to public understandings, so do they misconceive ("abuse") liberty and give it a "specious name" when they take it as a "Private Inheritance, and Birth right," and fail to understand that liberty "is the right of the Publique only" (267). The liberty of which we should make "frequent and honorable mention," says Hobbes, "is not the Libertie of Particular men; but the Libertie of the Commonwealth," which is at liberty to defend its borders and interests and thereby to protect the citizens who live not in liberty but in obedience to the sovereign's laws. It is "not that any particular men had the Libertie to resist their own Representative"—which would be the case were liberty a personal birthright and not a condition (the condition of being free to move around) secured by the *general* institution of public restraints—"but that their representative had the libertie to resist or invade other people" (267). If resistance were the right of every man according to what he was pleased to call his "conscience," that is, if there was a "full and absolute Libertie in every Particular man," if men always had the liberty of "doing what their own reasons shall suggest," the result would be "no inheritance, to transmit to the Son, nor to expect from the Father; no propriety of Goods or Lands; no security" (266). How can anyone desire *that* liberty "by which all other men may be masters of their lives" (264) and not be "absurd"?

The absurdity follows from the mistake of defining liberty as "an exemption from Lawes" in favor of some inner law invoked as a higher authority (264); the true meaning of liberty can be nothing but the "corporall Liberty" of not being "imprisioned, or restrained, with walls or chayns" (264, 262). *That* liberty, Hobbes points out, is enjoyed by every citizen who has not been incarcerated for failing to respect the corporal (not essential) liberty of fellow citizens (by stealing, assaulting, embezzling, and so on), and therefore it is once again absurd "for men"—that is those who live within the constraints of the law—"to clamor as they doe, for the Liberty they so manifestly [already] enjoy" (264). In order to keep things straight, Hobbes observes, all you have to do is refrain from applying "the words *Free* and *Liberty*" to "anything but *Bodies*" (262). Any other application will be metaphorical and open the way to internalizing a concept whose true meaning and utility must remain public and external. Either liberty—properly understood as the liberty to walk in the streets and "buy, and sell, and otherwise contract with one another" (264)—is already the possession of those who abide by established authority, or liberty is the name of an anarchic right to go one's own way with no regard for the ways of others, and as such must be repudiated either as a political condition or a legitimate aspiration.[10] One must give up liberty in this second sense in order to secure it in the first. Unless every man lays down his *"Right, of doing anything he liketh,"* he will have no defense against another who would assert "his own Right to the same" (190).

2.

It is clear from these passages that getting the definition of liberty (or freedom or conscience or tyrannicide) wrong is not simply to have made a conceptual or philosophical error, but to have endangered the good order and security of the society. Let the wrong ideas get into people's heads and there is no telling what they will do, although you can be pretty sure that what they do will be bad. That is why Hobbes follows the paragraphs parsing the correct and incorrect understandings of liberty with a call for indoctrination and censorship. For, he says, "when the same errour [of taking liberty in a private rather than a public sense] is confirmed by the authority of men in reputation for their writings in this subject, it is no wonder if it produce sedition, and change of Government" (267). Especially dangerous are those "Greek, and Latine Authors" who teach that *"no man is* Free *in any other Government"* than a democracy, and that therefore it is lawful and virtuous to depose one's monarch. Those who read in these authors,

> From their childhood have gotten a habit (under a false shew of Liberty) of favoring tumults, and of licentious controlling the actions of their Sovereigns; and again of controlling those controllers, with the effusion of so much blood; as I think I may truly say, there was never any thing so deerly bought, as these Western parts have bought the learning of the Greek and Latine tongues. (267–68)

And the remedy? Care by the sovereign that the right and not the wrong doctrines are taught and read:

> [The sovereign must] be Judge of what Opinions and Doctrines
> are averse, and what conducing to Peace; and consequently, on
> what occasions, how farre, and what men are to be trusted with-
> all, in speaking to Multitudes of people; and who shall examine the
> Doctrines of all bookes before they be published. For the Actions
> of men proceed from their Opinions; and in the wel governing of
> Opinions, consisteth the well governing of mens Actions. (233)

This conclusion follows from everything that has preceded
it—from the discussions of conscience, freedom, liberty and
countless other matters; given the relentless unfolding of Hobbes's
argument, it makes perfect sense. But once again it is a sense delib-
erately counter to the sense that usually accompanies the rejec-
tion of censorship in the liberal tradition of which Hobbes is one
founder. In that tradition the question, Why allow the free publi-
cation of opinions and doctrines?, has always been answered with
the reasons Milton gives in his *Areopagitica*—to encourage dis-
sent, to prevent the state from criminalizing criticism of itself, to
provide self-governing citizens with the information necessary to
make informed decisions, to foster civic virtue and judgment by
allowing opposing views to contend with one another in a free and
open encounter. But these are all *bad* reasons if you distrust and
fear the very abilities a regime of unfettered publication promises
to produce (because you fear and distrust the unfettered energies of
humanity), if you fear that dissent will lead to dissatisfaction with
the present order of things, if you fear that a state that allows itself
to be challenged will lose its authority and its ability to keep the
peace, if you regard the notion of citizens governing themselves
with horror because each of them will want to go in a different
direction with no one to stop them, if you identify civic virtue
with obedience to established authority and regard private judg-
ments, especially those that have been well developed and exer-
cised, as the source of all troubles.

But what, one might ask, about truth? In Milton's *Areopagitica*,
and in every free expression defense that has followed his, the
importance of facilitating and encouraging the search for truth
is always a main reason for rejecting censorship. Since we are all

fallible, the argument goes, and since we are all prone to mistake our necessarily partial views for the true ones, it is necessary that there be a mechanism for ensuring that no view that has the potential of advancing the search for truth will be suppressed: "If it come to prohibiting, there is not ought more likely to be prohibited than truth itself; whose first appearance to our eyes bleared and dimm'd with prejudice and custom, is more unsightly and unplausible than many errors" (YP 2:565). Hobbes is ready for this objection and indeed raises it himself in the same paragraph: "And though in matter of Doctrine, nothing ought to be regarded but the Truth; yet this is not repugnant to the regulating of the same by Peace. For doctrine repugnant to Peace, can no more be True, than Peace and Concord can be against the Law of Nature" (233). Hobbes agrees that if it repressed the truth, regulation would be censorship, and therefore bad; but, he reasons, since the highest truth of all is the truth that peace and stability must always be preserved, any regulation of opinions tending to tumult and sedition is not a violation of truth's primacy, but a protection of it. What he has done here is substitute for the idea of *searching* for the truth—a truth by definition not fully available to us now—the idea of *hewing* to a truth that has been stipulated in advance. Rather than being a mysterious and elusive entity whose location is always shifting—Milton's definition—truth in Hobbes's argument is quite simply and formally defined as that which conduces to peace. The questions "What is Truth" and "Is this or that assertion true" are no longer deep questions—remember, Hobbes is the philosopher of surfaces—provoking sophisticated metaphysical contortions, but easy and automatic questions. Is the assertion, whatever it is, in harmony with the imperative of peace? If the answer is yes, it is true; if the answer is no, it isn't.

Once again Hobbes has taken a supposedly substantive concept—in this case *the* substantive concept—and made it into a matter of a settled convention which, once established, gives operational force to the judgment that something is or is not true. In another chapter, exactly the same formalization or "thinning" of a substantive value is performed with respect to the question, Is it or is it not just? In some philosophies the quest for justice—undertaken within the conviction that justice cannot be identified with existing positive law—takes a long and tortured and uncertain path. In Hobbes's philosophy, justice is found quickly and unproblematically in the idea of contract. It is easy to see why contract would be the branch of law Hobbes finds congenial. A contract is an agreement between persons who bind themselves to reciprocal actions as they are stipulated by the terms of a writing. A breach occurs when one of the parties ceases to abide by the terms; that party is then subject to a penalty. The sequence is entirely formal in that no independent assessment of the terms—no questions like, Are they fair, or Do they square with religious or moral or social norms?—is to the point; for the point is simply whether or not someone has or has not kept his or her word irrespective of the wisdom or prudence of having given it in the first place. You cannot receive either the credit for having kept your word or blame for having failed to keep it unless there is a public record of your word that can serve as the measure for assessing your actions. That is to say, the possibility of doing something good or bad exists not in the abstract—in some overarching moral system—but only in relation to a published contract. Morality, or at least this part of it, follows from certain speech acts and has no substantive form.

Hobbes says all this and more in a brilliant paragraph (202). First he explains what the moral life is like before there are covenants: "Where no Covenant hath preceded, there hath no Right been transferred, and every man hath right to every thing." In the state of nature, where there is no natural bar to the fulfilling of one's desires, nothing prevents a man from believing that everything should belong to him; everyone can justify his desires to himself and no independent public norm sets limits to those desires and labels them legitimate or illegitimate. "Consequently," says Hobbes, "no action can be Unjust." But once contractual terms have been formulated and agreed to by two or more, those terms immediately define the proper limits of desire and determine what will subsequently be deemed lawful and unlawful behavior. "But when a Covenant is made, then to break it is *Unjust*." All you need is a compact in relation to which you can default, and "unjust" becomes a possible description of your action where before the only descriptions available were successful and unsuccessful (you got away with it or you didn't.) It follows then, says Hobbes, that "the definition of INJUSTICE, is no other than *the not Performance of Covenant."* By "no other than," he means no *more* than; there is no deep moral content to injustice, just the fact of not having abided by your word, whatever it is and in whatever circumstances you gave it. It is an entirely procedural account of injustice, and along with it comes an entirely procedural, nonsubstantive account of justice: "And whatever is not Unjust, is *JUST."* No agonizing debates about conflicting duties or about the tension between natural law and positive law; no grand battles between utilitarian and normative justifications for action. Just a simple question: Is the action in accordance with the covenant? (Not the wise covenant or the fair covenant or the mutually beneficial covenant, but the agreed-upon covenant.) If the answer is yes, the action—however you might like or dislike its consequences—is just; if not, unjust. That's all there is to it, just as all there is to the truth of a doctrine is its conformity to the imperative of seeking peace.[11]

For Hobbes, this point is the whole of morality and is introduced as his third law of nature: *"That men performe their Covenants made"* (201). Just do what you said you would do, and you earn the description "moral." What drops out in this view is any inquiry into whether what you have pledged to do and done is good by some independent measure.[12] And that is why Johann Sommerville declares, "it is doubtful whether it makes sense to describe Hobbes as having any genuine moral system at all."[13] By "genuine" Sommerville means a system the content of which would be a set of general normative obligations which is prior to, and can be invoked as a check on, any particular act—including the act of entering into a covenant—we might perform. To this Hobbes would reply that the problem with any such "genuine moral system" is that there is more than one, indeed as many as there are people with different passions, and that therefore one would purchase moral depth at the cost of surface stability—at the cost, that is, of conflict, and, eventually, of civil war.[14] The way to stabilize surfaces—to provide for the orderly conduct of domestic, civic, and commercial business—is to remain resolutely on the level of surfaces, on the level of conventional forms (of stipulated meanings, of negotiated terms of contract, of political allegiance) whose chief recommendation is not that they correspond to reality or are in touch with goodness and virtue, but that they have been publicly proclaimed and so can serve as the artificial constraint made necessary by the unavailability of a natural constraint everyone would recognize and obey.

The only requirements are publicity and perspicuousness: if the definitions of words are settled and generally known, if the terms of contract are unambiguous and published, if the hierarchy of political authority is clear and not subject to dispute, life will work irrespective of whether the definitions, the terms, and the political arrangements have the content God and nature would approve (who's to know?). When people flourish in a state, says Hobbes, it is not because the man who rules them has the "right"—because of his superior wisdom and virtue—to rule them, but because he is the man "they obey" (380). The moral status of the one who is obeyed is irrelevant to the function he performs, the function of assuring "concord of the Subjects" (380).[15] It follows then that if the one chosen ceases to be wise and a person of integrity, he should be removed. In Hobbes's account removal of a sovereign is justified only if he is not keeping up his end of the bargain; that is, if he is no longer able to protect those who swear fealty to him: "Take away in any kind of State the Obedience (and consequently the concord of the People), and they shall not onley not flourish, but in short time be dissolved" (380). And, by the same reasoning, when a legal system flourishes, it is not because it embodies or reflects the ideal of justice, but because it has set up procedures by which citizens can order their lives and avoid penalties.

Earlier in the *Leviathan*, Hobbes provides a parallel account of the growth and establishment of knowledge. When science flourishes, he explains, it is because words have been precisely defined and then combined by rules of "Connexion" into "general

Affirmations" (the generality being entirely conventional, a matter of adhering to what has been set down), leading finally to a "Conclusion" that follows not from the shape of the world or from a Platonic idea of nature, but from the order of discourse. But, warns Hobbes, "if the first ground of such Discourse be not Definitions; or if the Definitions be not rightly joined…then the End or Conclusion is…OPINION" (131), no more than what some private person said; and if opinion is unchecked and allowed to proliferate, you will soon find yourself "wandering amongst innumerable absurdities; and their end, contention and sedition" (117). Always the same lesson: absurdities are ready at any moment to enter and disrupt discourse and life. The only way to keep them at bay is to resist the temptation of the private and the substantive and put your faith—a word deliberately chosen—in the public enforcement of artificial, stipulated conventions.[16]

Everything, then, depends on the order of words, but at the same time the order of words is the source of danger. Salvation is linguistic, but so is disaster. Both parts of this lesson are spelled out in the fourth chapter of *Leviathan* where Hobbes tells us first that there is "nothing in the world Universall but Names" (102), and second that the rightness of the names is synthetic not natural; the world does not suggest them; rather, their imposition (his word) and subsequent combining of them into general affirmations delivers to us a world—entirely discursive—about which we can then reason: "By this imposition of names…we turn the reckoning of the consequences of things imagined in the mind, into a reckoning of the consequences of Appellations" (103). The mind registers some images—the residue of *"decaying sense"* Hobbes has explained earlier (88)—and the same mind brings order to that random profusion by first coming up with, and then adhering to, the names it has set down. Once the order of names has been established (the reasoning is exactly the same as the reasoning that derives justice from contract), it is then possible to say of an assertion that it is true or false; not because some thing in the world pronounces either verdict, but because some name artificially instituted now stands as a measure of accuracy or its opposite. "For," says Hobbes

in a pronouncement as postmodern as anything said by Richard
Rorty, who indeed says exactly the same thing, *"True* and *False*
are attributes of Speech, not of Things. And where Speech is not
[that is, where there is no conventional system of signification],
there is neither *Truth* nor *Falsehood"* (105).[17] Without an in-place
system of signification, an artificial system devised by people with
no privileged relationship to the world, true and false statements
about the world (forever removed from direct inspection) cannot
be made.

The methodological conclusion follows immediately: "Seeing
then that *truth* consisteth in the right ordering of names...a man
that seeketh precise *truth,* had need to remember what every name
he uses stands for," not because he will thereby be in touch with
the thing the name refers to, but because in a world where every-
thing is in motion, where experience is made up of sense impres-
sions decaying even as they register, where people are driven by
the diverse desires of their diverse passions, there has to be some-
thing stable in relation to which mental life and civic life can be
organized, and that something can only be artificially devised
names and the strict logic by which they are combined and con-
nected. The person who loses a grip on that conventional stability
loses meaning, truth, and everything else: "He will find himselfe
entangled in words, as a bird in lime-twiggs; the more he struggles,
the more belimed" (105). This is not a warning against the dan-
ger of being seduced by words into forgetting about things on the
model of Cato's *rem tene, verba sequentur* ("hold to the thing, the
words will follow"). Hobbes's advice is exactly the reverse: hold
to the words, and things will follow and will sit still long enough
for you to begin and conclude your reckonings. The precise truth
Hobbes promises is not the truth of things, of an independent real-
ity, but the truth that follows upon precision (and consistency)
in definitions. The truth of things, Hobbes says, is absolute and
unconditioned, but it cannot be ours. The truth that can be ours
is entirely discursive and entirely "Conditionall": "No man can
know by Discourse, that this, or that, is, has been or will be, which
is to know absolutely [without mediation]; but onely if this [some

settled verbal signification] be, That is...which is to know conditionally; and that not the consequence of one thing to another; but of one name of a thing, to another name of the same thing" (131). As Victoria Silver puts it, "In Hobbes's view science does not manipulate facts, but words; its formulae do not describe the operations of external bodies, but rather the mind's concepts; its predictions remain conditional upon a precise, concrete use of language...and not upon a close and repeated observation of some world beyond ideas."[18]

3.

It is this ability to manipulate words and build out of them descriptive and predictive structures that distinguishes human beings from animals. Both humans and beasts, says Hobbes, react to an experienced effect in the same way: "wee seek the causes, or means that produce it" (96). So when a loud noise is made in the vicinity of a human and a dog, both will look around and try to identify its source, and if the noise is unpleasant both will move away from the source once it has been identified. But the human will then proceed to mental actions beyond the dog's capacity. The human might ask, Who is responsible for this noise? Do I have a legal remedy? If I build a wall around my house could I keep it out? Should I move to another neighborhood? In short, the human projects into the long-term future and makes plans. Rather than simply registering an effect, "Wee seek all the [other] possible effects, that by it can be produced; that is to say, we imagine what we could do with it," and this imagination, which Hobbes identifies with curiosity, is unique "to man onely" and withheld from an animal "that has no other Passion but sensuall, such as are hunger, thirst, lust and anger" (96). Only humans have the capacity of "designe," otherwise known as "the faculty of Invention" (96). This faculty, in excess of the "five Senses" we share with animals, is not natural but "acquired, and encreased by study and industry" (98). What enables us to acquire it and go far beyond what animals can do in the way of planning is speech: "For besides Sense, and Thoughts, and the Trayne of thoughts, the mind of man has no other motion" and is in this no different from the beast. But "by the help of Speech and Method, the same Facultyes may be improved to such a height, as to distinguish men from all other living creatures" (99).

It is a happy story and an old one, told first by Cicero in the *De inventione* and *De oratore* and repeated by every humanist who follows him: the arts of speech and eloquence civilize.[19] But it is a story of humanity's perfectibility and the possibility of substantive moral progress, and Hobbes will not let it stand.[20] He drops the other shoe in the fifth chapter where he revisits what he had said in chapter 3, "That a Man did excell all other Animals in this faculty, that when he conceived any thing whatsoever, he was apt to enquire the consequences of it, and what effects he could do with it" (113). "Apt to enquire" means apt to speculate, imagine, and devise. But, Hobbes quickly adds, "This priviledge"—of being able to think creatively—"is allayed by another, by the priviledge of Absurdity to which no living creature is subject, but man onely; and of men those are of all most subject to it, that professe Philosophy."

Why? Because philosophers are least content with the "Definitions, or Explications of...names" currently in use (113). Philosophers, rather than hewing to what has been conventionally settled, wish above all else to go beyond what is conventionally settled, and their ability to do so causes endless troubles in the form of metaphorical flights of fancy, definitions made up out of whole cloth, and projects which because they float free of any "orderly Method" (115) threaten the stability both of reckonings and political administration. If only humans were like animals, and had "no other direction, than their particular judgments"—judgments of the moment and therefore not built up into a narrative or a vision of life—and "appetites" (225). If only humans were, like animals, without the gift and burden of speech, "that art of words, by which some men can represent to others, that which is Good, in the likenesse of Evill; and Evill, in the likenesse of Good; and augment, or diminish the apparent greatnesse of Good and Evill [thereby] discontenting men, and troubling their peace at their pleasure" (226). Animals, because they lack reason and cannot generalize from the present moment of satisfaction or distress to a theory of the just distribution of goods and honors, have no sense of private injury and no capacity for being unhappy with the present arrangement of things.

> [Animals] do not see, or think they see, any fault, in the administration of their common businesse; wheras amongst men, there are very many, that think themselves wiser, and abler to govern the Publique, better than the rest; and these strive to reform and innovate [hear the scorn], one this way, another that way; and thereby to bring it into Distraction and Civill warre. (226)

In short, and with apologies to *My Fair Lady*, why can't a man be more like an animal?

Two answers to this question have already been given — reason and speech, faculties that mark a superiority that is dearly bought. To these Hobbes adds a third — equality, that most cherished of Enlightenment doctrines. What happens to equality in his hands is what happens in other chapters to freedom and liberty. It is stripped of its substantive aura and redescribed as a physical fact with no moral implications. The physical fact (and the new definition of equality) is that "though there bee found one man sometimes manifestly stronger in body, or of quicker mind then another; yet when all is reckoned together, the difference between man, and man, is not so considerable" (183). That is to say, people are roughly equal in bodily and mental endowments. That's all there is to equality; it is not an abstract condition that confers an abstract right, but an inconvenient empirical fact that presents us with problems of political management. For if every person is more or less equally endowed, there is no measure *in nature* for adjudicating the claims of one as opposed to another: "The difference between man, and man, is not so considerable, as that one man can thereupon claim to himselfe any benefit, to which another may not pretend, as well as he" (183). Whereas in the animal kingdom precedence follows natural abilities — the strong takes things from the weak, the swift outrun the slow — in the world of human beings precedence is continuously disputed and there are no natural marks by which it might be determined: "The question who is the better man has no place in the condition of meer Nature" (211). If people were born with the signs of superiority and inferiority emblazoned on their persons (here is the entire history of heredity and racism), the distinctions better and worse, deserving and undeserving, master and servant, would declare themselves. In the absence of any such signs, everyone is justified in believing that he or she is the one who should lead, possess, and rule: "From this equality of ability, ariseth equality of hope in the attaining of our ends. And therefore if any two men desire the same thing, which nevertheless they cannot both enjoy, they become enemies; and in the way to their End...endeavour to destroy, or subdue one an other" (184).

Equality in this account is not, as it is in the Enlightenment tradition following Milton and Locke, a reason for denying one person the right to rule over another. Rather, it is the reverse. Instead of subscribing to the proposition that everyone is created equal and therefore absolute authority is against nature, Hobbes says that everyone is created equal and therefore absolute authority is absolutely necessary. If nature will not tell us who is superior and deserving of rule, we must supply nature's defect by stipulating to the superiority of some person who will occupy the role of sovereign—not because the person deserves it, but because we need it. We must, that is, establish a precedence rooted in nothing more substantive than our declaration of it; we must establish a "common Power to feare" (187). Without such a power firmly ensconced, the passions and desires of those who are to all appearances equal will go unchecked, for they will not "know a Law that forbids them" (187). Without that law, without the imposition of conventional and artificial constraints, "nothing can be Unjust" and the "notions of Right and Wrong, Justice and Injustice have...no place" (188).

Conclusion

Here, in the concluding paragraphs of this essay, I finally reach the thesis for which Hobbes is most often remembered and most often excoriated:

> The only way to erect such a Common Power, as may be able to defend [men] from the injuries of one another, and thereby to secure them in such sort, that by their owne industrie...they may nourish themselves and live contentedly; is to conferre all their power and strength upon one Man...and therin to submit their Wills every one to his Will, and their Judgements to his Judgment.... This is the Generation of that great LEVIATHAN...of that *Mortall God*, to which wee owe under the *Immortal God*, our peace and defense. (227)

I did not introduce the thesis earlier because, in isolation, at the beginning of an explication, it would have struck the reader, as it strikes so many who first hear of it, as at once preposterous and evil. I would have then ignored the lesson Hobbes learned from Euclid, as Aubrey tells it: that a proposition nakedly offered may seem impossible, but if it comes at the end of a succession of proofs, it will seem inevitable.[21] As I trust it is now evident, the proposition of a sovereign will is no more or less startling than the proposition that conscience is a public matter, not a private one, and therefore requires a public, that is, conventional, baseline. Indeed, it is the same proposition, issuing from the same repudiation of substance in favor of artificially stipulated form. Once one gets the hang of the basic move—exchange a substantive vocabulary for a vocabulary of bodies and motions, take away the putative depth and interiority of concepts like conscience, justice, injustice, better, worse, true, false, liberty, freedom, merit, and equality—and once one grounds that basic move in an account of human nature—variable, competitive, voracious, and radically insecure—absolutely everything follows and seems, if I can use the word, natural.

Michael Oakshott, responding to those who seek and fail to find an architecture in Hobbes's thought, observes, "the coherence of his philosophy, the system of it, lies not in an architectonic structure but in a single 'passionate thought' that pervades its parts."[22] "Passionate thought" is Hobbes's phrase; it appears near the beginning of *Leviathan* where it serves both as a general direction for composition and as a description of how *this* composition works. What is required, says Hobbes, if discourse, thought, and life are not to "wander...as in a Dream" (95), is a "Passionate Thought to

govern and direct those that follow," an end and point kept always
in mind and acting "as the thing that directs all your thoughts"
(96). *Leviathan* answers perfectly to this description, and this per-
fection is the object both of Victoria Silver's praise and complaint.
The praise is for the tightness of the performance, for the degree
to which the prose generates, from sentence to sentence, an intel-
ligibility that leaves no seams or cracks that might disrupt it.[23] So
powerful is the effect that the "source of all true statement and
the criterion of self-evidence in *Leviathan* is its own terminology"
(366). The complaint is for the very same thing. Hobbes's argu-
ment, says Silver, "is consumed by the obsessive definition and
reiteration of terms, often to the detriment of its ostensible sci-
ence, which degenerates into verbal engineering."[24] Degenerates?
Verbal engineering, as Silver well knows, is the entire point, not
because Hobbes is trying to put something over on the reader, but
because, as he passionately believes, no other engineering, grounded
in something more substantial than words and the conclusions
they compel, is available. There is, according to Hobbes, nothing
to degenerate from, and it can hardly be a criticism of *Leviathan*
that its own performance is, as Silver also sees, an instance of what
it urges. The fact that on its own terms Hobbes's masterwork is
irrefutable should be the occasion not of complaint, but of wonder
and awe.

Of course we may challenge those terms and ask, after explain-
ing how Hobbes's argument works, whether or not it works in the
world beyond its own rhetorical unfolding. Many, from the very
day of its publication, have judged that it does not, and have said
that the argument fails at its core because, as Jean Hampton insists,
the right of subjects to determine whether or not the sovereign's
rule does in fact contribute to their self-preservation and so ful-
fills the contract, is a fatal undermining of the sovereign power
on which the entire scheme rests: "Indeed as long as the subjects
retain the right to preserve themselves in a commonwealth"—and
self-preservation is the reason for setting up the authority in the
first place—"they cannot be said to have surrendered *anything* to
the sovereign," and, consequently, Hobbes is unable "to make the

sovereign's rule permanent and secure."[25] But Hobbes knows this at least as well as Hampton and her predecessors, and—surprise, surprise—he builds it into his exposition:

> But as men, for the atteyning of peace, and conservation of themselves thereby, have made an Artificiall Man...so also have they made Artificiall Chains, called *Civill Lawes*, which they themselves, by mutuall covenants, have fastened at one end, to the lips of that Man...to whom they have given the Soveraigne Power; and at the other end to their own Ears. These Bonds, in their own nature but weak, may nevertheless be made to hold, by the danger, though not by the difficulty, of breaking them. (263–64)

That is to say, I know how fragile are both the argument I am making and the strategy that argument recommends. It all depends on the willingness of the unbridled will to bridle itself, to submit for no substantive reason, but for a prudential reason, to an authority it alone upholds. Nothing is easier than the breaking of these bonds; and nothing is more disastrously consequential. Put this way, the Hobbesian creed bears an uncanny resemblance to the faith-based creed proclaimed by his great opposite, John Milton. In a key passage, Milton's Raphael observes that the only guarantee of the happiness of free agents is an act of obedience rooted in nothing firmer than itself: "On other surety none" (*PL* 5.538).[26] On this point the arch-antinomian apostle of the inside and the arch-formalist champion of the outside agree. The security of the world is in peril at every moment, and the slightest wrong movement—eating an apple, or deciding to call a king a tyrant—can bring everything crashing down, as it, in fact, did. Of course the difference between the two remains: one stakes everything on an internal law that has no necessary external form; the other clings desperately to external forms and fears any invocation of the internal as a prelude to chaos. But even in this opposition, they stand allied against the facile rationalists, the believers in perspicuous and easy political solutions, of their day and ours.

5 ⇸ God's "Red Right Hand"
Violence and Pain in *Paradise Lost*

Diana Treviño Benet

1. Introduction

Among the many "firsts" in *Paradise Lost,* pain stands out by happening for the first time *twice.* Both first experiences belong to Satan, but as many readers have noticed, the poem ascribes the new sensation to different moments. Chronologically, the first time Satan experiences pain is when Sin bursts from his head while he conspires with the seraphim "against Heav'n's King."[1] The second "first time" occurs when Michael's sword "shear'd / All his right side" during the war in heaven (*PL* 6.326–27). Dolor permeates the first half of *Paradise Lost.* An essential aspect of human experience, pain plays a central role in Christianity. It is present at the beginning and at the end of the human story, according to the Bible, which defines its spiritual significance. God designates pain in childbirth as Eve's punishment for disobedience: "In sorrow

89

thou shalt bring forth children" (Gen. 3:16); finally, after the end-of-time battle, God will cause Satan and other sinners to be "cast alive into a lake of fire" (Rev. 19:20) and to "be tormented day and night for ever and ever" (Rev. 20:10). Religion and language come together in "the very word 'pain' [which] has its etymological home in *'poena'* or 'punishment.'"[2] To represent the causal relationship the Bible establishes between sin and corporal punishment, Milton must treat pain, which means he must deal with the punitive God: pain in *Paradise Lost* is the direct consequence of divine violence, of what Michael Lieb identifies as the *odium Dei*.[3]

A consideration of God's violence must focus on the war in heaven as the event that witnesses his invention of pain for the rebels,[4] and on hell, the place he designs for eternal suffering. Readers over the years have found fault with numerous aspects of the war, and Milton's hell is riddled with as many inconsistencies and seeming absurdities. These noticeable strains in the fabric of the poem highlight the difficulties Milton confronts in representing his supernatural characters' actions and motivations—his theology—but scholars either ignore the strains, or they argue or assume coherence where none exists. One of the few exceptions is John Wooten. Though Wooten writes exclusively about the war (which he characterizes as "a flawed effort"), he comments, also, on the critical stance that glosses over evident problems in the epic:

> The tendency in criticism, and an admirable one it is, is to arrive at, if at all possible, an interpretation that will hand a great poet success on as many levels as possible. Miltonists, like critics of other great writers, regularly make such an appropriately humbling effort.... Yet at times it is necessary for the sake of a truer understanding to say something else: namely, that the poetic intention is betrayed by the poetry itself. In this instance, what I wish to do is to urge the view that *Paradise Lost* shows unmistakable signs of finding the issue of violence an intractable one, despite Milton's best efforts.[5]

In this essay, I shall focus on some of those signs of Milton's struggle with violence and pain in hell and the war in heaven. I approach them neither as unconscious errors that must be silently ignored for the sake of postulating artistic "unity" nor as inadvertent slips that expose flaws in the poet's theodicy. Instead, I adduce three underlying contexts with a straightforward relevance to the topic of pain. The medical treatment of pain, its spiritual significance, and the thinking on Christian warfare are contemporary matters that threaten to subvert Milton's stated objective of justifying God's ways to men in several ways: by creating an unacceptable sympathy for the apostates; by elevating them to heroic stature and simultaneously lowering the stature of the obedient angels; by pointing to the intrinsic unfairness of the war in heaven; and by exposing God's undisguised violence. I use the cultural contexts as guides to understanding how Milton deals with his knotty material. My working assumptions are that Milton was cognizant of the problems inherent in his material, and that he used various more or less successful strategies to save the appearances of his divine apparatus. Inconsistencies and incongruities remain in hell and heaven as emblems of the poet's struggles with his material, but he does his best to mitigate the image and actions of a wrathful God who deliberately causes his creatures pain. Milton uses all the resources of a great poet to vindicate his represented God.

Milton's hell and war in heaven are multifaceted, complex topics. To focus as clearly as possible on pain and divine violence or the *odium Dei*, I shall not comment below on the requirements of plot that occasion some of the inconsistencies of the poem—we all know that (and why) Satan's detention in hell is not a creative option, for instance. Similarly, when I discuss Milton's treatment of the war between passible and impassible angels, I omit comment on his other efforts (with the cooperation of the Father) to create the utterly necessary illusion of equality between Satan and the omnipotent God.

2. Hell: The Pain of Unextinguishable Fire

Many details in Milton's early descriptions of hell combine to create the impression that infernal pain is unendurable. The instant that Satan regains consciousness, he is in torment, thinking "Both of lost happiness and lasting pain" (*PL* 1.55). Hell in *Paradise Lost* is a place of "torture without end" (1.67). Satan boasts "though in pain" (1.125); he strides with "uneasy steps / Over the burning Marl" (1.295–96) to muster his troops, who themselves awaken into "fierce pains" (1.336). Every speaker at the council in hell addresses the agony they all feel. Satan claims to be exposed "to greatest share / Of endless pain" (*PL* 2.29–30). Moloch suggests that the "pain" (2.88) renders the possibility of annihilation less undesirable. Belial hopes that, the apostates not further offending God, the "raging fires / Will slack'n" (*PL* 2.213–14). Mammon restates Belial's idea (*PL* 2.215–19) that their essence might eventually change: "Our torments also may in length of time / Become our Elements," an alteration that "must needs remove / The sensible of pain" (*PL* 2.274–78). Beelzebub, finally, and needlessly, reminds his fellows that they must suffer thus because they are God's slaves, sentenced to "custody severe, / And stripes, and arbitrary punishment" (*PL* 2.333–34).

Milton's hell conforms to the biblical and literary traditions: the angels of the Son of Man will gather up the wicked, according to Matthew, and "cast them into a furnace of fire: there shall be wailing and gnashing of teeth" (13:40–42). Like Dante, Milton never lets us forget that the flaming dungeon is the "place Eternal Justice had prepar'd / For those rebellious" (1.70–71), but only once does he present a tableau reminiscent of the *Inferno*. He describes a place beyond Lethe where "cold performs th' effect of Fire." Here the damned are brought to

> Feel by turns the bitter change
> Of fierce extremes, extremes by change more fierce,
> From Beds of raging Fire to starve in Ice
> Thir soft Ethereal warmth, and there to pine
> Immovable, infixt and frozen round.   (*PL* 2.598–602)

Though the broad outlines of the landscape and the purpose of Milton's hell are traditional, this image of passive suffering is unique to the first two books of *Paradise Lost*.

Milton's description of unendurable pain is deliberately negated by the behavior of the fallen angels. While they are supposed to be in agony, they are engaged continually in something other than hurting. Hell is populated by soldiers, musicians, miners, builders, explorers, and even philosophers, who—fairly soon after regaining consciousness—are actively pursuing their usual occupations. Hellish torment, it seems, can be whiled away with games, races, and other entertainments (2.525–42). It can be suspended with music (2.552–55) and charmed with intellectual pursuits such as philosophy and theology (2.566). This combination of agony and singing probably did not seem so bizarre in Milton's time as it does today. In fact, it suggests the ordinariness of pain in a pre-anesthetic culture. Milton's awareness that that very ordinariness might arouse readers' sympathy for the apostates results in his anguished but recreating angels.

An account of a famous sufferer, two common ailments, and two of their seventeenth century remedies will sketch the familiarity of pain in Milton's England. Anne Conway, a near-contemporary of the author (1631–78), is famous because Thomas Willis wrote about her in *De anima brutorum* (1672) and because she had a long correspondence with Henry More. Conway spent a large part of her life in darkened rooms because she suffered for more than 30 years with a headache so excruciating that the light hurt her. She tried every nostrum and treatment available, with the exception of trepanning (perforation of the skull), without ever getting sustained relief. In spite of the pain, however, Conway read, married, bore children, and engaged in a vigorous and extensive correspondence with friends and relatives.[6]

Pain was not familiar only to the victim of a spectacular and unique headache. "Since medical cures were often ineffective, the victims of illness or accident faced days of pain in which to contemplate their impending mortality."[7] "Intestine Stone" and "Joint-racking Rheums" (*PL* 11.484, 488)—gallstones and gout—have a place in the vision Michael gives Adam because they were common and dreaded ailments in Milton's day: "hardly a statesman whose attention could not be distracted in the sternest moments by news of a cure for the gout or the stone."[8] Thomas Sydenham usually prescribed "small beer" for those, like himself and Milton, who suffered the pains of gout. The standard treatments were bleeding, purging, and sweating. The physician John Symcotts wrote a letter in 1633 to a patient, G. Powers, with a recommendation: "For the pain in your toe and finger take this medicine. Beat yolks of raw eggs with twice as much black soap in a dish so long till the soap hath lost his color, with fine flax apply it as a plaster for three or four days, if the pain will cease not sooner." Seven years later, the still-afflicted Powers made a note on a letter from the doctor's assistant: "The black soap and yolks of eggs made the top of my foot swell and to itch exceedingly. I rubbed them, they rose in blisters and issued water exceedingly; at last I applied cowdung, vinegar, and butter poultice-wise, as hot as I could endure, at 4 times dressing the heat." It is hard to believe that the plaster ever did anything but distract Power. For pain relief, it sounds useless.[9]

Analgesics were not entirely unknown. In ancient times, cannabis, alcohol, mandragora, and opium were used,[10] and alcohol was still indicated for pain in the seventeenth century. Women in labor, for instance, were often given spiced wine. Since childbirth was expected to be painful, the limits of alcohol as an anodyne were not considered a problem. Also known in early modern England were the properties of Atropa mandragora, "called love apple, devil's apple, mandrake, or mandragora officinarum," but "physicians [who] tried to use 'narcotic' herbals in the middle of the seventeenth century...were condemned, arrested, and fined or tried for practicing witchcraft."[11] As for opium, it was known in England, "but not by any means familiar until Thomas Sydenham described it in 1669."[12] Moreover, it did not come into general use until about 1683 when Sydenham revolutionized the treatment of pain with his concoction of laudanum, which could be controlled by careful dosing, and "which he named and used not only to alleviate pain and induce slumber but also to treat dysentery epidemics, hysteria, nervous illnesses, attacks of gout," and so on.[13]

Carrying on—working, writing, singing, discussing theology—
carrying on in spite of pain is what people did in the seven-
teenth century. Understandably, such people were likely to react
to descriptions of intense pain with that "animal pity by which
all normal men are affected in the presence of...suffering."[14] To
avoid creating inappropriate sympathy for the fallen angels in such
readers, Milton has recourse to a glaring incongruity. While they
are supposed to be in agony, the residents of hell (like ordinary
Englishmen) march, build, explore, sing, discuss theology, and
generally get on with their eternal lives. Milton first stresses the
severity of the apostates' pain, and then tries to make readers
forget it.[15]

3. Hell: Torture without End

Hell is "torture without end" (*PL* 1.67); Satan's troops are
"condemn'd / For ever" (1.607–08); the reprobates are "decreed,
Reserv'd and destin'd to Eternal woe" (2.160–61): the pains of
Milton's hell are eternal. This obvious aspect of hell deserves
emphasis because permanent, punitive suffering must be distin-
guished from the transitory pain seen by Milton's contemporaries
as divine participation in their lives through the medium of their
bodies. More than punishment, such pain was seen as a discipli-
nary tool the deity used to instruct and correct his people: "All
afflictions, whether of mind, body, or estate, were sent by God as
a correction for sin, for the good of the sinner.... The affliction
would only be lifted when it had done its work of reformation."[16]
This religious interpretation did not prevent efforts to lessen or
eliminate pain. But the message God inscribed in flesh demanded
interpretation, and the only appropriate response to his sensible
communication was patient endurance.

Milton's contemporaries did not invent the theology of afflic-
tion, but they certainly emphasized it. This theological develop-
ment arose from the long historical inability of medicine to offer
adequate pain relief. Blaise Pascal's "Prayer to Ask God for the

Good Use of Sickness" is one of the many examples of affliction theology in popular parlance:

> Make me fully understand that the ills of the body are nothing else than the punishment and the encompassing symbol for the ills of the soul. O Lord, let them be the remedy, by making me aware, through the pain that I feel, of the pain that I did not feel in my soul, deeply sick though it was and covered with sores. Because, Lord, the greatest sickness is insensibility.... Let me feel this pain so sharply, so that I can make whatever is left of my life a continual penance to wash away the offenses I have committed.

A poet like George Herbert challenges the reader to select the best of many possible citations: "Sicknesses cleave my bones: / Consuming agues dwell in ev'ry vein / And tune my breath to groans," the poet writes in lines 27–28 of "Affliction (I)." The final line of "Easter-wings" states the standard belief that justifies the experience: "Affliction shall advance the [spiritual] flight in me."[17]

So entrenched was the teaching on affliction that even chronic pain was given a spiritual function. Anne Conway wrote to Henry More in May 1664:

> I still indure those violent paines (which I alwayes thought would be accounted intollerable by a stronger body than I ever had) and that more frequently than ever. I cannot dissemble so much as not to professe myself very weary of this condition. I pray God enable me with patience to bear whatsoever my sad fate hath designed for me and give me that entire resignation to his will which I endeavour after and do stand in so much need of.

Almost ten years earlier, in June 1654, More had offered counsel, encouraging Conway to interpret her pain as "an opportunity...to exercize that most lovely and divine virtue of all virtues, patient Humility." He advised her to think of "those dreadfull agonies Christ underwent on the crosse" as a way to "sweeten and mitigate [her] present torments" and practice patience while she was "under the rod of our heavenly Father as [Jesus] then was."[18]

The possibility of pain that was permanent and void of redemptive potential — the kind of pain, that is, suffered by the disobedient angels — was bound to make early modern Christians uncomfortable because of what it implied about God. Such uneasiness is evident in *Religio medici* (1643), where Thomas Browne confesses that his "greener studies" were "polluted" by several heresies. One of these "was that of *Origen*, that God would not persist in his vengeance for ever, but after a definite time of his wrath hee would release the damned soules from torture; Which error I fell into upon a serious contemplation of the great attribute of God, his mercy."[19] The problem was not that God inflicted the pains of hell but that he exacted endless retribution.

In *Paradise Lost* Milton deals with the mercilessness of eternal pain in two ways. First, he gives considerable emphasis to the impenitence of the reprobates. The most extended reconsideration and confirmation of sin belongs, as we might expect, to Satan. The first iteration of his conscious sin is in book 1, where he assures Beelzebub that, despite appearances, he does not "repent or change" (*PL* 1.96–97). Again, in his soliloquy on the sun, Satan examines his conscience only to confirm his deliberate alienation from God.[20] The other leaders also repeat their sin in book 2. Moloch's declaration that "the Scourge / Inexorably, and the torturing hour / Calls us to Penance" (*PL* 2.90–92) is a deliberate reminder of the theological link between pain and repentance. But Moloch embraces evil with his subsequent proposal that the disobedient angels continue fighting, for the sake, at least, of disturbing heaven, "Which if not Victory is yet revenge" (*PL* 2.105). Belial advocates "ignoble ease, and peaceful sloth, / Not peace" (2.227–28). Mammon's confirmation of sin takes the form of imagining "Forc't Halleluiahs" in heaven (2.243): "how wearisome / Eternity so spent in worship paid / To whom we hate" (2.248–50). Beelzebub declares that what he and the rest offer God is "hostility and hate / Untamed reluctance, and revenge though slow" (2.336–37). The infernal population does not suffer endlessly only because of their initial disobedience; by their ongoing sin, they merit their ongoing torture. Moloch uses that word with special emphasis when he suggests that the rebels should turn "our Tortures into horrid Arms / Against the Torturer" (2.63–64).

The second way that Milton mitigates the cruelty of eternal, entirely punitive pain is with an astounding loophole: in *Paradise Lost*, the agony of damnation can be escaped. The text deliberately emphasizes the strange fact that eternal pain can be circumvented (albeit with the permissive will of God). Satan tells Sin and Death that he is adventuring "to set free / From out this dark and dismal house of pain, / Both him and thee" along with the rest (*PL* 2.822–24). When he is forced to explain his presence in the unfallen garden, he says he has sought to go "Farthest from pain . . . to change / Torment with ease" (4.892–93). Gabriel mockingly asks if Satan is "Less hardy to endure" pain than his fellows (4.920). One and all understand that when Satan leaves the precincts of hell, he leaves behind pain. Against the considerable weight of his own descriptions of eternal torment, Milton creates an escapable hell and then tries to offset that incongruity with the assertion that the real tortures of hell are internal. As Satan famously declares, "Which way I fly is Hell; myself am Hell" (4.75). But there is no getting away from the amazing fact that God's "own invented Torments" (2.70) can be exchanged by the enterprising damned for "gentle gales / Fanning thir odoriferous wings" and wafting sweet perfumes (4.156–57).

4. *The War in Heaven: Unequal Work against Unequal Arms*

As William Poole points out, the war in heaven "is a theological necessity, because without it the Tempter in Eden remains just a mysterious snake, and not the instrument of a freshly-fallen devil."[21] It also enables Milton to link Satan with the origin of pain as the first sinner. But the war creates issues that many readers have pointed to as lapses in Milton's taste, conception, or performance.[22] Some scholars, with whom I disagree, have tried to account for the peculiarities of the war by suggesting that Milton wrote this section of the epic in a mock-heroic or comic mode. Wooten, for example, argues that the whole episode includes a lot of "comic debunking," and specifies other discordant elements: "God, before the actual fighting begins, disparages the ensuing war effort on his behalf," praising "the contest of words over that of arms" while still ordering Abdiel and the rest to fight. Furthermore, God lies by telling "Abdiel that victory in the 'brutish' contest will be easy for him" and the rest. In short, Wooten points out, there are many "absurdities of the epic battle Raphael describes" that evoke "conflicting responses on the part of unsettled readers."[23]

There is one essential absurdity from which a good many others follow. Like any war, the battle in heaven is about inflicting physical harm. As Elaine Scarry puts it, "the central activity of war is injuring and the central goal in war is to out-injure the opponent."[24] And since injuring spiritual beings is impossible, God embodies the disobedient angels. Raphael explains to Adam the degrees into which the creation is organized: every creature arises from "one first matter all...But [is] more refin'd, more spirituous, and pure, / As nearer to [God] plac't or nearer tending...Till body up to spirit work" (*PL* 5.472–78). But God makes the process reversible: the angels' essence changes as soon as they disobey. (Who knew?! as Satan exclaims about another surprise in 1.93.) When they are buried under the mountains hurled by God's warriors, Raphael explains, after the fact, what events have already disclosed. The mountains

> opprest whole Legions arm'd,
> Thir armor help'd thir harm, crush't in and bruis'd
> Into thir substance pent, which wrought them pain
> Implacable, and many a dolorous groan,
> Long struggling underneath, ere they could wind
> Out of such prison, though Spirits of purest light,
> Purest at first, now gross by sinning grown.   (6.655–61)

So are the apostates' sin and their punishment inscribed on their substance. The essence of Satan and the rest has been "thickened" in such a way that they are different creatures from what they were before, something between the entirely pure angels and the fully embodied human beings.[25] The change is not so great that it prevents Satan and the others from changing shapes, but their essence has been defiled. In the identification of incarnation with weakness, Milton follows biblical tradition:

> Throughout the Hebraic scriptures, the question of having or not having a body arises not only in man's relation to God but also in

man's relation to man. Even among human beings, the one with authority and power has no body for his inferiors. He cannot, for example, be seen without clothing: the family and people of Ham are enslaved by Noah after Ham accidentally sees Noah naked (Genesis 9:20–27).... No one, we are often told throughout the scriptures, sees God face to face and lives.[26]

Later in the poem, Satan laments that ambition compels him to enter the serpent, "with bestial slime, / This essence to incarnate and imbrute" (9.165–66). But he has already been incarnated and imbruted by sin, though under the logic of the poem every successive sin must increase the "brutedness" of his incarnation.

The (partial) embodiment of the disobedient angels permits Milton to show the effect of sin and to depict a war resembling a real conflict. But the poet faces a different set of problems because only one side has bodies (however porous or spiritual) to speak of. The chief of these, of course, is the inherent unfairness of a war between radically unequal parties. A war in which one side fights with arms capable of inflicting bodily harm while the other side brandishes impotent weapons would have been as outrageous to Milton's contemporaries as it is to our twenty-first century sensibilities. Seventeenth century soldiers were reminded often that there were rules of engagement, a Christian mode of warfare. In a just war, combatants could lay aside their compassion: "God himselfe in such cases casteth off pity."[27] But the just absence of pity did not justify ruthlessness. William Gouge, the Puritan divine, and Edward Symmons, the royalist clergyman and author of *A Vindication of King Charles* (1647), both preached that soldiers should exempt "Women, Children, and aged persons" because of the same basic principle: these were "such as cannot hurt thee."[28] The rebellious angels are such as cannot hurt God or the warriors of his army.

Nisroch's challenge to Satan after the first day of the war refers to the inequality between the two sides. Such a disparity must confer a different meaning on the efforts of the two armies. It is hard, Nisroch says,

> For Gods, and too unequal work we find
> Against unequal arms to fight in pain,
> Against unpain'd, impassive; from which evil
> Ruin must needs ensue; for what avails
> Valor or strength, though matchless, quell'd with pain
> Which all subdues, and makes remiss the hands
> Of Mightiest.   (*PL* 6.453–59)

But what about the other side? The reader might reasonably wonder, paraphrasing William Empson, what war can mean to those with no fear of death, injury, or pain, no death.[29] Milton must avoid presenting the passible warriors as heroic in daring to engage God's army and (equally) avoid presenting the impassible angels as negligible ciphers. "Pain is the worst disaster that can befall our being," avers Michel de Montaigne, and because it is so, it is accorded considerable cultural value: "If this were not so, what could have brought us to respect manly courage, valour, fortitude, greatness of soul and determination? If there were no pain to defy, how could they play their part?"[30] To ensure that no trace of heroism attaches itself to the rebels, Milton shows Satan and Moloch reacting to their wounds with something less than fortitude. Satan writhes and rolls—he "to and fro convolv'd" (6.328)—and gnashes his teeth "for anguish and despite and shame" (6.340). Moloch flees, with "uncouth pain...bellowing" (6.362), and finally the rebels finish the first day of the war "with fear surpris'd and sense of pain" and "ignominious" retreat (6.394–95).

To deal with the total absence of any danger that could exalt the efforts of the obedient angels, Milton creates the illusion of valor and orders his material with care. Raphael begins his account with a general description of the war in book 6 that emphasizes its nobility. From line 207 to line 246, he sketches a conflict full of actions deserving eternal fame without specifying that such glory belongs exclusively to either party: "no thought of flight, / None of retreat, no unbecoming deed / That argu'd fear" (*PL* 6.236–38). This loftiness holds until Satan is wounded by Michael and his injury described (6.353). At that point, Raphael broadens his perspective with the comment that, elsewhere, "like deeds deserv'd / Memorial" (6.354–55). And then, following Moloch's wounding, Raphael again emphatically asserts the heroism of God's angels:

> I might relate of thousands, and thir names
> Eternize here on Earth; but those elect
> Angels contented with this fame in Heav'n
> Seek not the praise of men.   (*PL* 6.373–76)

It is not until Raphael has created a strong impression of the courage and heroism of the heavenly army that he finally mentions, as if it were a minor detail, that God's saints are "Invulnerable, impenetrably arm'd" (6.400), "Unwearied, unobnoxious to be pain'd / By wound" (6.404–05).

But the loyal angels do not entirely avoid distress in the conflict. When Abdiel returns to his proper place before the war, the voice of God declares that he has done well because, for the sake of truth, he has "borne / Universal reproach, far worse to bear / Than violence" (*PL* 6.33–35). During the war, the loyal angels also experience "reproach" in the sense of "disgrace or shame; a...matter bringing disgrace or discredit upon one" (*OED*, s.v. 1). One of the well-known details of angelic lore in *Paradise Lost* is that spirits can be moved "from thir place by violence" (6.405). So when Satan's cannonballs smite the obedient angels, Raphael's language insists that they suffer: theirs is an "indecent overthrow" (6.601) which renders them "despis'd, / And to thir foes a laughter" (6.602–03). The apostates hold them in "derision" (6.608) and scoff (6.629), "and of [God's] Thunder made a scorn, / And all his Host derided" (6.632–33). The reader is supposed, I believe, to equate "reproach," the indignity of being knocked down and rolling about, with the agonizing and oozing gashes that wound the apostates.

We cannot doubt how much the loss of countenance disturbs the obedient angels because the ridicule they experience moves them to "Rage" (*PL* 6.635). Wooten points out that this emotion "compromises" them (140), causing them to tear up the mountains of heaven and thereby to earn the disapprobation of the Father, who refers to their "disorder'd rage" (6.696). "Rage" is the emotion the Son attributes as motive to the angels' rebellion (6.813); and rage, according to the Father, is what "Transports" Satan out of hell to seek the new world with malicious intent (*PL* 3.81). Here is another obvious inconsistency: the obedient angels experience a fallen emotion. The angels' disordered reaction to the wounding of their decorum moves the Father to enter the conflict.

5. *The War in Heaven and the* odium Dei

My consideration of pain in hell and in heaven has been a way of approaching the divine violence that expresses what Michael Lieb calls the *"odium Dei,"* the just hatred of God, the "all-consuming vengeance [he gives vent to] in response to those He finds entirely odious and fully deserving of retribution."[31] Satan refers to this divine attribute when he rejects the possibility of reconcilement, "Where wounds of deadly hate have pierc'd so deep" (*PL* 4.99). Representing a punishing deity, as we have seen, poses formidable difficulties for Milton. Divine violence, enacted first through the agency of the invulnerable angels against the semi-embodied rebels, is, as Scarry suggests in another context, chilling: "an absolute, one-directional capacity to injure [enemies]...may begin to approach the torturer's dream of absolute nonreciprocity, the dream that one will be oneself exempt from the condition of being embodied while one's opponent...is at any moment deeply woundable."[32] With the apostates' frequent attribution of pain to God, the poem acknowledges his violence. Belial refers most memorably to God's "red right hand" as the instrument that "plagues" the suffering inhabitants of hell (*PL* 2.174). Leading up to that, there are references in the first part of book 2 to "his Almighty Engine" (65), "His own invented Torments" (90), "his utmost ire" (94), "his rage" (144), "his ire" (155), "his anger" (158), "Heav'n's afflicting Thunder" (166), and the "breath that kindl'd those grim fires" (170).

Milton makes various efforts to mitigate the image of the "God who hates."[33] We have observed that the poem encourages the reader first to register and then to forget the punitive pains of hell that the apostates characterize as "torture." In heaven, one of the poet's strategies is to portray a God who is, on the brink of great violence, phlegmatic. Readers have complained about the Father's laughter at the expense of the rebels before the war (*PL* 5.735–37), and about the cold, uncaring tone of "Th' incensed Deity" of book 3 (187) when he foresees that man will fall: "ingrate, he had of mee / All he could have" (3.97–98). But there is nothing to complain of as the Father empowers the Son to drive the disobedient out of heaven:

> Go then thou Mightiest in thy Father's might
> Ascend my Chariot, guide the rapid Wheels
> That shake Heav'n's basis, bring forth my War,
> My Bow and Thunder, my Almighty Arms
> Gird on, and Sword upon thy puissant Thigh;
> Pursue these sons of Darkness, drive them out
> From all Heav'n's bounds into the utter Deep:
> There let them learn, as likes them, to despise
> God and *Messiah* his anointed King.   (*PL* 6.710–18)

The Father's tone is angry, stern—but measured. Readers who think his typical rhetorical coldness is unattractive have not considered properly what the impact would be of an expressive deity. Verbal articulation of the divine hatred would be as catastrophic as it is unnecessary. The Father's passion and wrath are given concrete expression in hell. The fiery, punishing landscape and the apostates' anguish in books 1 and 2 are forceful representations of the Father's feelings.

But Milton's two major strategies to temper the representation of a hateful deity involve the attenuation of the connection between omnipotent force and pain. Between the Father's red right hand and the apostates, the poet first interposes the Son, in whom the Father is "Substantially expressed," and in whose "face / Divine Compassion visibly appear'd" (*PL* 3.140–41), as if superimposing love on wrath would render wrath less painful. This emotional paradox was recommended by preachers like the aforementioned Gouge to seventeenth century soldiers: "What thou doest against thine enemies do in love."[34] In addition to making the Son the agent of the Father's wrath, Milton invents the Chariot of Paternal Deity, a device that displaces the Father's wrath and attempts to mitigate the Son's enactment of it with the impersonality of the machine.[35] David B. Morris comments on the significance of such instruments:

> Pain...is the universal instrument of force. Force uses pain—or threatens to use it—in order to get its way. That is why, as far back as the rack, strappado, and thumbscrews of the late Middle Ages, torturers have relied on increasingly diabolical machines. The machine is an impersonal artifact for generating and multiplying force.... Equally important...it represents the impersonal, mechanical power of whatever masked or unmasked authority stands behind its uses.[36]

The Chariot generates and multiplies the divine force:

> from the fourfold-visag'd Four,
> Distinct with eyes, and from the living Wheels,
> Distinct alike with multitude of eyes;
> One spirit in them rul'd, and every eye
> Glar'd lightning, and shot forth pernicious fire.   (*PL* 6.845–49)

Compared to this blazing, devastating machine, the Son himself is relatively mild. He sends out "ten thousand Thunders" before him (6.836), rides over the rebels felled by the Chariot, then raises and drives them before him, "Thunder-struck" (6.858), to the edge of heaven, but "His arrows" seem to issue from the living Chariot (6.845). Lieb points out, most significantly, that the Chariot has restorative and creative functions in addition to its punitive function.[37] Thus, economically the poet conveys the theological axiom that the power that punishes is identical with the power that raises and redeems.

But no matter who delivers the coup de grace to the apostates or how mechanically pain is inflicted, "Strength is what finally decides the outcome of the war in Heaven," as Michael Bryson argues.[38] Divine violence carries the day. The desire to believe that force can be justified and need not be reprehensible may be universal among all who wage war. Such a desire lies behind the royalist Edward Symmons's sermon to soldiers:

> Perhaps now you expect that by way of use, I should stir you up to
> be cruell: But (noble Gentlemen and Souldiers:) If I should do so, I
> should forget my self to be a Minister of the Prince of mercie.... The
> spirit of the Gospell is no bloody Spirit; *we* (saies the Apostle, speak-
> ing of himself, and all true Ministers) *have the mind of Christ*, which
> endeavoured the salvation, not destruction of men..... Though it be
> true Gallantry, and noblenesse of spirit, to bee fierce and courageous
> in the Battaile, yet 'tis no true valour to set your foot too hard upon
> the neck of a fallen foe... The generous Lion scornes to exercise his
> fury upon an enemy that's prostrate before him.[39]

This ideal of dispassionate ferocity is what Milton aims for with
the Son in the Chariot, but the divine lion does not forbear to exer-
cise his fury upon his prostrate enemy.

Milton's effort to combine the Father's wrath with the Son's
compassion is not successful, for reasons that Wooten details:

> The Son's *deus ex machina* role may make sense allegorically: for
> example, as representative of the apocalyptic Second Coming that
> will end the Strife on the battlefield of human history. But on the
> level of moral parable, the Son's intrusion is only confusing. What is
> one supposed to think: that war is indeed brutal but justified when
> divine or moral truths are at stake[?]...[The Son] justifies his own
> entry into battle by claiming that he is executing God's vengeance
> and "indignation."...[But] what is such language from the Prince of
> Peace meant to convey to readers?[40]

There, at last, is the intractable problem. Milton's representation
of the deity who inflicts pain on those he hates is bound to fail
because Milton cannot reconcile the God of love and the God of
wrath. It is an entirely honorable failure. Time out of mind, it has
been the refrain of theologians: efforts to comprehend the incom-
prehensible God can be made only by referring to divine attributes
that seem, to weak and imperfect human reason, irreconcilable.

6. Conclusion

Thomas Browne, with all the insouciance of a 30 year old, claims
that he "could lose an arm without a tear, and with a few groans,
methinks, be quartered into pieces." And Milton, according to

Aubrey, "would be cheerful even in his Gowte-fittes; & sing."[41] But these are seventeenth century men putting the best face on the uncomfortable reality of their world. At the end of *Paradise Lost*, when pain can be considered in its purely human guise, Milton gives it the respect it merits in his culture. The pathos of physical suffering overwhelms Adam when he sees "Spasm, or racking torture, qualms / Of heart-sick Agony" in the vision of the "Lazar house":

> Dire was the tossing, deep the groans, despair
> Tended the sick busiest from Couch to Couch;
> And over them triumphant Death his Dart
> Shook, but delay'd to strike, though oft invok't
> With vows, as thir chief good, and final hope.
> Sight so deform what heart of Rock could long
> Dry-ey'd behold? *Adam* could not, but wept,
> Though not of Woman born; compassion quell'd
> His best of Man, and gave him up to tears
> A space. (*PL* 11.489–98)

So pitiable is the sight that Adam twice asks Michael whether such pain must be suffered: can the "Image of God" not avoid such "inhuman pains," and be "for his Maker's Image sake exempt?" (11.507–14); and again, "is there yet no other way, besides / These painful passages" to death? (11.526–29).

The normal human response to suffering, Adam's reaction to the vision helps to explain Milton's care in his representation of hell, celestial warfare, and the *odium Dei*. The agonies of hell are, as Satan declares, the "Maker's work" (*PL* 4.380); the wounds inflicted during the war likewise have a divine source, as Gabriel reminds Satan at the end of book 4: all strength, all physical power to hurt, is not "our own, but giv'n" (4.1008). However justly the aches and pains of everyday illness might be blamed on sin in the primal first place or, more immediately, on "ungoverned appetite" (11.517), they also originate with God. Pain can be punitive or, as affliction, beneficial discipline, but all pain in *Paradise Lost* leads back to the deity, and Milton's poetic task is to mitigate the violence, the "red right hand" of God.

Pain is everywhere, too, and of different kinds, as is evident in Satan's two "first" experiences of it. When, conspiring, he is surprised by "miserable pain" in his head (*PL* 2.752), he is the first to experience the "pain [of] this intellectual being" (2.147), the pain of "inward torments" (4.88). Later, during the war, he is the first to experience the shock of physical pain. Michael Lieb is correct in his conclusion that the *odium Dei* functions to separate pure from impure, good from evil, so that hate will be expelled and love prevail;[42] eventually, *Paradise Lost* leads Adam and the reader to the promise that heavenly love shall outdo hate, hellish or divine. But that happy vision rests on inconsistencies, incongruities, and poetic problems of every variety that attest to the formidability of justifying God's ways to men.

6 ⇝ A World with a Tomorrow
Paradise Regain'd and Its Hermeneutic of Discovery

Joseph A. Wittreich

Fissures, rifts, crevices, conflicts, inconsistencies, contradictions—these terms are by no means new to Milton criticism. But now reinflected and newly deployed, they are fast becoming the language of an emerging criticism in which this vocabulary points not to aberrations, indiscretions, or a poet's noddings (much less snorings) but instead to acts of poetic engineering. These terms are important not as envelopes for isolated cases or curious phenomena but as component elements in a vast design. They achieve a gathering importance as it becomes apparent that contradictions in Milton's poetry function in consort. No longer cause for censure but now part of a rhetoric of commendation, these terms are also marks of Milton's modernity — indeed, postmodernity, evincing what Gordon Teskey describes as "a rift at the center of his consciousness," "a sort of invisible rift." It is here, according to Teskey, that "contradiction,...positive contradiction," creates a "friction," which, a principal signature of Milton's writings, is, by Teskey, then given the slip as "dissonances become harmonies," "incoherent moments" are recuperated, and "unity [is achieved] on a higher plane." The unity that Milton's detractors had once denied to his poetry is here represented as "the essence of a biblical poetics" that, integrating the fragments of Milton's vision, also affords a program for interpreting it.[1]

The uncertainty and contradiction, the "tangle" of competing codes and clashing meanings that Teskey attributes to Milton's poetry and eventually finds subdued therein, have become its defining features in a criticism that is ready to challenge the applicability to Milton's poetry of what Teskey understands to be the essence of biblical poetics, its harmonizing tendencies.[2] Milton's last poems—*Paradise Lost, Paradise Regain'd,* and *Samson Agonistes*—are all grounded in scriptural stories that, as A. J. A. Waldock explains, are "lined with difficulties of the gravest order." Further flawed in their retelling, says Waldock, those same stories are then projected by Milton onto huge canvases where rifts become gulfs and chasms.[3] Their ancient anchorings in Scripture are, paradoxically, the source of the postmodern aesthetic we are currently excavating from Milton's poems.

Michael Lieb's Milton, for example, "embraces...uncertainties": "my Milton is born of conflict, raised of uncertainty, and forever fulfilling all that is meant by the term *agonistes.*"[4] In their turn, Milton's writings are sites of contestation where uncertainties repeatedly destabilize a text; where what Lieb calls "a radical hermeneutic"[5] undermines rather than reinforces theological commonplaces, disrupting Milton's supposed alliance with "the traditional...well-established...unquestioned,"[6] and where, instead of creating a systematic theology, Milton moves against systems of thought, intent upon delivering us from them. Milton thus rejects the theological climate in which he writes—one that would close windows instead of opening them and that slides by contradictions rather than engaging them, one that answers questions instead of asking them. It is in the face of his own Milton that Lieb declares, "if there are contradictions, then there are contradictions."[7] What

distinguishes Lieb from Teskey and, more fundamentally, John
Milton from John Calvin is the fact that, while all parties allow
for ambiguities and contradictions, Teskey like Calvin eventually
explains them away; he contradicts Milton out of his contradic-
tions. Lieb and Milton, in contrast, thoroughly embrace them,
even if doing so means that supposed "faults" in Milton's poetry
are thus being numbered (as John Peter worried they eventually
would be) as "occult successes."[8] In the process, Milton criticism
becomes more than just a tuning fork.

Paradise Lost and *Paradise Regain'd* offer decidedly different
interpretive leads concerning the wilderness story. The narrator of
the first epic assumes that

> the Tempter set
> Our second *Adam* in the Wilderness,
> To shew him all Earths Kingdoms and thir Glory.
> His Eye might there [in the desert] command wherever stood
> City of old or modern Fame.[9]   (*PL* 11.382–86)

Like Adam, Jesus ascends in *vision* and *in spirit* sees (11.377, 405).
Alternatively, in *Paradise Regain'd*, as a prelude to the kingdoms
temptation, the narrator reports, "With that (such power was giv'n
him then) he took / The Son of God up to a Mountain high" (3.251–
52). Then, in the immediate aftermath of the kingdoms temptation,
Satan assures the Son: "the Wilderness / For thee is fittest place, I
found thee there, / And thither will return thee" (4.372–74), where-
upon the narrator confirms: "So saying he took (for still he knew
his power / Not yet expir'd) and to the Wilderness / Brought back
the Son of God, and left him there" (4.394–96). Correspondingly, as
the third temptation commences, the narrator relates: "he caught
him up, and without wing / Of hippograff bore through the air sub-
lime" and, there in Jerusalem, "on the highest pinnacle he set / The
Son of God" (4.541–42, 549–50), after which the angels "upbore"
the Son, "Then in a flowry valley set him down / On a green bank"
(4.584, 586–87), where now a celestial banquet awaits him.

How are we to account for narrative discrepancies, interpretive
differences? What are we to assume: that the narrator of *Paradise*

Regain'd corrects the erring suppositions of the narrator of *Paradise Lost?* Is either narrator's voice to be privileged, or is Milton's point, instead, that different narrators see, then relate, the same story differently; that competing interpretations have their own histories and sanctions within biblical exegesis, whose varying traditions sponsor rival hermeneutics of the wilderness story. On the one hand, if the Son remains in the desert for the duration of the kingdoms temptation and, by inference, for the pinnacle temptation as well; if as Luke says of the kingdoms temptation, it occurs "in a moment of time" (4:5), then, arguably, the entire sequence of temptations may be construed as a mental event and visionary experience. On the other hand, if, as Matthew reports, Satan transports the Son from the desert to the pinnacle and later from the desert to the mountaintop, then the temptation story, however fictional, may be read as real and actual.

Milton's way, in both his epic poems, is to formulate competing interpretations and then to let them collide with one another in our experience of reading those poems. When it comes to making interpretive choices, we must ask whose hermeneutic to privilege, the narrator's and Satan's in *Paradise Regain'd* or, rather, the narrator's in *Paradise Lost*, the latter's hermeneutic sanctioned by Luke, whose account, of course, Milton privileges in his dramatic ordering of the temptation sequence in *Paradise Regain'd* and whose account, perhaps more importantly, emphasizes the interiority of the wilderness experience: not the vehemence of the Spirit driving or bodily carrying Jesus as in Mark, but the gradual moving of the Spirit within, with the revelation eventually coming upon the mind epiphanically.

When Milton's thinking is viewed within the exegetical tradition summarized by Hugh Farmer—"*Calvin*...was of opinion, that several circumstances in this history agreed best to a vision. And the generality of later writers do readily admit, that the devil's shewing Christ all the kingdoms of the world, and all their glory, in a moment of time, was done in some visionary representation....if *one* of the temptations was presented to Christ in vision only; why might not the *two others be presented to him in the same manner?"*[10]—Milton occupies an interpretive middle ground, inflecting the visionary elements in the second and third temptations, then deepening such inflections through his supplementary banquet and storm temptations, as well as his representations of Mary pondering and Andrew and Simon Peter doubting. In this history, Milton is the segue from Calvin to Farmer—from literalist to figurative reading of the wilderness temptations. As he dramatizes the desert experience, Milton also creates a mindscape of it.

1. *Vying Versions of the Wilderness Story*

Different versions of the wilderness story, conflicted as they may be, are the various aspects of a single tale: one version giving the right order (as Matthew was credited with doing), and another (namely, Luke's) reducing the sequence to simultaneity, anatomizing "a moment of time" (4:5), and then attending to details that establish parallels and symmetries between the temptations of Adam, Eve (Eve especially), and Jesus and the wilderness experiences of Moses, Elijah, and the Son. Through such correspondences, Milton reinforces typological connections, with the temptation sequence itself emblematizing the drama of illumination experienced by the Son as he comes to understand his roles as prophet, king, and priest and, finally, to perceive not just his humanity but, on the pinnacle, his divinity. What may seem like an experience unique to Jesus is one that, instead, unites him with the rest of humankind, thereby legitimizing his role as epic hero: in the words of Richard Overton, "Every man [is] by nature...a King, Priest, and Prophet in his owne naturall circuite and compasse."[11]

Luke's temptation story, as John Lightfoot elucidates it, goes a long way toward explaining Milton's preference for this version over others. Indeed, *Paradise Regain'd* acts as a segue between earlier and later interpretations of the wilderness story, shifting attention to the interiority of the Son's journey, to its concerns with self-definition and discovery within a theater of the mind; then fixing on the fact that *the Spirit leads* (*PR* 1.189, 191–93, 290–92, 299) in a poem that, beginning and ending in moments of vision, is also ruled like its source-book by the spirit of contradiction as it eventually unites a hermeneutic of discovery with a myth of deliverance. How Lightfoot construes *the Spirit's leading* determines, at least initially, how he comprehends and interprets both the kingdoms and the pinnacle temptations. He glosses the verse, "was led by the spirit," in this way: "By which I would suppose our Saviour caught up by the Holy Spirit into the air, and so carried into the wilderness"—an episode later mimicked by Satan when he takes Jesus first to the summit of the mountain and later to the top of the pinnacle. Here we witness, as Lightfoot reports, yet another instance of the devil's deception, his pretending to be the Holy Spirit "who had caught...up [Christ] and brought him already into the wilderness....Christ...had been snatched up by the devil himself to the pinnacle of the Temple and to a very high mountain," although this order in Matthew is reversed by Luke.[12]

When different versions of scriptural stories are at variance, their differences from Lightfoot's point of view are, at least initially, to be construed as counterparts, not contradictions. Hence, the genealogy in Matthew's account places Jesus in the line of David, whereas Luke links Jesus to the woman whose seed bruises the head of the serpent. One typology is not ruled out by the other. Rather, both are important, both are in play. Luke's ordering of the temptations, his placing the temptation to violence last, reinforces the parallelism between Jesus' threefold temptation and Eve's. Describing Jesus as both the Son of Adam and Son of God, Luke conjoins the humanity and the divinity of the Messiah. Letting this tale culminate in the epiphany on the pinnacle, Luke makes clear, moreover, that the wilderness story is about the Son's discovery of his earthly offices as prophet, poet, and priest, yet still more importantly about the formation of the prophetic character, the building up of the human spirit, and about the moment he takes in his vision, as defined by the Milton of *Il Penseroso* only after "attain[ing] / To something like Prophetic strain" (173–74) he achieves a fully expanded prophetic consciousness.

If Jesus had been tempted for 40 days and thereafter is tempted again, it is by way of emphasizing that the Spirit first tempts Jesus invisibly and later visibly, that he is tempted in both the spirit and the flesh; and that he experiences all conceivable temptations, not once but repeatedly, in both his private and his public lives. Tempted in the desert, Jesus will be accosted anew, and more vehemently, once he assumes his messianic mission. Correspondingly, different versions of the temptation story emphasize that the Spirit sometimes leads (as in Luke) by "internal motion" and other times (as in Matthew) by "external compulsion."[13] That difference is marked by the different placements of the mountain and pinnacle temptations, Matthew placing the former last and Luke giving climactic place to the pinnacle temptation. Whatever the order, the end point of this temptation sequence is the moment of vision, achieved within an ascending order and progress, perhaps best encapsulated by Joachim of Fiore as he summons us to spiritual adventure:

> Clear the eyes of the mind from all dusts of the earth; leave the tumults of crowds and the clamor of words; follow the angel in spirit into the desert; ascend with the same angel into the great and high mountain; there you will behold high truths hidden from the beginning of time and from all generations.... For we, called in these latest times to follow the spirit rather than the letter, ought to obey, going from illumination to illumination, from the first heaven to the second, and from the second to the third, from the place of darkness into the light of the moon, that at last we may come out of the moonlight into the glory of the full Sun.[14]

From illumination to illumination—the movement in *Paradise Regain'd* is, correspondingly, from the darkness of the desert into the light of the mountain and from there onto the pinnacle and into the blaze of the sun. What Joachim of Fiore presents in prose Milton translates into poetry and, following him, William Blake puts into picture in the tenth of his designs for the *Paradise Regain'd* series:[15] the mountain and pinnacle temptations bring Jesus to new and ascending thresholds of vision, with the scene on the pinnacle representing the moment in which vision explodes upon the protagonist in this mental theater and in this very moment when Jesus appears in the full blaze of his glory.

Differences in Scripture are often disallowed as contradictions and thus weeded out by scriptural commentators, unlike in Milton's writings where, permeated by conflict, texts pause between competing interpretations, thereby bracketing moments of choice. The very fissures some commentators hide Milton highlights as he aligns himself with the interrogative casting of some seventeenth century biblical commentary where emphasis falls upon different, often competing, traditions of interpretation whirling around a single story, whether it be of Creation and Fall, or of Jesus tempted in the wilderness, or of Samson hurling down the pillars. That is, while some commentators tune and harmonize, others attend to fissures and conflicts, the plurality of traditions impinging on a text and the shifting contexts through which they may be interpreted. Milton's affinities are with this latter group of exegetes, and his strategy in the 1671 poetic volume is to choose stories wherein inspiration—how you know you have it, how you manifest your inspiration and convince others of it—is a core concern.

At the heart of the matter, especially with reference to the New Testament, is the issue of textual corruption. For harmonists like Hugh Broughton, it is axiomatic that a text "is not of God, if it be corrupted"; that "Gods Providence...keep[s] pure"—and is tuning—all books, their "two lips" (in the words of John Weemse) "breathing out one truth," their "kiss[ing] one another" (as Broughton puts it) in "glorious conjunction."[16] Such thinking may typify the Milton of *Tetrachordon* but not the Milton of *De doctrina Christiana* and the epics where, alternatively, Milton subscribes to the view (as stated in his theological treatise) that "the external scripture, particularly the New Testament, has often been liable to corruption and is, in fact, corrupt. This has come about because it has been committed to the care of various untrustworthy authorities" (YP 6:587–88). Milton then continues, "I do not know why God's providence should have committed the contents of the New Testament to such wayward and uncertain guardians, unless it was so that this very fact might convince us that the Spirit which is given to us is a more certain guide than scripture, and that we ought to follow it" (YP 6:589).

This view of the New Testament explains why, despite the retelling of the wilderness temptation in three of the four Gospels, in *Paradise Regain'd* Milton's narrator can claim (as if to fill in the white space in John's gospel) "to tell of deeds / Above Heroic, though in secret done, / And *unrecorded left* through many an Age, / Worthy t' have not remain'd *so long unsung*" (1.14–17; my italics). Milton models his brief epic by creating out of the Gospel stories a consolidated and extended work in which he strives, as Margaret Kean explains, "to re-invest his telling of events with the full impact of a revolutionary moment."[17] He makes one story, a continuous narrative from the conflicting and conflicted narratives in Scripture, revealing rather than concealing those rifts and, in the climactic episode on the pinnacle, capturing the moment when the God-Man discovers the divinity of which earlier he had been emptied.

Milton's "prompted Song" (1.12), *Paradise Regain'd* begins and ends in epiphany, in vision, with Jesus, at his baptism, reading the sign of the dove and, on the pinnacle, becoming an oracle to himself, thereupon fully comprehending both his humanity and his divinity as he readies himself now to "enter" the whirlwind of history and "begin to save mankind" (4.635). Thus, this epic-prophecy begins with the figure of the prophet doing Jesus reverence: "Before him a great Prophet, to proclaim / His coming, is sent Harbinger" (1.70–71; cf. 79–80); and ends with Jesus as a prophet emerging from the wilderness experience, the angels now doing him reverence, as an oracle not only to himself but of a better time: "by vanquishing / Temptation, [thou] hast regain'd lost Paradise / . . . A fairer Paradise is founded now" (4.607–08, 613). In *Paradise Regain'd*, a hermeneutic of discovery locks arms with a myth of deliverance. As William Cowper explains, "the first *Adam*, tempted by Sathan, was driuen from Paradise to the wildernes, but the second *Adam* by suffering himselfe to be tempted of Sathan, brings home the first againe from the wildernes into Paradise."[18]

2. *Competing Interpretations of the Wilderness Story*

"From shadowie Types to Truth, from Flesh to Spirit" (*PL* 12.303)—this movement within the concluding books of *Paradise Lost* replicates the movement from the Old to the New Testament and is replicated by the parallel movement from Milton's diffuse to his brief epic: "The old Testament is the occultation or hiding of the new, and the new is the manifestation of the old."[19] This insight is lost in Thomas Ellwood's complaint when, "after reading *Paradise Lost*," he says to Milton: "Thou hast said much here of *Paradise lost*; but what hast thou to say of *Paradise found?*"[20] The typology of the first and second Adams posits the habit of reading the New Testament without ever taking an eye off the Old, of then tracing Christ throughout the Old Testament. In the process, this habit of reading yokes together parallel temptation scenes, thus marking the beginning of our redemption even as it renders inseparable Adam and Eve's exile into the wilderness from the Son's triumph therein: "Sathan tempting the first *Adam* in Paradise, overcame him, and so caried him away and his posteritie, in a fearefull captiuitie, and bondage: but the second *Adam* suffering temptation by Sathan in the wildernes, overcomes him."[21] Or as Lightfoot argues, "He [Christ] is tempted, as Eve, . . . ; but overcometh . . . as did Moses and Elias" and did so "in the very same place." Lightfoot then goes on to explain that, here in the desert, "The war, proclaimed of old in Eden between the serpent, and the seed of the serpent, and the seed of the woman, Gen. iii. 5, now takes place."[22] Unsurprisingly then, and quite deftly, books 11 and 12 of *Paradise Lost* imply—indeed, they prophesy—the sequel poem of *Paradise Regain'd*. As Thomas Hayne remarks, "*the seed of the woman should breake the head of the Serpent*. That is to say, I will cause one to be borne of the womans seed, which shall subdue the Deuill, and the Deuill shall doe his endeavour to trip vp his heeles by tempting him."[23] The devil's temptation of Jesus, twice foreshadowed in *Paradise Lost*, is the subject of *Paradise Regain'd*, wherein this entire typological scheme involving Adam and Eve (especially Eve), Moses and Elijah, is appropriated and then reinforced by repeated citation, in the instance of Adam and Eve, each cited seven times and each implicated in more elusive allusions, echoes, and references as well.

Adam's dream in book 8 of *Paradise Lost*, one of Milton's supplements to the Genesis story, bears a haunting resemblance to both the Son's mountain and pinnacle temptations in *Paradise Regain'd*; that is, to Satan's transport of Jesus (whether that transport be in body or mind, in dream or in vision):

> suddenly stood at my Head a dream,
> Whose inward apparition gently mov'd
> My fancy...
> One came, methought, of shape Divine,
> And said
>
> ....
>   I come thy Guide
> ....
> So saying, *by the hand he took me rais'd*,
> *And over Fields and Waters, as in Air*
> *Smooth sliding without step, last led me up*
> A woodie Mountain; whose high top was plain,
> A Circuit wide, enclos'd, with goodliest Trees
>   that what I saw
> Of Earth before scarse pleasant seemd...;
>
> ....
> whereat I wak'd, and found
> Before mine Eyes all real, as the dream
> Had lively shadowd.   (*PL* 8.292–311; my italics)

And in *Paradise Regain'd*:

> So saying he caught him up, and without wing
> Of *Hippogrif* bore through the Air sublime
> Over the Wilderness and o're the Plain;
> Till underneath them fair *Jerusalem*,
>
> ....
> And higher yet the glorious Temple rear'd
> Her pile.   (*PR* 4.541–47)

Adam's narrative in *Paradise Lost* and the narrator's report in *Paradise Regain'd*, their perspectives jostling with one another,

pose the question of whether these temptations play out in a the-
ater of the mind or, by miraculous force, the Son is transported
bodily by Satan; whether the experience represented by these epi-
sodes is visionary or actual.

That at least the mountain temptation is visionary is an inter-
pretive inference suggested by the Argument to book 11—"the
Angel sets before him *in vision*" (my italics)—and thereafter cor-
roborated by narrative report:

> So both ascend
> In the Visions of God: It was a Hill
> Of Paradise the highest, from whose top
> The Hemisphere of Earth in cleerest Ken
> Stretcht out to the amplest reach of prospect lay.
> Not higher that Hill nor wider looking round,
> Whereon for different cause the Tempter set
> Our second *Adam* in the Wilderness,
> To shew him all Earths Kingdoms and thir Glory.
> His eye might there command wherever stood
> City of old or modern Fame, the Seat
> Of mightiest Empire
>
> . . . .
>
> in Spirit perhaps he also saw
> . . . the seat of *Montezume.*   (*PL* 11.376–406)

*Both ascend in the Visions of God . . . In Spirit perhaps he also
saw*—these figurative representations of the wilderness story,
countenanced by the narrator of *Paradise Lost,* are confounded
by the narrator of *Paradise Regain'd,* who credits a hermeneutic
ascribing to Satan a miracle. Here, as with a surfeit of strength
(such as Samson is also said to experience as he hurls down the
temple-theater), Satan transports the Son through air to the highest
mountaintop (and later to the pinnacle):

> With that (such power was giv'n him then) he took
> The Son of God up to a Mountain high.
> It was a Mountain at whose verdant feet
> A spatious plain out stretch't in circuit wide
>
> . . . .
>
> and so large

The Prospect was, that here and there was room
For barren desert fountainless and dry.
To this high mountain top the Tempter brought
Our Saviour.   (*PR* 3.251–66)

These competing interpretations of the wilderness temptations of
Jesus — the one reading the story metaphorically, locating its action
within the human mind and crediting the story as a visionary expe-
rience; the other reading the story literally and concluding that
Satan, miraculously empowered, carries Jesus to the mountain's
summit and then to the top of the pinnacle — these competing
interpretations swirl around the wilderness story during the early
modern era. They are central to the exegetical mix in Milton's last
poems where increasingly the pressures of the poetry point inward,
thus implying that the arena of epical activity, the theater of action,
is the human mind itself: Jesus "into himself descended" (2.111)
and, there, like the poet of *The Prelude*, engorging wonders from
the eye, experiences visions rising up in the suburbs of his mind.

3. *Tradition Transformed*

Some 60 years ago, when *Paradise Regain'd* was examined under
the lights of scriptural tradition, it was supposed that Milton wrote
his poem in conformity with received tradition and with what
were by Milton's time the fixed principles and settled opinions for
interpreting that tradition. "Entirely conventional," according to
Elizabeth Marie Pope, *Paradise Regain'd* was completely "consis-
tent with the established view of Milton's day" and thus was writ-
ten in conformity with "the most orthodox theologians."[24] This
poem is said, in Pope's words, to reject ideas of "temptation-by-
vision" and "temptation-by-thought" on the grounds that the devil
possessed no power over the Son's mind or imagination. Into the
mind of the Son Satan cannot go. Subsequently, Pope acknowl-
edges (within parentheses) a chief crux concerning the wilderness
temptations as she alludes to the time "when Satan took Christ
(whether bodily or by means of a vision) to the summit of the
Temple."[25]

Pope forgets an informing principle of *Paradise Lost:* that "Evil into the mind *of God* or Man / May come and go, so unapproved, and leave / No spot or blame behind" (*PL* 5.117–19; my italics). And she forgets, too, the key line of *Paradise Regain'd* where, with a swarm of "troubl'd thoughts" (*PR* 2.65; cf. 1.196–97), Jesus enters the desert as he "Into himself descended" (2.111); not to mention her own abandoned hypothesis that Milton is at times "vague and indeterminate."[26] Indeed, as Jeffrey Gore has remarked so brilliantly in public forum, *uncertainty,* which grips the Milton of *Paradise Lost* and *Samson Agonistes,* is thematized in *Paradise Regain'd,* where it characterizes a state of mind in which everyone at one time or another dwells.[27] Moreover, early receptions of *Paradise Regain'd,* rather than unquestioning, fret over the impropriety of taking for the subject of a poem about the retrieval of the lost paradise the story of regaining paradise in the desert rather than of recovering it on the cross. In the words of John Dennis, Milton here "err'd very widely" in his religion[28] as he craftily revised Atonement theory.

John Calvin focuses the crucial interpretive issue that subsequent commentators (at least initially) will skirt:

> It is sayd that Christ was set vpon a pinacle of the temple. But it is demanded whether he was caried vpon high in deed, or whether it was done by a vision. Many do boldly affirme that it was a true and a reall cariage of his body.... that which foloweth after, that all the kingdomes of the worlde were sette in the sight of Christ, and that also which Luke wryteth, that hee was caried far in the twinkling of an eye, doth rather belong to a vision.... I had rather suspende my judgement, then geue the contentious occasion of quarelling.[29]

Augustine Marlorate similarly shies away from this interpretive dilemma: "whether he were caried through the aire, or whether it were done by a vysion, it is not for the godly to searche." At first anyway, Marlorate is confident: "This truly was a vision,"[30] which fact makes clear, as others contend, that the Son is "the inward, and the new [man]," whose temptations "disturbe the tranquilitie of...mynde."[31]

However, as the seventeenth century presses onward, commentators, following Marlorate's initial instinct, begin to make choices, albeit different ones. Thomas Taylor summarizes one interpretive possibility as he opts for another:

> Some of great learning...hold, that Christs presence in the holy city, and on the pinnacle, was onely in vision, and not corporall. Their reasons are these: 1. Some of the Prophets thus are said in vision to goe from place to place....2. Because the *Evangelists* say, that the temptations were in the wildernesse, and therefore could not be actually in the holy Citie, or on a pinacle, but in vision. Because *Luke* saith, that the temptations beeing ended, Christ returned into *Galiley*, namely from the wildernesse. But it seems, Christs beeing in *Ierusalem*, and on the pinacle of the Temple, was not in vision, but in deed and truth.

To the matter of "whether Christ were...carried, and so set in vision onely, the Diuell deceiuing his senses," Daniel Dyke responds similarly, "I thinke the Diuell carried his body really."[32] John Diodati agrees:

> let confusion stop the mouthes of those blasphemous wretches, who pretending to new Lights and extraordinary Illuminations, belch out this damnable Heresie, That when Christ was tempted, he was tempted by his own Corruption: when it is evident, that the Devil *had nothing in him*, as himself professeth *John* 14.30. and therefore could not tempt him any way but Externally, and the *medium* of sense, by speaking to him, and presenting visible objects to his sight.[33]

Christopher Blackwood is emphatic: "neither were the eyes nor the imagination of Christ deluded." Yet others like John Downame demur: "That he shewed Christ here, all the kingdoms of the world in a moment, declareth that the shewing, was by a vision: otherwise all could not have been under view in a moment."[34]

Eventually swayed by the latter, Lightfoot initially aligns himself with the former: "Christ was bodily driven, or carried, into the wilderness"; and he continues that Matthew and Luke "bear the same sense,...they denote a real, and not a visionary action." "These transportations of our Saviour from place to place," Lightfoot concludes, "were really and actually done, even in the body, and not in a vision." On the matter of the pinnacle temptation, Lightfoot is uncompromising: "this taking him up, was bodily, and locally, and really, the devil catching him up into the air, and carrying him in air to the battlements of the temple."[35] Yet Lightfoot also reconsiders, then concedes, just as Milton will do in *Paradise Lost*, and hints at doing in *Paradise Regain'd*, that the mountain temptation is different perhaps inasmuch as there is no mountain from which all the temptations of the world are visible and none from which even the wisest of human eyes can see all the kingdoms, let alone each of them in all its glory. Here Lightfoot modifies his earlier literalism, suggesting that the Son, once transported to the summit of the mountain, in the Spirit sees: "here was something different from common prospecting or beholding: for men, looking upon a goodly prospect from a high place, view it successive, one part after another, and must turn themselves round; ... they must remove to another hill, where that prospect terminates; but here all this vast object, of all the kingdoms of the earth, is presented at one view, in a moment of time." It was, indeed, "fictious ... airy, delusory, and fantastical," Lightfoot concludes, "an airy horizon before the eyes of Christ."[36] In 1661, in a poem where temptation figures as pictures in the mind, Samuel Pordage (ten years before the publication of *Paradise Regain'd*) fixes attention to "the inner *Worlds*," their "divine irradiation" and their "sacred Visions" unfolding as an aspect of "the inner-World's varieties," yet also affording "true glances of Æternity."[37]

The way has been signaled for Milton's own revisionism, as we have noted already, by the declaration that Jesus "Into himself descended" (*PR* 2.111). In that moment, Jesus' horizontal journey into the desert is translated into a vertical journey into the self. The inward tilt of Milton's tale is marked by the swarming "multitude of thoughts" (1.196) that overtakes Jesus as the temptation story commences; it is accentuated by indicators such as "all my mind was set" (1.202), or "he still on was led, but with such thoughts / Accompanied of things past and to come" (1.299–300), or "with ... Meditations fed / Into himself descended" (2.110–11); and then underscored, in the conclusion to *Paradise Regain'd*, by the Son's "untroubl'd mind / After his aerie jaunt" (4.401–02).

What may have helped Milton map his revisionist reading of the wilderness story is metaphoric reading (popularized in the mid-seventeenth century) of the apocalyptic myth in which the forces of good and evil collide within the human psyche and on the battleground of the human soul, where Christ and Satan are enthroned within and where eventually Satan, defeated, is cast out and then cast off. This epitome of the action of *Paradise Regain'd* with one substitution—Milton for the Son—is, in epitome, the action of Blake's *Milton* as well, with Milton, here casting off Satan, readying himself for the Resurrection, for the moment when the natural man rises a spiritual man and a mind troubled achieves calm.

The inward tilt of Milton's version of the wilderness story is further evident in his representations of Mary meditating, of Andrew and Simon Peter doubting and later rendering of the mountain temptation. Whether the transport of Jesus be bodily or by vision (in *Paradise Regain'd*, "such power was giv'n" Satan that "he took / The Son of God up to a Mountain high" [3.251–52; cf. 4.541–43]), whatever the case, the Son's transport or ascent is *into* vision, both atop the mountain and on the pinnacle. Atop the mountain, Jesus sees before his eyes (3.245) and "beholdst / *Assyria* .../ ...thence on / As far as *Indus* .../ And...beyond" (3.269–73), "thou seest" (3.285), "he look't and saw" (3.310), "Before mine eyes thou hast set" (3.390). It is an optical extravaganza "presented to his eyes": "By what strange Parallax or Optic skill / Of vision multiply'd through art, or glass / Of Telescope" (4.38, 40–42). Thereupon, Jesus sees Rome and with "Aerie Microscope...behold[s] / Outside and inside both" (4.57–58). Finally, "Look once more .../ ...behold" (4.236–37), urges Satan, to whom Jesus responds, "these are false, or little else but dreams, / Conjectures, fancies, built on nothing firm" (4.291–92). Jesus dispels any doubt, declaring that the temptations here presented him belong to the realm not of actuality but of vision. Then, this temptation completed, and ending as it began, indeed as the whole series of temptations begins, Satan "took (for still he knew his power / Not yet expir'd) and to the Wilderness / Brought back the Son of God" (4.394–96; cf. 372–74). In Milton's rendering, the transport of the Son is physical, but the experience atop both the mountain and the pinnacle is visionary, both experiences essential to the formation of the Son as a prophetic character.

Milton neither twists nor turns Scripture, but he does draw inferences and supply inflections through interpolations like the banquet and storm temptations. Bracketing the kingdoms temptations, these interpolations reinforce the interiority of Milton's poem, its emphasis upon the mental landscapes and psychological inwardness of the wilderness story. These interpretations also elucidate the "narrative enigma"[38] created by Milton's gathering into focus, then highlighting, the whole question of whether the temptation sequence is to be read literally or figuratively, whether it is real or visionary, with Milton resisting the either-or answers of institutionalized interpretations and replacing them with both-and alternatives, which bespeak a salutary interpretive freedom and broker new interpretive possibilities. The banquet and storm scenes confirm that, in *Paradise Regain'd*, Milton embraces the ideas of temptation by vision, as well as temptation by dream and by thought. The pinnacle temptation is the very capstone to any argument that *Paradise Regain'd*, a poem that presents thought colliding with thought, minds thinking, involves temptation by thought, thought followed by thought, this poem's emphasis falling upon "the inner man, the nobler part" (2.477).

In book 1 of *Paradise Regain'd*, the first temptation ends with Satan, an apparition, "Into thin Air diffus'd" (1.499). In book 2, waking from sleep and finding "all was but a dream" (awakening into vision, as it were), the Savior "Up to a hill anon his steps he rear'd" (2.285). There he encounters Satan, who "spake no dream, for as his words had end, / Our Saviour lifting up his eyes beheld /.../ A Table richly spred" (2.337–40). Scornful of what he sees, we are told, "With that / Both Table and Provision vanish'd quite" (2.401–02). Then, newly empowered, Satan takes Jesus to a high mountain from which he beholds, as previously discussed and as an optical miracle, his eyes turning this way and that, and seeing from afar, all the kingdoms of the world, as well as those kingdoms in all their glory, though none allures eye or mind. The outcome of this visionary drama is a Savior patient of mind, but a Satan "Perplex'd and troubl'd" (4.1), although, once returned to the desert, the Savior finds that as "stormy blasts" "soon...ugly dreams / Disturb'd his sleep" (4.408–09; 418). "Infernal Ghosts, and Hellish Furies.../...some howl'd, some yell'd, some shriek'd" (4.422–23) and "grisley Spectres" too (4.430)—when morning comes, all are "chased" away, all these "terrors dire" (4.429, 431). When we recall that one of Milton's contemporaries, Jeremy Taylor (perhaps at Milton's own prompting), questions whether "the devils appeared in any horrid and affrighting shape," or as "ugly phantasms," thinking it more likely that while tempting Christ they appeared as angels;[39] when we remember assertions like these, we may also conclude that, in gestures of inclusivity, in *Paradise Regain'd*, as part of its epic endeavor, but also as part of its interpretive freight, Milton brings within the compass of his poem the very matters others would exclude from its story.

Finally, "caught...up" and, again by Satan, "bore through the Air" (4.541–42), our Savior stands upon the pinnacle, from where we hear, "Tempt not the Lord thy God, he said and stood. / But Satan smitten with amazement fell" (4.561–62). And the choir of angels responds, "Hail Son of the most High.../ Queller of Satan, on thy glorious work / Now enter, and begin to save mankind" (4.633–35). Having traveled to the very center of his being, having discovered himself as both man and God, and then having defined his roles in the world and his mission therein, now complete within himself and ready to complete his work as humankind's deliverer, Jesus returns to civilization, where he is also ready to trade a life of contemplation for one of action, to "work Redemption for mankind" (*PR* 1.267), thus allowing "Man fall'n...[to] be restor'd" (1.405). The Son is ready now, "to subdue and quell o'er all the earth / Brute violence and proud Tyrannick pow'r, / Till truth were freed, and equity restor'd" (4.218–20).

4. *Milton's Mental Theater*

Contemplation precedes but does not preclude action in *Paradise Regain'd*. In the poem proper, however, it does supersede action just as prophecy here supersedes epic, in the process scuttling so many of epic's time-honored conventions. Even if an example of what, in the preface to the second book of *The Reason of Church-Government*, Milton calls a "brief" epic (YP 1:813), *Paradise Regain'd* bears little resemblance to a miniature version (or even scaled-down model) of the diffuse epic poem. For the most part, epic conventions have been pared away, or persist only as signposts. Yet one of them is conspicuously retained and, in its retention, hugely amplified and completely reconstituted: namely, the descent into the underworld now figured as a descent into the wilderness of the self. In this way, Milton's remodeling serves the larger psychologizing tendencies and internalizing impulses of his project, even as it brings into relief its dramatic character. In *Paradise Regain'd*, epic poetry is transformed into a mental theater, its defining aspect, eventually and memorably epitomized by Blake in the phrase, "Visionary forms dramatic."[40] Here contemplation precedes action. The formation of the prophetic character is anterior to nation-building, now reconfigured in a major way so that the mind-transforming drama of *Paradise Regain'd* is prologue to a *world* transformed as the "Paradise within thee" of *Paradise Lost* (12.587) gives way to the newly recovered paradise—the "fairer Paradise...founded now" (4.613)—that is, *now to be found* in history. *Paradise Regain'd* is a reenactment of the prophecy in Isaiah 51:3: "the Lord...will make her wilderness like Eden, and her desert like the Garden."

Whether *Paradise Regain'd* is read as an epic prophecy or as exegesis in verse,[41] notably it never refers to, nor addresses, its hero (whom Milton describes in "The Passion" as "Most perfect Heroe" [13]) by the name of Christ. John Lightfoot (1602–75), Milton's contemporary and fellow student at Christ's College, Cambridge, is a useful point of reference here, not because influence can be established, but because their interpretive inflections are often the same, except when it comes to naming the hero of the wilderness story, whom Lightfoot regularly calls Christ, meaning the anointed one or the messiah. The protagonist of this story is never called "Christ" by Milton, perhaps because this name achieved its popularity and significance in terms of the Crucifixion story and with specific reference to the risen Christ and his followers. Christ's name, then, is irrevocably involved with a theology wherein reconciliation between God and man is achieved through Christ's Crucifixion and humankind's deliverance by his Resurrection.

Milton thus invites the double complaint, first, that he writes about Jesus in the wilderness, not on the cross, thereby getting this poem's "religion" wrong; and second, and simultaneously, that by never calling his hero Christ in *Paradise Regain'd* and, even in the numerological structure of the poem (four, not three books), inflecting the humanity of Jesus, Milton slights his hero's divinity, all the while magnifying his humanity. Thus Christ seems to be torn from the firmament, in the process inviting the further complaint that in its heresies *Paradise Regain'd* is Arian, even Socinian. One anonymous critique of the poem minces no words in its insistence that *Paradise Regain'd* stands "in open contradiction to the sacred Scriptures"; that here the Son's "*proper Divinity*...so unequivocally revealed in the Holy Scriptures, is kept entirely out of sight. Thus the Poet has injured himself no less than in excluding the scene of the crucifixion from the action of his Poem."[42]

Most important, in swerving from then current readings of the wilderness story, Milton also sets new interpretive directions for it. Felt before it is ever seen perhaps, Milton's presence is there in Matthew Poole's commentary, in the accent it places on Jesus, his very name, and its associations with savior and deliverer, as well as in the attention it gives (while acknowledging Lightfoot) to the optical splendor of the kingdoms temptation and its *"Airy Horizon,"*[43] also reminiscent perhaps of Milton's "aerie microscope" (4.57). It may also be owing to Milton that Abraham Woodhead conjectures, concerning the kingdoms temptation, that "It is likely that Satan set forth this...Temptation with many more words."[44]

It is perhaps owing to Milton as well that Laurence Clarke speaks of "troubled Thoughts and terrifying Apparitions in his [Jesus'] Mind," of "frightful Dreams when he [Jesus] slept, frequent Apparitions and Illusions of evil Spirits in the Night, and...unspeakable Terrors." Clarke may also be in Milton's debt when he remembers that "Satan was so thunder-struck, that he could keep the Field no longer" as he recognizes "Jesus was God incarnate." Then speaking of "that visionary Scene of all the Kingdoms and Glories," Clarke seems to swipe at Milton as he avers that "ugly Phantasms...disturb only feeble and imperfect Imaginations"; and in his rebuke of those "who would have all the History of our Lord's Temptation to be taken only as a Dream, or Vision," Clarke also brakes against the direction in which scriptural exegetes gesture and in which poets after Milton will follow.[45] The eighteenth and early nineteenth centuries afford some striking examples.

Between 1650 and 1700, a seismic change affects the way the wilderness story is read. *Paradise Regain'd* is one force for such change. At midcentury, Henry Hammond holds fast to the view that "Satan, as 'tis most probable, carried [Jesus] in the aire," even as he concedes of the kingdoms temptations the occurrence of "all this in a moment of time, Luke 4.5. not one after another," or in sequence.[46] By the end of the seventeenth century, the literalist and figuralist interpreters have formed separate camps. Thomas Manton represents the literalists as he asks "whether the Temptations of Christ are to be understood by way of Vision, or Historically; as things visibly acted and done. This latter I incline unto," says Manton, who then insists that the wilderness temptations are not "a piece of Phantasie," not "imaginary," even if Scripture remains silent on whether Satan carries Jesus through the air visibly or invisibly and even if the kingdoms temptation seems to fight against literalism inasmuch as the kingdoms of the world cannot all be seen from a single place. But then Manton explains the contradiction away by reading the kingdoms temptation as "a Synechdochial Hyperbole,...that sheweth a part of a thing," only "the chiefest part" and not the whole. Representing the figuralists and acting upon hints set forth earlier by Henry Hammond,

Jean Le Clerc argues, "What is here related, may more easily be conceived to have happened to *Christ* in a *Vision* or *Dream*, than *really*. It looks, methinks, very odd, that an Evil *Spirit* should be permitted to have such a power over our most holy *Saviour*, as to carry him through the Air; and then that prospect of the kingdoms of the whole World could no more be shewn from a *Mountain* than upon a *Plain*," hence Le Clerc's conclusion that things are shown to Jesus here "*in the Spirit, i.e., in a Vision.*"[47]

Paradise Lost employs the same language. *Paradise Regain'd* deepens its inflections. Remembering Milton's own language— "both ascend / In *the visions of God*" and "*in Spirit* perhaps *he also saw*" (11.376–77, 406; my italics)—we may also recall the coding of scriptural language as explained by Joseph Bretland for whom scriptural writers always tag visionary representations and experiences with "the words *in vision* or *in the vision of God*," these terms declaring that the narrative "is a vision."[48] By thus deploying the language of vision, Milton opens his narrative to being read as a visionary experience just as biblical writers, through such language, had both signaled their interpretive intentions and authorized such visionary readings. By Milton, the entire story of Jesus tempted is recast within a visionary mode.

Calvin, Lightfoot, and Milton are credited by Hugh Farmer with inaugurating a gradual shift in the wilderness hermeneutic that Farmer himself seems to have effected. What had been read "as a narrative of real facts, or outward transactions" is now being represented, in analogy with the book of Revelation, as "*a prophetic vision, under the afflatus of the Holy Spirit*" wherein "the things related were no where performed but upon the stage of fancy," "in vision," and where the things prophesied refer to the temptations undergone by the Son during his ministry. If Calvin concedes that the kingdoms temptation "was done in some visionary representation," "if *one* of the temptations was presented to Christ" in this fashion, Farmer asks, "why not the *two others*"? The entire temptation sequence is "a recital of visionary representations," with each of the temptations neither "a literal fact, nor diabolical delusion" but "a divine vision" and with Farmer now reinterpreting *led* into the desert to mean that the Son "was...conveyed thither in a spiritual manner, in vision or mental representation, under a divine inspiration." By telling us that Christ was carried into the wilderness *in vision,* such cues embedded within the wilderness story "lead us to conceive of every part of the temptation as visionary," each "vision exciting images within us."[49] Even when the broad outlines of Farmer's reading are rejected, Milton is invoked as an example of—and guide to—visionary literature.[50]

By the nineteenth century, Farmer's reading of the temptation story has taken hold. Thus Thomas Belsham contends, "The temptation of Christ was unquestionably a visionary scene intended as the vehicle of important instruction: and the introduction of the devil into this scenical representation, no more proves the existence of such a power and malignant spirit as the devil is commonly represented to be, than the symbolic figures in the apocalyptic vision, prove that such figures must have an external archetype." And Henry Cotes follows suit, crediting Farmer with having "remove[d] the veil of obscurity that so long concealed the nature and design" of the wilderness story, and then advancing this tale as "the narrative of a Divine Vision" in which "the future trials of his [Christ's] ministry are exhibited,...urging temptations correspondent with those real, actual trials, that he afterwards encountered." Cotes would promote *Paradise Regain'd,* this "neglected poem," as being as worthy of praise as *Paradise Lost,* even as he points out the absurdity in reading *Paradise Regain'd* as a real transaction, "according to the letter," and invokes Milton's authority as well, if not for interiorizing this story, at least for justifying an interval of time between the baptism of Jesus and his entrance into the wilderness.[51] If Milton did not invent this new wilderness hermeneutic, in big and small ways he paved the way for it, with William Blake, in his poem called *Milton,* finally giving this poet his due. Milton, experimental theologian, is equally and just as emphatically Milton, experimental exegete.

"No poet, outside the Bible," writes Northrop Frye, "was accorded the kind of authority that was given to a theologian."[52] With the exception of Milton, we should add, and then say: no theologian rivals Milton, even comes close to him, in terms of the impact he has registered on how the scriptural myths of Creation, Fall, Recovery, and Apocalypse are perceived today. _Paradise Lost, Paradise Regain'd_, and _Samson Agonistes_ form a trilogy of poems, each wrapped around a different myth and each transforming, as well as reinterpreting, the myth it appropriates. It is Milton's version of these stories that persists and prevails in the cultural consciousness of our time, each of these poems pressing toward a heightened understanding of the myth it inscribes. What Philip Pullman says of _Paradise Lost_ can be extended to _Paradise Regain'd_ and _Samson Agonistes_ as well: they just "will not go away."[53] _They will not go away_ because of the vastness of their hermeneutic field where we find multiplying, often discrepant meanings, as well as rival, sometimes irreconcilable interpretations. In such dialectics of counterparts, as Don Ihde explains, "if there is no closure or resolution of the conflicting interpretations, that, too, is a reflection of the position of the thinker in the present."[54] It is how Milton situates himself _in his own present_ and how we then situate Milton _in our present_ that matters. Milton dwelt in the uncertainties a newly emerging criticism now attributes to him.

By 1855, acknowledging what he might call the "mental culture" of the wilderness story, Harvey Goodwin, without reading Farmer yet partly agreeing with him, interprets this temptation story as "a spiritual history," "figurative, or symbolical," as an initiatory experience — "a preparation for the ministry" — and, as such, as a "prophetic vision." Following Dr. Nitzch, Goodwin concludes, "The history of the Temptation, in this form, is not a _real_, but a _true_ history." Nearly a decade after Goodwin, without an appeal to Milton's authority, T. T. Carter presents a reading of the wilderness story, which displays an amazing correspondence to Milton's own, as a counterpart to the story of the Fall, its closing off of the senses and its darkening of the mind, this story, instead, being of the "human consciousness [that] would...necessarily open and

expand in time"; of a mind's "progressive development," "advanc-
ing perfection," and "progressive realization."[55] The wilderness
story, especially in Milton's rendering of it in *Paradise Regain'd*, is
a prophetic poem about the evolution of human consciousness and
the building up of the human spirit. It is a prelude to *The Prelude:*
the delineation of a mental progress, involving self-definition and
self-discovery and engaging its readership in acts of thinking about
thinking. In the apocalyptic theaters of his epics, Milton stages
once and then once again, his mind-shattering, potentially world
transforming dramas in poems which, not singly but together, are
harbingers of the distinctly Romantic genres of mental theater
and epiphanic epic. By the early years of the nineteenth century,
Paradise Regain'd and *Samson Agonistes* have been disjoined and
published separately, thus paving the way for *Paradise Lost* and
Paradise Regain'd to be published together. Indeed, this pairing of
Milton's epics in publication in a distinctively nineteenth century
phenomenon.

In fixing attention on conflicting versions and interpretations of
the wilderness story (on Luke versus Matthew), and then following
Michael Lieb's injunction (if there are contradictions so be it, let
them stand), we begin to grasp that more is at stake in this conflict
than adding another footnote to Milton's place in literary history
or one more asterisk to yet another foray into Milton's poetics.
An interpretive controversy long repressed in the critical tradition
accruing to Milton's epics is now being released within them and
in a way that, bringing that controversy alive, forces us to experi-
ence it both as we move from *Paradise Lost* to *Paradise Regain'd*
and then as we travel within the boundaries of *Paradise Regain'd*
itself.

The Lucan precedent, seemingly privileged by Milton, spon-
sors—indeed, authorizes—reading the wilderness story as a
divine, not a demonic, vision; as not merely an episode in the biog-
raphy of Jesus but, more tellingly perhaps, as a page from history
and as a leaf of prophecy. The story of a perfect man is also the
story of humankind perfected, of trials yet to be endured and of
temptations still to be overcome. If it is really in keeping with its

Lucan model, *Paradise Regain'd* may be read anew as the anatomy of a moment stretched out in time, exhibiting events seemingly successive as actually simultaneous, thus suggesting in this and in still another way how *Paradise Lost* and *Paradise Regain'd* are counterparts: if *Paradise Lost* is not so much the story of Adam and Eve leaving paradise as the story of paradise departing from them, *Paradise Regain'd,* in a counter move, is the story of paradise returning to humankind; of the ordeal through which he travels and triumphs, in every episode leaving the vivid air signed with his honor. If Milton has made Scripture new through his supplements and retellings, in a parallel move we can renew Milton's texts, as well as our criticism of them, by developing and deploying new — or newly recovered — strategies for interpreting them.

7 ⮃ "Shifting Contexts"
Artists' *Agon* with the Biblical and Miltonic Samson

Wendy Furman-Adams and
Virginia James Tufte

> Perhaps better than any of Milton's poems, *Samson Agonistes*
> illustrates the proposition...that interpretation...provokes
> reinterpretation.
>
> —Joseph Wittreich

The past decade has abounded with readings of *Samson Agonistes*—a remarkable number of them published, with weird appropriateness, in 2001–02. Yet as Derek N. C. Wood remarks, "There is less agreement now than there ever has been about [its] meaning....Quite simply, even accounts given by belated liberal humanists and 'close readers' of what happens in the play can differ so startlingly from one another that the reader is left wondering if their authors have been reading the same text."[1] Nowhere is this disagreement sharper than with regard to the questions—all but suppressed by earlier readers—raised by the horrific violence suffered and inflicted in the play. "The still pressing question," Joseph

Wittreich writes, "is whether Milton, like Euripides and like the redactor of the Judges stories, deplores the culture of violence he depicts."[2]

Michael Lieb's provocative answer—worked out in a number of ways between 1994 and 2002—could not be more stark: "In no other work of Milton is the sparagmatic experience more germane than in *Samson Agonistes*. The drama is a work of violence to its very core. It extols violence. Indeed, it exults in violence."[3] Lieb also takes up, and answers, a corollary question: What, given the world represented in Milton's play, are we to make of Milton's God? Far from the rational, theodical God of Mary Ann Radzinowicz's 1978 reading, Lieb's godhead is revealed, incarnate, in Milton's shockingly primitive hero: "By virtue of his 'livingness,' God becomes ultimately a 'non-rational essence' that eludes all philosophical speculation. To appreciate the force of such a view of deity is to acknowledge 'the non-rational core of the biblical conception of God.'"[4]

Wittreich's contrasting answer—although worked out in ever more detail and in ever more contexts—is still essentially that argued in his earlier *Interpreting* Samson Agonistes: that "Samson is no type of Christ..., not at all of Christ triumphant and only ironically of Christ suffering." His deeds are entirely evil and reflect only inversely the justice of Milton and of Milton's God, whose nature can be read only through the Son in *Paradise Regain'd*. "Milton's point," writes Wittreich, "is obvious: evil is imputable to man, not God"; only his permissive will can possibly be read in Samson's deeds, as the epic voice explicitly reads it in Satan's. Samson is connected to the Son exclusively by inversion: the taker of life juxtaposed, as in the 1671 volume, with the giver of life and Savior of humankind.[5]

Yet to admit, with Wittreich—quoting Luther—that Samson is no model to be followed,[6] is not necessarily to reduce Samson's role to that of pure Antichrist. John T. Shawcross suggests that "disjunctive reading should, rather, be replaced by a reading that holds up multiple readings of the text in mind conjunctively, opposed though they may seem to be"—a discipline he models in *The Uncertain World of* Samson Agonistes.[7] And Derek Wood, benefiting from every reading mentioned here, substitutes synthesis for Shawcross's dialectic, bringing Wittreich and Lieb's horror together with a critical candor that allows Samson some possible redemption, while recognizing his ethic as barbaric. The tragedy, he writes,

> does not question whether Samson is a hero of faith, nor does it affirm that he is a "Christian" hero. Samson is tragically ignorant of the exemplary life of Christ as he shapes his own agonized moral choices, honestly but painfully and uncharitably.... Against Samson's divinely confirmed faith, Milton sets this questionable moral consciousness, this...condition of un-Christian savagery acted out in all honesty by human beings ignorant as yet of the living example of Christ's life in time.

Samson, for Wood, is no Christ figure. On the other hand, "Samson's final achievement was not satanic; he was, according to the Word of God [Hebrews 11:32–34], a hero of faith, but his morality was fashioned in the darkness under the Law, and Milton's text, for all its indirection, does not obscure what in that morality is ugly and un-Christian." Indeed, "the Nazirite's pre-Christian, literal and temporal conception of deliverance condemned all his efforts to futility.... In his commitment to serve God, he was prepared to give his life. And nothing came of his sacrifice."[8] No one has come closer to meeting the challenge Irene Samuel set a long 35 years ago: to read *Samson Agonistes* as tragedy.[9]

Out of Milton's nearly 200 illustrators, only 15 have chosen to represent *Samson Agonistes*. Nevertheless all the critical readings discussed above have been anticipated by these illustrators and by the literally hundreds of artists who have represented the biblical account of Samson (Judg. 13–16) in paintings and engravings.[10] Several hundred illustrations of the biblical Samson, ranging from the fourth to the twenty-first centuries, and about 70 illustrations of *Samson Agonistes* by a dozen artists from Milton's time to our own, provide another "shifting context" within which to read Milton's endlessly evocative drama. For artists, as for literary critics, the Judges narrative has been a site of contention—or at least of interpretations that can be held together only by the most determined effort at "conjunctive" reading. The Samsons of art range from types of Christ to types of Satan; from terrorists to romantic victims. Sometimes artists use the Samson story to reflect upon other, more contemporary issues. On the whole, as we shall see, representations of *Samson Agonistes* are characterized not by extroverted violence, but rather by profound interiority — something of a paradox when one considers both the violence of the Judges story and the difficulty of rendering emotional states in visual terms. Toward the end of the twentieth century — just as the problem of Samson heated to the boiling point in literary criticism — the most promising response to Milton's drama took the form of almost Rorschach-like abstraction — suggesting, perhaps, that the real story takes place, as Stanley Fish had told us it did, primarily in the mind of the reader.[11]

1. *Re-Visions of the Biblical Samson, ca. 350–1925*

Until the late fifteenth century, artists and their patrons were interested in the Hebrew Bible not primarily as narrative, but rather as a set of signs darkly but faithfully prefiguring the Gospel. Thus Samson, like other Old Testament heroes, was represented typologically, often in the role given him by the writer of Hebrews: one of a "great cloud of witnesses" anticipating "the author and finisher" of the Christian faith (Heb. 11:32, 12:1–2). As Augustine had argued in his *De doctrina Christiana*, "Scripture teaches nothing but charity, nor condemns anything but cupidity"; thus, "whatever appears in the divine Word that does not literally pertain to virtuous behavior or to the truth of faith [one] must take to be figurative."[12] And, as little in the Samson narrative could serve to exemplify such values, the medieval Samson, although frequently represented, was represented neither in terms of his terrible suffering nor of his incredible physical strength, but rather for his allegorical connections to other figures.

Samson's exploits could represent almost any moment of the Christ event. In one of the earliest extant images of Samson, a fourth century catacomb painting from the Via Latina, Samson raises the jawbone that, in Judges 15, he uses to slay 1,000 men. But in the fresco, he raises this strange object in a peaceable gesture that prefigures Christ's victory over death in his harrowing of hell (fig. 1). The toga-clad men to Samson's left appear not so much his Philistine victims as souls redeemed from Limbo. Likewise, on a twelfth century altar in Brussels, Samson carries the gates of Gaza (which he carries, in Judges 16, to "the top of the hill"). But, completely suppressing the action's narrative context—a visit to a Philistine prostitute—he carries it crosslike, directly under the parallel image of Christ carrying his actual cross. Samson could also serve, along with other typological heroes, to represent the Resurrection—as in a fresco from a church in Tirsted, Denmark, dating from around 1400 (fig. 2). Here Samson, again carrying the Gaza gate, is neatly paired with Jonah, who steps forth smartly from the whale's toothy mouth, and onto the welcoming shore.[13]

No event, moreover, in the Judges narrative resonated more seamlessly with the Gospels than the angel's annunciation of Samson's birth to Manoah's barren wife. The Klosterneuburg Altar, painted in 1181 by Nicolas of Verdun, represents parallel Annunciations and Nativities, using identical iconography: one representing the angel's appearance to Manoah's wife, the other to the Virgin Mary. And, as late as 1436–37, Jan Van Eyck painted a glorious Annunciation that demonstrated his near mastery of single-point perspective. Yet the very parquet floor that best shows that early modern mastery—and upon which his lavishly dressed Virgin and angel stand—is brilliantly etched with detailed scenes from none other than the life of Samson.

Early modern artists often rejected these earlier, typological readings of selected events, replacing them with more literal visual renderings of one episode or another from the Judges narrative. Some of these readings emphasized, as Wittreich has observed, the "horror" and savagery of Samson's exploits, "with sculptors and painters alike often capturing him in uncontrolled moments of rage and sometimes in scenes of mass destruction."[14] There are few more chilling examples of this violent strain than Andrea Schiavone's

Samson Killing a Philistine (fig. 3). In this Florentine work from around 1542–45, Schiavone brilliantly uses iconographic allusion to underscore his image of sparagmatic violence. For here, as nowhere in the far-from-pastoral Judges account, a dead lamb lies crumpled upon the ground to the left. Oblivious to this pitiful sight, Samson lifts a massive jawbone over his single pleading victim, with whom the viewer immediately identifies and who becomes, by his helpless posture, an innocent rather than a "foreskinned" infidel.[15] The scene recalls no biblical parallel so much as that of Cain and Abel. Indeed, were it not for the assailant's peculiar weapon, we could easily take this scene for the murder of the Bible's first shepherd by his envious brother.[16] Much of the visual horror lies, as one critic puts it, in "the aggressor's double action, pushing his victim down with one hand while striking with the other."[17] The rest lies, perhaps, in the total absence of redemptive imagery. For Schiavone, it would seem—as for Wittreich and others—Samson is simply another in a line of thugs and murderers, going straight back to Adam's firstborn son. Any lamb who has died to redeem *this* Samson will surely have died in vain.

Protestant prayer books and biblical illustrations often produced a somewhat more evenhanded effect, as their use of sequential narrative placed equal emphasis on the violent and the pathetic events in Samson's story—sometimes mimicking the detachment of the original narrative. At other times they return, at least by allusion, to the typological approach dominant in earlier art. A poignant *Mater Sampsonis* from a 1633 Scottish prayer book (fig. 4) represents the second, but not the first, of these effects. In this lovely engraving, the hero's mother sits, hands folded, in a thoughtful Marian pose. An inset in the background reveals the angel departing in the flames of the parents' sacrificial altar, as classical monuments domesticate the savagery of her son's future exploits into civilized heroism.[18] If such images by no means make up "*the* Christian tradition" in the interpretation of the Samson story, they do make up a strain within that tradition, one underscoring humanist values and baptizing Samson as a pre-Christian pattern of Christ.[19]

In other works, however, Samson's betrayal is linked by synoptic narrative not to his mysterious birth but rather to his terrible revenge. *Delilahs Falshood to Sampson,* from a Bible published at Oxford in 1682 (fig. 5), shows the agitated gestures of soldiers and attendants as Delilah intently wields the fatal scissors on Samson's sleeping head—underscoring, like many Baroque painters, his betrayal at her hands. An inset, however, shows the aftermath of her deed—in which a strangely childlike Samson breaks stylized pillars, and Philistines tumble from the temple's collapsing roof in a horrible if primitive preplay of 9/11.[20] And Matthäus Merian's Bible of 1630 represents Samson's story in four-color copperplate engravings, two of which foreground the violence of the Judges narrative.[21] In one of these images, Samson slays a thousand Philistines with the jawbone of an ass (Judg. 15:14–16), while, in a background vignette representing an earlier exploit, flaming pairs of foxes rush headlong into an already flaming field (Judg. 15:4–5). In another design—clearly related to the Oxford image, but reversed and more graphic in color—the victim Samson is again shorn by a deliberate-looking Delilah. But in a foreshadowing background vignette, he furiously avenges his two eyes—pulling down the temple as his enemies struggle in midair, falling upon and around him. We can even make out, as if in a child's nightmare, the round, open mouths of the victims' silent cries.

For seventeenth century artists, as for Milton, typological readings continued to have some resonance. But, as in scriptural illustration, they began to jostle with more literal readings, especially among radical Protestants, who sought to recover the original sense and context of the Hebrew Bible.[22] As W. A. Visser't Hooft has put it, artists like Rembrandt—working *within* the privileged space of Dutch religious tolerance, as Milton worked *for* such tolerance in England—"rediscovered the Bible and with joyous surprise found a new and fresh message in it."[23] Inspired by their individual, critical reading of the Bible—problematically illustrated in Milton's *De doctrina Christiana*—such artists used their art not to express the fixed, schematic meanings of medieval images, but to uncover new spiritual meanings in the ancient text. Interest in the actual Hebrew narrative began to register through the New Testament's great cloud of triumphant witnesses, and Samson's baffling narrative became even more worthy of exploration in its own right. Whether the emphasis fell upon the violence he inflicts or the violence he suffers, Samson at last moved to the center of his own story. Especially during Milton's lifetime (1608–74)—which almost exactly paralleled that of Rembrandt (1606–69)—Samson became less a type than an individual, displaying not Christ-like victory, but the passion and suffering so tragically common in human life and so hard to reconcile with the goodness of God. In short, the Samson story became, as it was to become for Milton, the singularly difficult site for an inquiry into the divine nature and purpose; a site, in other words, for raising the questions that G. W. Leibniz (1649–1716) would soon identify by the name "theodicy."

By Rembrandt's time—and Milton's—Samson's too-human story had already become a favorite subject of northern Baroque painters such as Peter Paul Rubens, Matthias Stom, Anthony Van Dyck, and Gerrit van Honthorst. These artists generally focus on the Nazarite, chosen of God, as spiritual prodigy, as lover, and, above all else, as victim. For them the heart of the narrative lies in the tragic scene of Samson betrayed: by his own sensuality, surely, but also by the woman he loves. Working a half century or so before Milton, they give that woman her major psychological role, as her motives become the crux of a story that now came to be known by its modern, operatic title: *Samson and Delilah*. In 1609, Rubens emphasized Delilah's sensual powers as a courtesan, while underscoring her own despairing subjection to others more powerful than herself. In 1630, Stom represented a coarser Samson and a cooler, more responsible Delilah, while Van Dyck, working in 1628 (fig. 6), shows us a woman who bluntly manipulates her body into a precision trap to capture an overgrown boy-man incapable of learning from experience. Yet the other, respectable-looking figures in Van Dyck's scene—including two women (one old and one young) and a kindly looking elderly barber—remind us too of Delilah's pact with her people: one based perhaps (as Milton's Dalila will argue) more on patriotism than on the 1,100 pieces of silver (from each Philistine lord!) promised in Judges 16:5.[24] Finally, in van Honthorst's meditative rendering (fig. 7), Delilah appears — even as she shears off Samson's locks — a tender and thoughtful matron, her face illuminated by a single candle like a seventeenth century Magdălene. A leanly muscled Samson, meanwhile, lies sleeping in childlike innocence upon his arm — creating an effect more elegiac than violent, more *Pietà* than soap opera.

But no artist seems to have found more fascination in Samson's story than Rembrandt van Rijn. In five paintings made between 1629 and 1641, he and his circle vividly dramatized various stages in the strong-man's life, as related in Judges 13–16. In these works which, although never shown together, have often been read as a series, Rembrandt and members of his workshop emphasize not only the hero's divine calling but also the pathos, cruelty, and waste of his subsequent career. Rembrandt's fascination with character and with moments of deep psychological drama, in addition to his scholarly interest in the recovery of Hebraic culture, seem to have drawn him especially to the character of Samson. Representing a number of scenes from the Judges account, he gives the great cipher of the Bible an inward life — anticipating, in another medium, the painful complexity of Milton's creation. Milton's tragedy, written within three decades of these visual works, moves Rembrandt's drama yet further inward, where it is staged primarily in the protagonist's tortured mind. Like Rembrandt and his circle, Milton uses Samson's story to explore the central problem of his own later life: that of discerning the benevolent presence of God through the seemingly irremediable darkness of human events.[25]

In Rembrandt's virtual narrative cycle of Samson's *agon*, the last painted of the five glorious oils is the first, and only nonlamentable, episode in the Samson story: *The Sacrifice of Manoah* (fig. 8). Here — in a work until recently attributed to Rembrandt, now believed to be by his associate Willem Dros — the artist shows his profound receptivity to the biblical text (Judg. 13:2–23), especially its deep chiaroscuro, ethical and spiritual as well as stylistic. Manoah and his wife kneel in shadow to the right of the picture, the wife bathed in mysterious light, as their nearly burned offering of kid and grain propels the ascent of their angel visitant upward—with a "secret" name "too wonderful to be spoken," and with white gown blurred by speed and darkness—from their modest human altar to the invisible and unfathomable heavens. The scene, although frightening and mysterious, is nonetheless clearly numinous and fraught with a marvelous sense of promise, prefiguring Samson's anguished recollections in Milton's text:

> O wherefore was my birth from Heav'n foretold
> Twice by an Angel, who at last in sight
> Of both my Parents all in flames ascended
> From off the Altar, where an Off'ring burn'd,
> As in a fiery column charioting
> His Godlike presence, and from some great act
> Or benefit reveal'd to *Abraham's* race?[26]

But shorn now of their ancient typological meanings, every other event in Samson's life is a tragic descent from this strange beginning, as Rembrandt himself goes on to demonstrate.

The next two images in the narrative take up Samson's stubborn attraction to and arrogant involvement with the woman of Timnah—which demonstrate, early in the story, both the hero's tragic vulnerability and his tendency toward gratuitous violence. Yet, the writer of Judges says, unbeknownst to either Samson or his parents, this attachment is also mysteriously "of the Lord": "he sought an occasion against the Philistines: for at that time the Philistines had dominion over Israel" (Judg. 14:4). Rembrandt articulates this odd mixture of human motive and divine intent in his 1638 representation of the wedding feast at which Samson propounds his riddle of honey out of the lion's carcass (fig. 9). At a perfectly rendered Dutch Jewish wedding feast, Samson ignores his gorgeously arrayed bride and is utterly intent on stumping three equally gorgeously arrayed men to his left, as two musicians watch warily from behind. On his fingers, Samson numbers the clues to what is, of course, an impossible riddle, clearly delighted by his auditors' pensive expressions and by the attention he thereby commands. Other guests gossip to the right of the bride, who sits in regal but lonely splendor, as an eerie light—perhaps that of an inscrutable Providence—illumines her dress and the robe of her inattentive bridegroom, both of them unwittingly "tangl'd," as Milton's Chorus will put it, "in the fold, / Of dire necessity" (*SA* 1665–66).

In the next scene (fig. 10), Samson returns to collect his bride who, having plied Samson with tears for seven days, has revealed his riddle to the "thirty companions." In the interim, he has killed 30 Philistines in order to provide the companions with the festal garments promised them if they learned his secret. The canvas is normally called *Samson Accusing* (sometimes "Threatening") *His Father-in-Law*. And indeed, in a scene Rembrandt does not represent, Samson will react to the old man's seeming betrayal by turning 300 foxes into living firebrands, destroying all the Philistine corn, along "with the vineyards and olives" (Judg. 15:4–5)—a dramatic moment often pictured in earlier art. But, like Milton, Rembrandt is far less interested in Samson's feats of destruction than in the mystery of an inner life that could possibly erupt in such behavior—and thus, by extension, of the kind of world in which such a man could possibly serve as God's champion. Thus, also like Milton, Rembrandt focuses on the moments of Samson's inward pain—pain never mentioned or even suggested in Judges' almost cynically flat account, or much emphasized in the relative objectivity of most biblical illustration.

Here Samson knocks on his father-in-law's door, face registering both anguish and longing, as the old man looks out with an expression of surprise and apprehension. The narrative mentions that Samson has brought his wife a kid, perhaps pictured in what looks like a large bag cradled in the bridegroom's left arm. The old man *should* be surprised by Samson's appearance—"I verily thought," he says in the text, "that thou hadst utterly hated her" (Judg. 15:2)—and having given his first daughter to Samson's best man, he offers the younger in her place. What we are left to consider, in this seemingly domestic moment, is how Samson's face will move, by some strange stirring, from the pain of rejected love (albeit a love of the most narcissistic and primitive kind) to the outsized violence that will soon bring death and destruction, both to the ordinary old man standing in Yahweh's headlights and to all his household.

By now Rembrandt has given us a pretty clear glimpse into Samson's less than perfect character. Yet no one who has seen it can forget Rembrandt's heartbreaking *Samson Betrayed by Delilah* (fig. 11)—a scene in which every figure seems to participate equally in Samson's anguish. Here, using the ochre and gold palette of his earlier work, Rembrandt represents the moment in which Delilah, having at last learned the secret of Samson's eerie strength, lets him "sleep in her lap," as she calls a man to "shave off the seven locks of his head" (Judg. 16:18–19). Two men creep into the room from behind a curtain, faces registering both apprehension and pity. The central figure, guarded from behind by a helmeted soldier who seems even less inclined to enter the scene, stretches his left arm ahead of him, as if in terror both of the sleeping strong-man and of the horrible deed he must do. The fatal razor disappears out of the picture to his right, as the soldier's long knife emerges clearly into the scene from his left. Samson's own knife, in contrast, hangs useless in its sheath, as he lies—childlike in his trust and "tired to death" (as the text tells us)—in the arms of the one woman in the entire narrative whom he unambiguously loves, his satin robe catching the strange light that seems to have entered the chamber with the invading men. Delilah looks up at the reluctant barber almost as if asking for pity, as if regretting too late her decision to betray this foolishly trusting lover. Her hands move in almost protective agitation over the beautiful brown locks of his hair. No one in the scene appears jubilant, or even content, with the role he or she must play in this miserable moment of sacred history.

But no moment can match the last moment in Rembrandt's virtual cycle: *The Blinding of Samson* (fig. 12). Ignoring Samson's own failings and the possible ambivalence of his enemies, this work clearly emphasizes their unspeakable cruelty, in a scene only Goya could match for brutality. In this horrible near reversal of Schiavone's *Samson Killing a Philistine* (fig. 3), a flailing Samson is pulled down onto his back, into the darkness of what appears to be a cave. Here he is held down by two intent and armored soldiers, one tightening a chain around his struggling wrist. And as a devilish-looking, turbaned assailant aims a massive spear at Samson's second eye—the other already bleeding like those of Oedipus or Gloucester—a jubilant if anguished Delilah lifts his shorn lock before her, like a torch or a flail, as the fatal shears still glisten in her menacing right hand.[27] Christopher Brown has described *The Blinding of Samson* as "without doubt the most violent picture Rembrandt ever painted." Other critics have referred to it as "his most gruesome," and as one "showing a hideous deed" with "dreadful accents."[28] Rembrandt painted these scenes during the years before Milton became totally blind: works that clearly portend Samson's God-given destiny, but show above all his tragic inadequacy, his suffering and betrayal.[29]

During the eighteenth, nineteenth, and twentieth centuries, the Samson of Judges continued to be represented alongside images of *Samson Agonistes*—sometimes by the same artists illustrating Milton's other works. In 1865, for instance, Gustave Doré represented five Samson episodes in his characteristic chiaroscuro style.[30] But it is hard, from these powerful engravings, to find a consistent interpretation of the man at their center. In earlier biblical illustrations, the slain and the fleeing are represented by relatively few figures. In Doré's far more sophisticated *Samson Destroying the Philistines* (fig. 13), they truly appear to number in the thousands. On the other hand, they do not look like the victims of a terrorist or madman. Rather, they stream, armed and armored, against a tiny and vulnerable-looking figure in their midst: a first draft of David taking on a host of Goliaths.[31] God's would-be champion acts without stealth against numberless men, many on horseback. Those in the foreground shadows appear quite terrifying—and much larger than Samson, who also appears smaller than most of the enemies falling away as he raises his small, simple weapon.

In Doré's final scene, the destruction of the temple of Dagon (fig. 14), the effect is nearly reversed: not lopsided combat, but unmitigated civilian disaster. The artist follows convention in his representation of the pagan temple—its antique magnitude and lavishness harking back to Piranesi's evocative engravings of ruins. Yet at Samson's gentle push with arms and one leg, the temple's huge columns topple, bringing the roof along, as if both were parts of a Styrofoam movie set. Dozens of extras—desperate men, women, even an infant in its mother's arms—fall, terrified, to their deaths, their terror easily read in their conventional gestures and postures. Although, as in the earlier scene, a relatively small figure amid the devastation he has released, Samson stands exactly at the center. And with his serpentine hair, he looks remarkably like a tiny devil, an entirely destructive force. Viewing this scene, one can easily believe that "the dead which he slew at his death were more than they which he slew in his life" (Judg. 16:30). And that hideous statistic remains, as in the Judges text, as Samson's final claim to remembrance. His story, for Doré—however cinematic—appears to have no redeeming spiritual meaning.

Robert Gibbings introduced a wholly different modernist aesthetic in his seven woodcuts for an edition of *Samson and Delilah* published by the Golden Cockerel Press in 1925.[32] Unlike Doré, who represented vast panoramic scenes drawn from Judges' literal narrative, Gibbings gave little attention to the drama's physical setting. Instead, like Milton, he filled all his small frames with the compressed energy of an archetypal drama—a drama taking place mostly in Samson's reflective and claustrophobic mind.[33] Gibbings's frontispiece (fig. 15) is the one work in the set that feels spacious—made up, as it is, largely of the soft tone of its watermarked Batchelor paper. About two-thirds of the way down the page kneels the unframed image of a dignified nude Samson—looking upward, broken chains hanging from each wrist—as if just released from the earthly shackles, both physical and psychological, represented in the slim volume to follow. This Promethean Samson can only be read symbolically. He appears nowhere either in the Judges narrative or in Milton's; for in both he is freed only by death, and in the Judges account there is no suggestion that Samson is freed into another dimension of existence—only, in the flat despairing tone of the Judges narrator, that at the time of his death he had judged Israel for 20 years. The spirit of the design, however, is Miltonic, suggesting a "reviv'd" Samson, surviving in fame, having brought at least the opportunity of freedom to his recalcitrant people and doomed tribe.

The Samson narrative itself is represented by six tightly filled black frames, each barely capable of containing, physically, the protagonist's largely psychological *agon*. The first episode pits the young hero against a lion (fig. 16). Here, in contrast to Doré's rather literal nineteenth century rendering of man against beast, Gibbings's Samson grapples with a young lion that appears a mirror of himself, an other self who has dared to "roar against him" (Judg. 14:5–6). Forcing open the lion's mouth, he gazes intently at the effect of his own strength, as though discovering a great and terrible secret. The entwined muscular structures of man and beast create a tension so palpable that the lion's desperately planted foot and Samson's powerful body transgress the frame at several points—almost like the potentially destructive power of modern machinery. Larger than life, Gibbings seems to suggest, the hero of Judges can barely be contained within the mythic structures of art, and that very uncontainability, much like the uncontainability of twentieth century human progress, becomes both his strength and his tragedy.

Yet if Gibbings emphasizes Samson's dangerous force, he nonetheless downplays, as Milton does, the narrative's literal, messy violence. Rather, he turns the violent scenes into stylized exercises in perspective and design. His scene of Samson with the jawbone represents him nude—feet planted firmly apart, back to the viewer—as armored and arrow-wielding Philistines fall right, left, and center. They turn their backs and arrows away from God's champion, as if unable even to look at his determined (although largely invisible) face, or at his gesture with what seems an enchanted bone (fig. 17). Whereas Doré's more operatic design (fig. 13) was at least as much about the soldiers as about Samson, Gibbings centers on the virile hero rather than on his opponents. Even though one soldier hangs headless next to Samson's raised right hand, the effect of the crisp white-on-black lines is too decorative to be violent: a symbolic tableau of unstoppable abstract power.[34]

The most important conflict for Gibbings's Samson, however, is clearly that of sex: in only seven designs, in fact, he represents all three of Samson's romantic entanglements. The overt sexuality of these engravings is characteristic of Gibbings's work and of some of the fine press books of the period. But it also typifies the erotic potential of the story, which, by the early twentieth century, had found its way into both opera and popular film. First, Gibbings represents the rarely shown woman of Timnah, weeping on a loin-cloth-clad Samson's chest, as he attempts to comfort her without giving away his riddle (Judg. 14:16–18). Two notably short-haired "men of the city" stand by, as if taking bets on her success on their behalf, under a charmingly starlit sky.

Perhaps alluding to early typological readings (compare fig. 2), most artists suggest Samson's dalliance with the harlot of Gaza only by showing him carrying away the door of the city gate (Judg. 16:1–3). Doré follows this prim convention. But Gibbings, the modern *bon vivant,* centers his picture on the sleeping harlot's sweeping hair and mesmerizing breasts — and the nude, muscular Samson bending over her in sensual enchantment, as if contemplating yet another primal mystery (fig. 18). In his scene with Delilah (fig. 19), the lovers' roles are fatally reversed. Now the nude Samson lies sleeping in the foreground — muscles relaxed and slack genitalia exposed — as a bare-breasted but self-possessed Delilah reclines at his side. The intensity of her gaze now mirrors Samson's own in earlier designs. But whereas Samson contemplates merely the wonder of the sleeping female form, caressing the prostitute's body with his eyes, Delilah caresses Samson's hair — and contemplates, with some sadness but with clear purpose, the betrayal she is about to undertake.

Gibbings's final design, that of Samson pulling down the pillars of the temple (fig. 20), is, like all the others, a stunningly original conception, and could hardly be more different from Doré's conventionally violent one (fig. 14). In a geometric composition that calls to mind the Russian constructivists, the artist reduces Samson's final conflict to a version of the man-versus-machine motif of his own anxious transitional era: in this case, Samson versus the pillars. The scene is elemental—entirely without context, without external violence, indeed entirely without other human figures, let alone victims. As with the opening lion scene (fig. 16), which it echoes formally as well as thematically, Samson seems here to be working out a problem both physical and metaphysical. His profile rapt in blind but intelligent contemplation, he takes on the dehumanizing machines and impersonal structures of the modern world. Moreover, he seems to be winning—not destroying others, "with these immixt, inevitably" pulling down the "same destruction on himself" (*SA* 1657–58). Rather, he appears to be *freeing* himself to rise (as on the title page) like "that self-begott'n bird / In the *Arabian* woods embost, / That no second knows nor third" (*SA* 1699–1701); readying himself, perhaps, for another century of mythic existence. Finally, although illustrating a book of the Bible, Gibbings is interested neither in its violent narrative nor in conventional Christian iconography, but rather in the psychological drama—especially (as the title, *Samson and Delilah*, suggests) the powerful drama of sex and the discovery of self in the modern world. Here both allegory and literal narrative give way to a new mythic vision of an age to come.

2. *Artists' Re-Visions of* Samson Agonistes, *1730–1978*

With the remarkable exception of Robert Gibbings, whose biblical illustrations are obviously informed by an equally close reading of Milton, most artists who have illustrated Milton's *Samson Agonistes* differ from those representing the biblical Samson by focusing, as the poet does, on the protagonist's inner life—an inner life completely absent in the Judges account. Beginning with Louis Chéron in 1720, one artist after another represents him blinded and in the hands of his enemies, *reflecting* on his painful plight and shameful past. Like seventeenth century artists working just before Milton, they generally represent Samson less as a type than as a human being—but a very different kind of human being: one who is above all thoughtful and contemplative, whether alone or with others. Most artists make his vulnerability clear, while giving him a dignity the Samson of Judges almost invariably lacks, even when portrayed as victim: a dignity born of intelligent interiority. This Samson is still strong and powerful, but generally not Herculean, not larger than life. Illustrations of the Miltonic Samson also occasionally represent, although less frequently, the conventional scenes of Samson with Dalila and Samson pulling down the pillars. But even in representations of these scenes, Samson's introspection distinguishes him from most representations of the biblical Samson.

In the earlier eighteenth century, Samson appears not totally alone, but in a social context. In the 1720 illustrated works, for instance, Louis Chéron portrays Samson sitting in chains as Manoa leans toward him in fatherly solicitude (fig. 21).[35] Three other companions, presumably members of the Chorus, gesture as if to say, "See... / Or do my eyes misrepresent? Can this be hee, / That Heroic, that Renouwn'd / Irresistible Samson?" (*SA* 118, 124–26). But Samson, for the moment at least, remains isolated in his own thoughts—"As one past hope"; yet not, as the text has it, "by himself given over; / In slavish habit, ill-fitted weeds / O'erworn and soild" (*SA* 120–23). A 1752 engraving designed by Francis Hayman (fig. 22) moves forward in the narrative to the most decorous imaginable encounter with a Dalila straight from the Georgian court, attended by a female servant and a small, elegantly dressed African boy.[36] As Dalila reaches out her hand in "conjugal affection," this Samson refuses her advances more in the manner of a chained Socrates than an enraged iron-age strong-man. And from the sage expressions of his listening companions, his discourse seems to consist of something more stoic and gracious than "Out, out Hyaena" (*SA* 748). Albeit "at a distance," he seems—not weakly, but chivalrously—to forgive her.[37]

Later eighteenth century artists tend to abandon narrative, simply to represent Samson in a variety of sorrowing poses. In J. H. Mortimer's 1777 frontispiece to Bell's edition of *The Poets of Great Britain*, Samson appears in an almost pastoral setting, "the breath of Heaven fresh-blowing" (*SA* 11), alone except for four quizzical onlookers in the background.[38] He sits on "a bank" with "choice of Sun or shade" (*SA* 3), his countenance thoughtful and troubled. But without chains, and with his simple garb and staff, he seems as much a candidate for *Lycidas'* "uncouth swain" as for the role of a violent Samson. In 1796, John Graham represents Samson with the caption, "Retiring from the popular noise, I seek / This unfrequented place to find some ease" (*SA* 17–18). Although he wears chains in this design, the pastoral landscape and his meditative pose again belie his violent past and future.[39] Richard Westall, in contrast, shows a muscular strong-man Samson in chains, eyes lifted heavenward in meditative appeal—"O impotence of mind, in body strong!" (*SA* 52)[40]—and uses light and shadow to suggest the possibility of some divine response, especially given the hero's striking halo of renewed hair.[41]

The nineteenth century brings fewer artists but a greater variety of representation to Milton's Samson. In one of six 1843 illustrations, William Harvey shows Samson in a posture similar to that represented by Graham, but with the Chorus in the background—as the hero ponders his former role: "Himself an army…O ever-failing trust / In mortal strength! And, oh what not in man / Deceivable and vain!" (*SA* 346, 348–50).[42] But the most dramatically introspective Samson appears in a woodcut made in 1898 by A. Garth Jones (fig. 23). Iconographically anticipating Christ's torment at the pillar of flagellation, Jones's Samson stands at the lowest ebb of his own physical and spiritual agon—arms tethered behind him, blinded eyes upcast above his tortured face and bare muscled chest—a man with the intelligence requisite for terrible mental suffering: "Thoughts, my Tormentors, arm'd with deadly stings / Mangle my apprehensive tenderest parts, / Exasperate, exulcerate, and raise / Dire inflammation" (*SA* 623–26).[43] This Samson is much more riddle than riddler—a figure of tragic, iconic stature and irreducible ambiguity.

Most artists illustrating *Samson Agonistes* have chosen to represent Milton's protagonist in thoughtful, meditative postures, imprisoned in Gaza. And even when representing Samson's final violent act, they have continued—despite the long tradition of extroverted violence in representation of the biblical Samson—to focus upon the interiority of his *agon*. In an engraving from 1904 (fig. 24), William Hyde represents not falling bodies, but the moment of stillness and meditation in the temple of Dagon before Samson pulls down the pillars. Appearing more like an ascetic desert saint or biblical prophet than a strong-man bent on avenging his own two eyes, "with head a while enclin'd / And eyes fast fixt he stood, as one who pray'd, / Or some great matter in his mind revolv'd" (*SA* 1636–38).[44] Yet we can make out to his right—in a building that looks more like a souk than a temple—four veiled figures and an armed guard whose seconds are numbered. To *our* eyes, they do not look drunk, with either idolatry or wine. If we feel for this Samson, as for Jones's, he nonetheless conveys in his very asceticism a purity of motive and indifference to self the modern world can neither countenance nor afford. His interiority isolates him both from his intended victims and from his equally helpless witnesses—neither seeking nor inviting the understanding that alone could avert the tragedy about to occur.

Of Robert Ashwin Maynard's 11 wood engravings of 1931, one shows a thoughtful Samson (fig. 25) still in prison, resisting the request to display his strength at the celebration in the temple of Dagon.[45] In representing this very unusual scene, Maynard follows Milton in adding a dimension to Samson's character completely absent in the Judges text. Unlike the inscrutably suffering Samson of Jones and Hyde, Maynard's Samson works within a recognizable ethical framework—albeit one he is willing to subordinate to Antinomian impulses. Norman T. Burns, with Sharon Achinstein, has carefully delineated this aspect in Milton's Samson, one rarely noticed either by critics or by artists.[46] As in Hyde's double image, a background scene represents—sympathetically elegant in white-on-black line—the people Samson will soon destroy. But as in Hyde's representation, too, it is not that destruction we see. Rather, Maynard complicates our reading by focusing on this rather Quakerly moment in Samson's Miltonic career—a moment dedicated not to violence, but to conscience and discernment. Another scene by Maynard shows an anguished, chained and naked Samson reexperiencing in his mind his violent past described in the accompanying text, which refers to his experience with the woman of Timnah (*SA* 1192–1204). But whereas in Milton's text his words of self-exculpation are addressed to Harapha and become a political argument, here they become part of the anguished soliloquy of a man, neither strong-man nor saint, who feels himself merely as one who has been betrayed and abandoned.

In contrast to all that has gone before, Robert Medley's designs for a 1979 edition of *Samson Agonistes* make use of what he called "organic abstraction" to represent scenes from Milton's drama.[47] Around 1950, Medley had made two figurative paintings: one of Manoa comforting Samson, and one of Samson being led out of prison. The artist came to believe, however, that figurative illustrations of the entire poem would "fall short" of the "imagined splendour" of the "rather baroque visual images" it called to mind. Influenced by Matisse's paper-cuts, Medley found "words among an enormous vocabulary" to create 23 full-page illustrations, many of them geometric, that he describes as "emblematic, drastically simplified images which relate directly to the text and indeed to the imagery of the poetry."[48] Meaning is expressed in these works not only by form, but also by color—22 different hues, including off-white, gray, and black—printed on folio sheets of off-white, watermarked paper. To make sure that viewers understood the relationship of each of his colorful images to the poem, Medley distributed with the book a two-page supplement with a thumbnail picture of each image and a quotation identifying it with particular lines.

Medley's striking illustrations, like so many others, are an attempt to face some of the agonizing questions raised by the Miltonic Samson's fate, his relation to his people, to Dalila, and to his enemies. The first 11 images, representing the period before Dalila's entrance, vividly convey the triumphs and especially the sorrows of Samson's past and present life. In the second image, for instance, Medley uses a horizontal tan bar and six black squares (three large and three smaller) to suggest the mill at Gaza—and the terrible, circular futility of Samson's' ignominious toil. The next vivid image crosses heavy black wisps with horizontal taupe bars to suggest the fatal shears—cutting off, at a seemingly arbitrary point, both Samson's hair and every human life. And the fourth stunning design (fig. 26), represents Samson's soliloquy—"O dark, dark, dark, amid the blaze of noon, / Irrecoverably dark, total Eclipse / Without all hope of day" (*SA* 80–82)—with four simple circles. In the upper half of the page, two mustard yellow circles, one large and one small, seem to float among cloudlike wisps of tan. But at the bottom of the page, a black circle literally eclipses a gray one, as both seem to sink into sharp black bars—abstractions, perhaps, of the instruments used to gouge out Samson's eyes.[49]

Medley also devotes three images to Dalila, expressing, for the most part, the usual harsh attitude of critics before Ulreich and others. His twelfth image uses a jerry-built mass of black rectangles and parallelograms to suggest her description by the Chorus as "a ship in full rig" (*SA* 710–23).[50] The next two images represent her (as does the Chorus) as slithery green serpents in the company of the black idol Dagon and illustrate her remark, after being rejected by Samson, that "Fame if not double-fac't is double-mouth'd" (971). Then, following Samson's encounter with and victory over Harapha, Medley moves on, through three images of Samson's seeming renovation, to the catastrophe (fig. 27), which he labels *The Destruction*. Here the artist returns to stark black on white: a tumble of squares and triangles, jostled into violent downward motion toward a floorlike base.

The last three designs in Medley's series make up the epilogue to Samson's story. In his twenty-first image, called *Prelude to the End* (fig. 28), he uses a variety of shapes and colors to build "A Monument, and plant it round with shade / Of Laurel ever green, and branching Palm, / With all his Trophies hung" (*SA* 1734–36). Soft green rectangles and tear-shaped blots of soft blue suggest the "sweet lyric Song" (1737)—the melodious tear—that seems never, in fact, to have become a part of Samson's story. The design, moreover, serves as a monument not only to Samson but also to his countless, suffering descendants—a monument that surely embraces the Holocaust as well as Samson's calamity. That this is so is quite clearly indicated by Medley's last design (fig. 29): his *Tablet for the God of Israel*. Using an unprecedented royal blue—along with the yellow, tan, and black that have appeared in previous images—the artist builds a stately monument out of rectangles, squares, and triangles. At the very center of that tablet or monument—gold ochre on a square of yellow, and pointed out from all sides by four black triangles—Medley places the most horrifying image of contemporary Jewry: a yellow six-pointed star. On the other hand, the blue of the tablet's base calls to mind the blue of the star on Israel's flag. Does Medley here suggest that—despite the particular disappearance of the tribe of Dan, even despite the incomparable horror of the Holocaust—Samson has at last won, with the foundation of the Jewish state in 1948, a tentative and fragile victory? The artist leaves this question to the reader of Milton's text, as well as his own visual one—in a Rorschach of history as ambiguous and tentative as a pattern written in tea leaves. As Shawcross writes, "We can understand why *the Chorus* says that there is 'calm of mind all passion spent'; but the uncertainty of the poem and of its ending asks whether there can be any calm of mind in these circumstances."[51]

If Milton's drama of Samson is the least illustrated of the longer poems, perhaps it is because of the problem Shawcross expresses in the very title of his *Uncertain World of* Samson Agonistes. A number of artists have made only one illustration, several only two or three, or created only decorative headpieces or tailpieces. Most seem to have been uncertain how to interpret the work or how completely to validate its main character. For to validate him seems to suggest approval of his actions as a model for Milton's time, perhaps even for our own—an approval too often and too clearly seen (on all sides) in recent and current events. The problem, as Wittreich has taught us, is older than Milton's play. He points out that even Luther, hardly a pacifist—yet horrified by the excesses of violence his own Lutheran movement unleashed—believed that although we should admire Samson, "he would be useless and dangerous to imitate." "All we know from the text," writes Derek Wood, "is that an unnaturally strong man kills vast numbers of his enemies out of revenge, probably believing that this is a good thing. Even critics who are privy to God's will should be modest about claiming the authority of *textual* evidence."[52]

Arguably the most ambitious artistic interpretation of Milton's *Samson Agonistes* is not visual but musical. George Frederick Handel's oratorio *Samson* was written in 1741–42, with librettist Newburgh Hamilton attempting to resolve some of the play's uncertainties by supplementing the text of Milton's drama with "several Lines, Words, and Expressions" taken from other poems by Milton.[53] The libretto, more clearly than the play, asserts that despite uncertainties, "All is best, though we oft doubt / What th' unsearchable dispose / Of highest wisdom brings about, / And ever best found in the close" (*SA* 1745–48). Yet, as music critic Donald Teeters says, throughout the oratorio "Grief [still] mingles with perplexity."[54]

One of the most perplexing moments of the work appears at the end of part 2, where the Israelites and Philistines sing a chorus in which they assert, in identical and echoing musical phrases, the supremacy and uniqueness of their own god — one cheering for Dagon, the other for Jehovah, using images borrowed from Milton's Nativity ode:

> Fixed in His everlasting seat
> [Jehovah/Great Dagon] rules the world in state.
> His thunder roars, heaven shakes, and earth's aghast.
> The stars, with deep amaze,
> Remain in steadfast gaze;
> [Jehovah/Great Dagon] is of Gods the first and last.   (#67)

Another gives us, in the cries of over 100 dying Philistines — sopranos and altos along with basses and tenors — a musical sense (albeit a quite decorous and orderly one) of the falling bodies we rarely see in the work of the tragedy's visual interpreters:

> Hear us, our god! O hear our cry!
> Death! Ruin! fallen! no help is nigh:
> O mercy, heav'n, we sink, we die!   (#85)

At most points in the work, of course, Hamilton and Handel do side with the protagonist—and with the Israelites. But not altogether. The almost postmodern ambiguity of these strange Baroque choruses hangs the otherwise clear message of the oratorio in suspension: both sides are certain they are completely right. Can the audience be equally certain? Perhaps that is why Stanley Fish has written that, at the end of *Samson Agonistes,* "There is simply nothing to be said..., no 'acquist' of wisdom with which we are 'dismissed,' despite the choral pronouncement to the contrary. The only wisdom to be carried away from the play is that there is no wisdom to be carried away, and that we are alone, like Samson, and like the children of Israel."[55]

Newburgh and Handel's interpretation plays with that assertion, but finally rejects it—more fully than Milton does. For in the place of the poem's somber ending, they return to the theme of light so poignantly introduced at the beginning (borrowing from both the Invocation to Light and, again, from the Nativity ode)—to suggest that outside Samson's dark and violent world there is a world of light and peace, where he has gone. For Handel, as for Milton, that world of light was also the world of harmony, of music, which rings out in praise of Samson and of the Israelites' God who "to the end / Not parted from him, but assisted still" (compare *SA* 1719–20). As promised at the end of Milton's play, a chorus of "virgins" sings,

> Glorious hero, may thy grave
> Peace and honor ever have,
> After all thy pains and woes,
> Rest eternal, sweet repose! (#93)

The end of the oratorio comes as a tremendous hymn of praise: "Let the bright seraphim in burning row, / their loud, uplifted angel trumpets blow" (#93, pp. 168–79). But that hymn does not entirely sweep away the questions the work's own shifting contexts, Samson's *agon,* or Milton's tragedy have raised.

Fig. 1. *Samson with a Jawbone Harrowing Hell* (fourth century catacombs, Via Latina, Rome). Eikon image database, Yale University, and Dr. Wayne Meeks.

Fig. 2. *Samson Carrying the Gaza Gates; Jonah Emerging from the Mouth of the Whale* (church in Tirsted, Denmark, ca. 1400). Courtesy of Index of Christian Art.

Fig. 3. Andrea Schiavone, *Samson Killing a Philistine*, ca. 1542–45 (Galeria Palantina, Palazzo Pitti, Florence). © Corbis.

Fig. 4. *Mater Sampsonis.* From *The Book of Common Prayer* (Edinburgh, 1633). The William Andrews Clark Memorial Library, University of California, Los Angeles.

Fig. 5. *Delilahs Falshood to Sampson.* From 1682 Bible. The William Andrews Clark Memorial Library, University of California, Los Angeles.

Fig. 6. Anthony Van Dyck, *Samson and Delilah*, 1618/20 (Dulwich Picture Gallery, London). By permission of the Trustees of Dulwich Picture Gallery.

Fig. 7. Garrit van Honthorst (Dutch, 1590–1656). *Samson and Delilah*, c. 1621. Oil on canvas; 129 x 94 cm. The Cleveland Museum of Art, Mr. and Mrs. William H. Marlatt Fund 1968.23.

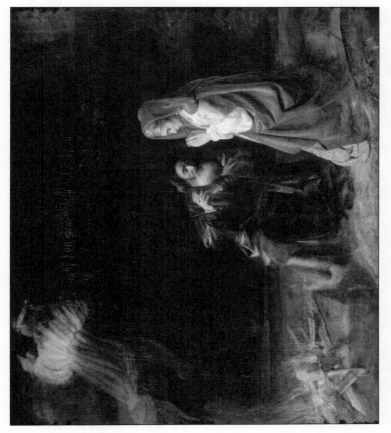

Fig. 8. Willem Drost (?), *The Sacrifice of Manoah*, 1641 (Alte Meister Gallerie, Dresden). Gemäldegalerie Alte Meister, Staatliche Kunstsammlungen Dresden, Photographer.

Fig. 9. Rembrandt van Rijn, *Samson Putting Forth the Riddle at the Wedding Feast*, 1638 (Alte Meister Gallerie, Dresden). Gemäldegalerie Alte Meister, Staatliche Kunstsammlungen Dresden, Photographer.

Fig. 10. Rembrandt van Rijn, *Samson Accusing His Father-in-Law*, ca. 1635 (Gemäldegalerie, Berlin). Bildarchiv Preussischer Kulturbesitz / Art Resource, N.Y.

Fig. 11. Rembrandt van Rijn, *Samson Betrayed by Delilah*, 1629–30 (Gemäldegalerie, Berlin). Bildarchiv Preussischer Kulturbesitz / Art Resource, N.Y.

Fig. 12. Rembrandt van Rijn, *The Blinding of Samson,* 1636 (Städlischer Galerie, Frankfurt). © Städel Museum — ARTOTHEK.

Fig. 13. Gustav Doré, *Samson Destroying the Philistines with the Jawbone of an Ass.* From *The Doré Bible*, ca. 1866.

Fig. 14. Gustav Doré, *Death of Samson.* From *The Doré Bible,* ca. 1866.

SAMSON AND DELILAH

FROM THE BOOK OF JUDGES ACCORDING
TO THE AUTHORISED VERSION, PRINTED &
PUBLISHED AT THE GOLDEN COCKEREL PRESS
WALTHAM SAINT LAWRENCE, BERKSHIRE
MCMXXV.

Fig. 15. Robert Gibbings, title page to *Samson and Delilah* (London: Golden Cockerel Press, 1925). The William Andrews Clark Memorial Library, University of California, Los Angeles.

Fig. 16. Robert Gibbings, *Samson and the Lion*. Woodcut for *Samson and Delilah* (London: Golden Cockerel Press, 1925). The William Andrews Clark Memorial Library, University of California, Los Angeles.

Fig. 17. Robert Gibbings, *Samson Killing His Enemies with the Jawbone of an Ass*. Woodcut for *Samson and Delilah* (London: Golden Cockerel Press, 1925). The William Andrews Clark Memorial Library, University of California, Los Angeles.

Fig. 18. Robert Gibbings, *Samson and the Harlot*. Woodcut for *Samson and Delilah* (London: Golden Cockerel Press, 1925). The William Andrews Clark Memorial Library, University of California, Los Angeles.

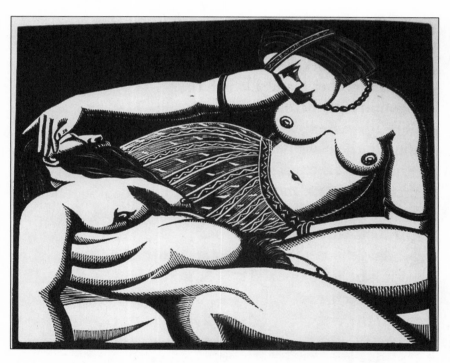

Fig. 19. Robert Gibbings, *Samson and Delilah*. Woodcut for *Samson and Delilah* (London: Golden Cockerel Press, 1925). The William Andrews Clark Memorial Library, University of California, Los Angeles.

Fig. 20. Robert Gibbings, *Samson Pulling Down the Pillars*. Woodcut
for *Samson and Delilah* (London: Golden Cockerel Press, 1925).
The William Andrews Clark Memorial Library, University of California,
Los Angeles.

Fig. 21. Louis Chéron, *Samson Sitting in Prison in Chains*. From *Poetical Works of Mr. John Milton*, 1720. Reproduced by permission of The Huntington Library, San Marino, California.

Fig. 22. Francis Hayman, *Samson Rejecting Dalilah.* From *Paradise Regained and Samson Agonistes,* 1752. Reproduced by permission of The Huntington Library, San Marino, California.

Fig. 23. A. Garth Jones, *Samson Tied to a Pillar*. From *The Minor Poems of John Milton*, 1898.

Fig. 24. William Hyde, *Samson Contemplating the Destruction of the Temple*. From *The Poetical Works of John Milton* (London: Astolat Press, 1904). Reproduced from copy owned by Virginia Tufte.

Fig. 25. Robert Ashwin Maynard, *Samson with the Philistine Officer.* From *Samson Agonistes* (Middlesex: Harrow Weald, 1931). The Mandeville Special Collections Library, University of California, San Diego.

Fig. 26. Robert Medley, *"O dark, dark, dark amid the blaze of noon."* From *Samson Agonistes: A Dramatic Poem by John Milton* (Norwich, Conn.: Mell Clark, 1979). Reproduced with permission from Susie Medley.

Fig. 27. Robert Medley, *The Destruction.* From *Samson Agonistes: A Dramatic Poem by John Milton* (Norwich, Conn.: Mell Clark, 1979). Reproduced with permission from Susie Medley.

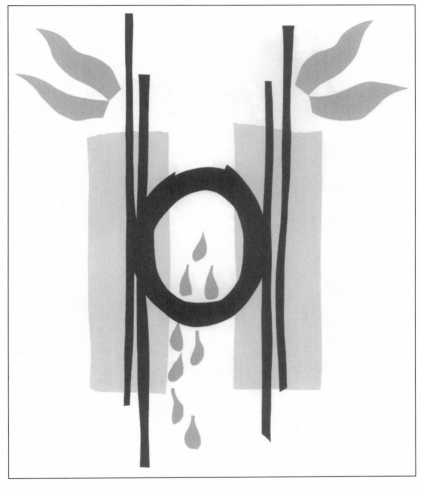

Fig. 28. Robert Medley, *Prelude to the End*. From *Samson Agonistes: A Dramatic Poem by John Milton* (Norwich, Conn.: Mell Clark, 1979). Reproduced with permission from Susie Medley.

Fig. 29. Robert Medley, *Tablet for the God of Israel.* From *Samson Agonistes: A Dramatic Poem by John Milton* (Norwich, Conn.: Mell Clark, 1979). Reproduced with permission from Susie Medley.

Part III

Milton's Visionary Mode and
Paradise Regain'd

8 ❧ Why Is the Virgin Mary in *Paradise Regain'd?*

Mary Beth Rose

1.

Published together in 1671, *Samson Agonistes* and *Paradise Regain'd* are parallel texts: each adapts a biblical narrative to tell the story of a divinely born redeemer of his people. Samson and the Son not only have in common divine pedigrees, guaranteed to their mothers by an angelic messenger of God. Each also has a miraculous public career, marked by temptation, betrayal, and a redemptive, sacrificial end. Interestingly, in his representation of both careers, Milton chooses episodes that exist outside of the traditional heroic narrative, which I am defining as the recounting of active public deeds of adventure—conquest, rule, or rescue—as they unfold in time, enacted and remembered as history. Although Samson's glorious accomplishments are related in the poem, they are told in flashback: his days of military victory are, pointedly, in the past. Milton instead focuses his drama on the present moment of the hero's defeat, his existence as a blind slave. He is interested not in Samson's famous battles, but in the ways in

193

which the hero endures suffering and failure after his conquests are over. If Samson's public heroism is belated, the Son's is potential. The encounters between the Son and Satan that comprise most of *Paradise Regain'd* precede Christ's ministry of preaching and healing, revealing instead his inner resistance to temptation; the Son's public deeds, as yet narratively unrealized, remain in the future. "My time I told thee.../...is not yet come" (*PR* 3.496–97), he insists.[1] With their steadfast decentering of the public careers of the protagonists, *Samson Agonistes* and *Paradise Regain'd* call attention to a Miltonic reconception of heroism and its relation to history and time.

   While the two texts are similar in focus and allied in purpose they are, of course, not matching. Samson is a hero of the Hebrew Bible, while the Son emerges from the Gospels. *Samson Agonistes* is a dramatic poem, which Milton defines as a tragedy. *Paradise Regain'd* is a brief epic with a promising end. Possessed of a magnificent physical strength, Samson slays hundreds of thousands of the enemies of the Jews with the jawbone of an ass. Human and therefore weak, he succumbs to female seduction and is defeated, blinded, and taken into slavery, doubted and betrayed not only by Dalila but by his own people. He nevertheless delivers his people from the Philistine enemy with an act of spectacular violence that is in its moral and even theological implications debatable: is this destruction suicide as well as murder, an act of tyranny and despair, or is it an act of faith and liberation, a sacrifice so stunningly devoted that it justifies all of the deaths it leaves in its wake? The Son also engages in occasional acts of violence, but his heroism is spiritual, internalized, and will eventually involve a ministry of preaching and healing. Arguably the Son endures an agon, moving through the poem darkly until he understands his divine identity by resisting temptation. Insofar as he is human, he suffers from doubt and is betrayed by his own people. But in *Paradise Regain'd* the hero's ordeal involves a grasping of origins to which there can be no real threat. Although the Son is alone in the desert and tormented by painful thoughts, there can be no narrative suspense about his ability to resist seduction. Like Samson, he ends his mortal career in an act of miraculous violence that saves others. Milton of course does not dramatize the Son's death, which remains potential in *Paradise Regain'd*. But, in contrast to that of Samson, the Son's death is perpetrated upon, rather than by him, and its redemptive implications are not historically limited, but infinite.

Theologically (and in terms of interpretation, typologically) the spiritual superiority of the Son's quest overwhelms that of Samson, improving and expanding immeasurably upon its devotion and its results. Milton's representation of the comparative superiority of the new Christian dispensation over the old Hebraic law as these are complexly deployed in the quests of the two heroes, along with his conception of heroic action, have been explored extensively.[2] Yet many salient aspects of the two texts, which enrich various perspectives on these issues, remain virtually unaddressed and certainly unexamined in relation to one another. Significant both in their sweep and their details, the unexamined issues have to do with gender and particularly with Milton's representation of maternal and paternal authority and agency.[3]

As mentioned, the biblical stories of both heroes begin with the divine annunciation of their births. Although Samson's mother plays a huge role in Judges 13–16 (the angel appears to her twice, and both times she is alone), Milton erases this entire biblical drama and focuses on Samson's relationship with his natural father, Manoa; except for a brief mention of "both my parents" (26), his mother disappears from the story. In contrast, adapting Luke (4:1–13), *Paradise Regain'd* recounts or alludes to the Annunciation to the Virgin Mary five times. Not only does Milton virtually erase Joseph, who plays a quite prominent part in Luke, but — even more surprising for reasons I will discuss — the Virgin herself becomes a major character in the poem. At the end of *Samson Agonistes* the body of the hero, whose exhausted career has ended in his death, is returned "Home to his father's house" (*SA* 1733), destined to become a public monument. In contrast, the father's house is seen from a satanic perspective in *Paradise Regain'd:* transporting the Son to the top of the pinnacle, Satan deviously observes, "I to thy father's house / Have brought thee, and highest placed, highest is best" (*PR* 4.552–53). Having overcome temptation at the end of the poem, "our Savior meek," his public life yet to begin, "unobserv'd / Home to his Mother's house private return'd" (*PR* 4.636–38). Given Milton's intentions to exalt the Son and all he represents, it is important that he emphasizes privacy and maternal authority at the expense of public heroism and paternal power in *Paradise Regain'd*. In what follows, drawing on *Samson Agonistes* for comparative purposes, I hope to shed light on the uses Milton makes of paternal and maternal authority and their relation to heroism in *Paradise Regain'd*.

2.

The literary representation of heroism during the long seventeenth century in England reveals an accelerating idealization of passive fortitude, replacing in prestige the idealization of that which is public and active. Rather than deeds of killing and conquest, the patient suffering of error, misfortune, disaster, and malevolence is celebrated in a newly and self-consciously constructed heroism of endurance that privileges the private life and pointedly rejects war. Milton's later texts present the supreme example of this aesthetic transformation. One need only think of *Paradise Lost*, in which the arena for human heroism is neither war nor politics, but marriage. At the beginning of book 9, for example, he assaults traditional military heroism as anachronistic, deluded, and trivial:

> Since first this Subject for Heroic Song
> Pleas'd me long choosing, and beginning late;
> Not sedulous by Nature to indite
> Wars, hitherto the only Argument
> Heroic deem'd, chief maistry to dissect
> With long and tedious havoc fabl'd Knights
> In Battles feign'd; the better fortitude
> Of Patience and Heroic Martyrdom
> Unsung; or to describe Races and Games,
> Or tilting Furniture, emblazon'd Shields,
> Impresas quaint, Caparisons and Steeds;

Bases and tinsel Trappings, gorgeous Knights
At Joust and Tournament; then marshall'd Feast
Serv'd up in Hall with Sewers, and Seneschals;
The skill of Artifice or Office mean,
Not that which justly gives Heroic name
To Person or to Poem. Mee of these
Nor skill'd nor studious, higher Argument
Remains.   (*PL* 9.25–43)

"They also serve who only stand and wait," he quietly assures us, when rejecting the necessity of external action in his famous sonnet on his blindness.[4]

As I have argued at length elsewhere, the elevation in the status of private endurance over public adventure involves a transformation in the gendering of heroism. With its multiplicity of sources, including Seneca and the Stoics, the lives of the Catholic saints, the continuing popularity of medieval treatises on the art of dying, Patient Griselda stories, and the careers and tribulations of both Protestant and Jesuit martyrs related to Renaissance audiences, the heroics of endurance is not so clearly gendered as the straightforwardly male heroics of action, and includes both sexes among its protagonists. Nevertheless it is striking that the terms that constitute the heroics of endurance are precisely those used to construct the early modern idealization of women: patient suffering, mildness, humility, chastity, loyalty, and obedience. As I hope to have demonstrated in my previous work, by the end of the seventeenth century the terms in which heroism is constructed and performed as the endurance of suffering are predominantly gendered female.[5]

Milton's epics and dramatic poem are the outstanding examples of this development in the representation of heroic action and identity. According to prescriptive gender norms in the Renaissance, Samson in Milton's dramatic poem clearly inhabits a subject position gendered female. As a slave of the Philistines, he occupies a passive position as object of the hostile gaze (*SA* 33–34), a predatory look which, blind, he is initially helpless to return or combat. He conflates his present slavery with his position as spouse, thus inscribing himself within a seventeenth century critique of marriage that equated wifehood with slavery, ironically implying in the process a self-definition as a wife.[6] Bound to silence, a female virtue, by his gifts from God, he breaks his vows with "shameful garrulity," an allegedly female transgression (491). Furthermore Samson spends a great deal of time trying to convince his father and the Chorus that for him the arena of significance — the arena in which he seeks both happiness and salvation and where he mourns his failures — is not the battlefield, but marriage.

Noteworthy for the concerns of this essay, Samson's slavery and passivity, which take up the present moment of Milton's poem, do not represent a loss of his heroic identity; rather, they are constituent of it. The failure of his hypermasculinity and demise of his physical strength clarify a reconceptualization of heroic experience itself as internal struggle and achievement. While Samson's female heroism becomes the location of significance in the text, Milton nevertheless provides an alternative model. After Samson's destruction of himself and the Philistines, his father delivers a ringing endorsement of his son's death. Praising his son's legendary military exploits with insistent eloquence — however tautological and wrongheaded (a point to which I will return) — Manoa demands attention be paid to traditional male heroics by insisting on the need for interpretation. Samson's death, his father argues, is "nothing but well and fair"; Samson "hath quit himself / Like Samson, and heroically hath finish'd / A life Heroic" (*SA* 1723, 1709–11). Insofar as Samson's bringing down the pillars of the theater on himself and the Philistines represents a desirable revival (in theological and political terms) of his phallic strength, Manoa's concluding view commands assent. Yet it is finally the Chorus who, in a departure from the conformity inherent in its role, asserts the need for a new mode of heroism, one that, matching Samson's present experience, is superior to "the brute and boist'rous force of violent men / Hardy and industrious to support / Tyrannic power" (*SA* 1273–75). Characterized by patience and fortitude and decidedly gendered female, that heroism takes the form of the Phoenix as image of regeneration and renewal:

From out her ashy womb now teem'd
Revives, reflourishes, then vigorous most
When most unactive deem'd,
And though her body die, her fame survives
A secular bird ages of lives.   (*SA* 1703–07)

At the end of *Samson Agonistes*, Manoa and the Chorus present alternative versions of heroism that compete with each other in gendered terms, a contest that is never fully resolved. Thus Milton concludes with two distinctively gendered heroic positions that are represented as rivals and never reconciled. The unresolved competition between the two models creates dramatic tension in the poem. In contrast, *Paradise Regain'd* is notoriously devoid of tension. "Narrative suspense and dramatic sympathy go together," Northrop Frye observes; "We have them in *Samson Agonistes*, but they must be renounced here [in *Paradise Regain'd*]."[7] The Son is self-contained, without need of sympathy. His heroism is singular, certain, and in its insistently private, patient, enduring nature, unambivalently gendered female: "who best / Can suffer best can do," the Son announces, rejecting with moralized finality the power displayed in external deeds (*PR* 3.194–95).

Scholars long have debated the reasons for the lack of traditional action and narrative suspense in the brief epic, connecting this structural peculiarity with the Son's heroic identity as *sui generis*. Addressing the issue of plot, Barbara Lewalski is adamant that the Son does undergo a tension-creating agon: "For the encounter between Christ and Satan to constitute a genuine dramatic action and a real conflict, Christ's character must be conceived in such a way that the test or temptation is real: he must be able to fall, must be capable of growth, and must be genuinely (not just apparently) uncertain of himself." Yet Stanley Fish brilliantly demonstrates that there *is* no "real conflict" in *Paradise Regain'd*, at least not in the conventional terms Lewalski describes, and that is precisely the point. That the Son's internal struggles do not manifest themselves in the dramatic tension that traditional action creates is purposeful: any suspense-generating belief that the Son actually could be tempted or fall is counterintuitive both to the reader's foreknowledge and experience of the poem. Preoccupation with public action and historical experience are satanic in *Paradise Regain'd*, and throughout the poem it is Satan, not the Son (or the reader), who is unsure of Jesus' true identity as Satan's successful adversary and the eventual savior of humanity.[8] The Son is not quite certain precisely *how* he will conduct his career, but his future actions are not the subject of the poem. The Son (unlike Samson) never doubts his mission: "His weakness shall o'ercome Satanic strength" (*PR* 1.161).

In what follows I would like to connect the lack of narrative suspense, the unusual static quality of *Paradise Regain'd*, both to the Son's female heroism and, in particular, to Milton's representation of motherhood. Once again, comparisons with *Samson Agonistes* are revealing. In Judges 13, the angel of the Lord appears twice to Samson's barren mother to announce his birth, and both times she is alone. When he does encounter the angel, Manoa fails to recognize him; finally realizing that he is confronting a divine messenger, Manoa assumes wrongly that "we shall surely die, because we have seen God" (Judg. 13:22). It is Samson's mother who corrects her husband's misperception and who goes on to bear and name the baby. Rachel Havrelock's insights in her essay on barren mothers who eventually, miraculously, give birth to biblical heroes can help shed light on the reasons for Manoa's obtuseness. The "gap between humanity and God, promise and fulfillment cannot be repaired by male loyalty or devotion, but only by female initiative," Havrelock explains. "The female journey from barrenness to fertility parallels the migrations through which the patriarchs achieve intimacy with the Divine."[9] Given the biblical emphasis on the heroic agency of Samson's mother, it is all the more striking that Milton eliminates her crucial role in her son's story.

The erasure of mothers from narratives in the West is not in itself surprising, particularly if we consider the omnipresent literary configuration I define as the dead mother plot. In this plot, which has been and continues to be reiterated throughout Western literature, the mother often literally is dying or dead; yet, for this aesthetic structure to do its work, she is not necessarily dead. The important fact becomes that, if the mother is alive, she presents an impediment in the life of the hero: the mother's position obstructs the hero's destiny. But matters are complicated further. The mother's position as obstacle does not inevitably carry a negative psychological or moral valence. Thus *Hamlet* is a dead mother plot, but so is *The Winter's Tale,* wherein sympathy rests with Hermione, whose desired pregnancy suddenly elicits the hero's injustice, irrationality, and self-destruction.

The dead mother plot is related to the gendered distribution of authority in the family. Maternal authority is first and foremost an authority of origin. Second, as the Samson story makes clear, maternity by definition constitutes an authority of knowledge, the mother's knowledge of authentic fatherhood and the legitimacy of children. These conjoined authorities are not only singularly empowering but are of necessity acknowledged by all. "No uncertainty can exist about knowledge of maternity," Carole Pateman explains: "A woman who gives birth is a mother and a woman cannot help but know that she has given birth; maternity is a natural and a social fact." In contrast, "paternity has to be discovered or invented."[10]

Despite almost universal recognition of maternal authority in the West, and despite its inevitability, this power and its impact do not find their corollary in most significant cultural formations of adult social and political life. The workplace and professions are not organized around the fact of maternal power. Political structures do not embody it. Until very recently, legal systems do not encode it: a good counterexample is primogeniture, an entire system of inheritance organized around fathers and eldest sons. A problem seems to arise not from the recognition of maternal authority, but from the disposition of it in cultural life. We are left with two simultaneous truths, one about the necessity and omnipresence of maternal power and another about the erasure of that power or the inability to give it cultural form. The dead mother plot, I am arguing, is designed to represent this paradox.

According to the logic of this plot, Milton's erasure of Samson's mother indicates that the hero's destiny remains to be worked out as a historical experience, by which I mean that it must unfold through action and in time. No maternal presence will impede or alter this process, which conjoins individual destiny to cultural forms. Milton dramatizes Samson's internal struggle in three encounters: with his father, his unfaithful wife Dalila, and the Philistine bully Harapha. The authorities of both Dalila and Harapha are unquestionably discredited, leaving only Manoa to intervene in Samson's destiny, which he does, tirelessly. Devastated by his son's suffering, the father tries with unfailing, poignant energy to restore Samson's status as a triumphant military hero. But Milton represents Manoa's enthusiastic interventions ambiguously, picking up on the Bible's focus on his cluelessness. Passionately desiring to repair his son's dignity, Manoa is nevertheless conceptually trapped, insensitive. He cannot listen to Samson's repeated attempts to explain his internal experience of anguish, dismissing (in one of Milton's infrequent bad lines) what his son tells him: that the source of his desperate sorrow is not military defeat, but marital failure. "I cannot praise thy marriage choices son," he retorts, inadequately (*SA* 420), before changing the subject. When his efforts to keep his son alive fail, Manoa does not respond to the Chorus's eloquent praise for the passive endurance of suffering and rejection of brute strength in its evocation of the Phoenix. Instead he remains caught in the failed terms of traditional male heroism, tautologically and so unconvincingly praising Samson's death as legendary: "Samson hath quit himself / Like Samson, and heroically hath finsh'd / A life Heroic" (*SA* 1709–11). Taking the dead Samson home, Manoa wants to build a public monument as a memorial; intending to honor his son's valiance, he disregards with oblivious sadness Samson's passionate interiority and desire for privacy.

While there is some pathos to Manoa's suffering, his sense of loss does not match that of Samson; nor does his conception of heroism provide an adequate correlative to Samson's experience. As noted, Milton grants the ideological edge of moral superiority in the poem to the female heroism of endurance reflectively celebrated by the Chorus, rather than to the generic male version of militant action that Manoa idealizes. Paternal authority in the play is present, but radically compromised. But what of maternal authority? The Chorus represents its image of the regenerative Phoenix as maternal (*SA* 1699, 1703–07); and Samson evokes God himself as a mother (633–35).[11] Yet there is no actual mother taking part in the text. One result of Milton's erasure of Samson's mother is the effect of mysterious ambiguity surrounding Samson's birth. Samson alludes to his divine origins, his inner promptings, but we never see them dramatized: there is no representation, even in flashback, of the twice-repeated annunciation that plays so prominent a part in Judges. For the divinity of Samson's birth we have only the word of the bitter, anguished hero himself, who tends to have serious doubts.

3.

The problems raised in the ambiguous treatment of Samson's heroism are solved in Milton's unconflicted representation of the Son in *Paradise Regain'd*. As noted, Samson must reckon with an unresolved destiny, to be performed through action and suffering. In contrast, the Son has not a destiny to be worked out, but origins to be recognized. The Son of course will engage in a future plot. But in *Paradise Regain'd* Milton does not present that future as constituent of the Son's heroism. Instead the Son's heroic identity in the present moment of the poem involves accepting his origins, which exist already; they are definite, rather than ambiguous, profound but uncomplicated; by definition they do not remain to be achieved: rather, they are revealed in order to be understood. Another way to make this point is to say that for the Son, origins and destiny are the same thing: the former contains and makes explicit the latter. To clarify this distinction, I would like to return to the idea that maternal authority is an authority of origins and knowledge, both of which take only vague, indefinite form in the motherless text, *Samson Agonistes*. In *Paradise Regain'd*, however,

it is the Virgin's presence that confirms the Son's origins and pro-
vides knowledge of his birth. I am arguing that the prominent pres-
ence of the Virgin Mary in *Paradise Regain'd* is an essential part of
the picture that consolidates the Son's identity, making it perfect:
both human and divine.

Given Milton's radical Protestantism, it is all the more striking
that he should foreground the Virgin Mary in *Paradise Regain'd*. In
a lively and thorough account, Frances Dolan traces the trajectory
of Marian devotion in Protestant seventeenth century England and
concludes that Protestants saw in the worship of Mary "a radical
and blasphemous reorientation."[12] Moving away decidedly from
Catholic theological emphases (treasured in popular piety) on
the Virgin birth and the Assumption of the Virgin into heaven,
Protestants demoted the worshipful apparatus surrounding Mary,
doing away, for example, with the saints and relics that comprised
her cult. Insofar as Protestants took notice of Mary, they empha-
sized her humanity; fearing that worship of the Virgin would
rival worship of her son, they directed their attention to Christ
alone.[13] In his prose writings Milton aligns himself with standard
Protestant thinking on the issue of the Virgin's humanity. For
example, he vehemently denies that Mary could be a cause of sal-
vation for herself or others, indignantly rejecting the idea of her
as a divine agent. Instead he praises her for her obedient, reverent
political sentiments about human misery, expressed in Luke, and
for her status as the ideal wife.[14]

Milton virtually ignores Mary's motherhood per se in the few
instances when he mentions the Virgin in his prose. This is all
the more interesting, given that, as Dolan shows, it is the idea and
representation of Mary's motherhood that evoke the most fervent
anxieties in the seventeenth century. Dolan points out, "Mary's
pregnancy, however unusual, reveals that motherhood alone
always embodies 'coverture' at its most literal; the mother of a son,
let alone the son of God, inverts the expected operations of cover-
ture in particularly threatening ways....During pregnancy, Mary,
like other mothers, 'overshadows,' covers, or subsumes her fetal

son."[15] While Protestants responded to these issues with hostility and alarm, their fears about Mary's maternal power and agency were shared to a lesser degree and experienced from slightly different angles by Catholics.

Aligning himself staunchly with Protestant thinking on the Virgin's humanity and disregarding her motherhood in the few mentions he makes of her in his prose, Milton nevertheless presents her as a major figure in *Paradise Regain'd*, occupying a great deal of space precisely because she is a mother. In her recent investigation of the subject, Marjorie O'Rourke Boyle finds "Milton's characterization [of the Virgin] seriously at odds with the scriptural sense restored by authoritative Renaissance philology and sanctioned by magisterial Reformation theology." Indeed, she argues, recommending sources to back up her claim, "*Paradise Regained* depends on Catholic interpretations of the gospel." Boyle's interesting observation has considerable evidence to substantiate it.[16]

The rich, extensive scholarship of Michael Lieb and others makes clear that Milton's theological positions and the passion with which he assumes them are always critically important for any understanding of his work.[17] As we have seen, Protestants, including Milton, ardently denied the Virgin Mary's divinity, fearing her rivalry with Christ and moving toward worshipping Christ alone. In *Paradise Regain'd* Milton makes no claims for Mary's divine agency, although he does represent repeatedly and at length her intimacy with the divine and her role as affective mediator between God (or his messengers) and the Son. Most interesting for purposes of this essay is the way in which Milton deviates in emphasis and tone from the range of Protestant positions he characteristically occupies. Far from fearing and so erasing the Virgin's powerful, miraculous maternity as competitive with Christ's divinity, Milton focuses intensely on Mary and her motherhood precisely in order to fulfill his intention to exalt the Son.

Milton's treatment of the idea that the Virgin Mary redeems the sin of Eve confirms the point. In *Paradise Regain'd* Milton presents this issue primarily through satanic eyes, but his representations are curiously devoid of the misogyny that often accompanies this theme. It is Satan who observes that his fatal wound "Shall be inflicted by the seed of Eve / Upon my head" (*PR* 1.52–54). "For this ill news I bring," he continues, "the woman's seed / Destined to this is late of woman born, / His birth to our just fear gave no small cause" (1.664–66). The fact that the Son is "of woman born," a reality that fatally contributes to the destruction of so many heroes (for example, Macbeth, Hamlet, Oedipus, and Coriolanus, to name only a few) is precisely what scares Satan. "His mother then is mortal," Satan observes, recognizing the guarantee of his doom. Comparing the Son to Job, God reveals his scheme to outwit Satan once again; but this time the triumphant result will be even better: Satan, God gloats,

>   might have learned
> Less overweening, since he failed in Job,
> Whose constant perseverance overcame
> Whate'er his cruel malice could invent.
> He now shall know I can produce a man
> Of female seed, far abler to resist
> All his solicitations, and at length
> All his vast force, and drive him back to hell,
> Winning by conquest what the first man lost
> By fallacy surprised.   (*PR* 1.146–55)

My point is not simply that Jesus' relation to Mary is the sign and symbol of his humanity, which it is; what I emphasize instead is that Milton locates the origins of the Son's eventual triumph over Satan in his relationship with his mother.

The Virgin's role as guarantor of the Son's origins—and so of his destiny—is evident whenever she appears in *Paradise Regain'd*. As noted, the Annunciation is alluded to (always in flashback) five times in the poem: once by God, who recalls it to Gabriel (*PR* 1.33–40); next by the Virgin, whose account the Son recollects (1.227–58); the Virgin then alludes to it for the third and fourth times, during her lament in book 2 (67–69, 107); finally, Satan returns to it in book 4, declaring that "thy birth at length / Announced by

Gabriel with the first I knew" (4.503–04), in order to one-up the Son with his superior knowledge.

But knowledge of the Son's birth in *Paradise Regain'd* is the property of the Virgin.[18] Interestingly, her first account of the Annunciation is longer than God's account. Milton fills it out with Mary's detailed rendition of the Son's Nativity and childhood, adapted for the most part from Luke. It is precisely this account that leads the Son to discover his identity:

> This having heard, straight I again revolved
> The law and prophets, searching what was writ
> Concerning the Messiah, to our scribes
> Known partly, and soon found of whom they spake
> I am.   (*PR* 1.259–63)

As Dayton Haskin demonstrates, this passage, connecting the Son's origins with his destiny, constructs the Virgin's authority as containing but not limited to a very specific kind of knowledge, knowledge of the written law.[19]

4.

Milton's emphasis on the Virgin's authority in *Paradise Regain'd* is indeed theologically quirky and, as noted, seems at first to run counter to his intention to exalt the Son. However, a clearer picture of Milton's strategies in the brief epic emerges when we consider his focus on Mary's maternity not solely in theological terms, but in relation to a more inclusive discourse about the early modern family that debated and discussed motherhood, revealing it as a problematic status.[20] Dolan argues correctly in her analysis of anxieties about the Virgin's motherhood that "whether or not Mary was viewed as a remarkable exception, the sustained and passionate public debate over her status in seventeenth-century England did not take place in a vacuum, remote from other contests over women's authority and agency or from historical women."[21]

Debates about the gendered distribution of authority in the early modern family stem perforce from a set of assumptions about sexual equality and/or hierarchy, issues that during the second half of the seventeenth century frequently were considered in relation to sovereignty and the state. During Milton's lifetime this debate, although falling far short of asserting equality between the sexes, was taking a more liberal turn. Building on decades of Protestant attempts to redefine the family, political philosophers, theologians, and moralists were beginning at least to weigh the possibility of mothers and fathers having equal authority. As Pateman notes, the extreme conservative Robert Filmer, most famous for being the object of Locke's scorn, comes at "*the end* of a very long history of traditional patriarchal argument in which the creation of political society has been seen as a masculine act of birth."[22] Using Pateman's insights in a recent study of Dryden, Susan Greenfield points out that in the late seventeenth century familial theory was becoming ideologically flexible and could be "shaped to suit various purposes."[23] Milton himself, weighing and rejecting the possibility of equality between husband and wife, sees husbandly abuse as a potential problem; nevertheless, he affirms the God-given stakes of male superiority:

> So had the image of God bin equally common to them both, it had no doubt bin said, In the image of God created he them. But *St. Paul* ends the controversie, by explaining, that the woman is not primarily and immediately the image of God, but in reference to the man, *The head of the woman,* saith he, 1 Cor. 11. *is the man: he the image and glory of God, she the glory of the man:* he not for her, but she for him. Therefore his precept is, *Wives be subject to your husbands as is fit in the Lord, Col.* 3. 18. *In every thing, Eph.* 5. 24. Nevertheless man is not to hold her as a servant, but receives her into a part of that empire which God proclaims him to, though not equally, yet largely, as his own image and glory: for it is no small glory to him, that a creature so like him, should be made subject to him. Not but that particular exceptions may have place, if she exceed her husband in prudence and dexterity, and he contentedly yeeld: for then a superior and more naturall law comes in, that the wiser should govern the lesse wise, whether male or female. But that which far more easily and obediently follows from this verse, is that, seeing woman was purposely made for man, and he her head, it cannot stand before

the breath of this divine utterance, that man the portraiture of God, joyning to himself for his intended good and solace an inferiour sexe, should so becom her thrall, whose wilfulness or inability to be a wife frustrates the occasionall end of her creation. (YP 2:589)

Apparently more interested in spousal relations, Milton does not mention parenthood in this discussion of marital hierarchy, never directly considering the issue of differential parental authority over a child. At the end of the century Locke, arguing against patriarchal sovereignty, underscores the "joint dominion" of parents over children, who "must certainly owe most to the mother." Despite his respect for and defense of maternal power, however, Locke in the end overrides motherhood in his consideration of women's familial status. Succumbing to the tenets of male superiority, he asserts that rule "naturally falls to the man's share," because man is "abler and stronger."[24]

It is Hobbes's account of the gendered distribution of parental power in *Leviathan* (1651) that is of primary interest for the purposes of this essay. As I noted when introducing the idea of the dead mother plot, early modern discussions of maternity assign to mothers a contradictory status: while they have the immense authority of knowledge and origins, that authority remains only indirectly, often obscurely, connected to public cultural forms. In contrast to other thinkers, Hobbes clearly acknowledges that the conceptual inconsistencies in the early modern family as debated and defined have to do not only with the positioning of women in relation to their husbands, but specifically and explicitly with the paradoxes surrounding mothers. In what follows I will examine at some length Hobbes's discussion of maternal power and agency because his logic provides a close and revealing parallel to Milton's deployment of the Virgin in *Paradise Regain'd.*

As Carole Pateman puts it in her study of the sexual contract, "Hobbes differs from the other classical contract theorists in his assumption that there is no natural mastery in the state of nature, not even of men over women; natural individual attributes and capacities are distributed irrespective of sex." While other theorists insist that "men's right over women has a natural basis," in Hobbes "both sexes are pictured as naturally free and equal."[25] Hobbes is indeed startlingly clear on the subject of equality between the sexes in his discussion of the distribution of authority in the family: "Whereas some have attributed the dominion to the man only, as being of the more excellent sex; *they misreckon in it.* For there is not always that difference of strength, or prudence between the man and the woman, as that the right can be determined without war." Hobbes therefore begins his discussion of "the right of dominion by generation" by considering that, logically speaking, parents should have equal rights over their children: "there are always two that are equally parents: the dominion therefore over the child should belong equally to both." The important slippage in Hobbes's logic results from these assertions about sexual equality. As it turns out, in the natural state, mothers in fact are not equal but superior to fathers. "In the condition of mere nature, where there are no matrimonial laws," mothers have dominion over children because "it cannot be known who is the father, unless it be declared by the mother." Not only does the mother have positive knowledge of the infant's origins, it is also in her power to preserve or expose the child: "every man is supposed to promise obedience to him in whose power it is to save, or destroy him." Given the natural fact of maternal superiority, how does it come about that "there be always two that are equally parents" and "the dominion over the child should belong equally to both"?[26]

A partial answer is that Hobbes does not place his faith in nature. He is famously convinced that, if left to its natural devices, humanity would destroy itself. There must be a humanly constructed political and social structure—a contract—that improves upon the given, natural one. Hobbes perceives that paternal dominance is artificial, a fiction that exists because although "there be always two that are equally parents...no man can obey two masters." Granting (along with the scriptural injunction) his fearful premise that the natural tendency of humanity is toward the war of all against all, there is still no logical reason why a person cannot "obey two masters." More important, given his belief in the equality of the sexes, the dangerousness of the natural state would not lead with inevitable logic to the social fact of *male* dominance. Even postulating the necessity of obeying one master-parent, why should not the parent who must be obeyed be the mother, particularly since Hobbes goes to pains to unveil assumptions about male superiority as erroneous: "they misreckon in it"? My point, then, is not that paternal dominance is artificial rather than natural: for Hobbes the construction of social fictions is both necessary and desirable. Instead I emphasize that, within the terms of Hobbes's own logic, paternal dominance is a tautology, circular, an incoherence. Fathers are dominant because they are and always have been dominant. In the struggle for power between parents, "for the most part, but not always, the sentence is in favour of the father; because for the most part commonwealths have been erected by the fathers, not by the mothers of families."[27]

Hobbes wants to clarify and nail down where the power lies. His arguments about the distribution of parental power repudiate both male superiority and a hypothesized nature/culture divide that would (naturally or artificially) relegate women to a private sphere. He makes clear that the logical slippage, or point of instability, in the construction of the patriarchal family is not the status of women per se, but motherhood, because of the natural and social authority inherent in that position. However, while directly acknowledging and exploring this problem at some length, Hobbes does not solve it. Instead motherhood begins to disappear from his formulations of familial authority. "He that hath the dominion over the child, hath dominion also over the children of the child," he reflects; and, in his considerations of the traditional analogy between the family and the commonwealth, he observes that the family consists "of a man and his children; or of a man and his servants; or of a man, and his children and servants together."[28] My point is not that Hobbes erases mothers; they are neither eliminated from nor invisible in his analysis. Rather, I am interested in the way in which his discussion of family structure describes with adamant elaboration the immensity of maternal authority and is then unable to develop it conceptually, or to give it cultural form. Maternal authority exists, prominently; but it is undertheorized. It is strikingly formulated, but no account is made of its consequences. It is in fact unaccountable: its components exceed the family system.

In Hobbes's analysis maternal authority, for all its prominence, does not take historical form, by which I mean that, while it never disappears, it does not unfold in time. This lack of a historical trajectory in time is what gives Hobbes's discussion of motherhood its relevance to literary representation and, specifically, to plot. As Peter Brooks demonstrates, plotting is an interpretive activity, concerned not only with "the underlying intentionality of event," but also with the ways in which "meaning can be construed over and through time." Plot establishes the relation of events to their origins and endpoints; it embodies "the sense of those meanings that develop only through textual and temporal succession."[29] Hobbes argues that maternal authority is crucial, but fails to imagine its enactment in time or history. Embodying the authority of origin and knowledge, mothers legitimize the patriarchal family; yet the exercise of maternal power exceeds the parameters of that same family as defined. In the literary terms corresponding to this logic, maternal authority can be said to exceed the dimensions of plot.

As we have seen, Milton's conception of the Son's heroism also exceeds the dimensions of plot, in the conventional sense of plot as the enactment and achievement of a destiny. Milton's focus on the Virgin as the authority figure in the first part of *Paradise Regain'd*, therefore, points to his conception of the Son's heroic identity as bound up in his origins. The exact parameters of the Virgin's maternal authority and agency are made manifest in her lament in book 2 (66–105). Here she reveals her uniquely expansive knowledge of the Son's past and his birth, legitimizing his status as God's child ("O what avails me now that honour high / To have conceived of God") and filling in details of his early biography (for example, the bleak conditions of his Nativity; the flight into Egypt). Importantly, she couches her observations in terms of the contrasting public and private dimensions of Christ's life. Milton emphasizes the Son's privacy at several points in the poem, from first—he is "obscure, / Unmarked, unknown" (*PR* 1.24–25)—to last, when "he unobserved / Home to his mother's house private returned" (4.638–39). As the final line of the poem indicates, Mary has been the presiding authority over this segment of the Son's life, which, with her, has been "Private, unactive, calm, contemplative, / Little suspicious to any king" (*PR* 2.81–82). Despite the framework of privacy that encompasses the Son, the whole point of the Virgin's lament is her realization that this part of the Son's life is nearing completion. It is clear that her authority does not extend to his future ministry. She has heard about, rather than witnessed, the baptism: "but now / Full grown to man, acknowledged, as I hear, / By John the Baptist, and in public shown, / Son owned from heaven by his father's voice" (*PR* 2.83–86). Recalling the predictions of Simeon, along with her son's independent journey to the temple at age 12, the Virgin realizes that, when he publicly undertakes "his father's business," she will not be there (*PR* 2.99). Indeed, as soon as the Son begins his struggle with Satan, his mother disappears from the poem, returning only in the final line, not as an embodied presence but as an allusion.[30]

Considering the extent as well as the limitations of the Virgin's maternal power and presence can focus us precisely on Christ's heroic identity as Milton construes it in *Paradise Regain'd:* the Son inhabits human history and time temporarily; he is suspended between the future and the past. When debating why Milton, given the title of his poem, did not choose to dramatize the Passion, several scholars have argued for a typological interpretation that conflates the Son's resistance to Satan's temptations in the wilderness with Christ's harrowing of hell after his Crucifixion.[31] While such a reading may be theologically sound, it does not correspond to the narrative logic of the poem, which exalts the Son as a hero not for what he does, but because of what he is: a son. In the present moment of *Paradise Regain'd* Milton insists that Jesus' public life has not happened yet, a fact that is underscored by the adamant finality of the Son's private return to his mother's house.

9 ➤ Charles, Christ, and Icon of Kingship in *Paradise Regain'd*

Stella P. Revard

When Milton published *Paradise Regain'd* in 1671, England had experienced more than ten years of the kingship of Charles II. On the eve of the Restoration, Milton had denounced in *The Ready and Easy Way* the excesses of royal rule that were likely to ensue with the restoration of the monarchy and had called for the return of Christ the King rather than Charles the King. With Charles II's propaganda machine in full force during the decade after his triumphant return, poets such as Abraham Cowley and John Dryden extolled the wonders of his kingship, comparing Charles to Moses, Joshua, David, and yes, to Christ himself. By the late 1660s it was time to assess the nature of kingship in England, and to refute the insistent claims of royalist poets that Charles had inherited the mantle of the Old Testament prophets and kings and that he was playing as son to the royal martyr the role of a Christological ruler as well. It has long been recognized that a major part of *Paradise Regain'd* concerns the nature of kingship itself. However, because

Satan offers the Son an earthly crown and Jesus rejects it, readers of *Paradise Regain'd* often misconstrue Milton's view of earthly kingship. Jesus is often viewed as a nonpolitical protagonist and *Paradise Regain'd* a nonpolitical poem, the product of Milton's retirement from the arena of politics in the wake of the failure of the commonwealth. Nothing, however, could be further from the truth.

As I have previously argued in an essay on Milton's millenarianism and as a recent volume of *Milton Studies* devoted to *Paradise Regain'd* also makes clear, *Paradise Regain'd* is a deeply committed political poem.[1] The reasons we have been slow in realizing this are many. One is the simple assumption that Milton's brief epic is functioning as a sequel to *Paradise Lost*—that it was composed to satisfy Milton's Quaker friend, Thomas Ellwood, who requested that Milton fulfill the promise of the previous epic and write of paradise found. Such a view places foremost the Son's role as the god-man who obeys God's commandments and installs humankind in a renewed paradise—the paradise within. But as some critics argue, Milton's description of the Son's wilderness experience is not a withdrawal from the world.

Long ago Michael Lieb pointed out that Jesus, as he enters the wilderness, is both a type of Moses, the leader of the people, and of Elijah the prophet.[2] Milton describes the Son's trials in the wilderness as a Mosaic journey that prepares him for leadership. In so doing he is also subtly contrasting the Son's trials with those of another much celebrated Moses figure, Charles II, who allegedly in the wilderness of exile in the 1650s was preparing himself for his role as king. Charles emerged from the "wilderness," as the poets and preachers often pointed out, to become the nation's savior and king. Jesus after his own solitary retreat returned to take on his mission as savior and begin his ministry. The wilderness experience also formed Jesus as a future king, the earthly ruler of the New Jerusalem—the Messiah in the fullest sense and a ruler who contrasts with the present ruler of England. If in *Paradise Regain'd* Milton is contrasting Jesus' role as the new Moses, Joshua, and David with Charles II's claims to these types, he is also contrasting

Charles's alleged role as anointed king or messiah with that of the true Christ.

From the moment of Charles's birth—and even before, when the royal child was expected—Charles was compared to Christ. Milton, the Puritan poet, as I have argued elsewhere, reacted to these prophecies when he was composing the Nativity ode by implicitly contrasting the expected royal heir—Prince Charles—with Christ.[3] Poets at the time were fond of comparing the infants, both heirs to royal thrones and born of Marys (or Marias, as Henrietta Maria was often called). They pointed out that when the prince's father, Charles I, was on the way to a thanksgiving ceremony for his newborn son, a noonday star reportedly was seen proclaiming the event. Throughout his life, and even in the poems eulogizing him at his death, poets remarked that only Charles and Christ were proclaimed at birth by a star.[4] At the time of Charles's return to England in 1660, Cowley and Dryden and a number of university poets, writing in an Oxford volume to celebrate the Restoration, reminded England how at Charles's birth a star had heralded the miraculous birth. Now the royal child was mature, and according to the poets, the prophecies promulgated at his birth were about to be fulfilled.

In his "ODE, Upon the Blessed Restoration and Returne of His Sacred Majestie, Charls the Second" (London, 1660), Cowley begins with an apostrophe to the peaceful stars that calm the stormy world, and recalls Charles's natal star, which, "in despight / Of the proud *Sun's* Meridian Light" shone forth 30 years before with a "powerfull *Ray*, / Which could out-face the *Sun*, and overcome the *Day*" (1.14–15, 18–19). He invokes the star to shine again:

> Auspicious *Star*, again arise,
> And take thy *Noon-tide station* in the skies.
> Again all *Heaven* prodigiously adorn;
>   For loe! thy *Charls* again is *Born*.
>   He then was *born with, and to Pain;*
>   *With*, and *to Joy* he's *born* again.
>   And wisely for this *second Birth,*
>   By which thou certain wert to bless
> The Land with full and flourishing *Happinesse.*[5]   (2.1–9)

Implicitly, by alluding to the star, Cowley connects Charles not only with Christ at his miraculous birth but also with Christ come again—returned to earth to assume his rightful kingdom at his Second Coming. The pain that Charles and Christ experienced in their "first coming" will be turned to joy at this second advent—the so-called "Second Birth"—which proclaims not only joy for Charles, but also joy for the land that he will fill with prosperity and happiness.

The university poets who celebrated Charles's return to England took a similar view. Charles is the sun, an Apollo returning to dispense his light.[6] The star that shone at Charles's birth is not forgotten, nor is the connection it announces with the birth of Christ. An Oxford poet, John Ailmer, puts it this way:

> That Star, Heav'n's Herald, that at's Birth in *May*
> Shone amidst all the Glories of the day,
> Bespoke him Monarch, and th' auspicious thing
> Led all our Wisemen unto CHARLES our King
>   Of whose fair Reign, if Poets can divine,
> And prophesie been't ceas'd, then hear you mine.[7]

Throughout the collection, poets exploit images of light to proclaim the returned king's divinity, and the star of his birth is called upon again and again to testify to his kinship with Christ the King.

Endeavoring to erase the memory of the "Heroic Stanzas" he had composed in 1659 to mourn the death of Oliver Cromwell, John Dryden quickly put in a claim as a royal poet, publishing in succession "Astraea Redux" in 1660 and "A Panegyric on His Coronation" in 1661. Consistently he portrays Charles not only as the legitimate sovereign but also as a heaven-ordained ruler, summoning in "Astraea Redux" a wide range of types with which to compare the returning monarch. Charles is Jupiter who has finally put down Typhoeus-Cromwell's attempt to scale heaven; he is David come into a rightful kingdom after long suffering. Also he is the semidivine son of the royal martyr, "whose goodness [his] descent doth shew, / [His] heav'nly parentage and earthly too."[8] Dryden reserves the star of Charles's birth until almost the end of the poem—"That star that at your birth shone out so bright,

/ It stain'd the duller sun's meridian light" (288–89). The heavenly star now renews "its potent fires, / Guiding our eyes to find and worship you" (290–91). Combining Christian with classical, Dryden concludes the poem with another messianic reference, here to Virgil, whose fourth eclogue had promised an age of gold with the birth of a child. Now grown to maturity, Charles is to establish himself as Augustus: "O happy age! O times like those alone / By fate reserv'd for great Augustus' throne!" (320–21). In the "Panegyric on the Coronation," published in the year following, Dryden, like Cowley and the university poets, makes Charles into a sun-king, returned to warm the land after the devastation of the flood, the "wild deluge" (1), which, though leveling the land, also left it open for "new-born nature" (8) to take hold and bloom again. Charles is led to the sacred temple to be crowned, the very church he preserved from ruin and restored.[9]

In 1660 the preachers as well as the poets proclaimed the divine nature of Charles's return. The arrival of Charles on England's shores was greeted with no less excitement, as one enthusiastic preacher announced, than if Christ had arrived in Ezekiel's fiery chariot at the Second Coming.[10] Many sermons begin by comparing Charles's sojourn on the Continent to Moses' trials in the wilderness or David's adversities before he came to kingship. William Godman, for example, pleads that God gave Moses the authority of a king, if not the name, when he led him through the wilderness and so Moses serves as a type for the returning king. Godman also names David as a type for Charles—David, son of heroes, who before he became king had been rejected and persecuted as Charles had. All this leads up to a comparison of Charles to Christ, the stone that had been rejected by the builders. This text from Psalm 118, first applied to David, became a prophetic text that announced the kingship of Christ. Now Godman applies it to another king: King Charles is the stone refused by the builders who is now become the head of the corner.[11] Psalm 118 becomes a favorite text for the preachers, who wish to exalt not only Charles II's return to kingship, but also his reestablishment of the Church of England. Verses from Psalms and Proverbs are cited to support not only Charles's likeness to David but also his divine prerogative. Another preacher, Gilbert Sheldon, after celebrating how Charles, like David, was delivered and raised to kingship, goes on to affirm his likeness to Christ: "*David* [was] no ordinary *King* or *Saint*, but eminent in both relations; an excellent Person, and a gracious *King*, one *after Gods own heart*, a type of *Christ*; and no marvel if such be delivered by him, if God have an especial care of him."[12] No one, however, pressed the likeness between Charles, David, and Christ further than a certain J. W. in a sermon preached to mark Charles's return to England in May 1660. Citing the verses from Psalm 118, he advances Charles in Christ's place as the stone rejected by the builders who is now become the head of the corner and the head of the Church. But he is not content merely to cite the verses from Psalms that were used typologically of David and Christ to mark Charles's ordination as king. He also draws upon Daniel's citation of Christ as the stone cut out of the mountain who is to return as king to rule all the earth in his Second Coming: "In Daniels vision, He is the stone cut out of the mountain without hands, which grew so fast and great that it filled the whole earth Dan. 2. 34, 35 and 44, 45." In the eyes of the preacher, Charles's return to England to assume the kingship is no less an event than Christ's millennial assumption of his earthly office as king. J. W. asserts a direct parallel between these three rulers appointed by God: "David in his Kingdom, Christ in his Kingdome, so King CHARLES in his Kingdome is a stone, a tried stone ... in his faith, life, nature, vertue ... only to bear the weight of his Kingdome." Further, the very promise of Christ's Second Coming is a warrant for Charles's and his successors' continuance as earthly monarchs: "As Christ was so made and continues for ever, for to him is given, Imperium sine fine [kingdom without end]; so we hope and pray that King Charles may be so and his Posterity in these Kingdomes till Christs second coming, ever so long as the Sun and Moon endureth."[13]

Milton did not agree. The man who had smashed the false idol of Stuart kingship in *The Tenure of Kings and Magistrates* and in *Eikonoklastes* anticipated the preacherly and poetic eulogies of Charles by launching into a final attack on kingship in *The*

Ready and Easy Way. Writing just months before the preachers and poets delivered their fulsome welcome to Charles as the new David and the returning Christ, Milton presents a different view of the proposed sovereign and of kingship itself. Contrasting rather than likening the returning king to Christ, he disjoins rather than links God and king. Vindicating the commonwealth's abolition of kingship, Milton asserts, "we could not serve two contrary masters, God and the king, or the king and that more supreme law sworn in the first place to maintain our safety and our liberty."[14] He reminds the English people that contrary to the royalist propaganda that God approved kingship, "God in much displeasure gave a king to the Israelites" (885). Indeed, rather than sanctioning kingship, the government that Christ would have recommended was a commonwealth where brother was not exalted over brother.[15] As a Protestant, Milton affirms that he is fundamentally opposed to regarding any man as Christ's stand-in: "Christ in his church hath left no vicegerent of his power; but himself" (887). No Christian can claim to derive the authority over others from Christ, he continues, citing the spurious nature of both the pope and those kings who claim divine ordination. While he strongly rejects the divine foundation of kingship and thus Charles's claim of divine authority, Milton does not elaborate in *The Ready and Easy Way* on the question of Moses' or David's authority or David's claim as king and precursor to the Messiah—examples, which he will readily cite, though in a covert way, in *Paradise Regain'd*. However, Milton twice vehemently exhorts the English people not to return to Egypt, that is, to the slavery of kingship. He warns his countrymen that kingship, like the fleshpots of Egypt, would reinstate exorbitant luxury and excess into government. Moreover, in this final prose tract before the Restoration he does not hesitate to invoke the example of Christ the King. Dismissing Stuart kingship and invoking the imminent coming of Christ to assume his earthly crown, he contrasts Charles to Christ: "to the coming of our true and rightful and only to be expected King, only worthy as he is our only Savior, the Messiah, the Christ, the only heir of his eternal Father, the only by him anointed and ordained since the work of our redemption finished, Universal Lord of all mankind" (891–92). Of course, Milton has a political agenda in invoking Christ's earthly kingship at the very moment he is warning against restoring an earthly king to power. Christ the King is the foil to Charles the King—Christ's legitimate kingship contrasts with Charles II's spurious and tyrannical kingship. Milton is urging his countrymen that until King Messiah comes, a commonwealth and not a restored monarchy will assure England peace, justice, and prosperity. Moreover, Milton is not hesitant to join a millenarian message to his call for urgent political action to found a republic and resist the restoration of monarchy. The expectation of Christ's arrival to assume an earthly kingship undergirds the political aspirations of the nation.[16]

After the Restoration, Milton, constrained if not to quietism, at least to silence because of political censorship, must have nevertheless viewed with dismay the realization of his predictions about the extravagance of the royal court, now empowered by the Restoration. Even the poets and clergymen who had so enthusiastically welcomed the return of the divine king found it more difficult to make a case for Charles's sacred presence in England. Not long after Charles II had assumed power, as Nicholas von Maltzahn and others have reminded us, the English began to express widespread misgivings—political, religious, and moral—concerning Charles's kingship. The excesses of the prince's court in exile, which Milton had alluded to in *The Ready and Easy Way,* could now be witnessed first hand in the misdoings of the king at Whitehall. Charles's marriage to Catherine of Braganza rapidly failed—without producing a legitimate heir. His mistress Barbara Palmer was present at court, and the court itself had a reputation for dissolution, aggravated by reports such as that of Sir Charles Sedley's disgraceful night out (June 1663).[17] Besides, already in 1661–62 there was serious political and religious polarization that resulted from the failure of the Worcester House Declaration, the Corporation Act, the Hearth Tax, the Act of Uniformity (which ejected the Presbyterian ministers from Parliament), and the sale of Dunkirk to the French. By late 1662 the Venetian ambassador could report the common saying in London that the monarch only hunts and lusts.[18]

Nevertheless, Charles's encomiasts were constant in promoting the royal image throughout the 1660s. In 1666–67, however, different tactics were needed to preserve Charles's image in the face of the worsening political situation in England. Dryden responded in 1667 with the semiheroic poem *Annus Mirabilis*, his strongest plea for Charles's kingship. He dubbed 1666 the year of wonders, but it might have more properly been referred to as the year of disasters. The years 1665–66 saw the renewal of the naval wars with the Dutch; a virulent outbreak of the plague (which drove many, including Dryden and Milton, from London); and the Great Fire of London. For the millenarians, 1666 was a crucial year as well. They had long viewed the coming of the triple sixes as a possible moment when Christ's kingdom would come, when the Son of God would begin his thousand-year reign on earth. It is impossible to ignore the renewal of the murmurs of millenarianism, a movement that had been so important during the decade of the commonwealth and that continued to impact the politics of the era and ultimately Milton's view of the christological kingship in *Paradise Regain'd*. The year 1666 was also when Milton presented *Paradise Lost* to the press and perhaps embarked on the composition of *Paradise Regain'd*.

Paradise Regain'd and Dryden's *Annus Mirabilis* express contrary views of kingship. *Annus Mirabilis* is an unusual propaganda piece.[19] Dryden casts Charles in the role of a warrior-king despite the fact that Charles never actually took part in the war. He merely spurred on his brother, the Duke of York, Prince Rupert, and George Monk.[20] Dryden's models for the poem, as he explains in a letter to Sir Robert Howard, are classical.[21] Although the poem is no longer than one book of the *Iliad* or of the *Aeneid*, Dryden invokes these examples for this "historical" poem. He refrains, but barely so, from calling *Annus Mirabilis* an epic, though clearly it was composed, as was *Paradise Regain'd*, on the model of the brief epic. In the first part Dryden endeavors to make Charles into a Caesar, who undertakes war reluctantly to defend his nation against unruly neighbors—the Dutch who are harming the English trade. Also as king he must oversee the French and the Spanish, who were engaged in policies against each other that involved Britain and the Netherlands. Dryden manages to make Charles seem both a sagacious ruler who "griev'd the land he freed should be oppress'd," and a generous monarch who was moved by "fair ideas...of fame and honor" (*Annus Mirabilis*, 39, 40–41). Moreover, though Charles undertakes war, he is depicted more truly as a prince of peace. In the second part of the poem, Dryden makes Charles a savior-king who succors his people after the great devastation of the Fire of London.[22] Charles is the careful father of his people, who, when the fire devastates London, beseeches God to spare his subjects. Dryden is countering in *Annus Mirabilis* the widespread view that both the war and the fire are God's judgment on the English people and on their king for slackness and wickedness.[23]

Dryden's initial aim in *Annus Mirabilis* is to portray the Dutch naval war as an undertaking wherein Charles as Caesar Augustus through his deputies brings glory and victory to England. His secondary purpose is to argue that the Fire of London, though a disaster, was not God's doom, but a trial that the English must pass in order to enter into a new era. Like an Old Testament prophet, Charles intercedes with God on behalf of his people while the fire rages. When the fire abates, he gives thanks to God for favor and mercy and, like the Savior, relieves the people with bread. Discreetly, Dryden endues the king's person with the overtones both of King David and Messiah-King.

We have noted how important the Davidic persona was in Dryden's first poems for Charles in the early 1660s. In "Astraea Redux" Dryden had chosen, like the preachers, to link Charles's exile from England with David's banishment from Israel, remarking how both suffered adversities before they could assume the crown. In "A Panegyric on His Coronation" Dryden once again likens Charles to young David tried by adversity. However, by the time he wrote *Annus Mirabilis*, Dryden could no longer simply link the young David with the young Charles. He had to deal with the sins of the mature monarchs—namely, both David's and Charles's flagrant sexual misconduct. He astutely observes that if he could argue that David's sins were redeemed by his care for his people, so he might make a similar case for Charles. Therefore, in *Annus Mirabilis* Dryden boldly makes Charles a Davidic king who is both savior to his people and also justly, as David was, a type for Jesus Christ.

At the very same time that Dryden was vigorously defending Charles as a monarch after God's own heart, Milton was contemplating in *Paradise Regain'd* a poem that might be both a sequel to his long epic and a work with strongly political implications for the current situation in England. *Paradise Regain'd* may have been begun as early as 1666 and was completed before July 1670 when it was licensed for the press.[24] We should therefore consider the brief epic in the context of the late 1660s when propagandists such as Dryden were attempting to bolster Charles II's kingship by reminders of his Davidic heritage. If the question of Charles's Davidic heritage is crucial to *Annus Mirabilis*, the Son's Davidic heritage is no less so for *Paradise Regain'd*. From the beginning of Milton's brief epic to its very end, the issue of Jesus as a Davidic king engages us no less than the issue of his person as the Son of God. In the opening scene of *Paradise Regain'd,* John the Baptist trumpets that "Heaven's Kingdom [is] nigh at hand" (*PR* 1.20) and identifies Jesus both as Son of God and as the Messiah who will inherit the Davidic kingdom prophesied by Hebrew prophets such as Daniel and Isaiah. The disciples Andrew and Simon Peter immediately recognize, as Milton tells us at the beginning of book 2, that Jesus is the long-awaited Messiah who will deliver Israel and restore the kingdom. Conversely, Satan, as he confides to his fallen compatriots, is determined to forestall this restoration, "Ere in the head of Nations he appear / Their King, their Leader, and Supreme on Earth" (*PR* 1.98–99).[25] For Jesus, also, as he reflects to himself in the long soliloquy in book 1, the nature of this Davidic kingship must be determined. His mother Mary has told him he would inherit David's throne: "Thou shouldst be great and sit on *David*'s Throne, / And of thy Kingdom there should be no end" (*PR*

1.240–41). The context of this prophecy, as Milton's audience well knows, is millenarian, for the promise of the kingdom without end was drawn ultimately from Daniel 7:27, a text frequently cited by millenarians as predicting Jesus' Second Coming.

Throughout *Paradise Regain'd*, as Satan tests Jesus, the nature of Jesus' prophesied kingship appears undetermined. Is it earthly or heavenly? Will Jesus assume the throne immediately or in future time? Will he acquire it by force or through persuasion? During his soliloquy in book 1 of *Paradise Regain'd*, Jesus contemplates some of the paradoxes of his vocation as king. On the one hand, he acknowledges that he once aspired to "victorious deeds" and "heroic acts.../ To rescue *Israel* from the *Roman* yoke, / Then to subdue and quell o'er all the earth / Brute violence and proud Tyrannic pow'r" (*PR* 1.215–19). Yet, on the other, he declares that he now deems it "more humane, more heavenly, first / By winning words to conquer willing hearts, / And make persuasion do the work of fear" (*PR* 1.221–23).

In testing Jesus, Satan adjusts the temptations to different notions of what earthly kingship might entail. The first overt temptation after Satan's preliminary encounter with Jesus—the banquet of book 2—is a temptation that Milton interpolates into the text, for the biblical texts do not speak of Satan setting a banquet before Jesus. Satan has already addressed the issue of Jesus' hunger when he tempts him in book 1 to turn the stones into bread. However, the temptation of the banquet, though ostensibly designed to make Jesus break his fast, deals covertly with a larger issue directly concerned with the kingly state to which Jesus might aspire. The lavish offering that Satan sets before the Son of God is a feast for a king, and it is presented with the trappings and perks suitable for the kingly state, a state notably enjoyed in England by Charles II and in France by Louis XIV, the Sun King. The symbol is the royal table, a "Table richly spread, in *regal mode,* / With dishes pil'd, and meats of noblest sort / And savor, Beasts of chase, or Fowl of game" (*PR* 2.340–42; my italics). This is the kind of feast that might have been set before Charles himself after one of his hunts. Not only is there abundant food, but also royal luxury; the attendants are sexually appealing stripling youths and nymphs—the very "Ladies of th' *Hesperides*" (*PR* 2.357), who might have appealed to Charles II. Milton had predicted in *The Ready and Easy Way* that just such luxury and expense as Satan lavishly presents to the Son would follow upon a restored monarchy. When Milton has Jesus refuse Satan's banquet—"Thy pompous Delicacies I contemn" (*PR* 2.390)—he is also implicitly critiquing the lifestyle of the monarch who was on the throne of England.

Still in the royal mode is the next temptation—to acquire riches and that which pertains to wealth—"Honor, Friends, Conquests, and Realms" (2.422), the sort of wealth that Satan specifically implies that Herod and Antipater possess, and which Milton obliquely implies also pertains to the kingly state in England. Riches pave the way to a throne, Satan tells Jesus, while "Virtue, Valor, Wisdom sit in want" (2.431). Jesus astutely replies that power is impotent without virtue, valor, and wisdom to guide those in authority, another telling criticism of *Realpolitik* as it was being practiced in England. With a certain stoicism, Milton seems to imply that it is not necessarily those who wear a crown who are the most kingly. If virtue does not attend on the king, then the virtuous man, who rules himself, is more truly a king—"To know, and knowing worship God aright" (*PR* 2.475), to govern "the inner man, the nobler part" (2.477) and thereby "to guide Nations in the way of truth / By saving Doctrine" (2.473–74).[26] The work of a "king" is made to resemble that of a Socratic teacher, the philosopher king of Plato's republic. Besides, as Jesus enigmatically adds, "to give a Kingdom hath been thought / Greater and nobler done, and to lay down / Far more magnanimous, then to assume" (*PR* 2.481–83).

The aim of an early modern king was the aggrandizement of his state. On the Continent, Louis XIV was busy trying to annex the Spanish Netherlands and lay claim to the Spanish throne. Charles II was defending England's interests in the Dutch wars. Both could argue that the classical model for kingship involves the kind of military conquest that would enhance the kingly image as well as enlarge the kingdom's domain. Milton begins book 3 with Satan's attempt to revive in Jesus' heart aspiration to "victorious deeds" and "heroic acts." He sets before him a line-up of classical warriors and generals—Alexander, Scipio, Pompey, and Julius Caesar—ancient models that royal encomiasts had traditionally used, particularly in the Renaissance, to flatter princes. Satan employs them here to tempt Jesus to flex his royal muscles. Some of these very types Dryden names in *Annus Mirabilis* as he describes how Charles II plans his campaign against the Dutch. In justifying Charles's undertaking of the wars against the Dutch, Dryden recalls how Rome had responded when Carthage had threatened Rome's ships. Like Scipio, Charles must quell a dangerous neighbor. Ever judicious, Charles reluctantly responds to his subjects' call for war, finally gathering his warships to set forth. As the expedition is about to sail, Dryden points out how one star, "that bright companion of the sun," smiles on the enterprise, even as once its "glorious aspect seal'd our new-born king" (*Annus Mirabilis*, 69–70). Dryden cannot miss the opportunity once more to remember the star of Charles's birth and to compare Charles II and Christ.

For the Son, glory signifies something different from setting forth on a military expedition. Jesus sets Satan straight about attributing glory to "things not glorious, men not worthy of fame" (*PR* 3.70). The very warriors that political encomiasts such as Dryden were so eager to place before us as exemplars of honor are the ones Jesus censures as "scarce men, / Rolling in brutish Vices, and deform'd" (*PR* 3.85–86). Milton here indicts not only the ambitious conquerors themselves but also the kind of jockeying for political power and prestige that Dryden praises in *Annus Mirabilis*. The impulse to "count it glorious to subdue / By Conquest" (*PR* 3.71–72) that Jesus censures would apply not only to Alexanders and Caesars and their undertakings, but also to Louis XIV's ambitions to conquer Spain and the Netherlands as well as to those of his cousin Charles II to put down Dutch ambitions.

Yet the larger issue of the Son's future kingdom remains both for him and for Satan. It was the announcement by John the Baptist that the Messiah's future kingdom was at hand that spurred Satan to tempt Jesus in the first place. Now Satan tests Jesus by suggesting that he needs strategic military assistance to attain it, reminding him that "to a Kingdom thou art born, ordain'd / To sit upon thy Father *David's* throne" (*PR* 3.152–53). It is not Satan, but Jesus, who first alludes to David and the throne: "the Shepherd lad, / Whose offspring on the Throne of *Judah* sat / So many Ages, and shall yet regain / That seat, and reign in *Israel* without end" (*PR* 2.439–42). But there is a difference between Jesus' and Satan's perception of the Davidic kingship. Jesus praises a lowly boy raised to a throne; Satan praises a powerful king who maintains his kingdom though military might. Therefore, when Satan at last alludes to David, he slyly turns Jesus' praise of David about, implying that if Jesus is to ascend to David's throne he must, like his warlike predecessors, use requisite military power. The Jewish hero, Judas Maccabaeus, like Jesus, went into the desert alone but returned with an army. Jesus' reply is ambiguous: he does not deny the kingdom he is destined to rule, but he does defer his active pursuit of it. Indeed, in deferring his pursuit of kingship, he implies that he must first be tried in lowly state. For readers, the reference to lowly state might seem merely an allusion to Jesus' future ministry as a teacher. But inevitably this reference to trial in lowly state also points to a paradigm with which we are familiar. For so David was first tried, and so also, as the preachers who welcomed Charles back from exile suggest, was Charles in his continental exile.

The temptation of the kingdoms that follows in the final books of *Paradise Regain'd* must be read on multiple levels. Based on the texts in Matthew 4:8–10 and Luke 4:5–8, which recount how Satan took Jesus up to a high mountain to offer him the kingdoms of the world, these temptations might be interpreted as no more than satanic ploys to make Jesus forsake obedience to God for worldly power. But Milton does not simply allude in general to the kingdoms of the earth. He chooses specific kingdoms, and in choosing Parthia and Rome as the exemplars for power, Milton is attentive to several subtexts. One of these necessarily involves the millenarian prophecies that were being revived in the late 1660s. According to the millenarians, the prophecy in Daniel that foretold the Messiah's kingship stated that four kingdoms must fall before the Messiah could assume the fifth as his own and begin the thousand-year reign on earth that Revelation 20:1–4 promises.[27] The first three kingdoms are the Assyrian, the Persian or Babylonian, and the Greek—kingdoms that once composed the Parthia that Satan offers to Jesus. The fourth is Rome, the kingdom Satan offers Jesus after Jesus has rejected Parthia. Three of these kingdoms have already fallen, and Satan, himself knowing the prophecy, tempts Jesus to destroy the fourth—Rome—and begin his reign. But Jesus, who also is attentive to the prophecy, does not wish to anticipate a reign that is not yet forthcoming: "my time...is not yet come" (*PR* 3.396–97), he tells Satan. And here Milton is pointing to the millenarianism of his own time. For, according to seventeenth century millenarians, the Rome of Daniel's prophecy was not the ancient Roman Empire, but contemporary papal Rome. As Jesus has no doubt realized at this point, he is not to ascend to David's throne at his first, but at his Second Coming.[28]

If the millenarian subtext impacts upon Jesus' refusal to anticipate his ascent to David's throne, it also relates to his refusal to deliver "[his] brethren...the Ten Tribes" (*PR* 3.403). The Son's denial of his brethren is not absolute but conditional. He describes the Jews of his time as "impenitent" and "distinguishable scarce / From Gentiles but by Circumcision vain" (*PR* 3.423–25). Looking ahead, Jesus allows that in the future his countrymen might return "repentant and sincere" (*PR* 3.435). Milton is covertly referring to the return of the Jews to Jerusalem immediately before the institution of the millennium, when the Messiah will assume that much-awaited kingship that Milton in *The Ready and Easy Way* had contrasted with the spurious reign of the about-to-be-restored Charles.

There is another meaning to this passage. At first, Milton seems only to be alluding to the Jews who after the captivity forsook the God of their forefathers and betrayed their ancient patrimony. To deliver such people, Jesus states, would be futile, for, though freed, they would continue to devote themselves to idol worship, "Unhumbl'd, unrepentant, unreform'd" (*PR* 3.429). However, the accusation could also apply to the English, who had so often in the

1650s and 1660s been equated with the Jews. In *The Ready and Easy Way* Milton had warned his fellow citizens of returning to the idol of kingship from which they had been delivered. Moreover, this is not the only time in *Paradise Regain'd* that Milton under the veil of another name indicts the English for backsliding. Jesus' harsh description at the beginning of book 3 of the crowd as "a herd confus'd, / A miscellaneous rabble, who extol / Things vulgar" (*PR* 3.49–51) could have contemporary resonance. Similarly, Jesus' denunciation of the Roman people in book 4 recalls Milton's comparison of the English in *The Second Defense of the English People* to the "ancient Romans, wasted by excess, and enervated by luxury" (837). When Satan tempts Jesus to free the Roman people, Jesus indicts them for ambition, vanity, cruelty, and luxury: "Luxurious by thir wealth, and greedier still, / And from the daily Scene effeminate" (*PR* 4.141–42). "What wise and valiant man," he queries, "would seek to free / These thus degenerate, by themselves enslav'd, / Or could of inward slaves make outward free?" (*PR* 4.143–45). In this context the Romans, like the Jews, serve as stand-ins for the English.

If Milton is denouncing in *Paradise Regain'd* the slackness of the English in forsaking the commonwealth for monarchy, he is also indicting the monarchy itself for its dependence on corrupt policies and its attempt to settle disputes with its neighbors through force of arms. Once more Dryden's *Annus Mirabilis* gives us indirect insight into how England was managing the political issues of the time and how a ruler through his royal poet could manipulate public opinion. As he describes the Dutch war, Dryden works hard to turn a dodgy military enterprise into a glorious undertaking. In actuality the victories of the Dutch war that he glorifies did not lead to victory; England had to negotiate a peace with the Dutch. Nonetheless, Dryden in the first half of the poem makes it seem as though the English will win the war through those victories that Monk and Prince Rupert had actually narrowly achieved. Dryden dramatizes the battles Rupert and Monk waged and glamorizes how English weakness (their inferior forces as compared to the Dutch fleet) impelled Rupert and Monk to greater exertions.

Monk is compared to Scipio intent on defeating the Carthaginians whom he had once before tamed (*Annus Mirabilis*, 197–200). As the fleet appears to take on the Dutch, Rupert is compared both to a new Messiah and a Joshua leading his troops (453–54, 471–72). Moreover, it is God who is directing the fight, keeping the English safe, as he once kept "Israel safe from the Egyptian's pride" (367). The military strategy the English employ resembles in some way that which Satan advocates in *Paradise Regain'd*. Just as Monk and Rupert engage Sweden as an ally in an effort to defeat the Dutch, so Satan proposes that Jesus should secure Parthia's aid to defeat Rome. Milton critiques both the kind of strategy that Dryden praises and the view that the pursuit of arms is a worthy endeavor. The "luggage of war" (*PR* 3.401), as Jesus astutely points out, is an argument of human weakness rather than strength. In *A Treatise of Civil Power* Milton makes a similar point when he cites Jesus' refusal to advance his kingdom through force (847).

Book 4 of *Paradise Regain'd* takes us to Rome and Athens and finally to Jerusalem, cities that could be and had been compared with the London of Milton's time. In one way or another all these cities represent paradigms of power and prestige. Ostensibly, as the devil shows Jesus Rome and Athens or even as he takes him to the pinnacle of the temple in Jerusalem, he is tempting the Son of God to assert his power, indeed his kingship over one or all of these realms. Moreover, as we view in turn Rome, Athens, and Jerusalem, their likenesses and their differences from London and from one another become apparent. For in one way or another the London of Milton's time was emulating all three, its citizens having been compared by Milton and others to the Romans, the Athenians, and the Jews. By choosing and describing these cities as the kingdoms Satan sets before Jesus, Milton poses for us the question how they not only resemble London but also how London might appear had it been governed by the Son of God as king and not the son of Charles I.

Let us first consider Rome, described by Milton as though it were a composite of the ancient and the Renaissance city and perhaps a model for the new London after the Great Fire. The commission headed by Christopher Wren and Robert Hooke that Charles II assigned the task of reconstructing London after the fire took baroque cities such as Renaissance Rome as the model for the new London. Both of these men had traveled on the Continent and were impressed that cities like Rome and Paris had cast off their medieval wooden buildings and narrow streets to rebuild in brick and stone, thereby emulating classical design. In the imperial era Caesar Augustus had ordained that Rome should be rebuilt in marble. With his advisers Charles envisioned an imperial plan, widening London's streets, including squares and improvising monuments, such as the one Wren actually designed to commemorate the fire. The rebuilding of St. Paul's Cathedral was to be the crowning achievement, and though it was not to be completed until years after Milton's and indeed Charles's deaths, it had been designed even in the 1660s as a Renaissance rather than a Gothic structure. Its dome, when completed, would vie with the Pantheon's or with St. Peter's in Rome.[29] Along with these ambitious architectural plans went a classical mindset that advanced the imperial values of the Restoration over the republican principles of the commonwealth era. Once more Milton was seeing Charles the King advanced over Christ the King.

In describing and praising Rome, Milton imitates a well-known Renaissance poetic form, the city ode. He puts into the devil's mouth a poetic encomium of Rome's architectural wonders, its institutions, and its people, together with praise of Jesus as the new prince, who might replace Tiberius:[30]

> The City which thou seest no other deem
> Than great and glorious *Rome*, Queen of the Earth
> So far renown'd...
>
> ....
>
>   there the Capitol thou seest,
> Above the rest lifting his stately head
> On the *Tarpeian rock*, her Citadel
> Impregnable, and there Mount *Palatine*
> Th'Imperial Palace, compass huge, and high
> The Structure, skill of noblest Architects,
> With gilded battlements, conspicuous far,

>Turrets and Terraces, and glittering Spires.
>Many a fair Edifice besides, more like
>Houses of Gods.   (*PR* 4.44–56)

Along with praise of Rome's monuments and people, Satan lauds Rome's preeminence in "Civility of Manners, Arts, and Arms" (4.83), presenting a value system that is based upon material display and outer grandeur and magnificence.

It is no surprise that Jesus should deconstruct the devil's praise, challenging the very premises on which Rome's so-called eminence is based: "Nor doth this grandeur and majestic show / Of luxury, though call'd magnificence, /... allure mine eye, / Much less my mind" (*PR* 4.110–13). Jesus refuses to value what seems to him only lavish consumption and superficial display. Calling Satan's praise of Rome to account, the Son points out that Satan's view of excellence overpraises human pursuits and human achievement and fails to take into account divine authority and inner vision. On the basic level Milton is here juxtaposing classical and Christian values, the classical placing Man and not God at the center of a value system, the Christian looking to the relationship of Man and God. Yet it is not only classical civilization that Milton calls to account in the Son's denunciation of the luxury, consumption, and superficial display of classical Rome, but also the London of Charles II in which the king was promoting the very values that Satan has lauded and the Son has critiqued. Clearly, Charles II was hoping to rebuild London as a new Rome.

As he offers Rome to the Son, Satan has not left unnoted the deficiencies of Rome's ruler Tiberius and the desirability of the Son replacing him:

>This Emperor hath no Son, and now is old,
>Old, and lascivious, and from *Rome* retir'd
>To *Capreae*, an Island small but strong
>On the *Campanian* shore, with purpose there
>His horrid lusts in private to enjoy,
>Committing to a wicked Favorite
>All public cares, and yet of him suspicious,
>Hated of all, and hating. With what ease,

> Endu'd with Regal Virtues as thou art,
> Appearing, and beginning noble deeds,
> Might'st thou expel this monster from his Throne.   (*PR* 4.90–100)

Assuredly, the reigning king of England was no Tiberius, but certain resemblances between the two are obvious. Like Tiberius, Charles "hath no Son," and in court and in retirement enjoyed what might be called "horrid lusts" (*PR* 4.90, 94). Moreover, in 1667 Charles had agreed to the impeachment and banishment of his experienced adviser, the Earl of Clarendon, and appointed to a comparable office George Villiers, the second Duke of Buckingham, a companion since youth, who had indulged the king's excesses, a man whom Milton might well have designated "a wicked favorite" (4.95).[31] There is enough in Milton's description of Tiberius's court to remind many how the corruption of ancient Rome was being replicated in the Caroline court of the 1660s.

Although he rejects both Parthia and Rome, Jesus does not deny kingship itself, but as the heir of David lays claim to a kingdom that will transcend both and displace all the corrupt tyrannies of the world,

> Know therefore when my season comes to sit
> On *David's* Throne, it shall be like a tree
> Spreading and overshadowing all the Earth,
> Or as a stone that shall to pieces dash
> All Monarchies besides throughout the world,
> And of my Kingdom there shall be no end.   (*PR* 4.146–51)

The texts that underlie this passage are drawn from Daniel and are millenarian in implication. The tree (Dan. 4:10–12) is symbolic of the Son's everlasting kingdom predicted in Daniel 2:44, and the stone (Dan. 2:31–35) is the means by which the Son will destroy all other kingdoms and which itself will grow to a mountain as a kingdom will fill all the earth.[32] Undergirding these millenarian texts from the Old Testament is a prophecy not yet written in Jesus' time, the passage in Revelation 20:1–4 that predicts the Son's assumption of kingship at the millennium. Therefore, although Milton's readers would understand the allusion to Revelation's prediction of the Son's future kingship, the Satan of *Paradise Regain'd* would be wholly in the dark. Moreover, Milton's Jesus declines to enlighten him: "Means there shall be to this, but what the means, / Is not for thee to know, nor me to tell" (*PR* 4.152–53).

The temptation of Athens is not directly connected to the offer of the worldly kingdoms represented by Rome and Parthia. For these, Milton, following the texts of Matthew and Luke, had clear biblical precedent, and Jesus firmly refuses Satan's usurped dominions as blasphemous offers (*PR* 4.170–94). But when Satan, fixing his airy microscope on "*Athens,* the eye of *Greece,* Mother of Arts / And Eloquence" (*PR* 4.240–41), praises classical knowledge—the eloquence of Athenian philosophers and orators, the charm of Greece's lyric poets, the power of Homeric verse, and the teachings of "lofty grave Tragedians" (4.261)—he is offering a different perk of royal rule. In one way, Jesus' refusal of classical knowledge is predictable, for Jesus has refused all of Satan's previous offers. However, the issue is slightly different here. Satan presents Athens as a kingdom of the mind, a desirable supplement, so he pleads, to the wisdom in biblical scripture:

> Be famous then
> By wisdom; as thy Empire must extend,
> So let extend thy mind o'er all the world,
> In knowledge, all things in it comprehend.   (*PR* 4.221–24)

The real issue becomes not a question of kingdom or power but that of classical versus biblical values.

In recovering the poetic legacy of Greece and Rome during the fifteenth and sixteenth centuries, humanists on the Continent had constructed a man-centered rather than a God-centered poetics. They had often, like the classical poets, lauded princes as the new Caesars, the equals only of Jove on earth. With the Restoration of Charles II, the classicism of the Continent was being imported into England by the king, who had spent his youth in France, and by the poets who were praising him. In France, classicism had reigned supreme in the sixteenth century with poets such as Pierre de Ronsard and his imitators. In the seventeenth century, dramatists such as Pierre Corneille and Jean Racine had imitated classical drama. Critics such as Nicolas Boileau had lauded classical poetics, and court poets such as John Dryden had in turn praised Boileau.[33] During the commonwealth period, Milton had begun to construct a biblically based poetics, producing one biblical epic and now in the late 1660s composing another. With *Samson Agonistes,* which would be printed with *Paradise Regain'd,* Milton was revising classical tragedy into an apocalyptic model. Also, turning in the 1650s from lyrical poetry based on classical models to Hebraically inspired poetry, Milton had translated the Psalms, not Horace, into English. Jesus' preference for Hebraic hymns and the psalms seems to echo Milton's own predilections: "*Sion's* songs, to all true tastes excelling, / Where God is prais'd aright" (*PR* 4.347–48). Milton's aim in the Athens passage in *Paradise Regain'd* was not to add one more kingdom for the Son of God to reject, but to grasp the opportunity to expand on his own biblically based poetics. Milton wished to counter the poetics that was then being trumpeted by Restoration poets such as Dryden, where the principal aim is to enhance and protect the reputation of kings, such as Charles II. Biblical poetry does not flatter rulers but praises God. Biblical prophets do not expound philosophic theories of government, but investigate the divine principles that should guide those who govern. Therefore, as his final commentary on classicism, Milton has Jesus juxtapose Roman and Greek orators and Hebraic prophets. Jesus extols the prophets as "men divinely taught," who better than classical orators teach "The solid rules of Civil Government" (*PR* 4.357–58).

> In them is plainest taught, and easiest learnt,
> What makes a Nation happy, and keeps it so,
> What ruins Kingdoms, and lays Cities flat;
> These only, with our Law, best form a King.   (*PR* 4.361–64)

In this passage, Milton reiterates a view of kingship that he had expounded during the Interregnum. Rulers must be responsible to higher authorities, both to the wisest and best advisers of the nation and to God and his Scriptures. Not able to counter directly the ideology of the government led by Charles II, Milton indirectly teaches lessons of responsible kingship, which ultimately had their model in the kingdom that would be ruled by Christ.

In the survey of models for London, there is one more city to consider—Jerusalem. If the London that was being rebuilt could be lauded as the new Rome, or if the literary London that emulated Greek and Latin literature could be a new Athens, then modern London could also be considered a new Jerusalem. However, this name for London had more often been espoused by Puritans than by royalists. In 1641–42, the Puritans who assumed control of Parliament proclaimed that Babylon had fallen and that the new Jerusalem or Sion was rising in its place.[34] In *Areopagitica* Milton had envisioned London as a new Jerusalem, the city that Moses, looking down from heaven, might see rising in the place of the ancient Hebraic capital (744). The English people of this period were building their nation in its image; they were metaphorically reconstructing the temple that had been destroyed in Jerusalem by the Romans. But with the restoration of Charles II, plans for the new Jerusalem had been thwarted.

When Satan sets Jesus on the pinnacle of the temple in Jerusalem and Jesus stands while Satan falls, it is a deeply symbolic moment. Its implication extends beyond the testing of God or the Son of God that the incident as described in Matthew and Luke suggests. Michael Lieb has rightly called the temptation of the pinnacle a theophanic moment that confirms the Son's sacrificial office and prepares for his Passion, death, Resurrection, and Ascension. Clearly his standing confirms his divinity and results in a victory over Satan, who "smitten with amazement" falls (*PR* 4.562).[35] However, the Son's standing, as I have argued previously, also presages his defeat of Satan at the millennium with his assumption of earthly kingship. As such it has a contemporary application for modern London as the new Jerusalem. When Christ the King will come to the throne, he will defeat the tyrant kings who reign through Satan's power. As Jesus symbolically breaks Satan's power when he stands and Satan falls, so, Milton implies, will the Son defeat earthly monarchies when he becomes king. Those monarchies would include the Stuart monarchy. However, even if the new Jerusalem is not achieved in the 1660s and 1670s in England's green and pleasant land, the victory of Jesus on the pinnacle assures its eventual establishment. With this vision, Milton offers an alternative to the rule of Charles II and his heirs and an affirmation of Christ's kingship.

In 1685 after Charles II's death, poets remembered the star of his birth and the prophecy that he would be a messianic ruler. In "Threnodia Augustalis," Dryden lauded Charles both as a classical hero and a Christian king. The printer Henry Playford put out a volume of eulogies for Charles with pindarics by Aphra Behn, Francis Fane, Edmund Arwaker, and Nahum Tate. Comparing Charles's passing to Christ's, Aphra Behn lamented, "That such a *Monarch!* such a *God* should dye!" (2.6).[36] Edmund Arwaker announced the king's apotheosis, describing how the father Charles welcomes the son Charles into heaven. Such extravagances simply proved that Charles II's propaganda machine was still in place.

However, in 1671 when *Paradise Regain'd* appeared, Milton had had his own say about kingship. Although the free discourse he had earlier enjoyed as a pamphleteer had been curtailed, Milton in his poem could challenge the images of kingship that had been set forward during the Restoration era for Charles II. He could once more speak forth on the subject of kingship, shattering, as he constructs Jesus' replies to Satan, one by one the false idols of power and prestige and promoting in their place a redeemed view of kingship. Thus *Paradise Regain'd* affords Milton the opportunity to reaffirm the political positions of the 1640s and 1650s: both to speak out against the false icon of kingship and to set up the true image of the king that the returned Son will eventually erect.

10 ⤳ From Last Things to First
The Apophatic Vision of *Paradise Regain'd*

Michael Bryson

1. *The Visionary Mode*

How can a poet write God? How can *anyone*—even a poet who doubles as a theologian—describe the indescribable? Milton struggles with this in his *De doctrina Christiana*, attempting to describe God in terms of such ideas as may be found in the Scriptures; however, he is emphatic in pointing out—as a kind of preface or qualification to all that follows, that "God, as he really is, is far beyond man's imagination, let alone his understanding."[1] If God is beyond imagination, let alone understanding, how can he be represented at all, much less *represented accurately* in literary form? The key to this question lies in Milton's single most iconoclastic character—the human Jesus (more often referred to as the Son), in *Paradise Regain'd*.

In an attempt to understand Milton's use of this character, I propose that we read both *Paradise Lost* and *Paradise Regain'd* as examples of what Michael Lieb calls the "visionary mode." In his book of the same name, Lieb begins by carefully analyzing the vision of Ezekiel, finding in its imagery and logic that the visionary mode is a way of representing, if not bridging, the gap between God-with-qualities and God-without-qualities, what Lieb refers to as the *ma'aseh bereshit* and the *ma'aseh merk-abah*—roughly, the "lore of creation" and the "lore of the chariot" (shorthand for the knowable and unknowable God). According to Lieb, Ezekiel presents the reader with a veritable textbook of the mechanics and techniques of Western mystical thought, and the deconstructive relation of that thought to the traditions within which it stands:

> [Ezekiel's] vision simply refuses to be domesticated. Emerging from a rich and complex milieu of traditional source material, the vision ultimately subverts its own lineage.... The vision is conceptualized in such a way so as at once to suggest associations with identifi-able objects and at the same time to undermine those associations at every point.[2]

Lieb's crucial point here is that Ezekiel's vision—as a pattern of the visionary mode itself—is contextualized, that it comes from a long and complex tradition. But, grounded in that tradition though it may be, it contests the tradition, questions its categories, images, and assumptions even as it uses them in the contestation and questioning. The associations the visionary mode relies upon are at the very same time the associations it undermines. The vision-ary mode, as Lieb will argue, is a deconstructive reading of the symbols and narratives of the tradition within which the vision appears.

Lieb goes on to demonstrate that the visionary mode uses the motif of ascent through the known categories and objects of this world, to the unknown, and unknowable in strictly human terms, divine itself. One of the most famous examples of this ascent motif is to be found in the work of Pseudo-Dionysius. As Lieb argues, "Pseudo-Dionysius maintains that [cataphatic, or positive, the-ology] embodies a descent from first things to last, that is, from the most abstruse conceptions of deity to their concretization in symbolic form," while its necessary complement, apophatic (or negative) theology, "involves a return or *epistroph*" upward from last to first things. In this return we discover an obliteration of knowing, understanding, naming, speech, and language as the seer travels into the realm of unknowing, divine ignorance, the nameless, the speechless, and the silent" (*Visionary*, 236–37).

Pseudo-Dionysius's method, most notably as embodied in the works *The Divine Names* and *The Mystical Theology*, is to move from the knowable "God"—knowable because conceived in and through human terms—to the unknowable God which cannot be described, and finally cannot be grasped at all except through negation, in other words, except through the refusal of description. The movement is from a figure identifiable in terms of a name, a set of characteristics, a history of actions and interactions, to a figure without figuration, a blank, an absence of characteristics, an ahistorical, nonactive, and noninteractive hidden and unimaginable no-thing. But as Lieb explains, Pseudo-Dionysius proceeds along this path in two ways: directly from affirmation to negation (as demonstrated in *The Divine Names* and *The Mystical Theology*), but also *indirectly* toward negation through a paradoxically heightened (and exaggerated) form of affirmation. It is this latter method (as discussed in *The Celestial Hierarchy*) that provides a particularly powerful lens through which to see Milton's use of his characterizations of the divine. As Lieb writes,

> [In *The Celestial Hierarchy*] Pseudo-Dionysius...distinguish[es] two modes of revelation in the Bible. Corresponding to his cataphatic and apophatic views of mystical theology, these modes articulate a theoretics of scriptural interpretation. Whereas the first mode "proceeds naturally through sacred images in which like represents like," the second mode uses "formulations which are dissimilar and even entirely inadequate and ridiculous."...According to this [second] mode, the Deity is manifested through "dissimilar shapes" that embody an essential paradox: the more *unlike* God and the celestial realms they appear to be, the more they lead us to a knowledge of the unknowable....We are to read...apophatically by distancing

ourselves from, indeed denying (*aphairesis*), "the sheer crassness of
the signs" in order to understand what the signs truly signify. This is
essentially a deconstructive reading. (*Visionary*, 240).

In Pseudo-Dionysius's terms, such "crassness" is "a goad so that
even the materially inclined cannot accept that it could be permit-
ted or true that the celestial and divine sights could be conveyed
by such shameful things." The exaggerated, crass quality of the
images used to represent "the celestial and divine" are designed
paradoxically to focus attention away from the images themselves,
the "last things" of cataphatic (positive) theology, and toward the
negations of such concrete conceptions of the divine, toward the
"first things" of apophatic (negative) theology. Visual and other
representations of deity serve a necessary function as "types for the
typeless, for giving shape to what is actually without shape." Why
are such types and shapes needed? Because, according to Pseudo-
Dionysius, even the best of us "lack the ability to be directly raised
up to conceptual contemplations." At most, even the best of us
(in terms of intellectual capacity and philosophical/metaphysical
learning) can be led only to brief glimpses and momentary insights
of the realities toward which our symbols merely gesture. More
to the point, however, is that most of us are *not* the best of us
(most of us, after all, are neither Plato nor Plotinus, neither Proclus
nor Pseudo-Dionysius), and from that majority of us "it is most
fitting...that the sacred and hidden truth about the celestial intel-
ligences be concealed." "Knowledge," Pseudo-Dionysius argues,
"is not for everyone."[3]

But this highest knowledge, as Pseudo-Dionysius argues, is hid-
den behind both the images of the biblical texts and the interpretive
traditions through which worshippers encounter and understand
them. These images, texts, and traditions are actually what stand
between worshippers and the recognition that they do not, and can-
not, know God except, in the formulation of Paul, "through a glass,
darkly" (1 Cor. 13:12). The Pauline insight is also the Dionysian
insight: the only possible knowledge of this God is "the *knowledge
of his unknowability*."[4]

The Pauline and Dionysian insight is also, finally, the Miltonic insight. Just as Pseudo-Dionysius's method of scriptural interpretation is, in Lieb's terms, "a deconstructive reading," so also, I contend, is Milton's poetic rendering of deity.[5] Milton's portrayal of God is "a deconstructive reading" of the divine. This deconstructive reading, with its use of dissimilar and crass shapes and signs, is part and parcel of the visionary mode's simultaneous use and contestation of the images and concepts of the tradition within which it works. In using "dissimilar shapes" as representations of the divine, Milton is trusting his "fit audience...though few"[6] to understand the significance of "the sheer crassness of the signs" he uses in his great poems, to understand his own simultaneous use and contestation of the images and concepts of the tradition within which he is writing and they are reading. His poems were not then, and are not now directed to all, but to a few. For Milton, as for Pseudo-Dionysius, knowledge is not for everyone.

2. *Milton's Dynamic of First Things and Last Things*

Milton's works, like the Son's rejections of Satan's temptations in *Paradise Regain'd*, are strongly infused with a dynamic of moving from last things to first things, a dynamic often illustrated as a movement from external to internal values and motivations. In order to understand what is at stake in *Paradise Regain'd*, it is necessary to understand the relationship between *Paradise Lost* and *Paradise Regain'd*, keeping in mind what exactly has been lost and regained. What is this "Paradise" that Adam and Eve lose and that Jesus (the Son) regains? There is an equivalency at work: a one-to-one correspondence is being suggested in the logic of the titles and the structure of the works. Each work features a temptation by Satan. In *Paradise Lost*, that temptation is successful, first with Eve, then soon afterward with Adam. In *Paradise Regain'd*, the temptation is a failure, as the Son rejects and even scorns Satan's blandishments. At the core of each temptation is an appeal to identify oneself with power, with knowledge, with divinity itself, but each of these things is considered, and offered, as a thing external to the one tempted. In Eve's case, she is promised all these things as a direct result of eating the fruit of the tree of knowledge:

> he knows that in the day
> Ye Eat thereof, your Eyes that seem so clear,
> Yet are but dim, shall perfetly be then
> Open'd and clear'd, and ye shall be as Gods,
> Knowing both Good and Evil, as they know.   (*PL* 9.705–09)

Satan portrays this knowledge—and the power that comes with it—along with divine similitude (being as Gods) as an effect of the fruit itself; he even implies that "the Gods" themselves get their knowledge and power and divinity from their food: "And what are Gods, that Man may not become / As they, participating God-like food?" (*PL* 9.716–17). In doing so, Satan is cleverly trying to cultivate the seeds of this same idea that were earlier planted by Raphael, when he tells Adam and Eve, while dining with them, that "from these corporal nutriments perhaps / Your bodies may at last turn all to spirit, / Improv'd by tract of time, and wing'd ascend / Ethereal as wee" (*PL* 5.496–99). Raphael ties this suggestion of physical transformation and attainment of "Ethereal" (divine) status to obedience ("If ye be found obedient" [*PL* 5.501]), an idea that Satan conveniently elides in his version. The elision highlights, however, the *external* nature of the idea Raphael introduces. Raphael conceives of both the effect of the "corporal nutriments" and the effect of being "found obedient" as physical, external transformations. Food is ingested from outside the self. Obedience is offered to a figure outside the self. Ethereal status (as near as Raphael comes to the idea of divine similitude) is something to be achieved, grasped for, taken into oneself from outside, and/or conferred on oneself from outside. It is these external mechanics that Satan highlights in his temptations of both Eve in *Paradise Lost* and Jesus in *Paradise Regain'd*.

What is lost, then, in *Paradise Lost* is a focus on divine similitude, a connection to the divine source of all things that is always already there in Eve and Adam. Satan (with a little help from

Raphael, and by extension, from the Father) is able to focus both Eve and Adam on externals—for Eve, knowledge as a means to gain a greater place in a hierarchy of two, and for Adam, the potential loss of Eve—and, in so doing, manages to pluck paradise, the "paradise within" (12.587), right out of the human pair's hearts. Paradise had always been within. Eden was merely a place, a wondrous and lovely place to be sure, but it was not, in and of itself, "paradise." *Paradise Lost* is not a narrative of the loss of Eden, but of the loss of the "paradise within," the sense of divine similitude, the realization of connection to all things and to the source of all things. *Paradise Lost* is a narrative of descent, and of a loss of focus on first things. *Paradise Regain'd* is a narrative of ascent, of a reclamation of the "paradise within," of a restoration of the focus on first things through a successful rejection of the temptations to focus on externals and last things.

It is in this dynamic of ascent and descent, in a tension between a focus on first things and a focus on last things that *Paradise Regain'd*, through its human protagonist Jesus, comes brilliantly to light. The contest between the Son and Satan is precisely a contest between first things and last things, and understood in this way, none of the things that Satan offers the Son is, in itself, problematic. It is as if each of the temptations is its own text, a text that, according to Lieb, "reveals more about the interpreter than the interpreter reveals about the text" (*Visionary*, 240). In offering food, wealth, power, knowledge, Satan offers things which are fine in themselves, but he offers them as "last things," as ends in themselves. The Son's rejections constantly focus the issue back on first things, on ascent to the origin of all.

Satan's temptations, modeled on the temptation sequence from Luke 4:1–13 and Matthew 4:1–11, form a kind of circle, as if they were an attempt to replicate a full cycle of ascent and descent all on their own. But that circle or cycle is an illusion, a trick of light and shade that Satan uses in an attempt to deceive the Son, who will have none of it. The temptations Satan places before the Son run from that of bread and divine identity (a temptation to use

divine power to transform stones into bread), to the more physi-
cally elaborate temptation of gourmet delicacies, to wealth, politi-
cal and military power, knowledge, and finally the temptation
to prove—through a display of divine power—his identity. The
appearance is of a descent from temptations that focus on divine
power and identity through the realms of physical and worldly
powers and an ascent back to the realm of divine power and iden-
tity. But each temptation is actually the *same* temptation pre-
sented in a different guise. Each temptation is designed to trick
the Son into identifying himself with, and through, externals and
a focus on last things. All of Satan's temptations are, as Stanley
Fish observes, "allied in their inferiority to an inner word and an
inward kingdom."[7] What the Son rejects are not the things (bread,
gourmet food, wealth, knowledge, even power) in themselves, but
the temptation of regarding them as ends. The Son's rejections of
each temptation relentlessly return the focus back to internals and
first things.

3. *The Temptations of Identity, Glory, and Power*

The first temptation, which seems the simplest in terms of
the physical object involved, sets the pattern for everything that
follows: "But if thou be the Son of God, Command / That out of
these hard stones be made thee bread" (*PR* 1.342–43). What could
be simpler, and more understandable, than the need to eat? And
what could be more basic to that need than bread? Bread, after all,
is a staple, the bottom-line necessity of a subsistence diet, hardly
a luxurious indulgence. But it is not the bread that is the point of
the temptation; rather, it is the *means of attaining* that bread. The
temptation here is one of identity and power—each of which will
run like a bright crimson thread through the tapestry of tempta-
tions that Satan weaves in a deceptively improvisational manner. *If
thou be the Son of God*—what Satan is testing here is not whether
or not the Son is hungry. Satan is not so banal as that. The test, and
the temptation, is an attempt to get the Son to show off. *Go ahead.
Show me who you* really *are. Give me a flash of that "heavenly"*

*power...*if *you are who they say you are.* There is something primal about Satan's approach here, something redolent of the battlefields of human life (physical and symbolic), something that is designed to raise the hackles of a lesser man and trick him into identifying his primary strength as an *external* strength: the ability to transform—through power of some kind—*external* objects.

The Son rejects—as he will throughout—Satan's external focus and instead refocuses the issue as one of internals, in this case, the true sustenance by "each Word / Proceeding from the mouth of God" (*PR* 1.349–50). He also gives evidence of his focus through his ability to see past external appearances to the exact nature of his tempter. Satan, having not identified himself, and having disguised himself as "an aged man in Rural weeds" (*PR* 1.314), is easily seen through by the Son: "I discern thee other than thou seem'st" (1.348). In addition to seeing through Satan's *physical* disguise—something Uriel was unable to do in *Paradise Lost,* since such "Hypocrisy...walks / Invisible, except to God alone" (*PL* 3.683–84)—the Son also sees through Satan's *mental* disguise as someone who honestly does not know whether or not the man Jesus is the particular Son of God known only as "the Son" in *Paradise Lost.* Jesus cuts through this latter disguise—one that Satan may not be admitting to himself that he is donning until he is "smitten with amazement" (*PR* 4.562) much later—by confronting Satan directly: "Why does thou then suggest to me distrust, / Knowing who I am, as I know who thou art?" (1.355–56). The implications of this line are radical: if only God can see through hypocrisy's guise, and Jesus knows who this "aged man in Rural weeds" really is, then in some sense the Jesus of *Paradise Regain'd* is God. But in what sense? Here is where the temptation of *Paradise Regain'd* itself—and its corresponding modeling of how to resist that temptation—comes into play. Look past the external, the surface, and focus on the internal, the substance. What this means for the Son is a focus on connection to the divine, through a constant remembrance and realization of divine similitude.[8]

Where a focus on identity and power will be the thread that runs through all of Satan's temptations, it will be this focus on divine similitude that runs through all of the Son's rejections of temptation. Even when Satan is tempting the Son to identify himself with the glory and power of the Father, he is missing the point. It is not the trappings of glory and power through which divinity can be found; those things, in fact, are distractions, accidents, *externals*. The key to divine similitude, and thus to the Son's rejections of temptation, is to be found in the "inward oracle" (*PR* 1.403), the "spirit of truth" (1.402) that dwells within, as does "the Spirit, which is *internal, and the individual possession of every man*" (YP 6:587; emphasis added).

It is this "inward oracle," this "spirit of truth" from which the Son draws his strength to fight off Satan's temptations. Even after having given considerable thought, in 2.245–53, to the fact that he is *hungry after 40 days with no food* (a time span that can be life threatening), the Son rejects Satan's offer of

> A Table richly spread, in regal mode,
> With dishes pil'd, and meats of noblest sort
> And savor, Beasts of chase, or Fowl of game,
> In pastry built, or from the spit, or boil'd.   (*PR* 2.340–43)

He refuses even the smallest nibble, much less the opulence of the feast that has been spread before him "at a stately sideboard by the wine" (*PR* 2.350). Why? What could possibly be wrong with eating, especially after having fasted for 40 days? Nothing, in and of itself. The food is not the point; rather, it is the focus that Satan is trying to tempt the Son into adopting, a focus on the physical, the palpable, the external. Satan is trying, in each of his temptations, to get the Son to look outside of himself for the good, to focus on "last things" as if they were ends in themselves.

In rejecting Satan's bounty, the Son declares that he could himself "Command a Table in this Wilderness" (*PR* 2.384), but has not. Again, why? Earlier, in his private meditation on his hunger, he established a hierarchy of value that placed physical food beneath his "hung'ring more to do [his] Father's will" (*PR* 2.259). The "will" the character called "the Father" has expressed in *Paradise Regain'd* is that the Son "drive [Satan] back to Hell" (1.153), and "conquer Sin and Death" (1.159) as part of an overall effort to show Satan that he (the Father) "can produce a man / Of female Seed, far abler to resist" (1.150–51) than Adam turned out to have been, and to show future generations of humankind "from what consummate virtue I have chose / This perfect Man, by merit call'd my Son, / To earn Salvation for the Sons of men" (1.165–67).

This all sounds rather grand and showy, admirable to be sure, as far as, at least, the concern with "Salvation for the Sons of men" is concerned, but otherwise focused on public relations, on the Father's reputation. The opening phrase, "He now shall know," sounds interestingly like what might be said by a man planning a comeback from an earlier defeat: "I'll show him," in other words. There is a great deal, in fact, of showing in this statement. The Father will show Satan. The Father will show humankind. The Father, it seems, will show *everyone*. A more dramatic focus on external displays would be hard to shoehorn into a few short lines. The rest of the statement is couched in metaphors of war and combat, not out of character for the Father as a reader has come to know him from *Paradise Lost*, to be sure, but oddly out of place considering the dynamic that will develop in *Paradise Regain'd*. The Father imagines the Son "Winning by Conquest what the first man lost," but before he achieves this conquest, the Father means to "exercise him in the Wilderness" where the Son will "lay down the rudiments / Of his great warfare" (*PR* 1.154, 156–57).

With all this, is it merely conquest that is the "Father's will" the Son is hungering for, even more than he is hungering for food after a 40-day fast? Satan certainly seems to assume so. In fact, what Satan argues will be most likely to bend the mind of this man is glory. After Belial suggests that Satan "Set women in his eye and in his walk" (*PR* 2.153), Satan scoffs, insisting that it will take "manlier objects... /...such as have more show / Of worth, of honor, of glory, and popular praise" (*PR* 2.225–27). Is "the Father's will," then, glory? Satan argues as much after the temptation of wealth fails miserably. After sounding like Iago ("put money in thy purse") with his "Get Riches first, get Wealth, and Treasure heap" (*PR* 2.427), Satan is exasperated with the Son's refusal and argues that he is depriving himself of the opportunity to have "All Earth...wonder at [his] acts" and simultaneously denying himself "fame and glory, glory the reward / That sole excites to high attempts" (3.24–26). The Son's response, that glory is merely the praise of "a herd confus'd, /A miscellaneous rabble, who extol / Things vulgar" (3.49–51), elicits this defense from Satan: *your Father seeks glory:*

> Think not so slight of glory: therein least
> Resembling thy great Father; he seeks glory,
> And for his glory all things made, all things
> Orders and governs, nor content in Heaven
> By all his Angels glorifi'd, requires
> Glory from men, from all men good or bad,
> Wise or unwise, no difference, no exemption.   (*PR* 3.109–15)

What is initially most interesting about the Son's response is not what he says, but what he does not say. Satan has nailed the Father's concern with glory, and the Son does not deny it. But as the Son's response unfolds, it becomes obvious that his definition of "glory" is radically different from that of Satan. More interesting, however, is how radically different the Son's perspective is from the concerns expressed in the Father's speech from book 1. For the Son, "glory" is merely thanks: "what could he less expect / Than glory and benediction, that is thanks" (*PR* 3.126–27).[9] Such "thanks" are hardly what the Father seems concerned with as he meditates on how he will "show" everyone that he can defeat Satan through the medium of a perfect man—despite the fact that he is 0–1 on that score to date. Such "thanks" are hardly what Satan has in mind when pushing the Son to seek glory on earth. When Satan describes glory in terms of "show / Of worth" and "popular praise" (*PR* 2.226–27), he is not describing thanks so much as adulation.[10] The Father and Satan, as so often in *Paradise Lost*, seem to speak the same language here, while the Son speaks in a dialect that is almost unintelligible to the two ancient combatants. Humans should not seek glory, according to the Son, because they have nothing to be thanked for, and no one from whom thanks would be anything but unworthy. What value, after all, would thanks be from a people "Of whom to be disprais'd were no small praise" (*PR* 3.56)?

Having dispensed with glory, and having delivered—through his redefinition of glory as thanks—a critique of both Satan and the Father, the Son is easily able to reject the temptations of political and military power that Satan offers in the forms of the Parthian and Roman realms. More subtle, however, is Satan's lead-in to this temptation, the appeal to duty:

> If Kingdom move thee not, let move thee Zeal
> And Duty
>   . . . .
> Zeal of thy Father's house, Duty to free
> Thy Country from her Heathen servitude;
> So shalt thou best fulfill, best verify
> The Prophets old, who sung thy endless reign.
>
> (*PR* 3.171–72, 175–78)

This appeal is quite literally fiendishly clever, tugging, as it does, on the strings of the Son's own earlier revealed desires. At the tender age of 12, the Son already felt that his "Spirit aspir'd to victorious deeds" and "heroic acts" to "subdue and quell o'er all the earth / Brute violence and proud Tyrannic pow'r" (*PR* 1.215–20). It is precisely these feelings at which Satan's appeals to duty and zeal are aimed. But in the Son's case, these feelings are presented, not as the noble thoughts of a hero, but as a remembrance of the fantasies of a child, fantasies that were quickly rejected in favor of higher, and more reasoned thoughts, as the Son "held it...more heavenly," even as a child, to "make persuasion do the work of fear" (*PR* 1.221, 223), though there still remained an element of the fantasy of force in the line "the stubborn only to subdue" (1.226). The thoughts, however progressive, of a 12-year-old boy (no matter how exceptional a boy), have by no means yet reached the levels of profundity that are revealed in the thoughts of the fully mature man now being tested and tempted by Satan. This is no longer the Son who in heaven's battles in *Paradise Lost* seems to be just as concerned with raw power as either Satan or the Father, casting the dispute between the two in remarkably satanic terms:

> Mighty Father, thou thy foes
> Justly hast in derision, and, secure,
> Laugh'st at thir vain designs and tumults vain,
> Matter to mee of Glory, whom thir hate
> Illustrates, when they see all Regal Power
> Giv'n me to quell thir pride, and in event
> Know whether I be dext'rous to subdue
> Thy Rebels, or be found the worst in Heav'n.   (*PL* 5.735–42)

The Son is no longer the all-or-nothing thinker he was before the war in heaven—declaring that he would either be covered in the glory of military victory or be revealed through failure as the *worst* in heaven. Nor is the Son any longer the 12-year-old boy who fantasized conquest, though he quickly—if incompletely—rejected the means of force. The now fully mature Son reveals an altogether more profound judgment than he has yet displayed in any previous situation. His answer to Satan's earthly appeal emphasizes patience, even suffering, rather than conquest (the conquest by which both Satan and the Father still seem obsessed):

> All things are best fulfill'd in their due time
>
>   . . . .
>
>   who best
> Can suffer, best can do; best reign, who first
> Well hath obey'd; just trial e'er I merit
> My exaltation without change or end.   (*PR* 3.182, 194–97)

In fact, by this point, the Son has made it quite clear what he thinks of the conquests to which Satan would urge him (the "Duty to free / Thy Country from her Heathen servitude") and to which the Father would urge him ("Winning by Conquest what the first man lost"). The Son rejects the idea of external conquest: "They err who count it glorious to subdue / By Conquest" (*PR* 3.71–72). He even more definitively rejects war and violence.as means of attaining *any* end:

> *if* there be in glory aught of good,
> It may by means far different be attain'd,
> Without ambition, war, or violence;
> By deeds of peace, by wisdom eminent.
> By patience, temperance.   (*PR* 3.88–92; emphasis added)

The failure of Satan's temptation of military and political power, especially after the Son's rejection of the appeals to duty and zeal, and his redefinition of glory and rejection of conquest, violence, and war, comes as no surprise to any reader who has been attentive to the Son's earlier summation of the real nature of power, authority, and reign. Again, he speaks a different language from that spoken by both Satan and the Father, for whom the above-mentioned things are externals, things to be wielded over others than oneself. The position the Son expresses is quite the opposite: at the end of book 2, he rejects the external model of government that "o'er the body only reigns, / And oft by force, which to a generous mind / So reigning can be no sincere delight" (*PR* 2.478–80). Instead of this kind of external, public reign, the Son chooses the internal, private government of truth:

> to guide nations in the way of truth
> By saving doctrine, and from error lead
> To know, and, knowing worship God aright,
> Is yet more kingly, this attracts the soul,
> Governs the inner man, the nobler part.   (*PR* 2.473–77)

For the Son, power, authority, and reign are *internal* and to be exercised, not over others, but over oneself. The Son's greatest expressions of contempt are reserved for those who do not wield such control over themselves: the "captive Tribes... / Who wrought their own captivity" (*PR* 3.414–15) by falling into "Idolatries" (3.418), and the Roman people,

> That people victor once, now vile and base,
> Deservedly made vassal, who once just,
> Frugal, and mild, and temperate, conquer'd well,
> But govern ill the Nations under yoke.   (*PR* 4.132–35)

In each case, the Son is describing a people who have become slaves *internally*, and have projected that slavishness *externally* onto their orientation toward the world.

In Milton's well-known argument from *The Tenure of Kings and Magistrates*, the internal serves as the base and root cause of the external; as a result, slavish people beget tyrannical regimes: "being slaves within doors, no wonder that they strive so much to have the public State conformably govern'd to the inward vitious rule by which they govern themselves" (YP 3:190). The Israelites and the Romans, who once were free inwardly—the Israelites through "worship[ping] God aright," and the Romans through being "Frugal, and mild, and temperate" and having "conquer'd well" *themselves*—are now slaves internally, and thus slaves externally: Israel as an occupied territory, and the Romans, once citizens of a republic, now merely vassals of a vast empire.

4. *The Temptation of Knowledge*

So far, each temptation has been a call to focus on things in themselves, on last things, on a world of objects that may have its origin in the divine, but looks resolutely away from that origin. Each rejection of temptation has been grounded in a call to look past these last things back toward first things, the divine as the origin of all. The famous temptation—and rejection—of knowledge makes most sense when viewed in this context. Since Satan sees the Son as being "otherwise inclin'd / Than to a worldly Crown, addicted more / To contemplation and profound dispute" (*PR* 4.212–14), his final temptation is at once his most powerful and profound—knowledge, study, wisdom, the very things to which the poetic creator of Satan and the Son had given his life, had praised as early as the gorgeous lines of *Il Penseroso:*

> Or let my Lamp at midnight hour
> Be seen in some high lonely Tow'r,
> Where I may oft outwatch the *Bear,*
> With thrice great *Hermes,* or unsphere
> The spirit of *Plato* to unfold
> What Worlds, or what vast Regions hold
> The immortal mind that hath forsook
> Her mansion in this fleshly nook.   (85–92)

A love letter to knowledge, *Il Penseroso* should be in the background of a reading of the exchanges between Satan and the Son when Satan extols the virtues of "the Olive Grove of *Academe,* /

Plato's retirement" (*PR* 4.244–45), and "Blind *Melesigenes* thence *Homer* call'd" (4.259). The poet who had once begged his own father not to "persist in [his] contempt for the sacred Muses" (Nec tu perge, precor, sacras contemnere Musas [*Ad Patrem*, 56]), and who had gone on to claim that that contempt was a mere pretense, "You may pretend to hate the delicate Muses, but I do not believe in your hatred" (Tu tamen ut simules teneras odisse Camenas, / Non odisse reor [*Ad Patrem*, 67–68]), is not writing the Son's response to Satan to portray a man with contempt for the Muses of philosophy and poetry. Far from it—the Son's abiding familiarity with both shines through in the very scenes in which he is ostensibly rejecting both.

Though the intellectual achievements of the Greek and Roman worlds are characterized by the Son as "false, or little else but dreams, / Conjectures, fancies, built on nothing firm" (*PR* 4.291–92), the Son goes on to deliver a concise account of the very thinkers and schools of thought he has just "rejected," and like the Milton of *Ad Patrem* I contend that the reader's reaction is supposed to be *non odisse reor*—"I do not believe in your hatred." The Son's characterizations of Socrates, "The first and wisest of them all [who] profess'd /...that he nothing knew" (*PR* 4.293–94), and Plato, who "to fabling fell and smooth conceits" (4.295), strike at the very heart of the mental labors upon which Milton has spent the bulk of his life and energy: the search for knowledge and the ability to present that knowledge in high literary form.

But Milton is not rejecting himself, his studies, his work here. Rather, he is having the Son, through the expression of what seems a radical, even shocking point of view, make a variation of the point that the great German mystic Meister Eckhart makes in his famous prayer to be able to "for God's sake...take leave of god."[11] Eckhart asks for the strength to be able to recognize the highest good, and to be able to separate himself, his affections, his desires, his piety and belief from all other goods, even to the point of abandoning all of his most sacredly held beliefs about the divine itself, in order to reach that highest good. In Milton's case, through the

Son, the desire is analogous: to be able to reach the highest good, expressed in this case as an internal realization of divine similitude, one must have the strength to be able to leave behind all that one loves most in the world, about existence itself, which in Milton's case is no other than the knowledge, poetry, beauty he has spent his entire life pursuing, mastering, and powerfully expressing. Even these things, finally, are *externals*, last things, which at their best and most powerful can only be guideposts along the way to the divine, but taken as ends in themselves are distractions, if not impediments and barriers.

This is the core meaning of the poignant phrase from Sonnet 19, "God doth not need / Either man's work or his own gifts" (9–10). No work or gifts or talents can bring humankind to the divine. The one thing, ultimately the *only* thing needed (not desired, not appreciated, not loved, but *needed*) is "Light from above, from the fountain of light" (*PR* 4.289). This "Light from above" is the knowledge that reveals, the teacher that teaches the all-important lesson of divine similitude, and it can only be accessed from within, which is the crucial point of the scene in the desert where the Son realizes what he must do, and how he must do it:

> [the] Son, tracing the Desert wild,
> Sole, but with holiest Meditations fed,
> Into himself descended, and at once
> All his great work to come before him set;
> How to begin, how to accomplish best
> His end of being on Earth, and mission high.   (*PR* 2.109–14)

The desert is the ideal location for a narrative the point of which is the withdrawal from the world—from external values and stimuli—that facilitates the kind of internality essential to realizing one's connection to the divine. It is here where the Son realizes "how to accomplish best" his mission, here away from even the extremely private life he has been leading up to this point, away from the expectations of Mary, who believes that he will "By matchless Deeds express [his] matchless Sire" (*PR* 1.233), away from the expectations of his followers, who are "missing him thir joy so lately found" (2.9), and above all, away from the expectations of the Father, for whom the Son's mission is first and foremost an extension of the Father's own agon with Satan, as he envisions the Son "Winning by Conquest what the first man lost / By fallacy surpris'd" (1.154–55). But the "Light from above" is not to be found in any of these clamoring voices with their urgent, even imperious demands. This light makes no demands of any kind; rather, it merely shows the Son who and what he is. It is this light that allows the Son to read "The Law and Prophets" and find "of whom they spake / I am" (*PR* 1.260, 262–63). After that, it is always and only the Son whose demands on the Son are obeyed.

The figure of whom "The Law and Prophets" were speaking, of course, is the Messiah. From *mashiach*—anointed one/deliverer—the Messiah, in the early years of what is now regarded as the Common Era (CE), was often conceived as a political and military figure who would lead the peoples of the occupied territory of Israel in a rebellion against their Roman occupiers, and reestablish the earthly kingdom of David.[12] Milton weaves similar expectations into several of his characters, among them Mary, who expects "matchless Deeds" from her son who will "sit on *David's* Throne" (*PR* 1.233, 240); Satan, who not only shares the belief that the Son is "ordain'd / To sit upon...*David's* Throne" (3.152–53), but also suspects that the Son is "rais'd / To end his Reign on Earth" (1.124–25); and finally the Father himself, whose main concern seems to be his ongoing struggle with Satan:

> He now shall know I can produce a man
> Of female Seed, far abler to resist
> All his solicitations, and at length
> All his vast force, and drive him back to Hell.   (*PR* 1.150–53)

But just as the kingdom of the biblical Jesus was "not of this world" (John 18:36), so the "Conquest" and "Reign" and "matchless Deeds" that so many expect of the Son in *Paradise Regain'd* are "not of this world," in the special sense of being not of the world of politics, military struggles, wealth, and even physical necessities like food—not, in other words, of the world of *externals*.

The Son's conquest is of himself. The Son's reign is over himself. The Son's matchless deeds are the rejections of temptations to which everyone else—including the Father—succumbs. The Son's most truly "matchless" deed is his choice to focus, not on the world without, but on the world within; to focus, not on last things—food, wealth, power, knowledge, and even divinity conceived of as an external force—but on first things—the quiet, but firm assurance of divine similitude. In himself, and through himself—as he realizes when he "with holiest Meditations fed, / Into himself descended" (*PR* 2.110–11)—is the only place and the only way that the "inner man, the nobler part" (2.477) can be accessed, that part of each man which is connected to, even comprised by, the "Spirit of Truth" the "inward Oracle" (1.462–63). The Son's conquest is achieved in the realization that for humankind, indeed, for all creation, the divine is only to be found by searching within, by heeding the promptings of "the Spirit, which is *internal, and the individual possession of every man*" (*De doctrina Christiana*, YP 6:587; emphasis added). It is this realization that gives his final response to Satan its tremendous power.

5. *Tempt Not the Lord Thy God*

This final scene between Satan and the Son has been the subject of much analysis and controversy. One common line of argument suggests the Son does not fully realize who he is in the poem; he does not know, until he formulates his rejection of the final temptation, what his true identity is, and even after coming to the realization of that identity he is merely declaring his faith in God—*a God that he is not*. In contrast to this, it can be, and has been, argued that the Son is fully aware of who he is, and is openly declaring his divine status.[13] At the very moment of refusing the final temptation of Satan, the Son utters these enigmatic words: "Also it is written, / Tempt not the Lord thy God" (*PR* 4.559–60). The crucial question to be asked is what exactly the Son means by this. Are readers to assume that the Son is merely refuting Satan by trading biblical quotations with him, countering Satan's quotation of Psalm 91:11–12 by hurling Deuteronomy 6:16 back at him? Is the Son merely declaring his faith in God, or is the Son openly declaring his divine status, declaring that he actually *is* God?

More radical than either of these alternatives is a third, which I believe to be the underlying reason for Satan's reaction when he "smitten with amazement fell" (*PR* 4.562). What the Son, significantly referred to here as the man Jesus, reveals when he says "Tempt not the Lord thy God" (4.561) is a threefold meaning: (1) *do not tempt me*—I am God; (2) *do not tempt anyone*—all creatures, sharing in the divine as their origin, are also God; and (3) *do not tempt yourself*—you, even you, Satan, are included in points 1 and 2.[14] All temptation is ultimately *self-temptation* in the scenario Milton has created here. Thus, though in a different sense than either Satan or the Father seems to have understood in *Paradise Lost,* Satan was "Self-tempted, self-deprav'd" (3.130), in that he—though not by "his own suggestion" (3.129) as the Father claims—did not simply refuse to indulge the feelings being played upon by the Father in the coronation scene of 5.600–15. It was in Satan's power to ignore the external provocation, to focus, not on last things (in this case, his fixation with finding meaning in rank and power within the confines of a rigid hierarchical system), but on first things, an inner awareness of divine similitude. Satan's failure ever to realize this, ever to understand who—and what—he has been all along is what truly amazes, not the realization that he cannot successfully tempt this man (or this God). What has smitten Satan with amazement is the profoundly horrific depth of his misunderstanding and miscalculation about the nature of himself and the origin of all things.

The crushing irony of Satan's situation is that he was right in characterizing the Father as a usurper, someone claiming solely for himself rights that belonged to all, but that he was tragically wrong about the way he confronted, and has continued to confront, the situation. The Father, in this scenario, is no more or less "God" than are any of the angels, "fallen" or "unfallen," than were Adam and Eve, than is Satan or the Son. In his rebellion, Satan had hit upon an essential truth, but as proves to be usual for his character, he understood that truth in precisely the wrong way, emphasizing the external rather than the internal, difference rather than similitude.

In making his radical claim, the Son redefines all of the expectations that have been laid upon him, most notably that of taking hold of what he refers to as "My everlasting Kingdom" (3.199). Mary, Satan, and the Father all seem to envision this kingdom as an earthly or heavenly variant on the political and military kingdom over which the conqueror David reigned. But it is *not* that kind of kingdom. The Son's kingdom is, as Donald Swanson and John Mulryan argue, "a spiritual kingdom that is neither accompanied by eschatological signs nor located in space.... The inner or spiritual nature of the kingdom might easily have been inferred from the parable of the seed growing secretly or from Luke xvii, 21b: 'for behold, the kingdom of God is within you.'"[15] *The kingdom of God is within you* — in some sense, everyone who attains what Milton elsewhere calls "the mind of Christ" (YP 6:583) has what the Son calls "The authority which I derived from Heaven" (*PR* 1.289). This authority is an internal authority, the "double scripture," especially the "internal scripture of the Holy Spirit" that Milton describes in *De doctrina Christiana* (YP 6:587). He who has "the spirit, who guides truth" (YP 6:583) has an authority that no "visible church...let alone any magistrate, has the right" (YP 6:584) to gainsay or oppose. The Son in *Paradise Regain'd* powerfully illustrates what John Shawcross calls "Milton's essential belief," that "worth does not lie in the external, in works for a public arena, in negation and prohibition, nor in a mere following of example, no matter how blest the example might be, if the inner being has not been enlightened."[16]

As the Son returns "unobserved / Home to his mother's house private" (*PR* 4.638–39), he has accomplished the regaining of paradise, making of *Paradise Lost* and *Paradise Regain'd* a complete cycle of descent and return. Where Adam and Eve move away from, the Son moves in return to the divine source. *But that source is not the Father.* The divine source is the "Spirit of Truth," the "inward Oracle" (*PR* 1.462–63), which the Son is at pains to tell Satan will replace the latter's oracles ("henceforth Oracles are ceast" [1.456]). The external "Oracles" which are "ceast," however, do not have their origin with Satan, but with "Heaven's King" (1.421). When Satan claims to have been allowed access to heaven, to have undertaken the assignment of filling "the tongues / Of all [Ahab's] flattering Prophets...with lies" (*PR* 1.374–75), the Son, though he berates and belittles Satan, does not contradict him; instead, he attempts subtly to shift the emphasis, arguing that Satan *chose* the task:

> But thou art serviceable to Heaven's King!
> Wilt thou impute to obedience what thy fear
> Extorts, or pleasure to do ill excites?
> What but thy malice mov'd thee to misdeem
> Of righteous *Job,* then cruelly to afflict him
> With all inflictions? But his patience won.
> The other service was thy chosen task,
> To be a liar in four hundred mouths;
> For lying is thy sustenance, thy food.
> Yet thou pretend'st to truth; all Oracles
> By thee are giv'n.   (*PR* 1.421–31)

This is true, as far as it goes, but it stops short of an important acknowledgment. Oracles may, indeed, be given by Satan, but everything Satan does (or is allowed to do) has its origin in the Father.

In *Paradise Lost* this is made abundantly clear when the narrator informs us that Satan would never have been able to get up off "the burning Lake" (1.210) except for the fact that "the will / And high permission of all-ruling Heaven" allowed it (1.211–12). In *Paradise Regain'd* this idea is reinforced. Satan does nothing beyond what he is allowed to do by the Father, as the Son makes clear by telling Satan: "do as thou find'st / Permission from above; thou canst not more" (1.495–96). In the specific cases of Job and Ahab being discussed by Satan and the Son, it is important to note that in the biblical accounts Satan (known in each case as *the Satan* or *ha satan* in the Hebrew, signifying that "Satan" is a title or a function rather than a proper name) undertakes his activities with the express permission of Yahweh. The origin of Job's sufferings is Yahweh. The origin of the "lying spirit" sent to Ahab in 1 Kings 22:20–23 is Yahweh. With these incidents serving as the background of the argument between Satan and the Son here in *Paradise Regain'd*, the scenario that Milton has created argues, not only for the irrelevance of Satan in the face of the "inward Oracle," but the irrelevance of the *source* of Satan's external oracles, the Father himself.

How does it do this? By sweeping the Father up, along with Satan, in the relentless focus on the "inner Paradise" first mentioned in *Paradise Lost*, and reinforced with each rejection of temptation in *Paradise Regain'd*. Where *Paradise Lost* was a narrative of descent, of moving away from a focus on first things, and toward a focus on appearances, surfaces, and last things, *Paradise Regain'd* is a narrative of ascent, or return, which restores a focus on first things, the true substance and nature of which are all too often obscured behind appearances. This process began with the temptations of food. In *Paradise Lost*, food was at the center of the question of what it meant to be like God. Satan's temptation of Eve focused on the fruit of the tree of knowledge as if it had, in itself, the power to transform human into divine, to make ethereal of physical. In so doing, Satan was merely following up on broad hints to the same effect delivered earlier by Raphael. In *Paradise Regain'd*, the very human (and very hungry) Jesus rejects Satan's offering of food, considering himself "fed with better thoughts" (2.258).

Satan's appeals, however, are no different, his focus no less external, than are the thoughts of the Father, who cannot seem to get enough recognition, enough in the way of accolades and affirmation from the creatures to whom he is ostensibly superior. The Father's fixation on his reputation, how he is regarded by others, shines through clearly in his desire that Gabriel, and "all Angels conversant on Earth / With man or men's affairs" (*PR* 1.131–32), bear witness to what he anticipates will be the Son's "Conquest" (1.154) of Satan. Given the Father's previous model of such conquest, the Son's piloting of "The Chariot of Paternal Deity" (*PL*

6.750), which "O'er Shields and Helms, and helmed heads he rode" (6.840), it becomes clear that the Father expects a display that can best be understood from without, visually, aurally, even kinetically.

But there is no sound and fury in the Son's "conquest" in *Paradise Regain'd*, because the Son's focus is not the value of appearances, but on how best to hear, understand, and obey the promptings of the "Spirit of Truth," the "inward Oracle" (1.462–63). In mastering this, the Son, existing in this time and place as the human male Jesus, realizes within himself the strength to easily withstand the all-too-transparent temptations of Satan, but he also realizes that the divine is to be found within, not without, that "Tempt not the Lord thy God" is an admonition, not against tempting a God conceived and understood as an external figure, but against *self*-temptation. In regaining paradise, Jesus neither regains Eden, nor does he shed a drop of sacrificial blood. In Milton's construction of the descent and ascent, the procession from and return to the divine, such externals are—at best—mere symbols, but at worst—and more typically—active and dangerous distractions from the one basic truth: *The kingdom of God is within you.*

Part IV

Milton's Visionary Mode and the Last Poems

11 ⁀ From Politics to Faith in the Great Poems?

David Loewenstein

1. Against Schematic Formulations

How helpful are the schematic formulations and patterns critics employ to characterize the shape or trajectory of the late Milton's responses to the political sphere in his great poems published during the Restoration? Is it at all helpful or even accurate to describe the visionary poet as withdrawing from politics into faith in the late poems, as though we can discern a consistent pattern of development or change in his dissenting reactions to Restoration politics and religion? Can we conclude with any certainty, by looking at the 1671 volume of poems, that Milton the disappointed revolutionary preferred the position of a pacifist or quietist (as exemplified by Milton's retiring Jesus) following his long career of political and polemical engagements during the English revolution? This essay questions the critical tendency to make the Milton of the late poems too consistent and predictable in his various dissenting responses to the religious politics of the Restoration milieu.

269

In 1990 Blair Worden published a now well-known essay on the politics of *Paradise Lost* ("Milton's Republicanism and the Tyranny of Heaven") in which he concludes that the great poems, beginning with *Paradise Lost* itself, not only signal Milton's "return to his right hand [of poetry]," but essentially signal the poet's Restoration withdrawal "from politics into faith," so that by the time of *Paradise Regain'd*, "written at the prompting of a Quaker [Thomas Ellwood], the retreat from the political sphere is complete." Thus, as Worden observes, by the end of the Interregnum we can see in Milton's controversial writings that "political language is beginning to yield to religious language," as if the two languages are finally disconnected in Milton's great poems.[1] I suspect that many readers today would disagree with Worden's formulation about the late Milton's retreating from politics into faith, finding it unsatisfactory because it seems to reject the idea of the politically engaged Milton after the disappointments of the Restoration or because it sets temporal politics against faith and apolitical quietism, universal spiritual values, and the "eternal verities" of Milton's greatest poetry.[2] Worden's voice, it should be noted, is one more in a distinguished line of commentators who suggest that the great poet, embroiled for so many years in political and religious controversies, finally sought solace in a personal, quietistic faith. In 1673, Andrew Marvell, no doubt aiming to protect his friend in a calculated observation, said of Milton, "it was his misfortune, in a tumultuous time, to be toss'd on the wrong side, and he writ *Flagrante bello* certain dangerous Treatises," so that "at His Majesties happy Return [he] did partake...of his regal Clemency and has ever since expiated himself in a retired silence." Similarly in 1818 Samuel Coleridge observed that the later Milton, "finding it impossible to realize his own aspirations, either in religion, or politics, or society, ...gave up his heart to the living spirit and the light within him, and avenged himself on the world by enriching it with this record of his transcendent ideal [that is, in *Paradise Lost*]."[3]

More recently, however, a wide range of historically informed criticism has given us a Milton who in the great poems is intensely political and polemically active in his responses to Restoration culture, politics, and religion. The poet-polemicist's "experience of defeat" in the Restoration was thus an occasion to make a weakness into a strength: Milton did not simply withdraw from the political sphere into faith and a posture of passive quietism—thereby striving to represent "eternal verities"—but was a profoundly political animal in his last poems; consequently, we have Milton the poet of dissent, of political resistance and activism, of republicanism, of radical religious politics, and so on.[4] Needless to say, I sympathize with these various versions of the politically engaged late Milton, although I myself have strongly resisted the tendency to secularize Milton's politics (as some of the critical work on Milton and seventeenth century republicanism has done)[5] and have argued for a much more polemically engaged radical religious poet in the great poems. Such a Milton does indeed unsettle the more traditional picture of quiescent Restoration dissent.[6]

Yet in this essay I wish to begin to argue for a more nuanced account of the later poet's divergent political responses and to challenge the schematic ways we often describe them. In particular, I want to question the adequacy of those formulations we often employ to characterize Milton's political responses after the Restoration, insofar as they are manifested in the great poems. Some of these formulations tend to be too schematic and ultimately too neat, predictable, and probably reductive: for example, arguing for the late poet's withdrawal "from politics into faith" versus arguing for his ongoing political and republican engagement in the poems; or, in the case of the volume of 1671 poems, arguing that Milton's radical quietism in *Paradise Regain'd*, represented by Jesus' abjuring force and militarism, is a kind of moral and imaginative triumph over the horrid Old Testament violence dramatized in *Samson Agonistes*. These formulations, I believe, do not fully account for the divergent and, indeed, sometimes agonized political responses we find expressed in the last poems.

Living by faith and remaining committed to political action, whenever the Lord may call the saints, were not necessarily conceived as irreconcilable responses by Milton's radical religious contemporaries biding their time during the Restoration. Writing in exile during the mid-1660s and waiting for the Lord's wisdom "to know when to goe forward and when to stand still," the regicide and godly republican Edmund Ludlow reflected that "by suffering we may be fitted for the doing of his will" and "being on our Watch Tower, and living by faith, we may see our duty so plainly, that when the Lord's tyme is come we may be up and be doing, and the Lord may appear to be with us and to owne us."[7] Knowing "when to goe forward and when to stand still": Ludlow's antithesis neatly conveys two options available to the besieged godly; the latter is especially pertinent to the retiring and unmoved protagonist in *Paradise Regain'd*, the former to the warrior protagonist in *Samson Agonistes* who shatters the Philistine temple in that dramatic poem's apocalyptic climax.[8]

Nevertheless, I suggest that there remain tensions in the late Milton's own diverse, multifaceted responses, which range between the poet's impulse to retire into a spiritual world of faith and "the light within him" (as Worden and Coleridge suggest in their different ways) and the poet's desire to remain polemically engaged and "up and...doing," even if this sometimes means taking action to subdue the stubborn enemies of God by means of violence. Here I want to stress that the responses in Milton's great poems to the trauma of the Restoration are more conflicted and—imaginatively and emotionally—more varied than we often acknowledge.

In a sense, then, I think that Worden is partially correct: we can find moments when the dispirited and bitter radical Puritan poet expresses the urge to retire "from politics into faith," and in this essay I will discuss one notable example from the postlapsarian history lessons at the end of *Paradise Lost*. However, these moments are countered or complicated by other moments when Milton's polemical voice and political and religious convictions are expressed as sharply and as distinctively as ever. Similarly, to argue that the great poems project a posture of quietism after the collapse of the English revolution is too simple and schematic as well, and overlooks or reduces the rich ambiguities of juxtaposing *Paradise Regain'd* and *Samson Agonistes* by publishing them together in the

1671 volume of poems. Indeed, Michael Lieb's scholarship, including his study *Milton and the Culture of Violence*, has done much to illuminate (persuasively in my view) "the politics of violence" depicted in *Samson Agonistes* in relation to Milton's controversial works, notably his *Defenses*.[9] As I will argue here, however, the terrifying violence of Samson and his dreadful God explored so well by Lieb is one manifestation of Milton's divergent, multifaceted, and sometimes conflicting political reactions to Restoration political and religious culture that we find in the great poems.

2. Weltering Responses

Milton famously tells us in the invocation to book 7 of *Paradise Lost* that "though fall'n on evil days" and "evil tongues," he sings "with mortal voice, unchang'd / To hoarse or mute,"[10] and many recent critics have rightly construed this as a bold assertion that the dissenting poet's voice remains unsilenced in the cold political climate and evil days of the Restoration.[11] But Milton does not sing or respond with only one political voice in the great poems. We need to be more attuned, I suggest, to the multiple, diverse, even conflicting voices with which Milton responds, in his three late poems, to what he regarded as the hostile, dissipated, and idolatrous world of Restoration England.

My point is that the deeply agonized Milton, having witnessed his own nation, once "chos'n before any other,"[12] now having "decline[d] so low / From virtue" (*PL* 12.97–98), must have indeed felt a great welter or agitation of emotions during the "evil days" of the 1660s and 1670s. His great poems enabled him to give those weltering feelings diverse imaginative expression. Milton uses versions of the word "welter" in the Nativity ode, *Lycidas,* and *Paradise Lost:* it can mean rolling, tumbling, or tossing about, and conveys a sense of turbulence. Here I use it in the sense of being in a state of agitation or turmoil—indeed, it once conveyed the sense of political agitation.[13] We need a historicized criticism, I am arguing, that acknowledges that even within dense passages of Milton's great poems we may find conflicting impulses and weltering reactions to the pressures of contemporary postlapsarian history and the political sphere of post-Restoration England.

We find powerful evidence for Milton's divergent, weltering reactions at the end of *Paradise Lost*. For example, in the midst of Michael's grimmest historical narrative near the end of the poem, a narrative that moves from the time of the apostles to the Apocalypse, we can indeed hear the visionary poet bitterly cursing history, expressing the impulse to retire (like "Truth") from such a faithless world empty of any reforming individuals or just men:

> Truth shall retire
> Bestuck with sland'rous darts, and works of Faith
> Rarely to be found: so shall the World go on,
> To good malignant, to bad men benign,
> Under her own weight groaning.   (*PL* 12.535–39)

In such a bleak postlapsarian world, devoid of "just men" and darkened by religious persecution and oppression, it might well be preferable to assume a posture of quiescent dissent or to withdraw altogether "from politics into faith" (to recall Worden's formula for the poet's retreat from politics). But such bleak lines are also set against the withering polemical voice of the antiauthoritarian radical religious poet who condemns the perversion of secular power, when consciences are forced, and "Whence heavy persecution shall arise / On all who in the worship persevere / Of Spirit and Truth," especially the radical godly who follow the Spirit and repudiate the "outward Rites and specious forms" of religion (*PL* 12.531–33), whether they be of the Church of England or any other religious institution. To be sure, Milton does not single out specific radical religious groups or contemporary individuals here: no Quakers, General (that is, non-Calvinist) Baptists, Congregationalists, or other English sectaries are mentioned by name and singled out as righteous or "just men." Yet his biting, emotionally charged language evokes a Restoration world of severe persecution, bitter disappointment, and uncertainty for dissenters. The poet's impulse to curse history and withdraw from it and his impulse to give a sharp voice to his radical religious convictions, in the midst of the dark world of Restoration England, are allowed to coexist. Both are movingly expressed in this unstable, haunting passage narrating the uneven course of postlapsarian history.[14]

Moreover, the apocalyptic release envisioned at the end of Michael's harsh narrative, in which we hear about "New Heav'ns, new Earth, Ages of endless date / Founded in righteousness and peace and love" (*PL* 12.549–50), hardly cancels out the appalling grimness of the preceding lines. Rather, these lines and the fluctuations I have been charting in Michael's dense historical narrative may remind us of *Lycidas* with its jagged emotional edges, its agonized poet's weltering responses, and its flagrantly conflicting transitions—such as the poet's command to "Weep no more" immediately following upon his plea that the guardian angel Michael "melt with ruth" (lines 165, 163). At the end of *Paradise Lost*, we also see the weltering reactions of the agonized visionary poet—this time torn between the urge to retire from the religious politics and tragedy of postlapsarian history and the urge to remain polemically engaged in the tragic world of politics, "carnal power," and "heavy persecution" (12.521, 531). My point is that we need to acknowledge Milton's conflicting and competing political reactions, and to recognize that they are the expressions of a great poet struggling to confront the bitter consequences of recent history and "a World perverse" (*PL* 11.701). The notion of the poet's withdrawing from politics into faith is only a partial truth: that sentiment is expressed at the end of *Paradise Lost*, but it is also complicated by other, more polemical responses that suggest the poet's competing and divergent reactions to the hostile religious and political world of Restoration England. No schematic formulation can fully convey the complexity of the poet's responses in this powerful and unstable prophetic depiction of postlapsarian history in *Paradise Lost*.

3. *Political Ambiguity in the 1671 Volume*

Yet how should we interpret the message or messages of the 1671 volume of poems where Milton seems to offer two apparently irreconcilable models of political behavior and heroism in

Jesus and Samson? *Samson Agonistes* has for some years now been construed as a major "political document" in Milton's oeuvre, an expression of his "political principles."[15] Yet "the politics of violence" in the drama (to borrow Michael Lieb's phrase) has disturbed many commentators, who find Samson's violence repellent, and has tended to encourage schematic accounts of the 1671 volume as a whole. Indeed, when it comes to interpreting the 1671 poems and the issue of violent action to achieve political ends, there has been a notable tendency among recent critics to argue that ultimately Milton wants his readers to sympathize with the pacifism, quietism, and patience of Jesus in *Paradise Regain'd* and to reject the Old Testament violence and militarism of Samson in its companion piece, *Samson Agonistes*. For example, Michael Wilding argues succinctly and forcefully for this point of view in a study that valuably places both poems in the context of the turbulent revolutionary years:

> Samson is the old-fashioned, active, military hero who uses the old, pagan, military, heroic means to save his people. Christ is the new hero whose method is *patience and heroic martyrdom, suffering for truth's sake* instead of killing. Samson suffers death, Christ offers life. Samson uses force and kills himself as well as his enemies; Christ abjures forces and saves mankind.[16]

Wilding is normally highly attentive to ambiguities in Milton's later poems,[17] but on this matter there should be no ambiguity at all: the militarism of Samson is surely superseded by the pacifism and spiritual wisdom of the contemplative, even quiescent hero of *Paradise Regain'd*, a hero who firmly rejects military means to accomplish his political ends, including deliverance from political oppression and servility.

This critical point of view has been strengthened even further by interpretations of *Samson Agonistes* that situate its depiction of spectacular violence—Samson's final act of apocalyptic power and cataclysmic destruction that turns the Philistine temple of Dagon into a "place of horror" (1550)—in the context of the so-called "war on terror." It is becoming almost commonplace to compare Milton's Samson to a terrorist on a suicide mission,[18] despite the fact that Milton clearly suppresses Judges 16:30 (Samson's prayer "Let me die with the Philistines") and despite the fact that Milton writes in the Argument to the poem—these are the author's own words, after all—that the destruction Samson brought upon the Philistines he did *"by accident to himself"* (Hughes, 551). Milton's words in the Argument, moreover, are reinforced by the Messenger, who observes of Samson's destruction and death that "Inevitable cause / At once both to destroy and be destroy'd" (*SA* 1587–88), and by the Chorus who reports that Samson was "self-kill'd / Not willingly, but tangl'd in the fold / Of dire necessity" (1664–66). Nevertheless, proponents of the negative Samson see him as a "deeply flawed" hero whose suicidal act of violence and dreadful vengeance must ultimately be rejected by the poem's readers.[19] Milton could never have condoned such horrific violence, so this line of argument goes, despite the fact, of course, that Milton fully supported the heroism of regicide in 1649 (and never retracted his support for this highly traumatic and historic act) and despite the fact that, based on all the evidence we have, Milton fully supported Oliver Cromwell's "shock and awe" campaign (to borrow a phrase from recent military parlance) to terrify and reconquer the stubborn anti-Christian Irish in the fall of 1649, thereby seeking to avenge the blood guilt of 1641 by means of a "war in Ireland in full accordance with the will of God" (*A Defence of the People of England;* YP 4:458).[20] From the perspective of commentators who see Samson's militant heroism as deeply flawed and outmoded, the introspective, retiring Jesus of *Paradise Regain'd*, who chooses to fight with words rather than with arms, is surely the heroic model of faith and true prophecy Milton wants us to admire.[21] If Milton is to be politically engaged in the Restoration, it is by means of verbal and spiritual weapons, not physical ones. *Samson Agonistes* is a tragedy of spectacular religious violence—a drama illustrating the utter fruitlessness of such militant action.

Consequently, distinguished Miltonists from Irene Samuel to Joseph Wittreich, from Michael Wilding to John Carey to other commentators who interpret Milton's drama in the context of the so-called "war on terror" have produced a series of compelling, but nevertheless (in my view) questionable critical accounts that insist that Samson's horrid violence and apocalyptic destruction must finally be rejected by the poem's readers, and that such violence is a profoundly flawed response to the politics of renewed servility. Some of this criticism—especially the major book-length studies by Joseph Wittreich—have given us richly nuanced readings of Milton's retelling of the Samson narrative in relation to Judges.[22] Nevertheless, one conclusion we are expected to reach is that Samson the negative Old Testament man of violence represents an outmoded, failed kind of militarism and is thus superseded by the introspective, quietist "perfect Man" (1.166) of *Paradise Regain'd*. Milton's violent Samson is to be seen in sharp, clear-cut contrast to his pacifist Jesus. I have not been counting books and articles, but my guess is that the proponents of the negative, deeply flawed Samson are beginning to gain the upper hand; indeed, anxieties about the so-called "war on terror" in the twenty-first century have encouraged fresh readings of Milton's drama that reinforce this negative interpretation of Samson's violence and destruction, so that it has even become something of a new orthodoxy in Milton criticism.

The problem with such a critical perspective is not simply that it tends to construe the bloody end of Milton's drama in a way that is shaped too uncritically by present political and religious concerns (including current anxieties about religious extremism and violence), a complex and interesting issue that deserves more rigorous and skeptical examination in its own right.[23] This critical perspective also tends to treat the late Milton in too consistent, too neat a fashion, which fits our own (more acceptable) image of the radical visionary poet who, unlike the Samson of his dramatic poem, could never or who could no longer, after the Restoration, condone an act of holy violence and vehement rage as a devastating yet creative and heroic political act. Moreover, it assumes, without strong evidence, that Milton's readers are meant to feel only or primarily a sense of revulsion at Samson's final terrifying act against the idolatrous Philistines, whose behavior and religious practices evoke the religious and political world of Restoration England, despite the fact that in *De doctrina Christiana* Milton argues, with the support of ample biblical proof-texts, that "hatred" — *odium* — is in some cases "a religious duty [*pium*], as when we hate the enemies of God or the church [*hostes Dei aut ecclesiae*]," and that we "are not forbidden to take or to wish to take vengeance upon the enemies of the church" (YP 6:743, 755).[24]

Reflecting on his political role, the contemplative, solitary Son of God of *Paradise Regain'd* observes in his first meditative soliloquy that, when it comes to rescuing "*Israel* from the *Roman* yoke," he

> held it more humane, more heavenly, first
> By winning words to conquer willing hearts,
> And make persuasion do the work of fear;
> At least to try, and teach the erring Soul
> Not wilfully misdoing, but unware
> Misled: *the stubborn only to subdue.*
>
> (*PR* 1.217, 221–26; my emphasis)

Jesus' important qualification here — "the stubborn only to subdue" — is easily overlooked (or misconstrued) by commentators who argue that Milton surely wants readers to reject the violence and futility of Samson's final act as "morally disgusting" (to quote from one of the poem's modern editors).[25] While the Son of God has chosen "winning words" over physical violence as his preferred weapons to "conquer willing hearts," that does not altogether exclude other means that may be necessary "to subdue" the stubborn enemies of God.

Now one might at first object to this line of argument by noting that in the 1671 edition of the poems, the word "destroy" is corrected to "subdue" in the Errata.[26] Admittedly, "destroy" to our ears may more unequivocally convey a sense of violence, and Milton probably wished to echo Luke 9:56 ("For the Son of man is not come to destroy men's lives") by changing the verb to "subdue." Thomas Newton noted the scriptural echo in his eighteenth century commentary on *Paradise Regain'd,* while also observing that "subdue," with its apparently less violent implications, is "the more proper word" because it is certainly "more suitable to the humane and heavenly character of the speaker." And Michael Wilding, who clearly wants to find unequivocal evidence for Milton's pacifism in the 1671 volume, concurs with Newton by stressing that "the correction shows Milton's anxiety to get the morality of Christian heroism right."[27] But does it?

The problem with this argument about Milton's emendation is that the verb "subdue" is hardly a neutral one in the Bible; nor is it less charged with violent implications. Indeed, it is an especially powerful verb in the Old Testament and evokes the violence of the Lord or of Israelite champions toward their enemies: in Psalm 47, where God is described as "terrible," he subdues the enemies of Israel, "the nations under our feet" (Ps. 47:3); in Judges 3:30 the nation of Moab, having subdued Israel in war, is then "subdued...under the hand of Israel" led by the liberating hero Ehud, whose forces slaughter "about ten thousand men...of valour; and there escaped not a man"; and in Judges 11:33 Jephtha, the Israelite military leader cited favorably in both *Paradise Regain'd* and *Samson Agonistes* (see *PR* 2.439 and *SA* 283), performs "a very great slaughter" so that "the children of Ammon were subdued before the children of Israel."[28]

Moreover, in Milton's Puritan culture the word "subdue" could also refer to the actions of the militant godly. Thus when Christian reaches Palace Beautiful in Bunyan's *Pilgrim's Progress,* he hears all about "the worthy Acts" of the militant godly in history: "how they had *subdued* Kingdoms, wrought Righteousness...stopped the mouths of Lions...waxed valiant in fight, and turned to flight the Armies of the *Aliens.*"[29] Consequently, the verb "subdue" in Jesus' meditation leaves open the possibility of other responses besides "winning words." Nor does it, as we have just seen, soften or dampen the implications for a more robust or violent response, if that is needed to overcome "the stubborn" enemies of God.

Jesus' speech in *Paradise Regain'd* may therefore highlight the potency of "winning words," but it also leaves room for the final act of Samson in the next poem of the 1671 volume: horrified by the Philistine's idolatrous religious rites in honor of Dagon, Samson does indeed subdue these "stubborn" enemies of God,

> thir hearts...jocund and sublime,
> Drunk with Idolatry, drunk with Wine
> And fat regorg'd of Bulls and Goats,
> Chanting their idol, and preferring
> Before our living Dread who dwells
> In *Silo* his bright sanctuary.   (*SA* 1669–74)

Milton's late poetry, including the 1671 volume, thus allows for divergent responses to what Milton regarded as the calamity of the Restoration, when (as Milton scathingly observed in 1673) the ungodly English "Nation of late years, is grown more numerously and excessively vitious then heretofore, Pride, Luxury, Drunkeness, Whoredom, Cursing, Swearing, bold and open Atheism every where abounding" (*Of True Religion*; YP 8:438).[30]

After all, who is to say that Milton altogether rejects Samson's violence, as horrid and as disturbing as that apocalyptic climax and final spectacle of destruction may be? In the introduction to *Samson Agonistes* Milton provides an extended and revealing commentary about his dramatic work in relation to Greek tragedy and in relation to the book of Revelation as a tragedy. Yet in the midst of this detailed commentary Milton *never* glances back at the brief epic that immediately precedes the dramatic poem in the very same volume where both major works were originally published together. Milton says nothing in the 1671 volume about the relation of *Samson Agonistes*—in aesthetic, political, or spiritual terms—to *Paradise Regain'd*. Presumably this relation is left to the discretion of the volume's discerning readers. There is no indication that Milton himself believes that *Paradise Regain'd* is somehow supposed to offer a corrective perspective when read in conjunction with the violent political world depicted in its companion poem.

Indeed, the 1671 volume of poems is provocative and suggestive precisely in terms of what it *does not* include: *Paradise Regain'd* is printed first, but there is no preface, no note on verse, and no argument summarizing the poem or the contents of its books. There is no statement from John Milton (whose full name appears on the volume's title page) about its relation to the dramatic poem that follows. My point is that the 1671 volume—by the way it prints the two poems together and by virtue of what it *does not say* about their relationship—encourages a relatively more open-ended interpretation from its readers. Moreover, by remaining more open-ended as readers, we allow the poet in 1671 a greater divergence of emotional and political responses to the Restoration, as well as a crucial element of ambiguity. Milton's dramatization of the deeply anguished Old Testament warrior Samson, who finally commits a spectacular, terrifying act of apocalyptic revenge, is allowed to coexist, as it were, with the poet's brief epic about an inward-looking, meditative Son of God who appeals, at the end of the poem, to the inspiration and illumination of that "Light from above" (*PR* 4.289), and who withstands every possible temptation presented to him, including the temptations of regal and imperial power.

Why not admit that Milton might wish to represent both scripturally based stories with deep sympathy, including the impulse to apocalyptic revenge with all its horror and preceded by Samson's terrible anguish? That anguish is presented so graphically in the drama (with Samson's intense "griefs" compared to "a ling'ring disease" or wounds that "Rankle, and fester, and gangrene, / To black mortification" [*SA* 617–22]) that Milton must surely have expected his readers to sympathize with Samson's humiliation and acute inward torment[31] while also allowing us to experience the dreadful horror of his gory end (with his body lying "Soak't in his enemies' blood" [*SA* 1726]). Why not admit that Milton could imagine in these two poems two differing responses (one of them a response of vehement rage) to the unwelcome world of Restoration conformity and religious rites and to the plight of the besieged, suffering godly and their calamities, including the many nonconformists who suffered from difficult physical conditions in "loathsome prison-house[s]" (*SA* 922) and who were subjected, as Manoa says of Samson, to "so foul indignities" (371)?[32] I believe that we close off imaginative possibilities when we argue too schematically that Milton was a quietist or pacifist after the Restoration or even that he was always expressing, in some fashion, political engagement in the great poems, and never expressing the urge to withdraw from the painful pressures of contemporary history. We thereby exclude the possibility that the three great poems enabled Milton to express imaginatively diverse responses to the disappointment and trauma of the Restoration and its triumphalism.

We need, then, to be more attentive to the dissonances of Milton's Restoration poems, to the ways, say, that *Samson Agonistes* and *Paradise Regain'd* not only complement each other, but *jostle against* each other, offering alternative responses to the religious and political crisis of the Restoration. Moreover, they do so without providing a clear signal that tells us that, in reading the two 1671 poems together, we must finally repudiate the violence of the tragic, militant Old Testament Samson (even as we register its horror) and instead embrace, as the only viable heroic response, the verbal resistance of Milton's faithful, unmoved, inward-looking Jesus. The 1671 volume, I suggest, remains much more ambiguous and more open-ended than that.

4. *Conclusion: Milton's Divergent Political Voices*

To conclude: we need not altogether agree with Coleridge, then, that the late Milton, "finding it impossible to realize his own aspirations, either in religion, or politics, or society, ...gave up his heart to the living spirit and the light within him." But we also need to acknowledge that Milton's political responses expressed in the great poems during the Restoration were more complex and more varied than models of spiritual withdrawal versus political engagement allow or of violence versus pacifism. I should like to urge scholars and readers of Milton to nuance or eschew such potentially reductive and schematic formulations and dichotomies. We need to recognize that they can never adequately account for the complexity of the poet's divergent imaginative and emotional responses as he struggled with the bitter political and religious consequences of the failures of the English revolution and the humiliation brought on by the Restoration. When it came to Milton's agonized engagements with Restoration politics and religion, his great poems allowed Milton to give voice to a multiple range of imaginative, emotional, and political responses—some of them in tension with one another, some of them remaining in ambiguous relation to one another.

In the case of the volume of 1671 poems, the dissenting poet indeed "avenged himself on the world," to recall Coleridge's words again. Yet rather than simply "enriching it" with another "record of his own transcendent ideal," Milton was able to publish, close to the end of his career, a particularly ambiguous, double-edged response to the religious politics of post-Restoration England.[33] The relation of Samson's cataclysmic violence to Jesus' apparent posture of pacifism or quietism, as I have suggested, remains more open-ended and less clear-cut in the 1671 volume of poems. There is no need to insist that Milton wanted readers to choose one response over another, just as there is no need to insist that the dispirited poet fallen on evil days chose politics over faith or faith over politics during the last part of his career. Together the companion poems explore divergent ways of acting or dissenting or remaining steadfast and unmoved in a hostile political sphere; their open-ended relation to each other—especially in terms of the volume's unresolved relation of pacifism to holy vengeance, retiring quietism to dramatic apocalyptic action—contributes to the volume's provocative ambiguity. To be sure, Milton the controversialist may well have felt, much like his contentious but retiring Jesus, that "winning words" is the preferable means "to conquer willing hearts"; nonetheless, by looking to the Bible, he could see that there are times of crisis when the stubborn political and religious enemies of God do indeed need to be subdued by force. The late Milton was not simply a quiescent dissenter disgusted by Restoration triumphalism; rather, he left open—especially in the imaginative and tragic world of *Samson Agonistes*—the possibility that the dreadful God of Israel might again need to subdue his idol-worshipping enemies, this time in post-Restoration England.

Consequently, Milton's defiant voice may have remained "unchang'd / To hoarse or mute" after the severe political and

religious disappointments of the English revolution and the catas-
trophes of the Restoration. Yet Milton's political voices, at the
culmination of his poetic career, could also be ambiguous and
divergent, sending more than one signal, while articulating more
than one reaction. His three great poems allowed the visionary
poet to express, in post-Restoration England, a much wider range
of imaginative responses and political reactions than we often
acknowledge. By stressing the varied responses we find in the great
poems to the religious politics of Restoration England, we have,
I admit, a less tidy and less predictable Milton at the end of his
career. Ultimately, I believe that this is a more accurate and per-
suasive depiction of a great and multifaceted poet painfully strug-
gling to confront and make sense of, in his final poems, "a World
perverse."

Notes

Notes to Introduction

1. Mary Ann Radzinowicz, *Toward* Samson Agonistes: *The Growth of Milton's Mind* (Princeton: Princeton University Press, 1978), 351–59; quotation at xix.

2. Joseph Wittreich, *Interpreting* Samson Agonistes (Princeton: Princeton University Press, 1986).

3. See Radzinowicz, *Toward* Samson Agonistes, 283–84, 346, 349.

Notes to Shawcross, "Milton and the Visionary Mode"

1. See *A Collection of the Works of That Holy Man and Profound Divine Thomas Iackson, D. D[.] Late President of Corpus Christi Colledge in Oxford* (London: Printed by R. Norton for Timothy Garthwait, 1653), book 1, chap. 14, 42–47; quotation at 43. The first two books appeared as *The Eternall Truth of Scriptures, in 2 books of Commentaries upon the Apostles Creed* (London: W. Stansby for J. Budge, 1613–14), entered on July 23, 1612. The epistle dedicatory to book 3 is dated "March 25. 1614."

2. *Paradise Lost*, 1.26. Milton's poetry (including translations) is quoted from my revised edition of *The Complete Poetry of John Milton* (Garden City, N.Y.: Doubleday Anchor, 1971), hereafter cited in the text.

3. Michael Lieb, *The Visionary Mode: Biblical Prophecy, Hermeneutics, and Cultural Change* (Ithaca: Cornell University Press, 1991), 1, 3, 10.

4. Carl Jung, "Psychologie und Dichtung," *Psychologie der Literaturwissenschaft* (Berlin, 1930), reprinted in *The Collected Works of C. G. Jung* (New York: Pantheon Books, 1966), Bollingen Series 20, *The Spirit in Man, Art, and Literature*, trans. R. F. C. Hull, 84–105; see 90. He writes, "the vision is a genuine primordial experience [*Urerlebnis*]"; "Great poetry draws its strength from the life of mankind, and we completely miss its meaning if we try to derive it from personal factors.... A work of art is

produced that may truthfully be called a message to generations of men" (94, 98).

5. Lieb, *The Visionary Mode*, 7–8.

6. Leland Ryken, introduction to *Milton and Scriptural Tradition: The Bible into Poetry*, ed. James H. Sims and Leland Ryken (Columbia: University of Missouri Press, 1984), 13.

7. Leland Ryken, *The Apocalyptic Vision in* Paradise Lost (Ithaca: Cornell University Press, 1970), and Joseph Anthony Wittreich Jr., ed., *Milton and the Line of Vision* (Madison: University of Wisconsin Press, 1975), xv, xv–xvi.

8. Ryken, "*Paradise Lost* and Its Biblical Epic Models," in Sims and Ryken, *Milton and Scriptural Tradition*, 74.

9. William Kerrigan, *The Prophetic Milton* (Charlottesville: University Press of Virginia, 1974), 17, 127, 270. See also M. V. Rama Sarma, *Milton and the Prophetic Strain* (New Delhi: Sterling, 1991), who discusses *Comus* and the three major poems.

10. Barbara Kiefer Lewalski, Paradise Lost *and the Rhetoric of Literary Forms* (Princeton: Princeton University Press, 1985), 33. See also William Kerrigan's discussion of vision in the poem in *The Sacred Complex: On the Psychogenesis of* Paradise Lost (Cambridge, Mass.: Harvard University Press, 1983), 141–43, 159–60, and 143–50 for remarks on "light."

11. Lieb, *The Visionary Mode*, 270, 267, 271.

12. Joseph Wittreich, *Visionary Poetics: Milton's Tradition and His Legacy* (San Marino, Calif.: Huntington Library, 1979), 33.

13. Milton, of course, here employs the prophecy of 2 Peter 3:12–13, which iterates the words of Isaiah 65:17–25: "For, behold, I create new heavens and a new earth: and the former shall not be remembered, nor come into mind." I have previously examined the significance of "Light after light well us'd" in its relationship to the myth of Exodus and the Hebraic concept of linear time, and its iteration of *Paradise Lost* 7.154–61. See John T. Shawcross, *With Mortal Voice: The Creation of* Paradise Lost (Lexington: University Press of Kentucky, 1984), chap. 11, 119–38, esp. 135–36.

14. *Paradise Lost*, for example, by Leland Ryken in *The Apocalyptic Vision*, and in *Lycidas*, for example, by Joseph Wittreich in *Visionary Poetics*. It has informed studies of *Paradise Regain'd*, for example, in Wittreich's *Angel of Apocalypse: Blake's Idea of Milton* (Madison: University of Wisconsin Press, 1975), and Charles Huttar, "The Passion of Christ in *Paradise Regained*," *English Language Notes* 19 (1982): 236–60. Relevant references in the poetry prior to 1637, when *Lycidas* was written, have appeared here and there, particularly in discussions of "Ode on the Morning of *Christs* Nativity" and "The Passion," and see Kerrigan, *The Prophetic Milton*. Additionally important studies that relate to the visionary mode and Milton are Michael Lieb's "Scriptural Formula and Prophetic Utterance in *Lycidas*," in Sims and Ryken, *Milton and Scriptural Tradition*,

31–42; "Ezekiel's Inaugural Vision as a Literary Event," *Cithara* 24 (1985): 22–39; and *Children of Ezekiel: Aliens, UFOs, the Crisis of Race, and the Advent of End Time* (Durham: Duke University Press, 1998).

15. Letter 5 in *Epistolarum Familiarium* (1674), my translation; see *The Prose of John Milton*, ed. J. Max Patrick (Garden City, N.Y.: Doubleday Anchor, 1967), 603.

16. The sonnet is quoted in the first version of the letter to an unnamed friend in the Trinity manuscript, the date of which is debated. For an examination of the significance of the parables of the talents (Matt. 25:14–30) and the laborer (Matt. 20:1–16) and for explication of this matter of career in the sonnet and the letter, see David V. Urban, "Mr. Milton: A Parabolic Laborer and His Identity," in *Milton Studies*, vol. 43, ed. Albert C. Labriola, 1–18 (Pittsburgh: University of Pittsburgh Press, 2004).

17. Since at least William Blake and William Ellery Channing, as Wittreich points out in *Visionary Poetics*, 218n5, a prophetic Milton has been recognized, and not only in the poetry but also in the prose. The assignment of a poet like Spenser or Milton to the line of prophecy, and contrastively, of a poet like Donne or Pope to the line of wit reduces their writing to *prophecy*, that is, a reader-oriented approach and conceptual intentionality on the part of the author, and to *wit*, that is, an author-controlled crafting and an almost exclusionary recognition of technique on the part of the reader. This oppositional bifurcation can serve a purpose, but it is simplistic and overlap will occur often in numerous ways, as we see in the next three elegies discussed here.

18. The final reference to "the mistress of Cephalus," that is Aurora, the dawn, and the last line, however, add something of the line of wit, and only readers well versed in Latin and in Ovid (his fellow schoolmates?) would recognize it. "I wept for the dreams disturbed by the mistress of Cephalus. / May such dreams often befall me" (Flebam turbatos Cephaeleia pellice somnos, / Talia contingant somnia saepe mihi"). On the serious level the lines say only that he awoke with the dawn and wishes for further dreams of reassurance of the visionary prophecy, which can be shaken easily by death and injustice. On the level of wit it implies that his dreaming has turned into a sexual and perhaps seminal dream.

19. Like "Elegia quarta," the fair infant elegy (January–February 1628) has a contemporary political theme in its background. See my "Milton's *Nectar:* Symbol of Immortality," *English Miscellany* 16 (1965): 131–41.

20. The odes are uncertainly dated, ranging from 1631 to 1637; the first two are transcribed into the Trinity manuscript, having been written elsewhere and probably prior to the inception of the manuscript, and the last being worked out in it through three and a half drafts. The argument that the manuscript was begun around September 1637, of course, places them, and especially "At a Solemn Music," closer to the pastoral elegy.

21. See also Michael Lieb, "Milton's 'Unexpressive Nuptial Song': A Reading of *Lycidas*," *Renaissance Papers* (1982): 15–26.

22. Among other studies, see Arthur Barker, "The Pattern of Milton's Nativity Ode," *University of Toronto Quarterly* 10 (1941): 167–81; Rosemond Tuve, *Images and Themes in Five Poems by Milton* (Cambridge, Mass.: Harvard University Press, 1957); and Maren-Sofie Røstvig, *The Hidden Sense and Other Essays* (Oslo: Universitetsforlaget, 1963), 55–58, for numerological analysis.

23. In "Elegia sexta," written to Charles Diodati in December 1629, Milton describes the Nativity ode thus: "I am singing the King, bringer of peace by his divine origin, / and the blessed times promised in the sacred books, and the crying of our God and his stabling under the meagre roof, who with his Father inhabits the heavenly realms; / and the heavens insufficient of stars and the hosts singing in the ark / and the gods suddenly destroyed in their temples." The completed poem, however, pays less attention to the actual birth and "stabling" than seems indicated here.

24. The poem was written in March or April 1630 (Easter Sunday was March 28 and the sermon, on Matthew 28:6, referring to the Resurrection was delivered at St. Paul's by Dean John Donne). Eastertide was a time when Milton introspectively meditated upon his personal world as the elegy and letter to Thomas Young, discussed before, confirm. Not only are the birth and life motifs of the Nativity ode replaced by sacrifice and death as themes, but the individual poet in his own world in the former ode gives way here to the poet recognizing that he must take a place in this world. The sermon stressed the auditors' being raised "from the bed of sin, in any holy purpose," raised "To that renovation, to that new creation." The poet of "The Passion," "hurried on viewles wing...[to] Mountains wild," is soon amid "The gentle neighbourhood of grove and spring" and a "race of mourners." Significantly, the liturgy for Easter Sunday included Matthew 28:16–20, part of which is "Go ye therefore, and teach all nations, baptizing them in the name of the Father, and of the son, and of the Holy Ghost; teaching them to observe all things whatsoever I have commanded you" (see *The Sermons of John Donne*, 10 vols., ed. Evelyn M. Simpson and George R. Potter [Berkeley and Los Angeles: University of California Press, 1958], vol. 9, no. 8, 212, 203).

25. See also John A. Via, "Milton's 'The Passion': A Successful Failure," *Milton Quarterly* 5 (1971): 35–38; Philip J. Gallagher, "Milton's 'The Passion': Inspired Mediocrity," *Milton Quarterly* 11 (1977): 44–50; and Frederic B. Tromley, "'Milton's Preposterous Exaction': The Significance of 'The Passion,'" *ELH, A Journal of English Literary History* 47 (1980): 276–86. In a forthcoming paper, Bryan A. Hampton, "All 'Passion' Spent: Hermeneutics and Theology in Milton's 'unfinish't' Poem," concerned that "The Crucifixion remains for Milton a distant and alienating text," argues that "Milton appropriates the Incarnation, rather than the Crucifixion, as a transformational text for himself." Jesus' "Consummatum est" does not allow for a "world projected 'in front' of the text" (to employ Paul Ricoeur's hermeneutical concept).

26. Joseph Wittreich, "William Blake: Illustrator-Interpreter of *Paradise Regained,*" in *Calm of Mind: Tercentenary Essays on* Paradise Regained *and* Samson Agonistes *in Honor of John S. Diekhoff,* ed. Joseph Anthony Wittreich Jr. (Cleveland: The Press of Case Western Reserve University, 1971).

27. The Geneva Bible's introduction to the Psalm is pertinent, representing a general reading and one that Milton would surely have encountered:

> David complained becavse he was broght into suche extremities, that he was past all hope, but after he had rehearsed the sorowes & greifs, where with he was vexed, He recouereth him self from the bottomles pit of tentations and groweth in hope. And here vnder his owne persone he setteth forthe the figure of Christ, whome he did forese by the Spirit of prophecie, that he shulde maruelously, & strongly be deiected & abased, before his Father shulde raise & exalte him againe.

Jesus' human cry appears in the report of the Crucifixion in Matthew 27:46 and Mark 15:34.

Compare also Margaret Justice Dean, "Choosing Death: Adam's Temptation to Martyrdom in *Paradise Lost,*" *Milton Studies* 46 (2007): 30–56,who explores the question of martyrdom, finding that Milton deploys "The Passion" narrative, the true martyrdom of the Son, in the epic as counterdistinction to Adam's false notions of martyrdom.

28. Huttar, "The Passion of Christ," 244.

29. Ibid., 258.

30. Marshall Grossman, "'In Pensive Trance, and anguish, and ecstatic fit': Milton on the Passion," in *"A Fine Tuning": Studies of the Religious Poetry of Herbert and Milton,* ed. Mary A. Maleski, 205–20 (Binghamton: Medieval and Renaissance Texts and Studies, 1989), 210, 207, 214. Quotation of *De doctrina Christiana* is from *Complete Prose Works of John Milton,* 8 vols., ed. Don M. Wolfe et al. (New Haven: Yale University Press, 1953–82), 6:440, hereafter cited as YP.

31. "The Passion is the suffering both interior and exterior endured by Jesus Christ from the Last Supper until His death on the Cross" (*New Catholic Encyclopedia. Second Edition* [Detroit: Gale, 2003], 10, 924, under "Passion of Christ, II [Devotion To]"). "In general, 'the Passion' is best taken in reference to the Last Supper, the agony in Gethsemane, the arrest, trials, crucifixion, death, and burial"; from *The Interpreter's Dictionary of the Bible* (Nashville: Abington Press, 1962), 3, 663, under "Passion, The." Thomas N. Corns, "'On the Morning of Christ's Nativity,' 'Upon the Circumcision' and 'The Passion,'" *A Companion to Milton,* ed. Thomas N. Corns (Oxford: Blackwell, 2003), may wisely curtail the critics' lament: "For this is a poem about the inadequacy of the poet's idiom

to capture the enormity of Christ's sacrifice. It is a poem about what the poet would like to do, but cannot, and just as Milton as believer cannot really bring himself to contemplate the tortured Christ, so Milton as poet cannot commemorate the event" (219).

32. I cite Lieb in *Milton and the Culture of Violence* (Ithaca: Cornell University Press, 1994), 10. We should, of course, remember that violence enters some visionary narratives that have been mentioned in this essay: the Crucifixion, the circumcision, Samson's act of destruction. It is not that the visionary mode will always proceed with violence encountered, but that the aims of the Son, of a Gideon or Samson, the covenantal results of Abraham's circumcision or Noah's flood, as well as James Baldwin's (that is, Peter's) "the fire next time," must too often go through ordeal and death and violent action to attain the "blissful Seat."

33. Kerrigan, *The Prophetic Milton*, 200; Huttar, "The Passion of Christ," 244.

34. Louis L. Martz, *The Poetry of Meditation: A Study in English Religious Literature of the Seventeenth Century* (New Haven: Yale University Press, 1954), 168. The grossness and the unintelligibility of having "infection" of "sorrows" make some fat-looking "cloud" "pregnant" render the last stanza unbelievably silly.

Notes to Lewalski, "Milton and the Culture Wars"

1. John Milton, *Doctrine and Discipline of Divorce*, in *The Complete Prose Works of John Milton*, 8 vols. in 10, ed. Don M. Wolfe et al. (New Haven: Yale University Press, 1953–82), 2:279–80. All citations to Milton's prose are to this edition and are noted parenthetically.

2. Michael Lieb, *Milton and the Culture of Violence* (Ithaca: Cornell University Press, 1994).

3. W. H. Auden, "In Memory of W. B. Yeats," 36.

4. Charles I, *The King's Majesty's declaration to his subjects concerning lawful sports to be used* (London, 1633); William Prynne, *Histrio-mastix; or, The Player's Scourge and Actors Tragedy* (London, 1633 [1632]).

5. Lines 87–89, "Patria dura parens, & saxis saevior albis / Spumea quae pulsat littoris unda tui, / Siccine te decet innocuos exponere foetus," trans. John Carey, ed. *John Milton: Complete Shorter Poems*, 2nd ed. (London: Longman, 1997).

6. Lines 9–12, "Tunc memini clarique ducis, fratisque verendi / Intempestivis ossa cremata rogis. / Et thera raptos, / Flevit memini Heroum quos vidit ad & amissos Belgia tota duces," trans. Carey, ibid.

7. John Milton, "Ode on the Morning of *Christs* Nativity," 28; Milton's early English poems are cited from *Poems of Mr. John Milton, Both English and Latin* (London: Humphrey Moseley, 1645).

8. In *Poems* (1645) these lines are added to the third song (106–07).

9. See Barbara K. Lewalski, "Milton's *Comus* and the Politics of Masquing," in *The Politics of the Stuart Court Masque*, ed. David Bevington and Peter Holbrook (Cambridge: Cambridge University Press, 1998), 296–320.

10. See Maryann Cale McGuire, *Milton's Puritan Masque* (Athens,: University of Georgia Press, 1983).

11. Cedric C. Brown, *John Milton's Aristocratic Entertainments* (Cambridge: Cambridge University Press, 1985), 57–77.

12. See Stella P. Revard, *Milton and the Tangles of Neaera's Hair* (Columbia: University of Missouri Press, 1997), 131–56.

13. Joseph A. Wittreich Jr., *Visionary Poetics: Milton's Tradition and His Legacy* (San Marino, Calif.: Huntington Library, 1979), 142–43.

14. When Milton agreed to be published by Moseley, he was not yet identified with the Cavaliers; save for Waller, all the volumes mentioned postdate Milton's *Poems*, as does Moseley's copyright for Sir John Denham's *Cooper's Hill* (1642) and Thomas Carew's *Poems* (1640). For a fuller discussion of the contestation between author and publisher within Milton's 1645 *Poems*, see Barbara K. Lewalski, *The Life of John Milton: A Critical Biography*, rev. ed. (Oxford: Blackwell, 2003), 226–29.

15. *Poems, &c. Written by Mr. Ed. Waller of Beckonsfield, Esquire; lately a Member of the Honourable House of Commons* (London: Humphrey Moseley, 1645), sig. A2.

16. David Loewenstein, "Milton and the Poetics of Defense," in *Politics, Poetics, and Hermeneutics in Milton's Prose*, ed. David Loewenstein and James Grantham Turner (Cambridge: Cambridge University Press, 1990), 187–88.

17. John Milton, *Paradise Lost: A Poem in Twelve Books*, 32–36 (London: S. Simmons, 1674); hereafter cited in the text. See Lieb, *Milton and the Culture of Violence*, 13–80, for discussion of the dismemberment of Orpheus in this passage as well as in *Lycidas* and elsewhere.

18. Laura Lunger Knoppers, *Historicizing Milton: Spectacle, Power, and Poetry in Restoration England* (Athens: University of Georgia Press, 1994), 67–122; John Dryden, *Astraea Redux* (London, 1660), 320–21.

19. David Norbrook, "Lucan, Thomas May, and the Creation of a Republican Literary Culture," in *Culture and Politics in Early Stuart England*, ed. Kevin Sharpe and Peter Lake (Stanford: Stanford University Press, 1993), 45–66; and Norbrook, *Writing the English Republic* (Cambridge: Cambridge University Press, 1999), 438–67.

20. John Dryden, *Annus Mirabilis: The Year of Wonders* (London, 1667), sigs. A5v–A6v; John Dryden, *Of Dramatick Poesie, An Essay* (London, 1667), 66–67.

21. Steven N. Zwicker, "Lines of Authority: Politics and Literary Culture in the Restoration," in *Politics of Discourse: The Literature and History of Seventeenth-Century England*, ed. Kevin Sharpe and Steven N. Zwicker (Berkeley and Los Angeles: University of California Press, 1987), 249.

22. For discussion of such comparisons and contrasts throughout the poem, see Barbara K. Lewalski, Paradise Lost *and the Rhetoric of Literary Forms* (Princeton: Princeton University Press, 1985), esp. 55–109.

23. John Milton, *Paradise Regain'd. A Poem in IV Books. To which is added Samson Agonistes* (London: John Starkey, 1671). Citations to these poems are to this edition.

24. Steven N. Zwicker, "Milton, Dryden, and the Politics of Literary Controversy," in *Culture and Society in the Stuart Restoration,* ed. Gerald Maclean (Cambridge: Cambridge University Press, 1995), 139–40, 151.

25. Edward Phillips, "The Life of Mr. John Milton," in *The Early Lives of Milton,* ed. Helen Darbishire (London: Constable, 1932), 75; Thomas Ellwood, *The History of the Life of Thomas Ellwood,* ed. J[oseph] W[yeth] (London, 1714), 314.

26. David Loewenstein, "The Kingdom Within: Radical Religious Culture and the Politics of *Paradise Regained," Literature and History* 3 (1994): 63–89.

27. Sharon Achinstein, "Milton, *Samson Agonistes,* and the Drama of Dissent," in *Milton Studies,* vol. 33, ed. Albert C. Labriola and David Loewenstein (Pittsburgh: University of Pittsburgh Press, 1996), 133–58.

28. For further discussion, see Barbara K. Lewalski, "Milton's *Samson* and the 'New Acquist of True [Political] Experience,'" in *Milton Studies,* vol. 24, ed. Albert C. Labriola (Pittsburgh: University of Pittsburgh Press, 1999), 233–51.

29. John Carey, "A Work in Praise of Terrorism? September 11 and *Samson Agonistes," Times Literary Supplement,* September 6, 2002, 15.

30. Michael Lieb, *Theological Milton: Deity, Discourse, and Heresy in the Miltonic Canon* (Pittsburgh: Duquesne University Press, 2006), 184–209.

31. On this point, see John T. Shawcross, *The Uncertain World of* Samson Agonistes (Cambridge: D. S. Brewer, 2001), 111.

Notes to Achinstein, "Red Milton"

1. Walter Benjamin, "Critique of Violence," in *Walter Benjamin: Selected Writings,* vol. 1, ed. Marcus Bullock and Michael W. Jennings (Cambridge, Mass.: Harvard University Press, 1996), 236–52. See Beatrice Hanssen's sensitive treatment of Benjamin's brush with the "battlefront of fascism," "On the Politics of Pure Means: Benjamin, Arendt, Foucault," in *Violence, Identity, and Self-Determination,* ed. Hent De Vries and Samuel Weber (Stanford: Stanford University Press, 1997), 238, and her brilliant study, *Critique of Violence: Between Poststructuralism and Critical Theory* (London: Routledge, 2000).

2. John Milton, *Samson Agonistes,* cited in *Milton: Complete Shorter Poems,* 2nd ed., ed. John Carey (London: Longman, 1997). See Michael Lieb,

"'Our Living Dread': The God of *Samson Agonistes*," in *Milton Studies*, vol. 33, ed. Albert C. Labriola and Michael Lieb (Pittsburgh: University of Pittsburgh Press, 1996), 3–25.

3. On the nexus of psychological and theological, see Michael Lieb, *Milton and the Culture of Violence* (Ithaca: Cornell University Press, 1994); and for violence and theology, see his *Theological Milton* (Pittsburgh: Duquesne University Press, 2006).

4. Thomas H. Kean et al., *The 9/11 Commission* Report (New York: Norton, 2004), 348.

5. Tom Rockmore and Joseph Margolis, eds., introduction to *The Philosophical Challenge of 9/11* (Oxford: Blackwell, 2005), 3.

6. Alan M. Dershowitz, *Why Terrorism Works: Understanding the Threat, Responding to the Challenge* (New Haven: Yale University Press, 2002), 11.

7. Slavoj Žižek, *The Puppet and the Dwarf: The Perverse Core of Christianity* (Cambridge, Mass.: The Massachusetts Institute of Technology Press, 2003), 37.

8. See my "Cold War Milton," *University of Toronto Quarterly* 77 (2008): 801–36.

9. Howard Mumford Jones, ed., *Primer of Intellectual Freedom* (Cambridge, Mass.: Harvard University Press, 1949); A. Whitney Griswold, *Liberal Education and the Democratic Ideal* (New Haven: Yale University Press, 1959), 11, 12.

10. See, for example, on Milton in the American Revolution, John S. Tanner and Justin Collings, "How Adams and Jefferson Read Milton and Milton Read Them," *Milton Quarterly* 40 (2006): 207–19; Tony Davies, "Borrowed Language: Milton, Jefferson, Mirabeau," in *Milton and Republicanism*, ed. Quentin Skinner, David Armitage, and Armand Himy (Cambridge: Cambridge University Press, 1995), 254–71; on Milton in the French Revolution, see Don M. Wolfe, "Milton and Mirabeau," *PMLA* 49 (1934): 116–28; and Christophe Tournu, *Milton, Mirabeau: Rencontre révolutionnaire* (Paris: EDIMAF, 2002); and on Milton in the Russian Revolution, see V. J. Boss, "*Areopagitica* and Freedom of the Press," *East European Quarterly* 24 (1990): 127–50.

11. Frances Stonor Saunders, *Who Paid the Piper? The CIA and the Cultural Cold War* (London: Granta, 1999), 157. On cold war academia, see Ellen Schrecker, *No Ivory Tower: McCarthyism and the Universities* (Oxford: Oxford University Press, 1986).

12. "The Tragedy of John Milton," in *To Illuminate Our Time: The Blacklisted Teleplays of Abraham Polonsky*, ed. John Schultheiss and Mark Schaubert (Los Angeles: Sadanlaur Publications, 1993), 345. All citations come from this edition. On Polonsky, see Paul Buhle, *A Very Dangerous Citizen: Abraham Lincoln Polonsky and the Hollywood Left* (Berkeley and Los Angeles: University of California Press, 2001).

13. See Paul Buhle and Dave Wagner, introduction to *The World Above* (Urbana: University of Illinois Press, 1999).

14. On the achievements of his film noir oeuvre, see Robert Sklar, *City Boys: Cagney, Bogart, Garfield* (Princeton: Princeton University Press, 1992).

15. Cited in John Shultheiss, "A Season of Fear: Abraham Polonsky, *You Are There*, and the Blacklist," in Schultheiss and Schaubert, *To Illuminate Our Time*, 8. See also Victor S. Navasky, *Naming Names* (New York: Viking, 1980), 421.

16. *Hollywood Reporter*, April 26, 1951, "Dmytryk Bares Giant Red Plot to Control Screen and Unions," cited in Buhle, *Very Dangerous Citizen*, 145.

17. Polonsky, *A Season of Fear* (1956; repr. Berlin: Seven Seas Publications, 1959), 112, 97; hereafter cited in the text.

18. Larry Ceplair and Steven Englund, *The Inquisition in Hollywood: Politics in the Film Community, 1930–1960* (New York: Doubleday, 1980), 191; Buhle, *Very Dangerous Citizen*, 136–45. See also Brenda Murphy, *Congressional Theatre: Dramatizing McCarthyism on Stage, Film, and Telelvision* (Cambridge: Cambridge University Press, 1999), 158.

19. See Shultheiss and Schaubert, introduction to *To Illuminate Our Time*; Robert F. Horowitz, "History Comes to Life and *You Are There*," *American History/American Television: Interpreting the Video Past*, ed. John E. O'Connor (New York: Frederick Ungar, 1983), 79–93.

20. See Frank R. Cunningham, *Sidney Lumet: Film and Literary Vision* (Lexington: University Press of Kentucky, 1991), 19.

21. Walter Bernstein, *Inside Out: A Memoir of the Blacklist* (New York: De Capo Press, 2000), 233.

22. Murphy, *Congressional Theatre*, 3. See also Daniel Aron, *Writers on the Left: Episodes in American Literary Communism* (New York: Columbia University Press, 1992); Paul Buhle and Dave Wagner, *Hide in Plain Sight: The Hollywood Blacklistees in Film and Television, 1950–2002* (London: Palgrave Macmillan, 2003).

23. "The Tragedy of John Milton," 329.

24. Polonsky, *The Box*, quoted in Murphy, *Congressional Theatre*, 1. On Polonsky, see Walter Bernstein, *Inside Out*.

25. *The World Above*, 312, spoken by the psychologist Curtin. Quotations from the play hereafter cited in the text.

26. Giorgio Agamben, "Beyond Human Rights," in *Means without End: Notes on Politics*, trans. V. Binetti and C. Casarino (Minneapolis: University of Minnesota Press, 2000); see also his *Homo Sacer: Sovereign Power and Bare Life*, trans. Daniel Heller-Roazen (Stanford: Stanford University Press, 1998), 8–9, 79, 82–85.

27. Giorgio Agamben, *State of Exception*, trans. Kevin Attrell (Chicago: University of Chicago Press, 2005), 2, 59.

28. Dominic LaCapra, *History in Transit: Experience, Identity, Critical Theory* (Ithaca: Cornell University Press, 2004), 191.

Notes to Fish, "How Hobbes Works"

1. Michael Lieb, *Milton and the Culture of Violence* (Ithaca: Cornell University Press, 1994), 10.

2. John Milton, *Paradise Lost,* 7.32, in *John Milton: Complete Poems and Major Prose,* ed. Merritt Y. Hughes (New York: Odyssey Press, 1957). All quotations of Milton's poetry come from this edition; quotations of *Paradise Lost* are noted parenthetically as *PL* by book and line(s).

3. Michael Lieb, *Theological Milton: Deity, Discourse, and Heresy in the Miltonic Canon* (Pittsburgh: Duquesne University Press, 2006), 193.

4. Lieb, *Milton and the Culture of Violence,* 69.

5. John Milton, *An Apology against a Pamphlet,* in *The Complete Prose Works of John Milton,* 8 vols. in 10, ed. Don M. Wolfe et al. (New Haven: Yale University Press, 1953–82), 1:937. All quotations of Milton's prose come from this edition and are noted parenthetically as YP by volume and page.

6. Compare Bunyan: "Things to come, and carnal sense, are... strangers to one another." See John Bunyan, *The Pilgrim's Progress,* ed. James Wharey; rev. ed. Roger Shattuck (Oxford: Oxford University Press, 1960), 32.

7. Thomas Hobbes, *Leviathan,* ed. C. B. Macpherson (Harmondsworth, England: Penguin Books, 1968), 186. All quotations of *Leviathan* come from this edition and are noted parenthetically.

8. Stanley Fish, *How Milton Works* (Cambridge, Mass.: Belknap Press of Harvard University Press, 2001), 24.

9. On this point, see David Panagia, *The Poetics of Political Thinking* (Durham, N.C.: Duke University Press, 2006), 41.

10. Mary Dietz, "Hobbes's Subject as Citizen," in *Thomas Hobbes and Political Theory,* ed. Mary G. Dietz (Lawrence: University Press of Kansas, 1990), observes correctly that "insofar as the virtues of Hobbes's citizen cultivate a disposition toward obedience to Leviathan, they conspire to deprive the citizen of precisely the sort of liberty that distinguished classical republicanism—a liberty Hobbes deemed specious" (112).

11. For a brilliant discussion of Hobbes's view of contract and its relationship to other views held by his contemporaries and predecessors, see Victoria Kahn, *Wayward Contracts: The Crisis of Political Obligation in England, 1640–1674* (Princeton: Princeton University Press, 2004). Kahn observes that in Hobbes's account of contract, "The contemporary discourses of natural law[,] covenant theology, and the common law appear, but each is systematically undermined" (155). She further notes, "To define breach of contract in formal terms as a logical and linguistic absurdity would have been shocking to Hobbes's contemporaries," who would have learned from Aristotle and Aquinas that "the idea that promises should be kept was a maxim of the moral law" (156). Kahn links Hobbes's position with the famous Slade's Case (1604): "If in the older view of obligation, promises were to be kept because of a transcendent moral law...in

Slade promises were to be kept because they had been articulated in the shared medium of language and ratified by the exchange of other material signs" (47).

12. M. M. Goldsmith *Hobbes Science of Politics* (New York: Columbia University Press, 1966), points out that Hobbes is a legal positivist, which means that he "denies that laws must be just, right, moral, and good in order to be laws. Instead law is distinguished by procedural...test" (274).

13. Johann Sommerville, "Hobbes on Political Obligation," in *Leviathan*, ed. R. Flathman and D. Johnston (New York: Norton, 1997), 334.

14. Richard Tuck, *Hobbes: A Very Short Introduction* (Oxford: Oxford University Press, 1989), explains that Hobbes "treated *moral* terms in exactly the same way he had treated color terms: though common language and common sense might lead us to think that something is really and objectively good, in the same way as we might think something is really and objectively red, in fact such ideas are illusions and fantasies, features of the insides of our heads only" (63). This relativism, Tuck notes, need not lead to toleration on the reasoning that everyone's judgments are equally unauthorized. It might lead instead to absolutism, on the reasoning that in the absence of a perspicuous authority in nature, we must invent one: "Moral relativism, thought through properly, might lead...to the Leviathan" (130).

15. Milton's position is exactly opposite. In *The Tenure of Kings and Magistrates*, he tells a more virtue-centered story of the origin of political authority. When humans first perceived the need for some form of governance, "they communicated and deriv'd [the authority] either to one, whom for the eminence of his wisdom and integrity they chose above the rest, or to more then one, whom they thought of equal deserving" (YP 3:199).

16. See on this point Bernard Gert, "Hobbes's Psychology," in *The Cambridge Companion to Hobbes*, ed. Tom Sorell (Cambridge: Cambridge University Press, 1966): "What was really important for Hobbes was to use words in such a way that everyone would agree that the terms referred to the same thing. He did not want to use words that were primarily expressions of the attitudes of the person using them" (163).

17. See Richard Rorty, *Contingency, Irony, and Solidarity* (Cambridge: Cambridge University Press, 1989): "To say that truth is not out there is simply to say that where there are no sentences there is no truth....The world is out there, but descriptions of the world are not" (5).

18. Victoria Silver, "The Fiction of Self-Evidence in Hobbes's *Leviathan*," *ELH, A Journal of English Literary History* 55 (1988): 360.

19. Marcus Tullius Cicero, *On Invention*, in *On Invention. The Best Kind of Orator. Topics*, trans. H. M. Hubbell (London: Loeb Classical Library, 1949), 1.1.1–3. Marcus Tullius Cicero, *On the Orator, Books I–II*,

trans. E. W. Sutton and H. Rackham (London: Loeb Classical Library, 1949), 1.8.33.

20. Rousseau tells still another story, one in which civilization corrupts the noble savage by socializing him to the point where the authenticity of his own inner existence disappears and is replaced by the artificial conventions insisted on by society. His fear is Hobbes's desire.

21. John Aubrey, *Brief Lives,* ed. O. L. Dick (London: Secker and Warburg, 1949), lxv.

22. Michael Oakshott, *Hobbes on Civil Association* (Oxford: Basil Blackwell, 1975), 17.

23. Sheldon Wolin, "Hobbes and the Culture of Despotism," in Dietz, *Thomas Hobbes and Political Theory,* observes that "Hobbes was not trying to persuade his readers but to compel them. The logical structure of his argument is a sequence of stark compulsions forcing on his reader-citizen the choice between controlled violence and violent oblivion" (26). In the same volume James Farr explains that Hobbes's "ideal reader...is the person persuadable in the ways of truth and peace, as Hobbes understood them." He adds, "Should Hobbes actually persuade readers he would not have only authored some new doctrines but created new vessels for them" ("Hobbes and the Politics of Biblical Interpretation," 188).

24. Silver, "The Fiction of Self-Evidence, 371.

25. Jean Hampton, "The Failure of Hobbes's Social Contract," in Flathman and Johnston, *Leviathan,* 354, 357.

26. See Fish, *How Milton Works,* 511–73.

Notes to Benet, "God's 'Red Right Hand'"

1. John Milton, *Paradise Lost,* 2.751, in *John Milton: Complete Poems and Major Prose,* ed. Merritt Y. Hughes (New York: Odyssey Press, 1957); hereafter cited in the text by book and line number.

2. Elaine Scarry, *The Body in Pain: The Making and Unmaking of the World* (Oxford: Oxford University Press, 1985), 16.

3. See Michael Lieb, "'Hate in Heav'n': Milton and the *Odium Dei,*" *English Literary History* 53 (1986): 519–39; and *Theological Milton: Deity, Discourse, and Heresy in the Miltonic Canon* (Pittsburgh: Duquesne University Press, 2006), 163–83.

4. William Empson, *Milton's God* (1961; rev. ed. London: Chatto & Windus, 1965), 54.

5. John Wooten, "The Poet's War: Violence and Virtue in *Paradise Lost,*" *SEL* 30 (1990): 136.

6. Sarah Hutton, "Of Physic and Philosophy: Anne Conway, F. M. van Helmont and Seventeenth-Century Medicine," in *Religio Medici: Medicine and Religion in Seventeenth-Century England,* ed. Ole Peter

Grell and Andrew Cunningham (Aldershot, Hants: Scolar Press, 1996), 230, 231–32.

7. David Cressy, *Birth, Marriage, and Death: Ritual, Religion, and the Life-Cycle in Tudor and Stuart England* (Oxford: Oxford University Press, 1997), 390.

8. *The Conway Letters: The Correspondence of Anne, Viscountess Conway, Henry More, and Their Friends,* ed. Marjorie Hope Nicolson; rev. ed. Sarah Hutton (1930; rev. ed. Oxford: Oxford University Press, 1992), 10.

9. On Sydenham, see Barbara K. Lewalski, *The Life of John Milton* (Oxford: Blackwell, 2000), 536. On standard treatments, see Annabel Hecht, "For Treating Arthritis, Start with Aspirin," *FDA Consumer*, January 1984; available at findarticles.com/p/articles/mi_m1370/is_v17/ai_3074217/ (accessed December 7, 2006). On Symcott's plaster recommendation to Powers, see Frederick George Marcham, "Letters of an English Physician in the Early Seventeenth Century," *Isis* 16 (1931): 64, 73.

10. Gillian R. Hamilton and Thomas F. Baskett, "In the Arms of Morpheus: The Development of Morphine for Postoperative Pain Relief," *Canadian Journal of Anesthesia* 47 (2000); available at www.cja-jca.org/ cgi /content/abstract (accessed December 11, 2006).

11. Robert S. Holzman, "The Legacy of Atropos, the Fate Who Cut the Thread of Life," *Anesthesiology: The Journal of the American Society of Anesthesiologists* 89 (1998): 1, 6; http://www.anesthesiology.org/pt/re/ anes/abstract.00000542-199807000-00030.htm (accessed November 14, 2006).

12. Nicolson, *Conway Letters,* 113.

13. Roselyne Rey, *The History of Pain,* trans. Louise Elliott Wallace, J. A. Cadden, and S. W. Cadden (Cambridge, Mass.: Harvard University Press, 1995), 83.

14. Hannah Arendt, *Eichmann in Jerusalem,* quoted in Scarry, *The Body in Pain,* 58.

15. Empson, *Milton's God,* 12.

16. David Harley, "The Theology of Affliction and the Experience of Sickness in the Godly Family, 1650–1714: The Henrys and the Newcomes," in Grell and Cunningham, *Religio Medici,* 227.

17. Blaise Pascal, "Prayer to Ask God for the Good Use of Sickness," quoted in David B. Morris, *The Culture of Pain* (Berkeley and Los Angeles: University of California Press, 1991), 44. Herbert quotes from *The Works of George Herbert,* ed. F. E. Hutchinson (1941; repr., Oxford: Oxford University Press, 1959).

18. Nicolson, *Conway Letters,* 224, 103.

19. Thomas Browne, *The Prose of Sir Thomas Browne,* ed. Norman J. Endicott (New York: New York University Press, 1967), 13.

20. I have written elsewhere about Satan's reenactment of his sin. See my "Adam's Evil Conscience and Satan's Surrogate Fall," *Milton Quarterly* 39 (2005): 2–15.

21. William Poole, *Milton and the Idea of the Fall* (Cambridge: Cambridge University Press, 2005), 176.

22. Regarding the war, there are so many inconsistencies and issues that the reader can pick and choose. Robert H. West, *Milton and the Angels* (Athens: University of Georgia Press, 1955), for instance, focuses on how the angels are "hampered by their armor." He asks, "Why did they not contract themselves and slip out of it? And why was the armor itself incontractible in heaven whereas the whole demonic host apparently contracted it to enter Pandemonium?" (110).

23. Wooten, "The Poet's War," 137, 139, 141.

24. Scarry, *The Body in Pain*, 12.

25. Empson, *Milton's God*, 53, points out that this thickening means the disobedient can no longer enjoy angelic sex; see *PL* 4.508–10. In *Comus*, the Elder Brother attributes to lust a like degenerate effect: "defilement" is let in "to the inward parts, / [And] the soul grows clotted by contagion, / Imbodies and imbrutes, till she quite lose / The divine property of her first being" (466–69).

26. Scarry, *The Body in Pain*, 30.

27. William Gouge, *The Church's Conquest over the Sword*, in *God's Three Arrowes: Plague, Famine, Sword*, 2nd ed. (London, 1631), 295.

28. Edward Symmons, *A Military Sermon, wherein by the word of God, the nature and disposition of a Rebell is discovered, and the Kings true Souldier described and Characterized* (Oxford, 1644), 25; Gouge, ibid., 295.

29. Empson, *Milton's God*, 54.

30. Michel de Montaigne, *The Complete Essays*, trans. and ed. M. A. Screech (1987; repr., London: Penguin Books, 1991), 59.

31. Lieb, "'Hate in Heav'n,'" 524.

32. Scarry, *The Body in Pain*, 80.

33. Lieb, "'Hate in Heav'n,'" 520.

34. Gouge, *The Church's Conquest*, 296.

35. Michael Lieb, *Children of Ezekiel: UFOs, the Crisis of Race, and the Advent of End Time* (Durham, N.C.: Duke University Press, 1998), 4.

36. Morris, *Culture of Pain*, 184.

37. Lieb, "'Hate in Heav'n,'" 530–33.

38. Michael Bryson, *The Tyranny of Heaven: Milton's Rejection of God as King* (Newark: University of Delaware Press, 2004), 135.

39. Symmons, *A Military Sermon*, 24–25.

40. Wooten, "The Poet's War," 142.

41. Browne, *Prose*, 74. Aubrey is quoted in Lewalski, *Life of John Milton*, 536.

42. Lieb, "'Hate in Heav'n,'" 533.

Notes to Wittreich, "A World with a Tomorrow"

1. Gordon Teskey, *Delirious Milton: The Fate of the Poet in Modernity* (Cambridge, Mass.: Harvard University Press, 2006), 5, 9, 114, 150, 149, 150–51. Some of the terms of this new Milton criticism are traceable to John Dryden, John Dennis, and the Jonathan Richardsons. The chief early practitioners of it are William Blake and Percy Bysshe Shelley, and recent examples and discussions of it are provided by Peter C. Herman, *Destabilizing Milton:* Paradise Lost *and the Poetics of Incertitude* (New York: Palgrave Macmillan, 2005), and also by Herman, "Paradigms Lost, Paradigms Found: The New Milton Criticism," *Literature Compass* 2 (2005): 1–26 (the Herman essay was retrieved January 19, 2007; available at http://www.Literature-compass.com/viewpoint.asp?section=2&ref=518); and by Joseph Wittreich, "Questioning and Critique: The Formation of a New Milton Criticism," *Why Milton Matters: A New Preface to His Writings* (New York: Palgrave Macmillan, 2006), 141–94, 225–40.

2. Teskey, *Delirious Milton*, 185.

3. A. J. A. Waldock, Paradise Lost *and Its Critics* (1947; repr., Cambridge: University Press, 1966), 18; see also 19, 42.

4. Michael Lieb, *Theological Milton: Deity, Discourse, and Heresy in the Miltonic Canon* (Pittsburgh: Duquesne University Press, 2006), 5. Compare John T. Shawcross, *The Uncertain World of* Samson Agonistes (London: D. S. Brewer, 2001), and also by Shawcross, *Rethinking Milton Studies: Time Present and Time Past* (Newark: University of Delaware Press, 2005).

5. Lieb, *Theological Milton*, 7.

6. See Elizabeth Marie Pope, Paradise Regained: *The Tradition and the Poem* (1947; repr., New York: Russell and Russell, 1962), 95.

7. Lieb, *Theological Milton*, 123.

8. John Peter, *A Critique of* Paradise Lost (1960; repr., New York: Columbia University Press, 1962), 159.

9. All quotations of Milton are from *The Complete Poetry of John Milton*, rev. ed., ed. John T. Shawcross (Garden City, N.Y.: Doubleday, 1971), and *Complete Prose Works of John Milton*, 8 vols. in 10, ed. Don M. Wolfe et al., (New Haven: Yale University Press, 1953–82), hereafter cited in the text.

10. Hugh Farmer, *An Inquiry into the Nature and Design of Christ's Temptation in the Wilderness* (London: Printed for A. Millar, J. Buckland, and J. Waugh, 1761), 24. See notes 49 and 50 below.

11. Richard Overton, "An Arrow against All Tyrants" (1646), in *The Levellers in the English Revolution*, ed. G. E. Aylmer (Ithaca: Cornell University Press, 1975), 69.

12. John Lightfoot, "Hebrew and Talmudical Exercitations upon the Evangelist St. Luke," in *The Whole Works of the Rev. John Lightfoot, D.D.*, 12 vols., ed. John Rogers Pitman (London: Printed by J. F. Dove, 1822–25), 12:62–63 (cf. "The Harmony of the Four Evangelists," 4:343).

13. Lightfoot, "The Harmony of the Four Evangelists," in ibid., 4:344.

14. Joachim of Fiore as quoted by Marjorie Reeves, *The Influence of Prophecy in the Later Middle Ages: A Study in Joachimism* (Oxford: Clarendon Press, 1969), 292.

15. These designs are reproduced and discussed by Joseph Wittreich, *Angel of Apocalypse: Blake's Idea of Milton* (Madison: University of Wisconsin Press, 1975), esp. 103–46 and figs. 34–45.

16. Hugh Broughton, *The Work of the Great Albionean Divine...Mr. Hugh Broughton* (London: Printed for Nath[aniel] Ekins, 1662), 373, 339; John Weemse, *The Christian Synagogue* (London: Printed for John Bellamie, 1623), 48.

17. Margaret Kean, "*Paradise Regained*," in *A Companion to Milton*, ed. Thomas N. Corns (Oxford: Blackwell, 2001), 429. Other important perspectives on how *Paradise Regain'd* intersects with the Gospel accounts are afforded by Ira Clark, "*Paradise Regained* and the Gospel according to John," *Modern Philology* 71 (1973): 1–15; Frank Kermode, *The Art of Telling: Essays on Fiction* (Cambridge, Mass.: Harvard University Press, 1983), 185–200; Mary Ann Radzinowicz, "How Milton Read the Bible: The Case of *Paradise Regained*," in *The Cambridge Companion to Milton*, 2nd ed., ed. Dennis Danielson (Cambridge: Cambridge University Press, 1999), 202–18; Stella P. Revard, "The Gospel of John and *Paradise Regained*: Jesus as 'True Light,'" in *Milton and Scriptural Tradition: The Bible into Poetry*, ed. James H. Sims and Leland Ryken (Columbia: University of Missouri Press, 1984), 142–59; and Annabel Patterson, "It Is Written: *Paradise Regained*," *Milton's Words* (Oxford: Oxford University Press, 2009), 114–45. Very simply, Milton would do for the wilderness story what John Foxe had earlier claimed to do for the Crucifixion story: he would envision a story "heard of by many but never *seen* before"; see John Foxe, "A Prologue to *Christ Triumphant*: An Apocalyptic Comedy," in *Two Latin Comedies by John Foxe*, ed. and trans. John Hazel Smith (Ithaca: Cornell University Press, 1973), 229; my italics.

18. William Cowper, *Three Heavenly Treatises, Concerning Christ* (London: Printed for John Budge, 1612), 123.

19. T[homas] W[ilson], *Theologicall Rules, to Guide Vs in the Vunderstanding and Practice of Holy Scriptures* (London: Printed for Fran[cis] Burton, 1615), 37. See also Tho[mas] Manton, *Christs Temptation and Transfiguration, Practically Explained and Improved in Several Sermons* (London: N.p., 1685), 11–15, 34.

20. Thomas Ellwood, quoted from *Milton: The Critical Heritage*, ed. John T. Shawcross (London: Routledge and Kegan Paul, 1970), 223.

21. Cowper, *Three Heavenly Treatises*, 114–15.

22. Lightfoot, "Rules for a Student of the Holy Scripture" and "Hebrew and Talmudical Exercitations upon the Gospel of St. Matthew," in Pitman, *Whole Works*, 2:43, 11:82.

23. Thomas Hayne, *The Times, Places, and Persons of the Holie Scripture* (London: Printed for Richard Ockould, 1607), 18.

24. Pope, *The Tradition and the Poem*, 121, 26, 84.

25. Ibid., 21, 80. For starters, let us remember with Annabel Patterson that the very name of "John Starkey," appearing on the title page to the 1671 poetic volume, is by then "an icon for radical publication"; see Wittreich, *Why Milton Matters*, 29. And let us remember, too, that there is, as Theodor Keim, *The History of Jesus Nazara*, 6 vols., trans. Arthur Ransom (London: Williams and Norgate, 1876), reports, a long tradition regarding these temptations as "an inner process in the soul of Jesus..., a vision (Origen), a dream (Paulus), or a course reflexion busied among the pictures of the people's and the world's imagination." The "domain" of this story is the "inner experience" of Jesus (2:314).

26. Pope, *The Tradition and the Poem*, 114.

27. As Jeffrey Gore remarked during the retirement celebration for Michael Lieb at the University of Illinois, Chicago, on November 1, 2008.

28. John Dennis, quoted in Shawcross, *Milton: The Critical Heritage*, 134.

29. John Calvin, *A Harmonie upon the Three Evangelists, Matthew, Mark, and Luke*, trans. E[usibius] P[age] (London: Printed by George Bishop, 1584), 131.

30. Augustine Marlorate, *A Catholike and Ecclesiasticall Exposition of the Holy Gospel after S. Mathewe* (London: Printed by Thomas Marshe, 1570), ff. 62, 65.

31. See both Richard Daye, "To the Christian Reader," in John Foxe, *Christ Iesvs Triumphant* (London: Printed by John Daye, 1579), unpaginated preface, and Foxe, ibid., f. 13.

32. Thomas Taylor, *Christs Combate and Conquest; or, The Lion of the Tribe of Jvdah* (Cambridge: Printed for Thomas Man, 1618), 189. Daniel Dyke, *Michael and the Dragon; or, Christ Tempted and Satan Foyled* (London: Printed by John Beale, 1625), 275.

33. John Diodati, *Piovs Annotations vpon the Holy Bible Expounding the Difficult Places Thereof*, 3rd ed. (London: Printed for Nicolas Fussell, 1651), second pagination, sig. A3. The possibility that a dispute now centers on this scriptural passage is evident in the fact that Diodati boldly repudiates an interpretive position that in the first edition of 1643 he casually acknowledges: "By a vehement motion of the Holy Ghost," Christ enters the desert and, later, "by some swift motion, but without any hurt, and that by the permission of God," Christ is taken to the pinnacle of the temple." Diodati then concedes that atop the mountain Christ is tempted "by some vision, or illusion...it appears"; see Diodati, *Piovs Annotations vpon the Holy Bible*, 1st ed. (London: Printed for Nicholas Fussell, 1643), second sig. A3.

34. Christopher Blackwood, *Expositions and Sermons upon the Ten First Chapters of the Gospel of Jesus Christ, According to Matthew* (London: Printed for Francis Tyton and John Field, 1659 [1658]), 103. John

Downame et al., *Annotations upon All the Books of the Old and New Testament*, 2nd ed., 2 vols. (London: Printed by John Legatt, 1651); annotation to Luke 5:4.

35. Lightfoot, "The Harmony of the Four Evangelists," 4:343 (see also 344), 363–64 (see also 365).

36. Ibid., 4:370–71. Downame et al., *Annotations*, had already hinted that Matthew and Luke, in their respective representations of the pinnacle and mountain temptations, sanction decidedly different readings of the temptation story. These commentators contend that Satan carries Christ atop the pinnacle, according to Matthew 4:5, whereas, according to Luke 4:5, atop the mountain Satan "shewed Christ...all the kingdoms of the world in a moment," thus "declar[ing] that this shewing was by a vision" (sig. [A4v] and sig. [J5]).

37. Samuel Pordage, *Mundorum Explicatio; or, The Explanation of a Hieroglyphical Figure:...A Sacred Poem* (London: Printed for Lodowick Lloyd, 1661), 197, 282; compare 195.

38. Kermode, *The Art of Telling*, 188.

39. Jeremy Taylor, *The Life of Our Blessed Saviour Jesus Christ* (Somerset, Pa.: Printed for T. and J. Patton, 1818), 59.

40. Blake, *Jerusalem*, in *The Complete Poetry and Prose of William Blake*, ed. David V. Erdman (Garden City, N.Y.: Doubleday, 1982), 257 (pl. 98, 1. 28). Among the foothills leading up to the publication of *Paradise Regain'd*, according to Barbara Kiefer Lewalski, *Milton's Brief Epic: The Genre, Meaning, and Art of* Paradise Regained (Providence, R.I.: Brown University Press, 1966), "the most important new theoretical basis for the production of biblical epic was supplied by Guillaume Du Bartas' *Urania* (1574), a short, dream-vision poem" (69). On this tradition and *Paradise Lost*, books 11 and 12, see ibid., 85. Moreover, notice that Milton, the author of the Arguments to *Paradise Lost*, asserts the relevance of the dream-vision tradition to books 11 and 12, in the Argument to book 11, saying that "the Angel...sets before...[Adam] in vision what shall happ'n till the Flood" and, correspondingly, in book 12, saying that in the final books of the poem, "*Eve*...with gentle dreams [is] compos'd to quietness of mind and submission." See also the important essays by Stuart Curran, "The Mental Pinnacle: *Paradise Regained* and the Romantic Four-Book Epic," in *Calm of Mind: Tercentenary Essays on* Paradise Regained *and* Samson Agonistes, ed. Joseph Wittreich (Cleveland: Press of Case Western Reserve University, 1971), 133–62; and Shawcross, "Milton and Epic Revisionism," in *Epic and Epoch: Essays on the Interpretation and History of a Genre*, ed. Steven M. Oberhelman, Van Kelley, and Richard J. Golsan (Lubbock: Texas Tech University Press, 1994), 186–207.

41. For the landmark readings of this poem, see Kermode, *The Art of Telling*, 185–200; Lewalski, *Milton's Brief Epic*; Shawcross, Paradise Regain'd: *"Worthy T'Have Not Remain'd So Long Unsung"* (Pittsburgh: Duquesne University Press, 1988); and Arnold Stein, *Heroic Knowledge:*

An Interpretation of Paradise Regained *and* Samson Agonistes (1957; repr., Hamden: Archon Books, 1965), 3–134.

42. Anonymous, "A Critique on *Paradise Regained,*" in *Paradise Regained and Other Poems* (New York: Published by J. H. Turney, 1832), 12–13.

43. Matthew Poole, *Annotations upon the Holy Bible. Wherein the...More Difficult Terms in Each Verse Are Explained. Seeming Contradictions Reconciled,* 2 vols. (London: Printed for Thomas Parkhurst, 1683, 1685), 2:sig. (2nd ser.) [A]. John T. Shawcross, *Milton: A Bibliography for the Years 1624–1700* (Binghamton, N.Y.: Medieval and Renaissance Texts and Studies, 1984), remarks upon Milton's "Influence and language from *Paradise Lost* in annotations to Genesis, without acknowledgment" (274). For discussion of Poole and Milton, see Jason P. Rosenblatt, "Milton's Chief Rabbi," in *Milton Studies,* vol. 24, ed. Albert C. Labriola, 43–71 (Pittsburgh: University of Pittsburgh Press, 1988).

44. Abraham Woodhead, *An Historical Narration of the Life and Death of Our Lord Jesus Christ: In Two Parts* (Oxford: At the Theater, 1685), 119. Milton is perhaps also comprehended in Woodhead's remark that "some think...[he] shewed himself in the habit of some religious Hermite" (114). Compare *Paradise Regain'd* 1.314–19: "But now an aged man in Rural weeds, / ...He saw approach."

45. Laurence Clarke. *A Compleat History of the Life of Our Blessed Lord and Saviour Jesus Christ* (London: Printed for the Author, 1737), 166, 176, 164, 172, 176.

46. H[enry] Hammond, *A Paraphrase, and Annotations upon All the Books of the New Testament* (London: Printed for Richard Royston, 1653), 21. These views persist through the fifth edition of this work (1681), 20.

47. Tho[mas] Manton, *Christs Temptation and Transfiguration,* 31, 32, 125; see also 124. Jean Le Clerc, *A Supplement to Dr. Hammond's Paraphrase and Annotations of the New Testament* (London: Printed for Sam. Buckley, 1699), 16.

48. Joseph Bretland, *Sermons,* 2 vols. (Exeter: Printed by S. Hegdeland, 1820), 2:286; see also H[enry] Cotes, *Lent Sermons; or, An Inquiry into the Nature and Design of Christ's Temptation in the Wilderness* (London: Printed for C. Cradock and W. Joy, 1813), 26, 55, 138, while remembering from *Paradise Lost* God's calling "by Vision" (12.121) and from *Paradise Regain'd* his warning "By Vision" (1.256).

49. Hugh Farmer, *An Inquiry into the Nature and Design of Christ's Temptation in the Wilderness,* 3, vi, 20, 24, 27, 32, 36, 49, 54; a second enlarged edition was published in 1765. A third edition appeared in 1768 (?) and yet another in 1882. For supplementation of his argument that the "whole" wilderness temptation sequence is "a *spiritual* and mental transaction," set forth in visions "*prophetical* and *premonitory,*" see also Farmer, *An Appendix to an Inquiry into the Nature and Design of Christ's Temptation in the Wilderness* (London: Printed for J. Buckland and

J. Waugh, 1765), esp. 41, 27, but also 28–30, 41. For another argument that the temptations arise in the mind of Jesus as a mental event, see Thomas Dixon, *The Sovereignty of the Divine Administration, Vindicated; or, A Rational Account of Our Blessed Saviour's Remarkable Temptation in the Wilderness* (London: Printed for Becket and De Hondt, J. Gore, and Clarke and Haslingden, 1766), 10. Dixon apparently did not read Farmer, but their respective interpretations coincide. See "The Preface," ibid., viii, as well as Dixon's avowal that "most...*good* commentators depart from the letter" (13; my italics) and Dixon's citation of Milton as an apt example of those good commentators who, like himself, exhibit a reforming spirit (12).

50. See Anonymous, *Christ's Temptations: Real Facts...In Answer to Mr. Farmer's Inquiry* (London: Printed for the Author, 1762), 3–31, 33. Farmer credits Milton in this way: "Some indeed, and particularly our famous countrymen *Hugh Broughton*...and *Milton* [in *Paradise Regain'd*] suppose that the Devil shewed our Saviour all the kingdoms of the world by the help of *optic instruments:* but it is now generally asserted, that he did it either by visionary impressions upon his mind, or by external representations to his sight"; see *An Inquiry into the Nature and Design of Christ's Temptation in the Wilderness, To which Is Added, An Appendix,* 2nd ed. (London: J. Buckland and J. Waugh, 1765), 34.

51. Thomas Belsham, *A Summary View of the Evidence and Practical Importance of the Christian Revelation* (London: Printed by R. Taylor, 1807), 86. Cotes, *Lent Sermons,* Av, Av–A2, 13, 126, 137; see also 122–30, 136–37. Cotes's Milton "deserts the letter of Scripture" (125) even as he breathes its "very spirit" (128).

52. Northrop Frye, *A Study of English Romanticism* (New York: Random House, 1968), 16.

53. Philip Pullman, introduction to *Paradise Lost: An Illustrated Edition* (Oxford: Oxford University Press, 2005), 9.

54. Don Ihde, "Editor's Introduction," in Paul Ricoeur's *The Conflict of Interpretations: Essays in Hermeneutics,* ed. Don Ihde (1974; repr., Evanston: Northwestern University Press, 2004), xxv.

55. Harvey Goodwin, *Christ in the Wilderness: Four Sermons* (Cambridge: Deighton and Bell, and London: Bell and Daldy, 1855), 82, 143 (see also 144–47), 6, 76, 143, 142. T[homas] T[hellusson] Carter, *The Passion and Temptation of Our Lord: A Course of Lectures* (London: Joseph Masters, 1863), 21, 22.

Notes to Furman-Adams and Tufte, "'Shifting Contexts'"

Epigraph from Joseph A. Wittreich, *Shifting Contexts: Reinterpreting Samson Agonistes* (Pittsburgh: Duquesne University Press, 2002), iv. We are grateful to Professor Wittreich for his permission, indeed encouragement, to borrow his evocative and appropriate title for the present essay.

1. Derek N. C. Wood, *Exiled from Light: Divine Law, Morality, and Violence in Milton's* Samson Agonistes (Toronto: University of Toronto Press, 2001), 30.

2. Wittreich, *Shifting Contexts*, 40.

3. Michael Lieb, *Milton and the Culture of Violence* (Ithaca: Cornell University Press, 1994), 237. In this magisterial work, Lieb situates *Samson Agonistes* in the context of Milton's prose—in particular the *Second Defense*—demonstrating in devastating detail how Milton avenges his symbolic rape and dismemberment by his critics (undergoes a process of "repristination") by "marshal[ing] those very forces through which sparagmos is executed" and turning them against his attackers. "Violence," Lieb concludes, is Milton's "signature" (263).

4. Mary Ann Radzinowicz, *Toward* Samson Agonistes: *The Growth of Milton's Mind* (Princeton: Princeton University Press, 1978). Michael Lieb, "'Our Living Dread': The God of *Samson Agonistes*," in *Milton Studies*, vol. 33, *The Miltonic Samson*, ed. Albert C. Labriola and Michael Lieb (Pittsburgh: University of Pittsburgh Press, 1996), 7. Lieb here quotes Rudolf Otto's *The Idea of the Holy*, trans. John W. Harvey (London, 1928), 79, and goes on to say that the play's catastrophe is "a manifestation of godhead at it most archaic form....If *Samson Agonistes* moves 'toward' anything, it certainly moves toward this most primitive conception of godhead" (17).

5. Joseph Wittreich, *Interpreting* Samson Agonistes (Princeton: Princeton University Press, 1986); quotations are from *Shifting Contexts*, 8, 49.

6. Wittreich, *Shifting Contexts*, 182.

7. John T. Shawcross, "Misreading Milton," in *Milton Studies*, vol. 33, 194; and *The Uncertain World of* Samson Agonistes (York: York University Press, 2001).

8. Wood, *Exiled from Light*, xxii, 61, 165.

9. Irene Samuel, "*Samson Agonistes* as Tragedy," in *Calm of Mind: Tercentenary Essays on* Paradise Regained *and* Samson Agonistes, ed. Joseph Wittreich (Cleveland: Case Western Reserve University Press, 1971), 235–57.

10. For the over 300 paintings and drawings of the biblical strong-man that have been catalogued from the seventeenth and eighteenth centuries alone, see Andor Pigler, *Barockthemen*, 3 vols. (Budapest: Akademiai Kiado, 1974), 1:122–32. An uncounted number of representations also exist from the centuries before and after. For the still-essential catalog of and introduction to Milton's illustrators, see Joseph Wittreich, "Illustrators," in *A Milton Encyclopedia*, vol. 4, ed. William B. Hunter, John T. Shawcross, John Steadman et al. (Lewisburg, Pa.: Bucknell University Press, 1978), 55–78.

11. See Stanley Fish, *Surprised by Sin: The Reader in* Paradise Lost (1967; repr. Cambridge, Mass: Harvard University Press, 1997). Robert Medley's abstractions were produced in 1978.

12. Augustine, *On Christian Doctrine,* trans. D. W. Robertson (1958; repr. Indianapolis: Bobbs Merrill, 1978), 88.

13. See http://www.the-orb.net, an online network for medieval studies. Jesus explicitly likens his resurrection to Jonas's emergence from the whale in the gospel of Matthew: "An evil and adulterous generation seeketh after a sign; and there shall no sign be given to it, but the sign of the prophet Jonas: For as Jonas was three days and three nights in the whale's belly; so shall the Son of man be three days and three nights in the heart of the earth" (12:39–40).

14. Wittreich, *Shifting Contexts,* 7.

15. See Michael Lieb, "'A Thousand Foreskins': Circumcision, Violence, and Selfhood in Milton," in *Milton Studies,* vol. 38, *John Milton: The Writer in His Works,* ed. Albert C. Labriola and Michael Lieb (Pittsburgh: University of Pittsburgh Press, 2000), 198–219. The painting is now in the Galleria Palatina (Palazzo Pitti), Florence.

16. The iconography of the lamb suggests exactly this parallel. See Genesis 4:1–16. As noted in the text, no lambs appear in the multiple slaying related in Judges 15:14–17. And, conversely, no weapon is mentioned in the Genesis story: a jawbone would work as well as any other when "Cain rose up against Abel his brother and slew him" (Gen. 4:8).

17. Francis L. Richardson, *Andrea Schiavone* (Oxford: Clarendon Press, 1980), 159.

18. Church of England, *The Book of Common Prayer, and Administration of the Sacraments: And Other Rites and Ceremonies of the Church of England: With the Psalter or Psalms of David* (Edinburgh, 1633). We are reminded here of Milton's representation of Mary in *Paradise Regain'd,* a work that likewise underscores the humanity of the Son.

19. For this strain in (mostly earlier) Milton criticism, see F. Michael Krouse, *Milton's Samson and the Christian Tradition* (1949; repr. New York: Octagon Books, 1974), and William G. Madsen's more nuanced *From Shadowy Types to Truth: Studies in Milton's Symbolism* (New Haven: Yale University Press, 1968).

20. *The Holy Bible Containing the Old and New Testament* (Oxford, 1682). The debate about Milton's Samson as "terrorist" began with an essay by John Carey, "A Work in Praise of Terrorism?" *Times Literary Supplement,* September 6, 2002, 15–16. In the article, Carey challenges a view advanced by Stanley Fish, *How Milton Works* (Cambridge, Mass.: Harvard University Press, 2001). For a review of the controversy, see D. D. Guttenplan, "Reading Milton: Unsafe at Any Speed?" *The New York Times,* December 28, 2002, B3, col. 9.

21. *The Bible: In Word and Art* (1630; repr., New York: Arch Cape Press, 1988). Text based on the King James Version. In colors vying with those of the great oil paintings of the time, Merian's 234 engravings, some familiar from earlier bibles, appeared several times during the seventeenth century: 1625 in Strasbourg, 1627 in Frankfurt, and 1628 in an Amsterdam edition in English, French, and German.

22. These radical Protestants ranged from Calvinists to Mennonite Anabaptists and Socinians, more groups arising with each new reading of the text, newly freed from papal authority. Interestingly, although nominally a member of the Dutch Reformed Church (where he was married and where his children by Saskia were baptized), Rembrandt, like Milton, moved in Mennonite and Remonstrant circles and numbered among his acquaintances Catholics as well as Socinians and Jews. And just as scholars still struggle to identify Milton's theology with any particular group, so Rembrandt scholars have been unable to identify Rembrandt's position beyond calling him a "Protestant," deeply attached to the Bible.

23. W. A. Visser't Hooft, *Rembrandt and the Gospel* (Philadelphia: Westminster Press, 1958), 283.

24. This latter detail may come from Josephus's *Antiquities of the Jews*, which was available in Latin translation, and of which Rembrandt (whose library was not remarkably extensive) owned a copy. Milton also knew Josephus and, according to Peter A. Fiore, *Milton Encyclopedia*, 4:172–73, paraphrases him when Samson speaks to Harapha of his nuptial feast: "I.../ in your City held my Nuptial Feast: / But your ill-meaning Politician Lords, / Under pretence of Bridal friends and guests, / Appointed to await me thirty spies" (*SA* 1193–97).

25. This, as we have suggested, has also been a major crux for Milton's readers. Some (like Krouse, *Milton's Samson*) have found such a God quite easy to discern in the text and have found a Samson capable, at least to some extent, of apprehending such a concept of God. Others (like Lieb) posit a Samson who understands God only too well—in his truest primitive, archaic identity as "our Living Dread" or, read more historically, as Milton's Puritan God. Others yet, like Wittreich, find God in the text only by his absence and in the horrific parody of God worshipped and embodied by the satanic Samson.

26. *Samson Agonistes*, 23–29. All quotations of Milton's poetry come from *The Complete Poetry of John Milton*, ed. John T. Shawcross (1963; rev., New York: Doubleday, 1971).

27. According to Josephus's account, Delilah is responsible for the actual cutting of Samson's hair; in the Judges narrative, "a man" is called to shave off "the seven locks of his head" (Judg. 16:19). Rembrandt seems to hedge his bets between the two versions of the story.

28. Christopher Brown, *Rembrandt: Every Painting*, vol. 1 (New York: Rizzoli, 1980), 72. This large 1636 oil on canvas (236 x 302 centimeters) is in the Stadelsches Künstinstitut, Frankfurt. Several copies also exist.

29. No paintings exist by Rembrandt's hand of Samson's final act—whether read as deliverance or revenge. Perhaps Rembrandt, like so many readers of Milton's *Samson*, could never quite decide how to read the end of his story.

30. *The Doré Bible Illustrations* (New York: Dover, 1974). This edition contains 229 reproductions from *The Holy Bible, with Illustrations*

by Gustave Doré, (London: Cassell, Petter, and Galpin, ca. 1866). Also included are 12 illustrations from *Die Heilige Schrift Alten und Neuen Testaments verdeutscht von D. Martin Luther. Mit zweihundert und dreissig Bildern von Gustave Doré,* 2 vols. (Stuttgart: Deutsche Verlags-Anstalt, ca. 1875).

31. Milton likewise calls attention to this parallel in his invented genealogy of Harapha and in Samson's offer to meet him in all his "gorgeous arms" with only "an Oak'n staff" (*SA* 1247–49, 1219–23).

32. *Samson and Delilah: From the book of Judges according to the authorized version,* printed and illustrated by Robert Gibbings (Berkshire: Golden Cockerel Press, 1925).

33. A longtime associate of artist, engraver, and typographer Eric Gill, Gibbings owned and directed the Golden Cockerel Press—generally regarded as one of Europe's finest small presses—between 1924 and 1933.

34. The source of that power is not made explicit in Gibbings's designs. Interestingly, however, fellow Golden Cockerel artist Mary Groom later used a black-on-white variation of this design for her representation of Satan rousing his troops (1937).

35. *The Poetical Works of Mr. John Milton,* 2 vols. (London, 1720). This edition has illustrations by Louis Chéron and James Thornhill, but the illustrations for *Samson Agonistes* are by Chéron alone.

36. The engraving can be found in *Paradise Regain'd. A Poem in Four Books, to which is added Samson Agonistes, and Poems upon several occasions* (London, 1752). This edition includes five illustrations by Francis Hayman, just one of which is for *Samson Agonistes.*

37. Perhaps this gesture of reluctant forgiveness suggests that readers before John Ulreich, "'Incident to All Our Sex': The Tragedy of Dalilah," in *Milton and the Idea of Woman,* ed. Julia M. Walker (Urbana: University of Illinois Press, 1988), 185–210, could discern in Milton's complex text a Dalila who is not entirely summed up in the Chorus's misogynic designation as "manifest Serpent" (*SA* 997).

38. *The Poetical Works of John Milton...In Four Volumes with a Life of the Author by William Hayley* (Edinburgh, 1779). The frontispiece to volume 3 has an illustration for *Samson Agonistes* by John H. Mortimer.

39. *Samson Agonistes* (London, 1796). The frontispiece to *Samson Agonistes* is by John Graham.

40. *The poetical works of John Milton, With a life of the author, by William Hayley and Plates from designs by Richard Westall* (London, 1794–97).

41. For a discussion of the "secret" location of Samson's strength, see John Rogers, "The Secret of Samson Agonistes," in *Milton Studies,* vol. 33, 111–32.

42. *The Poetical Works of John Milton, with a Memoir and Critical Remarks by James Montgomery and one hundred and twenty engravings*

by John Thompson, S. and T. Williams, O. Smith, J. Linton etc. from drawings by William Harvey, 2 vols. (London, 1843).

43. *The Minor Poems of John Milton, Illustrated and Decorated by A. Garth Jones* (London, 1898).

44. *The Poetical Works of John Milton with Etchings, Mezzotints and Copper Engravings by William Hyde* (London, 1904).

45. *Samson Agonistes—With Wood Engravings by Robert Ashwin Maynard* (repr., Harrow Weald, Middlesex: Raven Press, 1931).

46. Norman T. Burns, "'Then Stood Up Phinehas': Milton's Antinomianism, and Samson's," in *Milton Studies*, vol. 33, 27–46; and in the same volume, Sharon Achinstein, "*Samson Agonistes* and the Drama of Dissent," 137–49.

47. *Samson Agonistes—With Illustrations by Robert Medley* (Norwich: Mell Clark, 1979), a limited edition of 150. Wittreich mentions this wonderful series in *Shifting Contexts* (194) and uses Medley's designs as cover art for both that book and for *Interpreting* Samson Agonistes.

48. Medley's quoted comments are from an interview by Roger Berthoud for the London *Times*, August 18, 1980, 9.

49. This sun motif, moreover, reappears later in the series (image 16)—in this case a rising ochre ball in a pastel yellow field—to represent Samson's victory over Harapha—a formerly vast black shape (image 15), now a crumpled black heap at the bottom of the page.

50. Harapha, likewise (as noted above), is represented by a "swelling high-built pile" of black. Each represents a different kind of nemesis, both of which, for Medley, Samson clearly overcomes.

51. Shawcross, *Uncertain World*, 195.

52. Wittreich, *Shifting Contexts*, 182; Wood, *Exiled from Light*, 19.

53. George Frederick Handel, *Samson: An Oratorio for soprano, tenor, bass soli, SABT and Orchestra* (London: Novello, no date). The libretto, furnished by Newburgh Hamilton, uses lines from *Samson Agonistes*, freely rendered and often rhymed, in the recitatives; lines from other Milton poems are added in the airs and choruses. The first performance, in Lent of 1743 at Covent Garden Theatre, was a success; a performance in 1753 was especially poignant because by then Handel had become blind. Handel's oratorio is one of a number of musical works based on the story of Samson. For a list, see A. W. Verity, "Introduction to *Samson Agonistes*," in *John Milton's Samson Agonistes*, ed. Ralph E. Hone (San Francisco: Chandler Publishing, 1966), 157–58.

54. See "Concert Note: The Bible, Milton, Hamilton, and Handel," http/www.bostoncecilia.org/samson.html; accessed October 1, 2003.

55. Fish, *How Milton Works*, 473.

Notes to Rose, "Why Is the Virgin Mary in Paradise Regain'd?*"*

1. All citations of *Samson Agonistes, Paradise Lost,* and *Paradise Regain'd* are taken from *John Milton,* ed. Stephen Orgel and Jonathan Goldberg (Oxford: Oxford University Press, 1991); hereafter cited by book and/or line number in the text.

2. In *Milton Studies,* vol. 17, ed. Richard S. Ide and Joseph Wittreich (Pittsburgh: University of Pittsburgh Press, 1983), Stuart Curran, *"Paradise Regained:* Implications of Epic," 209–24; and John T. Shawcross, "The Genres of *Paradise Regain'd* and *Samson Agonistes:* The Wisdom of Their Joint Publication," 225–48. See also Barbara Lewalski, *Milton's Brief Epic: The Genre, Meaning, and Art of* Paradise Regained (Providence, R.I.: Brown University Press, 1966), and Elizabeth Marie Pope, Paradise Regained: *The Tradition and the Poem* (Baltimore: The Johns Hopkins University Press, 1947). For a recent and very interesting critique of Milton's typological thinking in relation to gender in *Samson Agonistes,* see Rachel Trubowitz, "'I was his nursling once': Nation, Lactation, and the Hebraic in *Samson Agonistes,"* in *Milton and Gender,* ed. Catherine Gimelli Martin (Cambridge: Cambridge University Press, 2004), 167–83.

3. For a different orientation to this subject than my own, see John Guillory, "The Father's House: *Samson Agonistes* in Its Historical Moment," in *Re-membering Milton: Essays on the Texts and the Traditions,* ed. Mary Nyquist and Margaret W. Ferguson, 148–76 (New York: Methuen, 1987).

4. Orgel and Goldberg, *John Milton,* 81.

5. See Mary Beth Rose, *Gender and Heroism in Early Modern English Literature* (Chicago: University of Chicago Press, 2002).

6. See Carole Pateman, *The Sexual Contract* (Stanford: Stanford University Press, 1988), 120.

7. Northrop Frye, "The Typology of *Paradise Regained," Modern Philology* 53 (1956): 227–38.

8. See Lewalski, *Milton's Brief Epic,* 135, and throughout; and Stanley Fish, "The Temptation to Action in Milton's Poetry," *ELH, A Journal of English Literary History* 48 (1981): 516–31; and "Things and Actions Indifferent: The Temptation of Plot in *Paradise Regained,"* in *Milton Studies,* vol. 17, 163–85. Also see Fish's discussions of these themes and of both poems in *How Milton Works* (Cambridge, Mass.: Harvard University Press, 2001).

9. Rachel S. Havrelock, "The Myth of Birthing the Hero: Heroic Barrenness in the Hebrew Bible," *Biblical Interpretation: A Journal of Contemporary Approaches* 16, no. 2 (2008): 154–78. See also Susan Ackerman, *Warrior, Dancer, Seductress, Queen: Women in Judges and Biblical Israel* (New York: Doubleday, 1998), 181–207.

10. Pateman, *The Sexual Contract,* 35.

11. See Trubowitz, "'I was his nursling once,'" for an extended treatment of this topic.

12. Frances E. Dolan, *Whores of Babylon: Catholicism, Gender and Seventeenth-Century Print Culture* (Ithaca: Cornell University Press, 1999), 103.

13. Helen Hackett, *Virgin Mother, Maiden Queen: Elizabeth I and the Cult of the Virgin Mary* (New York: St. Martin's Press, 1995), 68.

14. References to the Virgin Mary occur in *Of Prelatical Episcopacy*, in *The Complete Prose Works of John Milton*, 8 vols. in 10, ed. Don M. Wolfe et al. (New Haven: Yale University Press, 1953–82), 1:642. In this tract Milton criticizes Irenaeus for arguing the "heresy" that "the obedience of Mary was the cause of salvation to her self, and all mankind" and for the view that Mary was the corrector and redeemer of Eve. See also *The Judgement of Martin Bucer*, where Milton offers various Protestant orthodoxies about "one flesh," pointing out that Joseph was not the father of Jesus, which is interesting given that Milton erases Joseph from *Paradise Regain'd* (YP 2:465); *Tetrachordon*, where he again glosses the biblical marital ideal of "one flesh" in reference to Mary and Joseph, also pointing away from Joseph's fatherhood (2:610–11); and *Tenure of Kings and Magistrates*, where he praises Mary's "Magnificat" from Luke, the biblical text to which he is most indebted in *Paradise Regain'd*, in support of his arguments about Christ's opposition to tyranny (YP 3:217).

15. Dolan, *Whores of Babylon*, 107.

16. Margaret O'Rourke Boyle, "Home to Mother: Regaining Milton's Paradise," *Modern Philology* 97 (2000): 499–527; quotations at 506–07.

17. See, for example, Michael Lieb, *The Sinews of Ulysses: Form and Convention in Milton's Works* (Pittsburgh: Duquesne University Press, 1989); *Milton and the Culture of Violence* (Ithaca: Cornell University Press, 1994); and *Theological Milton: Deity, Discourse, and Heresy in the Miltonic Canon* (Pittsburgh: Duquesne University Press, 2006), to name only a few of Lieb's many studies of the multiple ways—both subtle and direct—that theological ideas permeate Milton's thought and representations.

18. For a very interesting account of the Annunciation to the Virgin in Luke and the scholarly debate about its meaning, see David T. Landry, "Narrative Logic in the Annunciation to Mary (Luke 1:26–38)," *Journal of Biblical Literature* 114 (1995): 65–79.

19. Dayton Haskin, "Milton's Portrait of Mary as a Bearer of the Word," in *Milton and the Idea of Woman*, ed. Julia M. Walker (Urbana: University of Illinois Press, 1988), 169–84.

20. See Mary Beth Rose, "Where Are the Mothers in Shakespeare?: Options for Gender Representation in the English Renaissance," *Shakespeare Quarterly* 42 (1991): 291–314.

21. Dolan, *Whores of Babylon*, 106.

22. Pateman, *The Sexual Contract*, 3. See also Diane Purkiss, *Literature, Gender and Politics during the English Civil War* (Cambridge: Cambridge University Press, 2005).

23. Susan C. Greenfield, "Aborting the 'Mother Plot': Politics and Generation in *Absalom and Achitophel*," *ELH, A Journal of English Literary History* (1995): 286.

24. John Locke, *Two Treatises of Government*, ed. Thomas I. Cook (New York: Hafner Press, 1947), 43, 162.

25. Pateman, *The Sexual Contract*, 41, 44.

26. Thomas Hobbes, *Leviathan*, ed. Michael Oakeshott (New York: Collier Books, 1962), 152; emphasis mine.

27. Ibid., 152.

28. Ibid., 153, 155.

29. Peter Brooks, *Reading for the Plot: Design and Intention in Narrative* (Cambridge, Mass.: Harvard University Press, 1984), 94, 35, 37.

30. For a different view of Mary's enduring influence, see John T. Shawcross, *John Milton: The Self and the World* (Lexington: University Press of Kentucky, 1993), 216–22; and discussions throughout his Paradise Regain'd: *Worthy T'Have Not Remain'd So Long Unsung* (Pittsburgh: Duquesne University Press, 1988).

31. See esp. Frye, "The Typology of *Paradise Regained*."

Notes to Revard, "Charles, Christ, and Icon of Kingship in Paradise Regain'd"

1. See Stella P. Revard, "Milton and Millenarianism: From the Nativity Ode to *Paradise Regained*," in *Milton and the Ends of Time*, ed. Juliet Cummins (Cambridge: Cambridge University Press, 2003), 42–81; N. H. Keeble, "Wilderness Exercises: Adversity, Temptation, and Trial in *Paradise Regained*," in *Milton Studies*, vol. 42, Paradise Regained *in Context: Genre, Politics, Religion*, ed. Albert C. Labriola and David Loewenstein, 86–105 (Pittsburgh: University of Pittsburgh Press, 2002). See also chapter 11 of this book, David Loewenstein's "From Politics to Faith in the Great Poems?"

2. See Michael Lieb, *Poetics of the Holy* (Chapel Hill: University of North Carolina Press, 1981), 50.

3. Stella P. Revard, "Apollo and Christ in the Seventeenth-Century Religious Lyric," in *New Perspectives on the Seventeenth-Century English Religious Lyric*, ed. John Roberts (Columbia: University of Missouri Press, 1994), 143–67, reworked in *Milton and the Tangles of Neaera's Hair* (Columbia: University of Missouri Press, 1997), 64–90.

4. Several poets allude to the star of Charles's birth in the volume of poetry produced in Oxford to mark the event: *Britanniae Natalis* (Oxford:

Iohannes Lichfiéld, 1630). See the discussion in Revard, *Milton and the Tangles*, 81–82.

5. Abraham Cowley, "ODE, Upon the Blessed Restoration and Returne of His Sacred Majestie, Charls the Second" (London: Henry Heringman, 1660). The ode was reprinted in *Works* in 1668 with a different title, "ODE, Upon His Majesties Restoration and Return," and with a slightly different text. I quote from the first edition.

6. See *Britannia Rediviva* (Oxford: L. Lichfield, 1660). James Vaughan writes, "You like the Sun (Great King) dispense your light; / And cherish with your Royall beams the land" (sig. Bbv).

7. John Ailmer, in ibid., sig. Bb3r.

8. John Dryden, "Astraea Redux," 256–57, *The Poetical Works of Dryden*, ed. George R. Noyes (Cambridge, Mass.: The Riverside Press, 1950); Dryden's poetry is cited in the text from this edition.

9. In the poem to the Lord Chancellor, Clarendon, published in 1662, Dryden also celebrates Charles as the sun of the universe. Clarendon argued that Charles had been providentially preserved during his years of exile—his trials in the wilderness—so that he could assume his kingship. See Keeble, "Wilderness Exercises," 94–95. Also see my discussion of the depiction of Charles as Moses in Stella P. Revard, *Politics, Poetics, and the Pindaric Ode: 1450–1700* (Tempe, Ariz.: Medieval and Renaissance Texts and Studies, 2009), 144, 146, 149–50, 160.

10. See Edward Reynolds, *The Wall and Glory of Jerusalem* (London, 1660), 15.

11. William Godman, *Filius Heröum, The Son of Nobles, Set forth in a Sermon Preached At St Mary's in Cambridge before the University on Thursday the 24th of May, 1660, being the day of Solemn Thanksgiving for the Deliverance and Settlement of our Nation* (London, 1660), 4–5, 24.

12. Gilbert Sheldon, *David's Deliverance and Thanksgiving. A Sermon Preached before the King at Whitehall upon June 28, 1660, Being the Day of Solemn Thanksgiving for the Happy Return of His Majesty* (London, 1660), 3.

13. J. W. Minister, *The Parallel Between David, Christ, and King Charles, In their Humiliation and Exaltation* (London, 1660), 1, 7, 9.

14. *The Ready and Easy Way to Establish a Free Commonwealth*, in *Complete Poetry and Major Prose*, ed. Merritt Y. Hughes (New York: Odyssey Press, 1957), 881. All citations of Milton's prose and poetry are to this edition.

15. In *The Ready and Easy Way* Milton interprets Jesus' rebuke of the ambitious desire of sons of Zebedee as a caution against kingship (885).

16. As I have argued previously, the apocalyptic views expressed in *Of Reformation* and *The Ready and Easy Way*—tracts written with political ends in mind—closely resemble views expressed in theological treatises such as *De doctrina Christiana* and Joseph Mede's *The Key of the Revelation*. See Revard, "Milton and Millenarianism," 54–55.

17. According to contemporary accounts, Sedley appeared on the balcony of the Cock Tavern in Bow Street with two companions. They stripped themselves naked, and "Sedley, after performing certain disgusting pranks," preached a mock sermon to the assembled crowd. Although he was an intimate friend of the king, Sedley was brought to court, fined, and briefly imprisoned for the incident. See V. De Sola Pinto, *Sir Charles Sedley, 1639–1701* (London: Constable & Company, 1927), 61–67.

18. See Ronald Hutton, *Restoration: A Political and Religious History of England and Wales, 1658–1667* (New York: Oxford University Press, 1985), 190.

19. See Michael McKeon, *Politics and Poetry in Restoration England: The Case of Dryden's* Annus Mirabilis (Cambridge, Mass.: Harvard University Press, 1975).

20. Dryden depicts three battles of the naval wars: the battle of Lowestoft (1665) between English and Dutch ships, the Four Days' Battle (June 1666), and finally the battle of St. James's Day (July 1666). Despite these English victories the Dutch war was unpopular and the English were on the losing side and were forced to negotiate a peace treaty in 1667. See David Ogg, *England in the Reign of Charles II* (Oxford: Oxford University Press, 1934), 283–303.

21. See "An Account of the Ensuing Poem," in Noyes, *The Poetical Works of Dryden*, 23–26.

22. The Great Fire of London took place between September 2 and 7, 1666. Although a greater part of the City of London was destroyed, the fire was eventually stopped. Charles II promised to rebuild the city, improving its streets and undertaking projects to renew it. Dryden presents the view that not only were the disasters averted, but also that God had miraculously saved England from destruction.

23. See Sophie Gee, "The Invention of the Wasteland: Civic Narrative and Dryden's *Annus Mirabilis*," *Eighteenth-Century Life* 29 (2005): 82–108.

24. See Gordon Campbell, *A Milton Chronology* (London: Macmillan, 1997), 203–04. In February 1666 *Paradise Regain'd* was shown to Ellwood. *Paradise Regain'd* was licensed in July 1670, and in September 1670 it was registered for publication with *Samson Agonistes*.

25. Though Satan does not realize it, he is referring to how the Messiah will appear at his Second Coming when he will be leader of a great army and will enter Jerusalem triumphantly and begin his reign over Jews and Gentiles alike. See Revelation 19:11–16.

26. Here Jesus appears to turn away from earthly kingship, preferring the role of a teacher to that of king. Milton is perhaps mindful that in the Gospel of John Jesus had firmly declared, as he stood before Pilate, that his kingdom was not of this world (John 18:36). For commentary on the Johannine echoes in *Paradise Regain'd*, see Revard, "The Gospel of John and *Paradise Regained:* Jesus as 'True Light,'" in *Milton and the Scriptural Tradition*, ed. James H. Sims and Leland Ryken (Columbia: University of Missouri Press, 1984), 142–59.

27. In the second chapter of Daniel, Nebuchadnezzar dreams of an image of gold, silver, brass, and iron; Daniel interprets the image as four monarchies that would perish before God set up a kingdom that could not be destroyed. Therefore, Satan's offer of Parthia to Jesus is strategic, for by it he hopes to subvert Daniel's prophecy. By offering Jesus only Parthia as the sum of the first three kingdoms, he tempts Jesus to act too soon, to anticipate his heritage by assuming rule over the first three monarchies, rather than waiting to destroy the still more powerful fourth.

28. See the commentary on Daniel's prophecy in Revard, "Milton and Millenarianism," 62–66.

29. See T. F. Reddaway, *The Rebuilding of London after the Great Fire* (London: Jonathan Cape, 1940); Christopher Wren, "Proposals for the Rebuilding of the City of London, after the Great Fire," in *Parentalia; or, Memoirs of the Family of the Wrens* (1750) (Farnborough, Hants.: Gregg, 1965); and Jim Bennett, Michael Cooper, Michael Hunter, and Lisa Jardine, *London's Leonardo: The Life and Work of Robert Hooke* (Oxford: Oxford University Press, 2003).

30. See my discussion of the Renaissance city ode and its application to Satan's praise of Rome and Athens in *Politics, Poetics, and the Pindaric Ode*, 310–15.

31. See Clayton Roberts, "The Impeachment of the Earl of Clarendon," *Cambridge Historical Journal* 13 (1957): 1–18.

32. See the commentary on Daniel's prophecy in Revard, "Milton and Millenarianism," 67–68.

33. For the spread of neoclassicism in Restoration England and the reaction against it, see Paul Spencer Wood, "The Opposition to Neo-Classicism in England between 1660 and 1700," *PMLA* 33 (1928): 182–89.

34. See, for example, William Bridge, *Babylons Downfall* (London, 1641).

35. Lieb, *Poetics of the Holy*, 72–73.

36. Aphra Behn, *A Pindarick on the Death of our Late Sovereign: With an Ancient Prophecy on his Present Majesty* (London: Henry Playford, 1685), discussed in Revard, *Politics, Poetics, and the Pindaric Ode*, 159–63.

Notes to Bryson, "From Last Things to First"

1. *De doctrina Christiana*, in *The Complete Prose Works of John Milton*, 8 vols. in 10, ed. Don M. Wolfe et al. (New Haven: Yale University Press, 1953–82), 6:133. All quotations of Milton's prose are from this edition, hereafter cited as YP, followed by volume and page number.

2. Michael Lieb, *The Visionary Mode: Biblical Prophecy, Hermeneutics, and Cultural Change* (Ithaca: Cornell University Press, 1991), 32; hereafter cited in the text.

3. All quotations in this paragraph are from *The Celestial Hierarchy,* in *Pseudo-Dionysius: The Complete Works,* trans. Colm Luibheid (New York: Paulist Press, 1987), 150, 149.

4. Hans Jonas, *The Gnostic Religion* (Boston: Beacon Press, 1963), 288.

5. Michael Lieb, *Theological Milton: Deity, Discourse, and Heresy in the Miltonic Canon* (Pittsburgh: Duquesne University Press, 2006), argues that Milton "reveals his determination to conceive the act of knowing God by arguing that God is beyond all power to know....Essentially at issue is...apophatic theology" (77). According to Lieb, "what emerges from the discussion [of God in *De doctrina Christiana*] is the unknowableness of God on any level" (79).

6. *Paradise Lost,* 7.31. All quotations of Milton's poetry are from *John Milton: Complete Poems and Major Prose,* ed. Merritt Y. Hughes (New York: Odyssey, 1957); hereafter cited in the text.

7. Stanley Fish, "Inaction and Silence," in *Calm of Mind: Tercentenary Essays on* Paradise Lost *and* Samson Agonistes, ed. Joseph Anthony Wittreich (Cleveland: Press of Case Western Reserve University, 1971), 41.

8. I have argued this point previously in chapter 5 of *The Tyranny of Heaven: Milton's Rejection of God as King* (Newark: University of Delaware Press, 2004). John T. Shawcross, Paradise Regain'd: *Worthy T'Have Not Remain'd So Long Unsung* (Pittsburgh: Duquesne University Press, 1988), also argues (quoting M. V. Rama Sarma) that *Paradise Regain'd* depicts "a human's ideal passage through life to salvation: any human being like the Son must first gain 'self-knowledge or awareness of divine similitude'" (1).

9. For a further discussion of "thanks" or gratitude, see Peter E. Medine, "Gratitude and *Paradise Lost:* A Neglected Context," in *Milton and the Grounds of Contention,* ed. Mark R. Kelley, Michael Lieb, and John T. Shawcross (Pittsburgh: Duquesne University Press, 2003), 115–49.

10. Anthony Low, "Milton, *Paradise Regained,* and Georgic," *PMLA* 98 (1983), argues, "Satan...cannot help thinking of heroic actions in terms of honor, glory, and popular praise—rewards he craves—because they constitute his definition of 'greatest.' For him, to be 'Above Heroic' must mean to win more applause than Alexander won" (163–64).

11. *Meister Eckhart: A Modern Translation,* trans. Raymond B. Blakney (New York: Harper & Brothers, 1941), 204.

12. Joel Marcus, "Mark 14:61: 'Are You the Messiah-Son-of-God?'" *Novum Testamentum* 31 (1989), argues that the titles "Messiah-Son-of-David" and "Son of David" refer to a Messiah understood as "one whose task is primarily to reestablish the Davidic empire," then goes on to argue that all three synoptic gospels claim "that Jesus is not just the Son of David [in other words, not a mere *military* messiah] because he is the Son of God" (137).

13. Shawcross, *Paradise Regain'd,* argues that the Son "knows he is the Son of God, despite the unintelligible readings of some critics who have tried to hinge the poem on that question" (39). Hill, *Milton and the English Revolution,* disagrees, taking the view that it is not until "the miracle of the pinnacle [that] Jesus arrives a full understanding of his nature" (422). Barbara Lewalski, *Milton's Brief Epic: The Genre, Meaning, and Art of* Paradise Regained (Providence: Brown University Press, 1966), 135–38, demonstrates that there has long been controversy over the nature—human or divine—of the Son in *Paradise Regain'd.* For example, Allan Gilbert, "The Temptation in *Paradise Regained,*" *Journal of English and Germanic Philology* 15 (1916): 606, maintains that the Son was taught directly by God, and therefore had no need for ordinary human education. Douglas Bush, *English Literature in the Earlier Seventeenth Century, 1600–1660* (Oxford: Clarendon Press, 1962), 412, characterizes the Son as a "sinless divine protagonist." Elizabeth Pope, Paradise Regained: *The Tradition and the Poem* (Baltimore: The Johns Hopkins University Press, 1947, argues that Milton himself viewed the Son as a divine being: "Milton was working under the influence of the tradition that Christ deliberately withheld from Satan all evidence of his own identity" (39). Among those who see the Son as human, however, are M. M. Mahood, who argues that the Son is a "perfect man, as yet scarcely aware of His divine progeniture"; Northrop Frye, for whom the Son "withstands the temptations as a human being until the tower temptation, at which time the omnipotent divine power 'takes over' the human will"; and A. S. P. Woodhouse, in whose account the Son "progresses from human beginnings to a full realization of his divinity in the tower scene" (all three quoted in Lewalski, *Milton's Brief Epic,* 137).

14. Milton's account of Creation as *ex Deo* (out of God) rather than *ex nihilo* (out of nothing) in both *De doctrina Christiana* (chapter 7, book 1), and *Paradise Lost* (7.168–69) supports the Son's meaning here. If all things (especially all living things) are of God, then all things share in the divine nature, and all things are—in that sense—God.

15. Donald Swanson and John Mulryan, "The Son's Presumed Contempt for Learning in *Paradise Regained:* A Biblical and Patristic Resolution," in *Milton Studies,* vol. 27, ed. James D. Simmonds (Pittsburgh: University of Pittsburgh Press, 1991), 250.

16. Shawcross, *Paradise Regain'd,* 76.

Notes to Loewenstein, "From Politics to Faith in the Great Poems?"

1. Blair Worden, "Milton's Republicanism and the Tyranny of Heaven," in *Machiavelli and Republicanism,* ed. Gisela Bock, Quentin Skinner, and Maurizio Viroli (Cambridge: Cambridge University Press, 1990), 244–45.

2. "Eternal verities" is likewise Worden's phrase where he distinguishes "between temporal politics and eternal verities" (ibid., 244). Compare my response to Worden in *Representing Revolution in Milton and His Contemporaries: Religion, Politics, and Polemics in Radical Puritanism* (Cambridge: Cambridge University Press, 2001), 240–41. And see William Walker, "Resemblance and Reference in Recent Criticism on *Paradise Lost*," *Milton Quarterly* 40 (2006): 189–206.

3. Andrew Marvell, *Rehearsal Transpos'd: The Second Part*, in *The Prose Works of Andrew Marvell*, 2 vols., ed. Annabel Patterson et al. (New Haven: Yale University Press, 2003), 1:417–18; Samuel Taylor Coleridge, "Milton (1818)," in *Milton Criticism: Selections from Four Centuries*, ed. James Thorpe (New York: Collier Books, 1969), 97.

4. See, among numerous studies, Mary Ann Radzinowicz, *Toward Samson Agonistes: The Growth of Milton's Mind* (Princeton: Princeton University Press, 1978); David Quint, *Epic and Empire: Politics and Generic Form from Virgil to Milton* (Princeton: Princeton University Press, 1993), chaps. 7–8; Sharon Achinstein, *Milton and the Revolutionary Reader* (Princeton: Princeton University Press, 1994), chap. 5; Achinstein, *Literature and Dissent in Milton's England* (Cambridge: Cambridge University Press, 2003), chap. 5; Laura L. Knoppers, *Historicizing Milton: Spectacle, Power, and Poetry in Restoration England* (Athens: University of Georgia Press, 1994); David Norbrook, *Writing the English Republic: Poetry, Rhetoric and Politics, 1627–1660* (Cambridge: Cambridge University Press, 1999); David Loewenstein, *Representing Revolution in Milton and His Contemporaries*, chaps. 7–9; Loewenstein "The Radical Religious Politics of *Paradise Lost*," in *A Companion to Milton*, ed. Thomas N. Corns (Oxford: Blackwell, 2001), 348–62; Barbara K. Lewalski, *The Life of John Milton* (Oxford: Blackwell, 2000), esp. chaps. 12–14.

The "experience of defeat" echoes, of course, the title of Christopher Hill's *The Experience of Defeat: Milton and Some Contemporaries* (Harmondsworth: Penguin Books, 1984), which studies the varied responses by both radical writers and more conservative ministers to the failure of the English revolution.

5. See, for example, *Milton and Republicanism*, ed. David Armitage, Armand Himy, and Quentin Skinner (Cambridge: Cambridge University Press, 1995); Quentin Skinner, *Liberty before Liberalism* (Cambridge: Cambridge University Press, 1998); and Skinner, "John Milton and the Politics of Slavery," in *Milton and the Terms of Liberty*, ed. Graham Parry and Joad Raymond, 1–22 (Cambridge: D. S. Brewer, 2002). Compare Loewenstein, *Representing Revolution*, and Walter S. H. Lim, *John Milton, Radical Politics, and Biblical Republicanism* (Newark: University of Delaware Press, 2006). See also, for some modification of his earlier secular emphasis, David Norbrook, "Republican Occasions in *Paradise Regained* and *Samson Agonistes*," in *Milton Studies*, vol. 42, Paradise Regained in Context: Genre, Politics, Religion, ed. Albert C. Labriola and David Loewenstein (Pittsburgh: University of Pittsburgh Press, 2003), 122–48.

6. Significant scholarly works that have challenged the picture of quiescent Restoration dissent include Richard L. Greaves, *Deliver Us from Evil: The Radical Underground in Britain, 1660–1663* (Oxford: Oxford University Press, 1986), and Greaves, *Enemies under His Feet: Radicals and Nonconformists in Britain, 1664–1677* (Stanford: Stanford University Press, 1990). See also the valuable study of the late Milton by the historian John Coffey, "Pacifist, Quietist, or Patient Militant? John Milton and the Restoration," in *Milton Studies*, vol. 42, 149–74; like my own essay, Coffey's challenges the notion that Milton reveals himself to be a consistent pacifist in *Paradise Regain'd* and the other late poems.

7. Edmund Ludlow, *A Voyce from the Watch Tower*, ed. A. B. Worden (London: Royal Historical Society, 1978), 309–10. This portion of *A Voyce* covers the years 1660–62.

8. See Loewenstein, *Representing Revolution*, chaps. 8–9; Coffey, "Pacifist, Quietist, or Patient Militant?," esp. 171.

9. Michael Lieb, *Milton and the Culture of Violence* (Ithaca: Cornell University Press, 1994), 226–63; Lieb, "'Our Living Dread': The God of *Samson Agonistes*," in *Milton Studies*, vol. 33, *The Miltonic Samson*, ed. Albert C. Labriola and Michael Lieb (Pittsburgh: Pittsburgh University Press, 1997), 3–25, revised in Lieb's *Theological Milton: Diety, Discourse, and Heresy in the Miltonic Canon* (Pittsburgh: Duquesne University Press, 2006), 184–209; Lieb, "Returning the Gorgon Medusa's Gaze: Terror and Annihilation in Milton," in *Milton in the Age of Fish*, ed. Michael Lieb and Albert C. Labriola (Pittsburgh: Duquesne University Press, 2006), 229–42. Also pertinent is Lieb's important chapter "The Theology of Strength," *The Sinews of Ulysses: Form and Convention in Milton's Works* (Pittsburgh: Duquesne University Press, 1989), 98–138, 161–69; see esp. 107–38 on the way that Milton's Samson is "able to manifest God's strength over his enemies in a final act of triumphant devastation" (135) so that the ending of the drama becomes an expression of apocalyptic strength (Lieb points to the context of Rev. 6:12–17).

10. *Paradise Lost*, 7.24–26, in *John Milton: Complete Poems and Major Prose*, ed. Merritt Y. Hughes (New York: Odyssey Press, 1957). Milton's poetry is quoted from this edition, hereafter cited in the text.

11. See, for example, Achinstein, *Literature and Dissent*; Norbrook, *Writing the English Republic*, chap. 10; Loewenstein, *Representing Revolution*, part 2; and Lewalski, *The Life of John Milton*, chaps. 12–14.

12. *Areopagitica*, in *Complete Prose Works of John Milton*, 8 vols. in 10, ed. Don M. Wolfe et al. (New Haven: Yale University Press, 1953–82), 2:255. All quotations from Milton's prose are taken from this edition, hereafter cited as YP. On the complexities of Milton's nationalism, including his agonized responses to the English nation, see the essays in *Milton's England and Early Modern Nationalism*, ed. David Loewenstein and Paul Stevens (Toronto: University of Toronto Press, 2008).

13. *OED* s.v. "weltering," def. 2. For variations of the word in Milton's poems, see "Ode on the Morning of Christs Nativity," 124; *Lycidas,* 13; *Paradise Lost* 1.78.

14. For a different but complementary account of the narrative of historical decline at the end of *Paradise Lost* in terms of competing configurations of history (including patterns of progress and regression), see my *Milton and the Drama of History: Historical Vision, Iconoclasm, and the Literary Imagination* (Cambridge: Cambridge University Press, 1990), 111–20.

15. Radzinowicz, *Toward* Samson Agonistes, 116–17; see part 3 (111–79) for a substantial account of the politics of the drama.

16. Michael Wilding, *Dragons Teeth: Literature in the English Revolution* (Oxford: Clarendon Press, 1987), 255. While Christopher Hill, *Milton and the English Revolution* (London: Viking, 1977), certainly deserves credit for positioning Milton fully in the contexts of the revolutionary decades, Wilding's 1987 book was in some sense the first *literary* study of the literature of the English revolution and deserves much credit for inaugurating the intensive study of the literature of this period in seventeenth century England.

17. See, for example, Wilding's acute account of Milton's Satan's ambiguities and the parliament of hell in *Dragons Teeth,* chap. 8.

18. Especially since John Carey's piece, "A Work in Praise of Terrorism? September 11 and *Samson Agonistes,*" published in *The Times Literary Supplement,* September 6, 2002, 15–16. For critical responses to Carey and the issue of religious violence, see Feisal G. Mohamed, "Confronting Religious Violence: Milton's *Samson Agonistes,*" *PMLA* 120 (2005): 327–40; Mohamed, "Reading *Samson* in the New American Century," in *Milton Studies,* vol. 46, ed. Albert C. Labriola (Pittsburgh: University of Pittsburgh Press, 2007), 149–64; Timothy J. Burbery, *Milton the Dramatist* (Pittsburgh: Duquesne University Press, 2007), 128–34; and the following essays in *Milton in the Age of Fish: Essays on Authorship, Text, and Terrorism,* ed. Michael Lieb and Albert C. Labriola (Pittsburgh: Duquesne University Press 2006): David Loewenstein, "*Samson Agonistes* and the Culture of Religious Terror," 203–28; Michael Lieb, "Returning the Gorgon Medusa's Gaze: Terror and Annihilation in Milton," 229–242; and Stanley Fish, "'There Is Nothing He Cannot Ask': Milton, Liberalism, and Terrorism," 243–64.

19. The phrase is Wittreich's: Samson "*is* deeply flawed and thus ambiguous in his heroism" (*Interpreting* Samson Agonistes [Princeton: Princeton University Press], 306). My emphasis here is clearly less on Samson's flaws and more on the ambiguous signals registered by the 1671 volume as a whole.

20. Lieb, "Returning the Gorgon Medusa's Gaze," 236–37, has used the phrase to describe the terrible violence of Samson against the Philistines, and I use it in discussing Cromwell's military campaign to destroy Irish

resistance in the Fall of 1649 in "*Samson Agonistes* and the Culture of Religious Terror," 210.

21. As Joseph Wittreich, *Interpreting* Samson Agonistes, puts it, "Samson emerges as a foil for the heroism of Jesus, the false and fallen prophet standing against Jesus who is the agent of divine vision and the spirit of true prophecy" (347). Compare Wittreich's comments on the "corrective" function of *Samson Agonistes* in relation to *Paradise Regain'd* (374); see also 376 on *Paradise Regain'd* offering "the possibility of renewal" in relation to the "fragmented" and violent world of *Samson Agonistes*. For a similar argument, see Derek N. C. Wood, *"Exiled from Light": Divine Law, Morality, and Violence in Milton's* Samson Agonistes (Toronto: University of Toronto Press, 2001), 120–25. On Samson as "outmoded hero," see also John Carey's argument in *Milton* (1969; repr., New York: Arco, 1970), 138–46.

22. Wittreich, *Interpreting* Samson Agonistes; and *Shifting Contexts: Reinterpreting* Samson Agonistes (Pittsburgh: Duquesne University Press, 2002). See also Irene Samuel's influential essay, "*Samson Agonistes* as Tragedy," in *Calm of Mind: Tercentenary Essays on* Paradise Regained *and* Samson Agonistes, ed. Joseph A. Wittreich (Cleveland: Press of Case Western University, 1971), 235–57. Samuel's essay challenges the notion that Milton's vengeful Samson is restored to divine favor and that *Samson Agonistes* is in any sense a martyr drama. Compare the very different view of Lieb, *Milton and the Culture of Violence*, who asserts that Milton's drama "extols violence. Indeed, it exults in violence" (237). Lieb, "The God of *Samson Agonistes*," 3–4, and *Theological Milton*, 184–85, however, also distinguishes his account of violence in the drama (a work "that is far from reassuring in its outlook") from the more assuring reading of divine providence, rationality, and progressive revelation offered by Mary Ann Radzinowicz, *Toward* Samson Agonistes.

23. For some astute reflections on the ways twenty-first century religious and political issues have reshaped critical discussions of Milton's drama, see Mohamed, "Reading *Samson*." Mohamed, however, somewhat misrepresents my argument in "*Samson Agonistes* and the Culture of Religious Terror": my aim is not to generate "a comfortable distance between seventeenth-century radicalism and that of today" or to consign Milton "to a distant and irrelevant past" ("Reading *Samson*," 157), but to argue against anachronistic readings of the drama which too readily equate Samson's violence with that of twenty-first century suicide terrorists. Despite important differences between Samson's violence and that of suicide terrorists, Samson's dreadful act at the end of the drama leaves readers profoundly uncomfortable or unsettled. But that does not mean that readers of Milton's drama need to reject altogether Samson as a certain example of heroism that subdues the stubborn enemies of God (as I argue below). Nor do my arguments there or in the present essay or in my other scholarship exemplify "intellectual work" that "declares its

allegiance with Western values of nonviolence and liberty and its uncomplicated cultural superiority to the religious violence of the Other" (159). This simplifies my position, which is that Milton remains much more open ended in the 1671 volume of poems; indeed, at moments of crisis and when faced with stubborn enemies, dissenters—the 1671 volume suggests—may need to pursue liberty by acts of religious violence. But the poet never provides a clear-cut directive in the 1671 volume.

24. For the original Latin, see *The Works of John Milton*, 18 vols. in 21, ed. Frank Allen Patterson (New York: Columbia University Press, 1931–38), 17:258, 288. Milton's scriptural proof-texts include, among others, 2 Chron. 19:2 and Ps. 139:21–22 in support of the former passage (on hatred of the Lord's enemies), and Ps. 18:38–43, Ps. 41:10–11, Ps. 94:2, Jer. 11:20 and 15:15 in support of the latter (on vengeance). See also Lieb's major discussion of the *odium Dei* in *Theological Milton*, 163–83, esp. 173–77.

25. John Carey's phrase in the first edition of his *Milton: Complete Shorter Poems* (London: Longmans, 1968), 333. See also Wilding, *Dragons Teeth*, who insists on "Christ's rejection of the role of military Messiah" as a major theme of *Paradise Regain'd* (251).

26. John Milton, *Paradise Regain'd. A Poem in IV Books. To Which is added Samson Agonistes* (London, 1671). The placement of the Errata for both poems at the end of the whole volume is another indication that, while the two poems are discrete works, they are also meant to be read in relation to each other. See also, on this issue, Stephen B. Dobranski, "Text and Context for *Paradise Regain'd* and *Samson Agonistes*," in *Altering Eyes: New Perspectives on* Samson Agonistes, ed. Mark R. Kelley and Joseph Wittreich (Newark: University of Delaware Press, 2002), 30–53, esp. 31. I discuss at greater length the implications of Milton's substitution of "subdue" for "destroy" in "Milton's Double-Edged Volume: On Religious Politics and Violence in the 1671 Poems," *Milton Quarterly* (forthcoming).

27. Thomas Newton, ed., *Paradise Regain'd. A Poem, in Four Books* (London, 1773), 1:25; Wilding, *Dragons Teeth*, 250.

28. For Milton's discussion of the Israelite deliverer Ehud, along with Samson, see *A Defence of the People of England* (YP 4:401–02). Compare *The Tenure of Kings and Magistrates* (YP 3:213, 215), and also *De doctrina Christiana* (YP 6:764).

29. John Bunyan, *The Pilgrim's Progress from This World* (London, 1678), 61; emphasis added.

30. Compare this passage in *Of True Religion* with the depiction of "fair Atheists" (11.625) in Michael's vision of Jubal and Tubal-cain and his vision of "luxury and riot, / Marrying or prostituting, as befell / Rape or Adultery" (11.715–17) during the sybaritic age of Noah.

31. Compare Wittreich, *Interpreting* Samson Agonistes, 56, 93, for the different view that Milton mocks or ridicules Samson's failings.

32. On Samson as a figure for the indignities suffered by dissenters dur-
ing the 1660s, see Janel Mueller, "The Figure and the Ground: Samson as
a Hero of London Nonconformity, 1662–1667," in *Milton and the Terms
of Liberty*, ed. Graham Parry and Joad Raymond (Cambridge: D. S. Brewer,
2002), 137–62.

33. See also my discussion in the afterword to *Representing Revolution*,
292–95.

Selected Publications by Michael Lieb

Books

Theological Milton: Deity, Discourse, and Heresy in the Miltonic Canon. Pittsburgh: Duquesne University Press, 2006.

Children of Ezekiel: Aliens, UFOs, the Crisis of Race, and the Advent of End Time. Durham, N.C.: Duke University Press, 1998.

Milton and the Culture of Violence. Ithaca: Cornell University Press, 1994.

The Visionary Mode: Biblical Prophecy, Hermeneutics, and Cultural Change. Ithaca: Cornell University Press, 1991.

The Sinews of Ulysses: Form and Convention in Milton's Works. Pittsburgh: Duquesne University Press, 1989.

Poetics of the Holy: A Reading of Paradise Lost. Chapel Hill: University of North Carolina Press, 1981.

The Dialectics of Creation: Patterns of Birth and Regeneration in Paradise Lost. Amherst: University of Massachusetts Press, 1970.

Collections (Coeditor and Contributor)

"Paradise Lost: A Poem Written in Ten Books": Essays on the 1667 First Edition. Coedited with John T. Shawcross. Pittsburgh: Duquesne University Press, 2007. Includes "Back to the Future: *Paradise Lost* 1667," 1–23.

Milton in the Age of Fish: Essays on Authorship, Text, and Terrorism. Coedited with Albert C. Labriola. Pittsburgh: Duquesne University

Press, 2006. Includes "Returning the Gorgon Medusa's Gaze: Terror and Annihilation in Milton," 229–42.

Milton and the Grounds of Contention. Coedited with John T. Shawcross. Pittsburgh: Duquesne University Press, 2003. Includes "Milton and the Socinian Heresy," 234–83.

Milton Studies, vol. 38, *John Milton: The Writer in His Works.* Coedited with Albert C. Labriola. Pittsburgh: University of Pittsburgh Press, 2000. Includes "'A Thousand Foreskins': Circumcision, Violence, and Selfhood in *Samson Agonistes,*" 198–219.

Milton Studies, vol. 33, *The Miltonic Samson.* Coedited with Albert C. Labriola. Pittsburgh: University of Pittsburgh Press, 1996. Includes "'Our Living Dread': The God of *Samson Agonistes,*" 3–25.

Literary Milton: Text, Pretext, Context. Coedited with Albert C. Labriola. Pittsburgh: Duquesne University Press, 1994. Includes "'Two of Far Nobler Shape': Reading the Paradisal Text," 114–32.

Milton Studies, vol. 7, *"Eyes Fast Fixt": Current Perspectives in Milton Methodology.* Coedited with Albert C. Labriola. Pittsburgh: University of Pittsburgh Press, 1975. Includes "*Paradise Lost* and the Myth of Prohibition," 233–65.

Achievements of the Left Hand: Essays on the Prose of John Milton. Coedited with John T. Shawcross. Amherst: University of Massachusetts Press, 1974. Includes "Milton's *Of Reformation* and the Dynamics of Controversy," 55–82.

Editions (Coeditor and Contributor)

"Paradise Lost: A Poem Written in Ten Books": An Authoritative Text of the 1667 First Edition. Coedited with John T. Shawcross. Pittsburgh: Duquesne University Press, 2007.

Book Chapters

"Milton and the Bible." In *The Blackwell Companion to the Bible in English Literature,* edited by Christopher Rowland and Rebecca Lemon. Malden, Mass.: Blackwell, 2009.

"John Milton and Theology." In *The Oxford Handbook of English Literature and Theology,* edited by Andrew Hass, David Jasper, and Elizabeth Jay, 413–30. Oxford: Oxford University Press, 2007.

Articles

"Brotherhood of the Illuminati: Milton, Galileo, and the Poetics of Conspiracy." In *Milton Studies*, vol. 47, edited by Albert C. Labriola, 54–85. Pittsburgh: University of Pittsburgh Press, 2008.

"Back to the Future: *Paradise Lost* 1667." In *"Paradise Lost: A Poem Written in Ten Books": Essays on the 1667 First Edition*, edited by Michael Lieb and John T. Shawcross, 1–23. Pittsburgh: Duquesne University Press, 2007.

"Returning the Gorgon Medusa's Gaze: Terror and Annihilation in Milton." In *Milton in the Age of Fish: Essays on Authorship, Text, and Terrorism*. Edited by Michael Lieb and Albert C. Labriola, 229–42. Pittsburgh: Duquesne University Press, 2006.

"Milton and the Socinian Heresy." In *Milton and the Grounds of Contention*, edited by Michael Lieb and John T. Shawcross, 234–83. Pittsburgh: Duquesne University Press, 2003.

"*De doctrina Christiana* and the Question of Authorship." In *Milton Studies*, vol. 41, edited by Albert C. Labriola, 172–203. Pittsburgh: University of Pittsburgh Press, 2002.

"Adam's Story: Testimony and Transition in *Paradise Lost*." In *Living Texts: Interpreting Milton*, edited by Charles W. Durham and Kristin Pruitt, 21–48. Selinsgrove, Pa.: Susquehanna University Press, 2000. With a response by J. Martin Evans, "Afterthoughts on Adam's Story," 48–56.

"Milton and 'Arianism.'" *Religion and Literature* 32 (2000): 197–220.

"'A Thousand Foreskins': Circumcision, Violence, and Selfhood in *Samson Agonistes*." In *Milton Studies*, vol. 38, *John Milton: The Writer in His Works*, edited by Michael Lieb and Albert C. Labriola, 198–219. Pittsburgh: University of Pittsburgh Press, 2000.

"Encoding the Occult: Milton and the Traditions of *Merkabah* Speculation in the Renaissance." In *Milton Studies*, vol. 37, edited by Albert C. Labriola, 42–88. Pittsburgh: University of Pittsburgh Press, 1999.

"'Our Living Dread': The God of *Samson Agonistes*." In *Milton Studies*, vol. 33, *The Miltonic Samson*, edited by Michael Lieb and Albert C. Labriola, 3–25. Pittsburgh: University of Pittsburgh Press, 1996. Reprinted in *John Milton: Twentieth-Century Perspectives*. 5 vols. Edited by J. Martin Evans, 5:211–33. New York: Routledge, 2003.

"Structures of the Self: Pico della Mirandola and Forms of the Merkabah." *Graven Images: A Journal of Culture, Law, and the Sacred* 3 (1996): 225–48.

"'Two of Far Nobler Shape': Reading the Paradisal Text." In *Literary Milton: Text, Pretext, Context*, edited by Michael Lieb and Albert C. Labriola, 114–32. Pittsburgh: Duquesne University Press, 1994.

"The Book of M: *Paradise Lost* as Revisionary Text." *Cithara* 31 (1991): 28–35.

"Reading God: Milton and the Anthropopathetic Tradition." In *Milton Studies*, vol. 25, edited by James D. Simmonds, 213–43. Pittsburgh: University of Pittsburgh Press, 1990.

"Ezekiel's Inaugural Vision as Jungian Archetype." *Thought* 54 (1989): 116–29.

"'The Chariot of Paternal Deitie': Some Visual Renderings." In *Milton's Legacy in the Arts*, edited by Albert C. Labriola and Edward Sichi, 21–58. University Park, Pa.: The Pennsylvania State University Press, 1988.

"Milton's 'Dramatick Constitution': The Celestial Dialogue in *Paradise Lost*, Book III." In *Milton Studies*, vol. 23, edited by James D. Simmonds, 215–40. Pittsburgh: University of Pittsburgh Press, 1988.

"Children of Ezekiel: Biblical Prophecy, Madness, and the Cult of the Modern." *Cithara* 26 (1986): 3–22.

"'Hate in Heav'n': Milton and the *Odium Dei*." *ELH, A Journal of English Literary History* 53 (1986): 519–39.

"Milton's 'Chariot of Paternal Deitie' as a Reformation Conceit." *Journal of Religion* 65 (1985): 359–77.

"S. B.'s '*In Paradisum Amissam*': Sublime Commentary." *Milton Quarterly* 19 (1985): 71–78.

"Scriptural Formula and Prophetic Utterance in *Lycidas*." In *Milton and Scriptural Tradition: The Bible into Poetry*, edited by James Sims and Leland Ryken, 31–42. Columbia: University of Missouri Press, 1984.

"Milton among the Monks." In *Milton and the Middle Ages*, edited by John Mulryan, 103–14. Lewisburg, Pa.: Bucknell University Press, 1982.

"Milton's 'Unexpressive Nuptial Song': A Reading of *Lycidas*." In *Renaissance Papers* (Southeastern Renaissance Conference, 1982), 15–26.

"Further Thoughts on Satan's Journey through Chaos." *Milton Quarterly* 12 (1978): 126–33.

"'Yet Once More': The Formulaic Opening of *Lycidas*." *Milton Quarterly* 12 (1978): 23–28.

"'Cupids Funeral Pile': Milton's Projected Drama on the Theme of Lust." *Renaissance Papers* (Southeastern Renaissance Conference, 1977), 29–41.

"'Holy Place': A Reading of *Paradise Lost*." *Studies in English Literature, 1500–1900* 17 (1977): 129–47.

"*Paradise Lost* and the Myth of Prohibition." In *Milton Studies*, vol. 7, *"Eyes Fast Fixt": Current Perspectives in Milton Methodology*, edited by Michael Lieb and Albert C. Labriola, 233–65. Pittsburgh: University of Pittsburgh Press, 1975.

"Milton and the Metaphysics of Form." *Studies in Philology* 71 (1974): 206–24.

"Milton's *Of Reformation* and the Dynamics of Controversy." In *Achievements of the Left Hand: Essays on the Prose of John Milton*, edited by Michael Lieb and John T. Shawcross, 55–82. Amherst: University of Massachusetts Press, 1974.

"*Paradise Lost*, Book III: The Dialogue in Heaven Reconsidered." *Renaissance Papers* (Southeastern Renaissance Conference, 1974), 39–50.

"'Holy Rest': A Reading of *Paradise Lost*." *ELH, A Journal of English Literary History* 39 (1972): 238–53.

"Milton and the Organicist Polemic." In *Milton Studies*, vol. 4, edited by James D. Simmonds, 79–99. Pittsburgh: University of Pittsburgh Press, 1972.

"Milton and the Kenotic Christology: Its Literary Bearing." *ELH, A Journal of English Literary History* 37 (1970): 342–60.

"*Paradise Lost* and the Twentieth-Century Reader." *Cithara* 9 (1969): 27–42.

About the Contributors

Sharon Achinstein is Reader in Renaissance English Literature at Oxford University and Fellow of St. Edmund Hall. She is the author of *Milton and the Revolutionary Reader,* which received the James Holly Hanford Award, and coeditor of *Milton and Toleration,* which received the Irene Samuel Award. Her edition of Milton's divorce tracts is forthcoming.

Diana Treviño Benet is professor of English at the University of North Texas. She is the author of *Secretary of Praise, Something to Love,* and articles on Milton in *Milton Studies* and *Modern Philology. Literary Milton: Text, Pretext, Context,* which she coedited, received the Irene Samuel Award. She was president of the Milton Society in 1996.

Michael Bryson is assistant professor of English at California State University at Northridge. He is the author of *The Tyranny of Heaven* and various articles on Milton in *Milton Quarterly* and *Milton Studies.*

Stanley Fish is Davidson-Kahn Distinguished University Professor of Humanities and Law at Florida International University. He is the author of *Surprised by Sin,* which received the James Holly Hanford Award, and *How Milton Works.* His most recent book is *Save the World on Your Own Time.* He was president of the Milton Society in 1980 and its Honored Scholar in 1991.

Wendy Furman-Adams is professor of English at Whittier College. She is coeditor of *Renaissance Rereadings* and *Riven Unities* and the author of articles on Milton in the *Huntington Library Quarterly, Milton Studies,* and *Philological Quarterly.*

Barbara K. Lewalski is the William R. Kennan Jr. Professor of English Literature and History at Harvard. She is author of Paradise Lost *and the Rhetoric of Literary Forms* and *The Life of John Milton,* both of which received the James Holly Hanford Award. She was president of the Milton Society in 1970 and its Honored Scholar in 1977.

David Loewenstein is Marjorie and Lorin Tiefenthaler Professor of English at the University of Wisconsin–Madison. He is the author of *Milton and the Drama of History: Historical Vision, Iconoclasm, and the Literary Imagination* and *Representing Revolution in Milton and His Contemporaries,* both of which received the James Holly Hanford Award. He is coeditor of the forthcoming *Complete Works of Gerrard Winstanley.* He was president of the Milton Society in 1994 and its Honored Scholar in 2006.

Peter E. Medine is professor of English at the University of Arizona. He has held research fellowships at the Huntington Library and the Folger Shakespeare Library and has directed six summer institutes on Shakespeare and Milton, which were funded by the NEH. He is author, editor, or coeditor of six books, the most recent of which is *Roger Ascham's* Toxophilus.

Stella P. Revard is professor of English emerita at Southern Illinois University at Edwardsville. She is the author of *The War in Heaven* and *Milton and the Tangles of Neaera's Hair,* both of which received the James Holly Hanford Award. Her edition of *The Shorter Poems of John Milton* appeared in 2009. She was president of the Milton Society in 1984 and its Honored Scholar in 1997.

Mary Beth Rose is professor of English at the University of Illinois at Chicago. She is author of various studies and editions of early modern literature. Her study *Gender the Heroism* appeared in 2002. Her coedited work, *Elizabeth I: Collected Works* appeared in 2002 and received the Professional/Scholarly Publishing Division Award of the American Publishers. She has been an ACLS, Folger, and NEH Fellow.

John T. Shawcross is professor of English emeritus at the University of Kentucky. He is the author, editor, or coeditor of over 30 studies of Milton and Renaissance authors. *Milton: A Bibliography for the Years 1624–1700* and *John Milton: The Self and the World* both received the James Holly Hanford Award. His most recent book is *The Development of Milton's Thought.* He was president of the Milton Society 1974 and its Honored Scholar in 1981. The Society inaugurated the John T. Shawcross Award in 2006.

Virginia James Tufte is distinguished emerita professor of English at the University of Southern California. Author of several books on early modern authors and topics, she has published extensively on Milton and the visual arts. Her book *Artful Sentences* appeared in 2006.

David V. Urban is assistant professor of English at Calvin College. He is the author of numerous articles on Milton, and his updated edition of *John Milton: An Annotated Bibliography, 1989–1999* is forthcoming from Duquesne University Press.

Joseph A. Wittreich is professor of English at the Graduate Center of the City University of New York. He is author of numerous studies of Milton and the Romantic poets. His study *Interpreting* Samson Agonistes appeared in 1986 and received the James Holly Hanford Award. His most recent book is *Why Milton Matters*. He was president of the Milton Society in 1979 and its Honored Scholar in 1993.

Index

Numbers appearing in italic refer to illustrations.